LOUISIANA CREOLE LITERATURE

Also by Catharine Savage Brosman

POETRY
   Watering (1972)
   Abiding Winter (1983) (chapbook)
   Journeying to Canyon de Chelly (1990)
   Passages (1996)
   The Swimmer and Other Poems (2000) (chapbook)
   Places in Mind (2000)
   Petroglyphs: Poems and Prose (2003) (chapbook)
   The Muscled Truce (2003)
   Range of Light (2007)
   Breakwater (2009)
   Trees in a Park (2010) (chapbook)
   Under the Pergola (2011)
   On the North Slope (2012)

CREATIVE PROSE
   The Shimmering Maya and Other Essays (1994)
   Finding Higher Ground (2003)

CRITICISM
   André Gide: l'évolution de sa pensée religieuse (1962)
   Malraux, Sartre, and Aragon as Political Novelists (1964)
   Roger Martin du Gard (1968)
   Jean-Paul Sartre (1983)
   Jules Roy (1988)
   Art as Testimony: The Work of Jules Roy (1989)
   An Annotated Bibliography of Criticism on André Gide, 1973–1988 (1990)
   Simone de Beauvoir Revisited (1991)
   Twentieth-Century French Culture, 1900–1975, edited with an introduction (1995)
   Visions of War in France: Fiction, Art, Ideology (1999)
   Existential Fiction (2000)
   Albert Camus (2000)

Louisiana Creole Literature

A HISTORICAL STUDY

Catharine Savage Brosman

University Press of Mississippi   Jackson

www.upress.state.ms.us

The University Press of Mississippi is a member
of the Association of American University Presses.

Copyright © 2013 by University Press of Mississippi
All rights reserved

First printing 2013

∞

Library of Congress Cataloging-in-Publication Data

Brosman, Catharine Savage, 1934–
  Louisiana Creole literature : a historical study / Catharine Savage Brosman.
    pages cm
  Includes bibliographical references and index.
  ISBN 978-1-61703-910-2 (cloth : alk. paper)—ISBN 978-1-61703-911-9 (ebook)
  ISBN 978-1-4968-5213-7 (pbk; alk. paper) 1. French-
American literature—Louisiana—History and criticism. 2. Creole literature—Louisiana
—History and criticism. 3. Creoles—Louisiana—History. I. Title.
  PQ3937.L7B76 2013
  840.9'9763—dc23
                              2013016686

British Library Cataloging-in-Publication Data available

CONTENTS

Preface vii

Chapter One. Louisiana and Its Population:
The Historical Background 3

Chapter Two. Features of Early Louisiana Literature
and the Cultural Milieu 17

Chapter Three. Père Rouquette
and Other Early Francophone Poets 28

Chapter Four. Mercier and Other Novelists Born
in the Early Nineteenth Century 45

Chapter Five. Mid-Nineteenth-Century Immigrant
Francophone Authors 57

Chapter Six. Fiction and Drama by Mid-Nineteenth-Century
Free People of Color 68

Chapter Seven. Poetry by Mid-Nineteenth-Century
Free People of Color 80

Chapter Eight. Cable and Hearn 93

Chapter Nine. Late Francophone Figures:
de la Houssaye, du Quesnay, Dessommes 104

Chapter Ten. Kate Chopin 121

Chapter Eleven. King, Stuart, and Others 131

Chapter Twelve. Some Twentieth-Century Louisiana Prose Writers 149

Chapter Thirteen. Louisiana Creole Poets
of the Twentieth and Twenty-First Centuries 168

Notes 189

Selected Bibliography 231

Index 241

PREFACE

This study is based on reading and research carried out principally in the Howard-Tilton Memorial Library of Tulane University and the Louisiana Research Collection. I consulted materials also at the Amistad Center of Tulane University, the Middleton Library of Louisiana State University, and the Fondren Library of Rice University. For twentieth- and twenty-first century literature, reading and research were supplemented by conversations and written exchanges with authors, editors, and publishers, including the late Donald Demarest (who communicated to me unpublished papers that he graciously allowed me to cite), Shirley Ann Grau, Maurice duQuesnay, Sheryl St. Germain, and Mona Lisa Saloy. I am grateful for these communications.

I was led to this general topic by my chief scholarly interest—French literature—and my *violon d'Ingres*, which is contemporary American poetry. I was drawn to the topic likewise by my acquaintance with the authors and editors just mentioned and others, plus long residence in New Orleans and familiarity with its literary landscape. I was thus able to appreciate how, in the words of one historian, "poets, novelists, songwriters, artists, historians, and essayists have found in [Louisiana's] past a wealth of material." An examination of Louisiana writing would allow me, I hoped, to extend readers' knowledge and share what Roland Barthes called "the pleasure of the text."[1]

The present work deals with writing in both French and English connected to the distinctive Louisiana Creole tradition and peoples (chiefly in the southeastern part of the state), whether *Creole* is defined broadly as in the past or in the more restricted manner frequent today. The study is directed to an audience of literary scholars, historians, and aficionados in America, Great Britain, and elsewhere in Europe. It consists in part of literary history and biography, following roughly the principles established in the *Dictionary of Literary Biography* series. Pertinent personal information on authors is furnished, as well as publishing facts; generic and other aesthetic matters are treated. Readers will find also summaries and descriptions of texts. In addition, judgments are made and opinions expressed, especially in order to challenge certain views. Emphasis is placed on poetry and fiction, reaching from early nineteenth-century writing through the twentieth century to selected works from the early twenty-first century. Works that appeared in Paris will be considered as well as those published locally, since much of nineteenth-century Louisiana literature was transnational.

The study is intended as broad and broadening. Social questions are treated principally in the contexts in which the works were produced and the terms set forth at the time, rather than through what Richard M. Weaver called *presentism*, or a filtering ideological vision of today. Postcolonial theory, the concept of *créolité*, feminist doctrine, cultural studies, and other critical theory thus have only a peripheral place here; I eschew the sort of approach that, in Norman Fruman's words, has metamorphosed "into a morally compromised and degraded branch of politics and the social sciences." Postcolonial theory is generally inappropriate, since it was developed in the context of twentieth-century colonial consciousness, whereas Louisiana was no longer French after 1803. Moreover, Louisiana literature in French was not *minoritaire*; French was the dominant language for many decades. Even the *gens de couleur libres* or Free People of Color—that caste composed of mixed-race people—were not an ordinary minority, and their literary aspirations and skills were close to those of the upper-class whites. While the racial and social axes were not unimportant—not at all—the linguistic axis, long shared with the majority, was even more significant for them.[2]

This is, in short, not an interdisciplinary undertaking, but a literary survey, shedding light on a corpus of writing, emphasizing its characteristics and insights, and employing what Terry Eagleton called "a venerable mode of discourse," that is, the language of literary criticism as established in France, especially—what Adolphe Jullien wished for, "praise and criticism [that] shall speak a language accessible to all." The thesis according to which "authenticity and 'truth'—if they exist at all—resist comprehension, expression, and definition" cannot be honored. I acknowledge some inevitable biases in the approach, as well as inevitable lacunae. But I do not practice the criticism of free association, and I endeavor to present others' views, as well as representative facts and quotations. If, as the postmodernists assert, there is no such thing as objectivity, all statements being subjective, partial, charged with secret messages and codes, then my own can be no more biased than those of certain critics with whom I differ.[3]

It will be obvious what debt I owe to predecessors. The earliest Louisiana literary historians include Charles Gayarré, Charles Testut, and Edward J. Fortier; two are treated below as novelists. Rodolphe-Lucien Desdunes, who published in 1911 *Nos hommes et notre histoire,* an assessment of achievements by the *gens de couleur libres,* deserves particular credit. His study was followed by Ruby Van Allen Caulfeild's *French Literature in Louisiana* (1929) and Edward Larocque Tinker's *Les Ecrits de langue française en Louisiane au XIXe siècle* (1932), which build on previous work. While having enduring historical value as indications of the interest and approaches of their time, these studies are inadequate now. Fortunately, later literary historians and critics have turned their attention to the field, and anthologies, bibliographies, monographs, translations of French texts, and numerous reprintings of nineteenth-century works have expanded the public's acquaintance.[4]

It remains true that, whereas certain authors to be examined here are well known to American literary historians, others have been nearly ignored or have been treated by local critics only. Few have been the subject of critical biographies; George Washington Cable and Kate Chopin are two exceptions. In 2011, poet Julie Kane noted that the *Princeton Encyclopedia of Poetry and Poetics* still had no entry on Francophone American poetry. A literary *tour d'horizon* and additional investigation (though not an exhaustive catalogue) seem justified, taking into consideration both literary qualities and the historical context. Certain older works seem young still, as if their authors self-consciously directed their writings some fifty years ahead, as Stendhal did his; others, while appearing dated, deserve nonetheless an audience today; new authors of importance have appeared. Old or new, these writings offer much for our appreciation; some acquire additional aspects or can be read differently in the light of changed circumstances and tastes. Little-known authors may reveal much about attitudes and conditions.[5]

The study is organized in part by chronology; as William M. Chase argued, it remains important, although it is never the whole picture. Two introductory chapters provide historical and cultural background and set forth the uses of *Creole*. The matter of changing reader reception, which does not entail rejection of earlier reception in different contexts, is addressed in due course. Language and literary genre are likewise principles of organization, though as such they inevitably entail awkwardness. In addition, authors are sometimes classified as "conservative" or "liberal" (occasionally "radical" or "socialist")—though these terms are fraught with difficulty, ill-defined, often misleading. Racial categories and labels as they prevailed in the past or present must be considered: however loath one may be to use such tags and thus appear to overemphasize their importance or stigmatize and essentialize those so labeled, ethnic terms do correspond to historical realities. The terms are not, certainly, to be viewed as prescriptive, normative, or judgmental, although in the case of "Creoles of Color" the label was and remains applied by authors to themselves, along with past or current terms (in which they take pride) such as *gens de couleur libres,* Free People of Color, black Creoles, and plain *Creoles.* These terms will often be used synonymously in the present work, as fitting the period.[6]

This study has been facilitated by the recent reprints mentioned and anthologies providing material that previously could be consulted in only a few libraries or scattered among collections. Les Editions Tintamarre (Shreveport) have republished numerous old, out-of-print materials in French; numerous texts have been put on line by La Bibliothèque Tintamarre. The Center for Louisiana Studies (now the University of Louisiana at Lafayette Press) and the Flora Levy Series have published useful material. From nineteenth-century newspapers, M. Lynn Weiss collected and annotated many poems, especially by Creoles of Color, that had simply been lost to literary historians and critics. Among other researchers, editors, and annotators whose work deserves commendation are Frans Amelinckx, Réginald Hamel, Christian Hommel, and Chris Michaelides. Mention should be made also of the volume edited by Mathé Allain, *Louisiana Literature and Literary Figures,* which includes new essays written for the bicentennial celebration of the Louisiana Purchase and reprints from quarterlies and books. In the last thirty years Louisiana State University Press, the University Press of Mississippi, and others have issued numerous pertinent volumes. Likewise, the accompanying interest in French-language writing of Louisiana for its own sake and as a source of documentation on earlier generations has expanded the field of investigation. Credit should be given to the Council for the Development of French in Louisiana, a state organism created in 1968, for its support of French in schools of the Acadian areas and elsewhere. With increased competence and awareness, the audience has grown for Francophone writing; courses in the field have multiplied at the university level.[7]

French is not quoted here extensively, however; where excerpts are given, English versions are provided also. With exceptions indicated, all translations are mine; the verse quotations are intended as aids to reading, not artistic renderings. What is chiefly folklore and oral tradition is not the concern of this study. Writing that concerns the experience of southern blacks in general is not examined. To limit the corpus, and for aesthetic reasons, contemporary Louisiana crime and detective novels (of varying quality) by authors such as James Lee Burke, John William Corrington and Joyce Corrington, James Sallis, Robert Skinner, and Julie Smith that draw on the history and ambiance of the New Orleans Creole communities will not be treated.

Although certain publications group together the Cajun (or Acadian) and

Creole traditions, and there is overlap (just as there are connections between black Creole folklore and some literary writing), the present investigation does not take into account Cajun materials. Linguistic and cultural factors are involved in this decision. As David Barry observed in 1989, French-language literature in the nineteenth century "was produced mainly by the aristocratic Creole society and those other social groups near the apex of this neo-colonial social structure." It was noted in 1945 that few Cajuns could read and write in French; there was still almost no written literary material, even of folk origin, among the Cajuns. Cajun speech was itself a barrier to literary development, since it was alienated from the literary language and tradition that would have supported it. "One looks in vain among the Cajuns for a written literary tradition," wrote May G. Waggoner. In a 1991 collection of essays called *Cajun Country*, there is no chapter devoted to written literary or quasi-literary work. Zachary Richard observed in his cover comment on David Cheramie's *Julie Choufleur ou les preuves d'amour* that "the young Acadians began to affirm their identity through poetry in the 1970s." James L. Cowan had a similar view, writing that a *littérature acadienne* dated only from 1977 or so, with Barry Jean Ancelet's anthology of Cajun poems and similar works.[8]

It is true that in the late twentieth and early twenty-first centuries, new tales and verses have been made up on the traditional subjects, and contemporary poets of Cajun descent, such as Cheramie, Darrell Bourque, and Kirby Jambon have drawn on the tradition, writing sometimes in English with a liberal sprinkling of Cajun words. New fiction in French has appeared also, such as *Baron Rouge 19-59* by Freddy de Pues, called by the publishers "the first French-language novel written in Louisiana for more than a century." Though it deals in part with New Orleans post-Katrina, it will not be treated here. Its author is Belgian; it has no clear connection to Creole matters; and, in aesthetic terms, it is unworthy of consideration.[9]

I should like to express appreciation to the staff of the Louisiana Research Collection of the Howard-Tilton Library, especially Leon Miller, and to the following friends and colleagues, who invited me to lecture at their respective institutions on topics treated here: Drs. Jamie Cockfield, Mercer University; Jean Duffy, University of Edinburgh; Alastair Duncan, University of Stirling; Patrick Henry and Mary Anne O'Neil, Whitman College; Raymond Mahieu, University of Antwerp; Walter Putnam, University of New Mexico; David Walker, University of Sheffield. Thanks go also to friends who assisted me in obtaining materials: Drs. Frank A. Anselmo of Louisiana State University; Jeannine Hayat of Paris; and Anne Schnoebelen of Rice University. I appreciate also the interest of Dr. Roger Jones of Ranger College, who invited me to read papers at the Popular Culture Association/American Culture Association meetings in 2010 and 2011. Several authors included below were the subject of studies or interviews I published in *Arkansas Review*, *Chronicles: A Magazine of American Culture*, *Explorations: The Twentieth Century*, and *Louisiana English Journal*; pertinent observations are found also in my preface to the translation (by Paul de Laup and Brosman) of Adolphe du Quesnay's *Un Été à la Grand'Isle* (Lafayette, Louisiana: Flora Levy Humanities Series, 1997). Although these studies have not been incorporated directly into the text below, they constituted initial steps, and I wish to acknowledge my debt to Drs. Janelle Collins, Maurice duQuesnay, Thomas Fleming, and Oliva M. Pass for publishing them. To my husband, Patric Savage, I owe a tremendous debt for his support and patience during the writing of this book; I want to thank him here.

LOUISIANA CREOLE LITERATURE

CHAPTER ONE

Louisiana and Its Population: The Historical Background

In what became a maxim of deterministic criticism, Hippolyte Taine, among the most influential French intellectual figures of the middle and late nineteenth century, asserted that human artefacts and creations such as literature and art were products of "la race, le milieu, le moment"—race, milieu or surroundings, and time. Race was understood as ethnicity or perhaps nation. However imperfectly the theory may hold elsewhere, it is highly pertinent to understanding literature by the early Louisiana settlers, their descendants, and others from the crucible of races, languages, and political and cultural elements that constituted the territory. Louisiana had an ethnic, linguistic, legal, and cultural history that set it apart; its legacy has endured into the twenty-first century, sufficiently to give it a distinctive character. Flags of ten different royal and imperial houses, republics, and a state have flown there. "Traversed by the Conquistadores of Spain, explored and colonized by France, and settled by Canadians, French, Germans, Acadians, Spanish, and Americans in successive waves, and with the Indians already there and blacks whose importation began early, Louisiana became the first 'melting-pot' in the present United States." It has been observed that New Orleans has an "organic connection" with multiculturalism. Thus, crisscrossed for three centuries by competing ethnic, civic, and cultural lines of force, and unique, as the only former French colony in what is now the United States, Louisiana gave rise, unsurprisingly, to a unique cultural patrimony, or what has been termed the state's "perverse complexity." "Situated on the northern rim of the historic Caribbean world, New Orleans in the eighteenth and much of the nineteenth century shared more with the people and languages and commerce of the French-African Caribbean than with the English colonies and states to the north." Louisiana is the only state that has a genuine and lengthy bilingual literary tradition.[1]

The Louisiana territory was discovered by the Spanish in the sixteenth century, perhaps as early as 1519. In 1526 Álvar Núñez Cabeza de Vaca made his way along the shore of the Gulf of Mexico toward Mexico. Hernando de Soto's party reached the Mississippi River in 1541. In the following century Robert Cavelier La Salle descended to the mouth of the river (1682). In 1699 Pierre Le Moyne d'Iberville, a Canadian, explored the Gulf Coast; he is given credit as the first to ascertain the main body of the stream from the Gulf side. He is said to have learned from an Indian of the portage from the river to Bayou St. John, the waterway which connects the city to Lake Pontchartrain. The Spanish having made no claim, both French explorers claimed "Louisiana" for France, and Iberville established a small post near the mouth of the Mississippi and others eastward.

With the help of Philippe II, duc d'Orléans, who was regent of France (1715–23), the territory, which had been held by the French crown or as a commercial monopoly by Antoine Crozat, was assigned in 1717 to the "Compagnie d'Occident," later "Compagnie des Indes." Shortly, the Scotsman John Law was charged with financing it by the sale of shares. The financial bubble burst in 1720, for lack of return on the investment. When the company was dissolved in 1731, Louisiana became a crown colony. New Orleans, named for the regent, was established officially in 1718 by Iberville's brother, Jean-Baptiste Le Moyne de Bienville. The feminine gender of the name *la Nouvelle-Orléans* was dictated, presumably, by the unacceptable vowel clash in *Nouveau-Orléans* and by the model of *Nouvelle-France*. Apart from small Indian tribes and African slaves imported shortly, the earliest occupants of the area were thus French or Canadian. They were, officially, subjects of a monarchy; excepting some later Huguenots, they and their descendants (and their slaves) were Catholics (public worship by Protestants was not legal until after the Louisiana Purchase). Among other colonists, Ursuline nuns arrived from France in 1727. Capuchin friars saw to the affairs of the Church.[2]

These early settlers (*colons*) were the original Creoles. The varying historical meanings of this word, applied variously along the Gulf of Mexico, in the Caribbean, and elsewhere, must be examined; as Robert Chaudenson observes, "The term has evolved extensively, depending on the place and time." The word *Creole* is derived from the Spanish word *criollo*, from Portuguese *crioulo*, "slave born in his master's house," probably from *criar* (to create). The French word *créole*, attested around 1670, originally designated a person of the white race born in the southern parts of the septentrional colonies.

According to Antoine-Simon Le Page du Pratz, "Créol [sic] est un enfant né dans un Pays éloigné, de père et mère de la même nation" [Creole is a child born in a distant country, of a father and mother of the same nation] (that is, the original European nation). In practice, the French word referred also to first-generation immigrants. In Louisiana, however, it served, originally, only for those of French descent, indicating Spanish or other origins only after considerable intermarriage had taken place in the colony. The Creoles of New Orleans and the surrounding plantation region, descendants of original French settlers, took pride in their high culture; many traveled to France, and they spoke good French (called eventually "Colonial French"), which became enriched lexically.[3]

The primary definition of the word *Creole* for southeastern Louisiana was long identical to this French meaning—as a noun, referring to the early settlers or their descendants, or, as defined by Chaudenson, "a white born in the colony." Adjectivally (not always capitalized), it applied to their language and culture, and, by extension, material features, products, and habits of local life (Creole tomatoes, "Creole goodbye"—an extended leave-taking). Throughout the nineteenth century, when Charles Gayarré, George Washington Cable, Lafcadio Hearn, Kate Chopin, Grace King, and Alcée Fortier wrote about Creole society, they meant chiefly the white Louisianans who were descended from the French, spoke French in most cases, and had a quasi-French culture with local variations. The appellation created status. In the mid-twentieth century, even as views were changing, the definition still held; one social historian noted that the Creoles "were always entirely Caucasian in race, and defiantly so." "No true Creole ever had colored blood. . . . Creoles were always pure white." This definition, even if inaccurate, endured in general use; the *Columbia Encyclopedia* of 1993 gave it as the only meaning, and French dictionaries such as *Le Petit Littré* and *Le Petit Robert* still support it.[4]

An enlarged nineteenth-century usage, parallel to the first, developed, however, that is, "a person of mixed Creole and black stock" (*Webster's New World Dictionary of the American Language*, 1964). In 1840 the New Orleans *Picayune* used the term for nonwhite slaves. Occasionally Hearn and others applied it to those of mixed race; without using it himself in that sense, Cable alluded to the belief that a Creole was of mixed blood. He, like Hearn, sometimes used the label *yellow* for such light-skinned Creoles. That identification likewise created status, though the uneducated among them spoke a pidgin language, or *patois*, derived from French or Spanish—called *Gombo* (from the Congolese word for okra), but also *Creole*, or sometimes "black Creole." Out of necessity whites as well as blacks spoke it, perhaps with differences but not so many that they could not communicate. Chiefly because of *Plessy v. Ferguson* (1896), a watershed legal decision widely viewed as unfortunate, this racial spectrum (white or various degrees of mixed blood) changed to become the binary classes of white and black (including those with only a small percentage of black ancestry). Having French or Spanish blood then became even more important as a marker of status within the nonwhite community. The historically based application of the word *Creole* to mean "descendant of white settlers" is unusual today in Louisiana, where it has come to be applied chiefly to mixed-race or black descendants of early families, who, following the enlarged usage, call themselves Creoles of Color (a variant of "People of Color," currently in wide use elsewhere) or simply Creoles. With the increased interest in creolization during the twenty-first century, Mona Lisa Saloy writes: "For us Creole is the African mixed with whatever landed here."[5]

Disagreements over cultural ownership of the term may be unfortunate, as they narrow the field. In contrast, the term can be too broadly applied. As Sylvie Dubois and Barbara M. Horvath observe, Creole ethnicity is, in practice, a "problematic ethnic category," which "wavers between inclusivity and exclusivity, positive and negative identity." H. Adlai Murdoch similarly remarks on the instability of the category. He is among recent commentators who view it as ambiguous because, referring to either white or black, colonizer or colonized, it is a nexus of differences, fraught with ultimate undecidability. Following Homi Bhabha, he treats creolity not as a duality but as a "third space." Such a wide understanding, by which creolization is treated as a transformation, even a reversal, of cultural patterns, is too broad for the present purposes and, for many authors, simply unsuitable.[6]

In 1743 New Orleans had two thousand inhabitants. Many Louisiana settlers (males) were of the nobility—younger sons without a fortune, explorers and adventurers with royal support. There were also former officers, whether minor nobles or *roturiers*; the latter sometimes added the particle *de* to their names. The earliest women in early Louisiana, who arrived in the 1720s, included criminals ("correction girls") and other riffraff, but also respectable peasant girls and orphans—*filles à la cassette*—though the numbers are uncertain. New waves of French, including aristocrats, immigrated following the Revolution of 1789 and the insurrections in Saint Domingue (Haiti) starting in 1791. Thirteen hundred of French stock came by 1804. (Black revolutionaries proclaimed the independent nation of Haiti in 1804.) A second wave—perhaps some twenty-seven hundred—arrived in 1809–10, having been expelled from Cuba, where they had spent a decade. Like their counterparts in France, Louisiana aristocrats declined generally to engage in business. Many early Louisianans who arrived from France settled in New Orleans, but others, with land grants or other advantages, established plantations up and down the Mississippi River—keeping a town house also, perhaps; still others settled close to what became the Acadian region, in south-central Louisiana. They remained politically conservative.[7]

Certain Indian communities survived throughout the nineteenth century; some became raiders around the settlements. Called *sauvages* generally, these natives survived "in the face of tremendous adversity and prejudice [and] actually challenged the dominant narrative that insisted on the inevitability of their disappearance. The 'vanishing Indian' refused to vanish from Louisiana." Fleeing from bondage, some blacks joined Indian tribes and produced children of mixed blood. The Mardi Gras Indians of New Orleans are a homage to black ancestors among the tribes, as is Brenda Marie Osbey's poetry collection *Ceremony for Minneconjoux*.[8]

Another group of great importance in early Louisiana consisted of Acadians or "Cajuns" (noun and adjective, invariable in the French feminine)— remnants of those Canadians removed forcibly from Nova Scotia and other territories by the British starting 1755. They were of peasant stock. Sent by boat to more southern colonies, some managed to reach the Mississippi, then south-central and southwest Louisiana, the heart of the bayou country. The earliest documented arrivals were in 1764. A half-million Louisianans claim Cajun heritage today. The early Acadians became hunters and trappers, chiefly. There was considerable intermarriage between them and members of Indian tribes. Until 1950 and beyond most members of the group remained ill-educated, their French decaying into a semipatois.[9]

The Spanish likewise left their mark on Louisiana. Before the conclusion of the Seven Years' War, France, by the secret 1762 Treaty of Fontainebleau, ceded to Spain the area west of the Mississippi; Louis XV was anxious to rid himself of the colonial burden and also hoped to keep the territory from Great Britain, the traditional foe and ultimate victor in the war. (It is said that Voltaire expressed opposition to this cession.) By the subsequent Treaty of Paris (1763) France was obliged to cede to the British everything to the east of the river—that is, what are now known as the Florida Parishes (eight modern parishes, or counties). New Orleans was excepted from this cession; it was treated as an island. In 1783, that territory passed back to Spain, however. Meanwhile, the rest of the Louisiana territory was returned to France, by the secret Treaty of San Ildefonso (1800), which was not announced until March 1803. In 1810 the residents of the Florida Parishes declared, briefly, the Republic of West Florida; it was annexed by the United States later that year.[10]

Spanish rule presented the first great cultural challenge to the French Creoles of New Orleans and upriver, who rebelled against the cession, though without violence, and drove away the first governor, Antonio de Ulloa, who arrived in 1766. Two years later the citizens were forced to capitulate when General Alejandro O'Reilly came with a strong expeditionary force. In response to the Spanish show of strength, a plan for an independent republic was drawn up; had it succeeded, it would have been the first republic in the Americas. Three of the conspirators were guests of O'Reilly on his ship; they were subsequently invited to attend on the twenty-first of August a grand party. They were trapped and arrested, along with their fellow plotters and such city figures as printers. The rebel leaders were either executed or exiled to Cuba. O'Reilly was loathed. Under succeeding and more accommodating Spanish governors, there was considerable reconciliation between the Spanish contingent and the French Creoles, through intermarriage and cooperation; and Hispano-Franco Creole society was the result. It was then tactful to blame O'Reilly as Irish.[11]

A first large wave of Germans and German Swiss arrived on the Gulf Coast in 1721 and by the following year reached New Orleans; they settled on the "Côte des Allemands" or "German Coast," upriver (that is, to the west of the city) on the west bank. Their names were generally Gallicized, wholly or partly, Zweig becoming Labranche, for instance. Although only Catholicism was officially permitted, there were Lutherans also. Isleños (Canary Islanders) arrived starting in 1778; in St. Bernard Parish they continued until well into the twentieth century to speak a somewhat antiquated Iberian tongue. Irish likewise arrived in large numbers after 1845 and at one time were the most numerous group in the city. Later groups included additional Swiss; Alsatians, after the Franco-Prussian War; Croats from the Dalmatian coast and other southern Slavs; further waves of Irish; and Italians, especially in the late 1800s. In 1883 Hearn discovered near Lake Borgne an almost-unknown fishing village settled by Malays from the Philippines.[12]

Nevertheless, it was the French who contributed most to shaping the mores and attitudes in the colonial and immediate postcolonial periods and whose legacy retained the greatest prestige thereafter. "French thought, literature, and art impregnated them so deeply that they existed in a completely French culture." The legacy of the early settlers was reinforced by continued immigration of French, following turmoil in France and Saint Domingue, the Bourbon Restoration (1815), the July Revolution (1830), the Revolution of 1848, and seizure of power by Louis-Napoleon (1851). Whether new arrivals were considered Creoles varied according to the social context and attitudes; radical thinkers (often refugees) from France, such as Louis-Armand Garreau and Charles Testut, were French and contributed to Francophone writing but did not share Creole attitudes.[13]

Blacks in Louisiana were brought directly from Africa, starting in 1719, and from the West Indies. Slave markets became a fixture of New Orleans; most slave merchants were Jews, including the father of the pianist Louis Moreau Gottschalk. Mixed-race residents were present as early as 1724. In 1729 a mixed-race child was baptized, the son of one Françoise, a slave, and Etienne de Périer, the governor of the colony. Interracial sexual relations, though denounced by the Church, were favored by the numerical disparity between men and women and later promoted by social ritual. They produced mulattos and ultimately quadroons, octoroons, and others, many of whom were born or became free—the *gens de couleur libres* or Free People of Color. By the time of Reconstruction, the white and nonwhite populations of New Orleans had more members with ancestors of the other race than any other American city or state. The early unions that produced these people were often a type of concubinage called, eventually, *plaçage*, whereby prosperous whites could take mistresses of color (usually free), whom they set up comfortably and by whom they often had children, born free. Gottschalk's father kept a mulatto mistress and had by her five children. Other Free Blacks were the legitimate offspring of free black or mulatto men and free or enslaved women; or they earned their freedom, many after having fought alongside the French in the Natchez Wars (1729–30). Their numbers increased particularly under the Spanish.[14]

The status of both *gens de couleur libres* and slaves was dictated by the Code Noir, drawn up originally in 1685 to regulate the slave trade in French colonies but emended by John Law and adopted for Louisiana in 1724. It was less severe than the Anglo-based codes used in the southern Atlantic colonies. Several articles, some modified later, stated the rights of slaves and owners' obligations to them, including humane considerations (decent clothing, adequate subsistence and shelter, even in old age). Article 43 stated that husbands and wives belonging to the same master should not be separated, nor children separated from parents. Article 54 granted to *affranchis* (manumitted slaves) the same rights, privileges, and immunities which were enjoyed by freeborn persons. According to article 22, however, slaves could not hold property; and marriage and concubinage between whites and blacks were forbidden (article 6).[15]

Modified again slightly in the blacks' favor by the Spanish, the Code Noir was replaced shortly after cession to the United States and modified once more by the first state constitution. The rights granted to manumitted persons were gradually curtailed until Free People of Color were almost as disenfranchised as slaves. They were forbidden to inherit property from a white (that law was often circumvented); at most, in the case of bachelor white fathers, the children could inherit only one-tenth of an estate. They could, however, sue whites and serve as witnesses in civil cases against them; and they had the right to trial.[16]

By 1810, the contingents of black and mixed-race immigrants from the islands were large; the smallest number cited is more than five thousand; one authority gives ten thousand. The mixed-race immigrants brought with them a developed system of distinctions and terminology of breeding, which contributed subsequently to the tripartite racial and class hierarchy in the city. Important connections, both direct and indirect, endured between New Orleans Free Blacks and Dominican and Haitian blacks; some traveled back and forth and others absorbed identical influences in Paris. Cable's story "Le Café des exilés" (which takes place in 1835) depicts with tenderness members of this exiled group and their nostalgia for their home islands.[17]

The influx of blacks was influential on the psyche of the white Creoles. As Doris Y. Kadish noted, the violent events on Saint Domingue in the 1790s "haunted the political unconscious of Europeans and Americans well beyond the abolition of slavery in the French colonies in 1848." It was believed that many black immigrants were seditious, and indeed in 1795 an insurrection—led, ironically, by whites—was attempted in Pointe Coupée Parish, followed in 1811 by a larger uprising, on the German Coast. In 1806 further immigration by free black males from the French islands was forbidden. Immigration of free nonwhites from elsewhere was restricted additionally later. In the early 1800s, the New Orleans city council prohibited assemblies of slaves for dancing except on Sundays, in an open space. Congo Square or Place des Nègres, as it was first known (located now within Armstrong Park), near the edge of the French Quarter, was opened for this purpose.[18]

Very briefly under French rule after 1800, the colony was transferred to the young American union in December 1803, at which time the territorial population was about fifty thousand or more, of whom ten thousand lived in New Orleans. Louisiana became a state in 1812 (over objections in Congress, owing to the "foreignness" of the culture). The 1803 transfer was not well received by the resentful Creoles, accustomed to thinking of themselves as French even under Spanish rule, suddenly residents of an Anglophone, generally Protestant republic. "Both Jefferson and [Governor] Claiborne anticipated difficulties in establishing the authority of the United States, as they had been advised by Spanish officials that the people of Louisiana 'are kept in order only by the hand of power.'" The Creoles "resented the Americans from the day and hour of the Louisiana purchase." Chafing under the humiliation of having their homeland sold, they found the Americans arrogant and disliked the imposition of English as the official daily language. They resolved to keep their culture and their languages (French and Spanish): "Already the determination to live within themselves must have been engendered in their minds. These Americans might come to New Orleans, but never would they enter its inner circles. They would always remain foreigners. The impregnable barriers went up. The bitter struggle against Americanization had begun." Evidence of their determination included the new French newspapers that were launched, as well as the petition lodged before Congress in 1804 pleading that the French language be maintained.[19]

The phenomenon of 1803 is curious: freedom-loving *Americans* became the oppressors of a formerly *European* colony and its European inhabitants, who for cultural reasons preferred their original colonizers. However, despite resentment at the Americans, the white Creoles were loyal to the United States in the War of 1812; siding with the British would have been inconceivable. As King wrote long after, "As much as the Creoles hated the Americans, they were not going to allow a foreign invader to occupy a land which they considered theirs by right of original discovery, occupation, and development." During the Civil War, they took, of course, the southern position; anti-Americanism found a new expression in their loyalty to the South and hatred of Yankee forces, carpetbaggers, and Reconstructionists. "A country given over to lawlessness, a people demoralized, swarming free negroes, an insolent soldiery, ruin, wretchedness and despair, . . . smug money-makers . . . who had shrewdly stayed home"—thus King described Louisiana after 1865. The contrast between Louisianans of European descent, conservative, cherishing their inherited culture, and the *criollos* of Latin America is striking; as Donald Demarest observed, almost all the Latin American independence movements were led by *criollos*. "Madame Délicieuse," a story by Cable, set in 1830, depicts the Creoles' early hopes of reclaiming their authority. "There was to be a happy renaissance; a purging out of Yankee ideas; a blessed homecoming of those good old Bourbon morals and manners which Yankee notions had expatriated."[20]

New Orleans was listed as having approximately 46,000 residents in 1830, and 102,000 in 1840—an enormous growth. In 1837 it was the fourth largest city in the United States; by 1850, with a population of 150,000, the third. By 1860, it had grown to 168,000. Ten years later, with the annexation of adjacent plantations and outlying small towns, it was 191,418. In the 1830s and 1840s, the struggle between the Creoles and the Americans reached its apex. The latter pushed through the legislature an amendment to the city charter by which the government was divided into three, serving the Vieux Carré or French Quarter, the Faubourg Marigny, and the American sector, or Faubourg Sainte-Marie. The last then had control of its own tax money and outstripped the Vieux Carré in improvements. This arrangement lasted until 1852. An epidemic of cholera added to yellow fever carried away in 1832 some 5,000 residents. Further yellow fever epidemics—"Bronze John"—in following years killed thousands; the 1853 rampage was the worst, and the combined death total for the three outbreaks of 1853–55 was almost 13,000. In 1837, 136 sugar plantations failed because of plummeting prices; 14 banks failed and numerous other bankruptcies followed; inflation was high, and the Depression continued into the early 1840s. By 1840 Americans outnumbered Creoles, whereas at the time of the Purchase the Creoles outnumbered the foreign Americans seven to one.[21]

By midcentury it was clear that the Americans had achieved political and commercial dominance, while the Creoles still had social and cultural prestige and the French language remained prevalent in the city. During Reconstruction (which lasted into 1877—the lengthiest occupation in any former Confederate state), the white Creoles, feeling twice ill-used, first by the transfer of their colony to America, then by the Confederate defeat, continued to cherish their traditions (including social structures and prejudices) and language. What was left of Creole culture was vulnerable, however, to the combined invasion of carpetbaggers and scalawags. After Admiral David Farragut occupied New Orleans in 1862 for the Union and General Benjamin Butler (nicknamed "Beast," "Butcher," or "Spoons") was appointed military governor, it was ordered that teaching in Louisiana public schools be done in English; not until 1868, however, was it specified that public laws and judicial documents must be in English, and French must not be taught in elementary schools. This law was subsequently emended to allow the teaching of French in French-speaking parishes. One manifestation of Creole resentment was the White League, which waged a paramilitary campaign against Reconstruction policies, notably the Battle of Liberty Place (1874).[22]

Affection for France lasted throughout the century and well into the following one. In the spring of 1871, after the Franco-Prussian War and the siege of Paris, sympathetic New Orleanians sent two hundred thousand francs in aid of the French wounded. James Barrie reported after his visit to New Orleans in 1896 that in their determination "to repel all encroachments of the despised Americans" the Creoles remained more French than the Parisians.

At the same time, they felt some ambivalence toward the former *patrie*. As late as 1882, the French consul in New Orleans could write: "Colonized and governed according to an authoritarian doctrine, ceded, taken back, sold by the fatherland, the very real affection of Louisianans for France is not without a sentiment of bitterness..."[23]

The Free People of Color or *gens de couleur libres* were largely industrious, often tasteful and cultured men and women who preserved their identity by marriage within their class. Though positioned ambiguously between two other classes and races, and defined both positively and negatively by what they were not, they did not merely *react*; they were agents, contributing to shaping their own situation. As early as 1830, some owned sugar and cotton plantations; many owned slaves. By 1850, they held some $2,200,000 worth of real property; by 1860 their real properties may have been worth as much as $15,000,000. By 1880 the per-capita wealth was $40, to be contrasted to that of blacks in Savannah, calculated at $7.31. A representative case was that of the Free Woman of Color Louise Vitry, who owned a large two-story house, given her by the white Achille Courcelle, for whom she bore four children; upon his death in 1858 his creditors sued her to recover unpaid debts, but she won the case.[24]

The ramifications of being in opposition to two groups—the Other to multiple Others, occupying the midposition between the valued and privileged (white) and the undervalued and unprivileged (enslaved black)—were various. The status accorded to *white* created a hierarchy, in which the lightest persons of mixed race occupied, and still occupy, the upper positions. Their education (including their speech) often justified this status, but education and other advantages reflected the hierarchy as well as contributing to it. Thus many Free Blacks drew their identity chiefly from whites, viewing their origin as *felix culpa*, or, as one of Cable's characters puts it, seeing the "taint of caste" as the "holiest and most precious of their virtues." During the German Coast uprising, local Free Blacks (and some slaves) joined the whites in opposing it. When slaves marched on New Orleans from outside the city in the 1850s, the Free People of Color resisted the rebellious slaves as vigorously as the whites did. Many clung tenaciously to their French ancestry and traditions; some continued long after the Louisiana Purchase to call themselves "French citizens." France represented and sometimes afforded true racial equality, not the restricted status available in Louisiana. "Their emotional allegiance was to the 'Marseillaise,' rather than the 'Star-Spangled Banner' or the drums and kalimbas of Africa."[25]

Many Free Blacks, who were listed in city directories, settled in the Faubourg Tremé (sometimes spelled Trémé), where descendants still live. It was created in 1810 as the first municipally funded subdivision in New Orleans, undertaken when Claude Tremé sold his Bayou Road plantation for forty thousand dollars; but in fact Tremé began selling lots in 1798. Located beyond North Rampart Street, a French Quarter boundary, it is claimed as the oldest surviving black neighborhood in the United States and is a crucible of black culture; it has been called the birthplace of jazz. The city's first brick manufacture (established around 1721) was located there; Osbey's poetry alludes frequently to slave-built brick walls and banquettes (sidewalks). According to the film *Faubourg Tremé: The Untold Story of Black New Orleans*, the district, which occupies part of both the Sixth Ward and the Seventh Ward, was at one time the largest community of Free Blacks in the Deep South; some families still used French as their principal language until the late 1960s. The New Orleans African American Museum is located on Governor Nicholls Steet in the Tremé Villa, built in the late 1880s. Another neighborhood with many black Creole residents was the Faubourg Marigny, likewise created shortly after 1800; early in its history three-quarters of the land belonged to Free People of Color.[26]

Prior to 1865, Free Blacks could practice medicine only with difficulty, but there were a few doctors—some trained in Paris—dentists, nurses, a pharmacist. Of the many businessmen, some became wealthy. From the early colonial period, when, to increase the skilled population, slaves were apprenticed to experienced tradesmen, many Creoles of Color practiced skilled trades, such as tailoring and furniture-making. The practice was continued under the Spanish. For example, Destrehan Plantation house, a few miles upriver from New Orleans, was constructed (1787–90), according to the building contract, by a Free Man of Color. Other Creoles of Color were musicians (performers, composers), architects, sculptors, painters. According to Mary Gehman, the 1850 New Orleans census listed 1,792 Free People of Color in fifty-four occupations, most of which required skill. There were more skilled workmen among them than among the local Irish. As anthropologist Nick Spitzer noted, the skilled tradesmen and artisans contributed greatly to "cultural creolization," particularly in architecture and music. Among accomplished painters was Julien Hudson (1811–1844), who trained in New Orleans with Italian and German teachers, then went to Paris.[27]

At the beginning of the Civil War, many Free Blacks were pro-Confederate and in some parishes formed Home Guards; three regiments of men of color fought on the Confederate side until the Federal troops took New Orleans. Blacks were subsequently recruited into Union regiments (the first colored units, constituted in September 1862), called Native Guards. After Butler's arrival in 1862, Armand Lanusse refused to follow his command that the Union flag should be raised over his school; he later apologized for what he recognized as a tactical mistake.[28]

Under the occupation, Reconstruction, and beyond, Free People of Color as well as whites suffered, for on top of the devastating impact of the war and occupation, the legal and social systems underpinning their privileged social position and status were dissolved by the emancipation of Negro slaves. As Anne Rice put it succinctly, "The close of the era of Reconstruction was the death knell for their caste. . . . The spirit and genius of the *gens de couleur libres* were forgotten." Though they had hoped for abolition of race barriers, the Creoles of Color, who were, as one historian put it, "aristocrats," were not generally pleased to be associated with former slaves. They felt more keenly than before that their ties to France, its language and literature, its Latin origins—important elements of their history and identity—were threatened by Americanization. While editors of *La Tribune de la Nouvelle-Orléans* and other opinion-makers believed that they should accept willingly the American decision to classify them as "black," some protested over their loss of identification and ascendancy. These decades were, according to one commentator, "the nadir of black life in the United States because of the increased violence, segregation, economic exploitation, and denial of citizenship rights that occurred."[29]

Thus the nonwhite Creoles in L'Isle Brevelle, an old and important Creole community near Natchitoches, who had publicly favored the Confederacy despite supposing that a Union victory would bring them political rights, "did not deign to go to school with the blacks who attended the new public institutions." The parents taught that "it's blood that counts." In Cable's "The 'Haunted House' in Royal Street," a girl protests, "Must I go to school with my own servants to escape an unmerited disdain?" while another cries, "The shame of it will kill me." Alfred Mercier's *L'Habitation Saint-Ybars* (1881) likewise suggests the dilemmas of the Creoles of Color and the deterioration of racial relations.[30]

The elimination of the caste called Creoles of Color would later be legally confirmed, as was noted above, by the definition of "Negro" in *Plessy v. Ferguson*. Of no help were the subsequent twentieth-century attempts to redefine "black" in legal terms, including the "traceable amount" law and particularly the 1970 statute (repealed in 1983) that held anyone having more than one-thirty-second of Negro blood should be considered black.

This chapter can conclude with a paradox. To the degree that *Creole* designates African Americans of partial French or Spanish ancestry in south Louisiana, or south Louisiana blacks in general, the category is a living, expanding one; in contrast, *Creole* as applied to whites is a shrinking category, no longer viable, practically. The concept and use have not disappeared entirely, as can be seen in New Orleans in circles where people take pride in their French ancestry—social and literary clubs such as Les Causeries du lundi, schools where French is taught throughout all grades, and churches. But, with a few exceptions, the category of "Creole (white) author" has not survived into the twenty-first century. Novelists considered in chapter 12 generally had roots early in the century or, though they treated Creole society, were not themselves Creole. Explanations for the change will be considered there.

CHAPTER TWO

Features of Early Louisiana Literature and the Cultural Milieu

The concerns of this chapter are the standing of literature by Louisiana Creoles (in all applications of the term) and its early features; the nineteenth-century cultural milieu; and features of the environment that contributed to the distinctiveness of Louisiana literature.

Initially, it should be considered to what degree this writing—by definition provincial or regional—is a discrete body of literary production, to be identified as such because of its distinctive characteristics and origin, and worthy of its own literary history—something like Scottish literature within the wider corpus of British writing. (The terms *provincial* and *regional* are not meant pejoratively, although, as Shirley Ann Grau remarked apropos of *southern*, a similar, if larger, category, they are often used in a condescending manner.) Bibliographies and compendia on an axis of "identity literature" call attention to bodies of writing but prove nothing about the critical value of such groupings. There is no doubt, at least, that Louisiana literature, even Anglophone, is not simply a point on the continuum of southern American literature—that is, an undifferentiated branch on the southern tree. The facts that the first Louisiana authors were, even if native-born, essentially foreigners, writing in a foreign tongue, and that many were, along with their fictional characters, Roman Catholics (with a French or Spanish flavor), are sufficient to distinguish Louisiana writing. This is so despite obvious overlap—especially, the centrality of blacks as authors and subjects and of the racial question, which marks so much writing from elsewhere in the South. Even less is Louisiana Creole writing generically "American": some is self-consciously *anti*-American.[1]

Letters in Louisiana were born from French roots in the eighteenth and early nineteenth centuries—that is, the declining decades of French classicism (with the great models still dominant), the *Age des Lumières*, pre-Romanticism, and Romanticism—generally liberal, though conservative and traditionalist Louisiana authors drew on it also. Whatever one's tastes, it was a literary inheritance to be envied, an established cultural foundation. Might Francophone nineteenth-century Louisiana literature thus be just a "colonial branch" of French literature? For decades it could be viewed thus—perhaps also as a "hyperliterature" or "hypernational," by its devotion to traditions; the enduring presence of French Romanticism, even as it waned, on the Louisiana literary scene constituted a *romantisme attardé*, a kind of colonial postscript. Yet its characteristic topics marked this body of writing also as intercultural, even as it developed in what Walter Putnam has called "espaces limitrophes." It evolved more slowly than writing did in France and, except for immigrant figures, local authors did not generally ascribe to revolutionary politics, nor did early Louisiana writers have to find new ground. Formal and thematic features of Louisiana writing, local authors' residence in Paris and connections there (schools, publishing houses, and theaters), and the French cultural life in New Orleans offer a prima facie case for considering Louisiana literature as an extension of French letters.[2]

Twentieth-century critics, even friendly, saw moreover that, as Edward Larocque Tinker asserted, nineteenth-century Louisiana literature did not constitute a body of great value, and that "most of these works are bizarre." He granted interest only to works in which authors depicted life around them. George Reinecke similarly observed that Louisiana literature was never *great*, only, sometimes, *good*. (Few bodies of literature can indeed be called *great*.)[3]

Nevertheless, it was not just imitative—neither distant outpost nor ingenuous parasite of another body of writing. While one must grant that there was no truly innovative literary movement and no Louisiana authors had the genius of nineteenth-century giants in France, that should not lead to broad condemnation of local writing, with its specific settings, themes, and concerns and its many skilled practitioners. By the 1840s, in full flower, it was a dual-culture, partly dual-language, and original product—transnational, somewhat transcultural, and yet singular, a unique phenomenon. Authors took as models the great French authors but also Shakespeare; they published their works in Paris and New Orleans, sometimes simultaneously, and saw their plays produced in one or another city; they read reviews of others' works from both continents, traveled back and forth, and used local materials, not just picturesque bits but unique cultural elements. While poetry, the most beloved genre of the nineteenth century, was broadly derivative, featuring the dominant Romantic forms and themes—nature, religion, exile, melancholy, and of course love—the genre still lent itself to the particular concerns of Louisiana authors, some of whom gave it distinctive directions. Local topics included the wilderness, the city, the peculiar racial system, expatriation, Creole linguistic and cultural inheritance, and white Creole opposition to Anglo-Americans. In the vein of Hippolyte Taine, one critic called for a distinctly indigenous literature that would "have an entirely local color, bear the impression of our ideas, undergo the influence of our climate." Ironically anticipating certain present-day views, Charles-Oscar Dugué, a poet and playwright, launched an appeal for Louisianans to affirm their heritage in literature. "Only a Louisiana historian can write the history of Louisiana; only a Louisiana poet can sing it."[4]

Local authors were Romantic partly by virtue of living in Louisiana, which for the French constituted the *désert* (wilderness) par excellence. As popularized by Jean-Jacques Rousseau and Bernardin de Saint-Pierre, then reinforced by François-René de Chateaubriand, Etienne de Senancour, Alphonse de Lamartine, Victor Hugo, and others, the view that nature is a home, a friend, a healer, a recourse and refuge from society could not have been better illustrated than by writers in the young colony. Antoine-Simon Le Page du Pratz, who traveled there in 1718, wrote upon returning to France in 1734:

> I was greatly taken by the beauty of the countries that I had seen; I should have liked to end my days in those charming places of solitude, far from the tumult of the world, from avarice and deceit; there, one enjoys a thousand innocent pleasures . . . there, one is exempt from criticism, . . . and calumny; there, charmed by the birds' concerts, which fill the neighboring woods, one can contemplate pleasantly the marvels of nature.

Similarly, the historical novel, as developed by Romantic writers in France, was well suited to Louisiana concerns, which invited colorful and dramatic treatment by means of Hugoesque devices such as hyperbole and antitheses. As one literary historian concluded: "The writings from the area and the era . . . must be viewed as constituting a distinct body of literature . . ." This was what Wendell Berry has called "a local commitment," the more so in that the language was widely shared in the same hemisphere only by inhabitants of some West Indies islands and Canadians.[5]

Such distinctiveness, contrasting with American culture elsewhere, was perceptible from Paris—as suggested by the reception given there to Louisiana authors. In Berry's view, "America was to Europe and to the deracinated Europeans who claimed it, a new place." Whether admired or criticized, the Creole attitudes toward pleasure, beauty, style, leisure, tradition, family, and place were both the source and the consequence of literary values. But, as Berry remarked, America was "unprotected by the cultural restraints of the Old World and therefore vulnerable to the Old World's worst impulses and desires." This lack of restraint is what the early Creoles disliked in Americans; even after 1900, they still resented the predominant exploitive economy of northerners, while other Americans, southerners included, viewed New Orleans as "that worldly and even foreign city," to borrow William Faulkner's words.[6]

Very early, in fact, New Orleans was known as the City of Sin, a New Sodom. Sister Madeleine Hachard de Saint-Stanislas, who arrived in 1727, described to her father the painted women and fancy dresses, adding, "The devil has a vast empire here." One of George Washington Cable's characters thinks of New Orleans as the "City of the Plain" and another alludes to the "Américain-Protestant-poisoned" Creole community. William Penn Brannan spoke of "the city of New Y'Orleans, the mother of harlots and hard lots . . . whar . . . gamblers, thieves, and pickpockets goes skiting about the streets . . . whar honest men are scarcer than hen's teeth." A century later Hamilton Basso spoke of the "Latin irresponsibility . . . found in New Orleans, the elevation of having a good time to the forefront of man's endeavor." "There were . . . no Puritans in New Orleans," wrote Lyle Saxon similarly. "These were Latins and they brought with them their Latin frankness as to eating and drinking and as to matters pertaining to sex."[7]

A distinctive feature of Louisiana writing is the remarkable body of nineteenth-century literary work in French by Free People of Color, who, with their racial mixture and their experience of difference, had unique viewpoints to offer. Writing expressed what their cultural marginality signified for them. Their cultural ties to the former colonial nation remained strong; France was the fatherland of equality, to which they could look with pride. The connection shored up their local image, moreover. Whereas elsewhere, the slave narrative (which arose in the 1830s, many perhaps ghostwritten) was by 1845 the principal literary mode of expression among black Americans, the *gens de couleur libres* cultivated standard European genres. "The literature of other black Americans of the period differed vastly from the romantic laments of the Creole poets." Literature by Free People of Color belongs thus to French colonial writing. It is also kin (linguistically, thematically) to Creole literature elsewhere and Atlantic literature—a broad category comprising writing from both shores of the Atlantic and, especially, the islands and the black diaspora, with its African connections.[8]

Literary products in Creole patois must be mentioned, although they occupy a minor place. Creole is a language of the Western Hemisphere, a singular cultural construct, whose birth coincides chronologically with the Enlightenment and its early anthropological understanding of singularity of nations and their products:

> If then each original language which is the native growth of a country develops in accordance with its climate and region, if each national language forms itself in accordance with the ethics and manner of thought of its people, then conversely, a country's literature which is original and national must form itself in accordance with such a nation's original native language in such a way that the two run together.[9]

Possessing a trilingual body of writing, with a fourth variety if one counts recent Cajun texts, Louisiana is unique among the states and closer to the Antilles. Poets such as Jules Choppin (1830–1914) and Edgar Grima (1847–1939), who wrote in standard French also, published fables in the Creole tongue. In addition, patois appears frequently, usually in conversations, alongside French or English, in Alfred Mercier's *L'Habitation Saint-Ybars*, Louis-Armand Garreau's story "Bras-coupé," George Washington Cable's *The Grandissimes*, and elsewhere.

Yet Louisiana literature is not simply a variety of Atlantic literature. It is older and was born of a stable and cultured society with considerable fluidity, despite the class system, and with a double center, two "lettered cities" (to borrow Ángel Rama's phrase). It is thus appropriate to see Louisiana writing in a European context also. As Bill Marshall has observed, "Louisiana literature in its diversity can be read as a tension between forces—of mimicry and authenticity, and of the translatlantic and the local." It was not until the twentieth century that such an advantage was gained by authors from the French-language Antilles. After English writing developed in Louisiana, the state had *two* splendid literary languages to draw on. This does not mean that they were culturally equivalent or that the choice to write in one or the other was neutral.[10]

While it will be granted, then, that Louisiana Creole literature constitutes a discrete body of writing and a rich literary legacy, not just a miscellany, one must recognize that it is not coherent and unified in all respects, nor should the materials be forced into tight categories. Between the Francophone poet

Adrien Rouquette (born 1813), a defender of white Creole society, and the popular Anglophone novelist Anne Rice (born 1941), who drew a sympathetic portrait of mixed-race Creoles in the 1840s, there is a broad gulf, not just chronological. Yet they and numerous others who present diverse faces of Creole culture can be examined together profitably, as the remainder of this book undertakes to do.

The milieu in which the Louisiana literature developed was a particular one. As early as 1803 it could be defined as a postcolonial territory; yet French culture did not yield readily to Anglophone influences (just as the Anglophone population granted value to Creole customs only reluctantly and partially). New arrivals, most speaking English, altered the demographic scene, and different attitudes toward mores, traditions, commerce, religion, and culture clashed with those of the original colony. When family fortunes permitted it, youth were sent to study in Paris; whole families went sometimes. The Lycée Louis-le-Grand was the favorite of Creole families. Many gifted men, such as Louis Moreau Gottschalk, Mercier, Michel Séligny, and Camille Thierry remained abroad for many years. At home, French-language schools afforded white Creoles a classical education. Among them was the Collège d'Orléans, conceived in 1805, which, after delays, finally opened in 1812. Its director later was Joseph Lakanal, who, having voted for the execution of Louis XVI, had fled from France in 1815. But Lakanal was looked on with great disfavor as a regicide by the conservative Creole majority, and the college closed in 1823.[11]

High culture flourished. Whereas Pierre-Louis Berquin-Duvallon could write in 1802 that New Orleans had a single school, a single printer, and no bookstore, only two decades later the cultural landscape was entirely different, and cultural life remained vigorous through 1860. There was a highly developed literary self-awareness, accompanied by dialogue and allusiveness, or intertextuality, by which authors echoed, supported, or opposed each other. Literary clubs as well as countless newspapers and magazines kept *amateurs* abreast of literary fashions and preserved for decades the tradition of a Creole literature. At midcentury, Charles Gayarré and Charles Testut published their respective studies *Literature in Louisiana* and *Portraits littéraires de la Nouvelle-Orléans*. In 1911 Rodolphe-Lucien Desdunes brought out his survey of the cultural achievements of the Free People of Color. Many twentieth-century works reflect and explore the cultural self-awareness and certain specific experiences of Louisianans.[12]

The first professional theatrical troupe was that of Saint Domingue refugees, who started performing in 1791. The first theater opened the following year, the Théâtre Saint-Philippe in 1808. The first opera was staged in 1796. Many European operas had their American premieres at the Théâtre d'Orléans—claimed as the first opera house in the United States—or the French Opera House (built in 1859, on Bourbon at Toulouse). (Theaters were segregated; Creoles of Color sat in the "Quadroon Boxes.") Grace King wrote: "When one said the 'Théâtre d'Orléans' in those days, and for forty years afterward, in New Orleans, one expressed a theatrical excellence second only to Paris." Figures for total performances vary and may not be reliable. In 1813, there were, on the boards, twenty-four operas, seventeen comedies, and seven tragedies; in 1816, seven operas, six comedies, and a tragedy. The plays were usually in verse (alexandrines), with Hugoesque topics and treatments. Later, some were performed also in Paris. One such may have been *Le Comte de Carmagnola* (1852; published 1856), by Louis-Placide Canonge, who had studied in Paris. It is alleged that it had one hundred performances, probably an exaggeration. Stephen Crane remarked that the best place to see opera in the United States was not New York but New Orleans, where both touring and resident opera and dramatic companies performed as well as numerous celebrated singers. In the American section, the St. Charles Theater, which seated four thousand spectators, opened in the 1830s. By the 1860s, New Orleans was surpassed only by New York in the number of theaters and reported quality of performances, and many famous actors and actresses appeared on its stages. Music was not confined to operas; the city was, according to S. Frederick Starr, long "second to none in the Americas with respect to the quantity, quality, and diversity of music performed there."[13]

In New Orleans the Free Blacks were not only industrious but largely literate; by one estimation, four-fifths met that standard by 1850, and over a thousand of their children were in school. One authority calls them "the most politicized and articulate free black community in the South." In the Isle Brevelle area near Natchitoches, the remarkable Métoyer family and others constituted a large, prosperous, hard-working, cultivated group. "It is obvious," wrote John Blassingame concerning the postbellum period, "that Negroes in New Orleans were far more articulate, literate, and cosmopolitan than blacks in most other Southern cities." Among the schools, all private, were the Académie Sainte-Barbe, founded by Séligny, and the Institut catholique des orphelins indigents, or Couvent Institute, a coeducational establishment under the supervision of the Catholic clergy, opened in 1848 in the Faubourg Marigny thanks to an endowment left at the death of Mme Bernard (Justine) Couvent, a woman of color, around 1836. One of its founders was the poet Armand Lanusse, who served as its second principal. Straight

University (later College), founded in 1868, which became Dillard University, had white students as well as blacks, especially in the law curriculum. Like white Creoles, Free People of Color traveled to France to study or live, thus carrying out the Romantic theme of exile. This was so especially after 1840, when restrictions on them were more strictly enforced and white hostility grew.[14]

In addition to the societies that ran the Quadroon Balls—the eighteenth-century Société du Cordon Bleu being the oldest—the Creoles of Color had the Société d'Economie, the Société des Artisans, and, after the Civil War, the Francs Amis and numerous other clubs. Their authors contributed to the local newspapers. The black Creoles also had their own churches, such as St. Ann's, built in 1852 (now St. Peter Claver), and St. Augustine, a parish founded in 1840–41; the building, completed in 1842, is the oldest African American Roman church in the nation. The parish included some whites and enslaved blacks, for whom the free parishioners purchased pews—an instance of a relatively liberal racial structure. Other Free Blacks attended services at the cathedral—St. Louis King of France.[15]

The 1840s and, for Anglophone writers, the 1880s and 1890s were especially productive in New Orleans, which some considered the cultural capital of the United States. One scholar estimated the mid- and late-century Louisiana audience as 100,000. As literacy figures elsewhere suggest, however, for letters to flourish, vast numbers are not required; what is needed is value placed upon literature. Of the 1850 population (150,000), perhaps 20,000 were *illiterate*. As a comparison, one may look at France, where in 1850 the population was 35,000,000; it grew to 36 by 1870; according to Robert Gildea, the reading public (adults over 14 who were literate) in 1871 was 17.8 million.[16]

As well as magazines and book publishers, some bilingual, there were dozens of newspapers, some in Spanish, most in French: *Le Moniteur de la Louisiane* (founded by Louis Duclos in 1794); *Le Courrier de la Louisiane*, launched in 1807; the *Louisiana Gazette*; *L'Abeille de la Nouvelle-Orléans*, or the *Bee* (since it was bilingual originally), founded by François Delaup in 1827 (which ceased publication only in 1923); *La Renaissance Louisianaise* (1861–71). Under the Federal occupation Dr. Louis Charles Roudanez, a Creole of Color, and two associates founded *L'Union* (1862-64, in French and English), essentially a caste paper, unlike *La Tribune de la Nouvelle-Orléans*, the first black daily in the United States (1864–69), which was intended to be the voice of all nonwhites, freedmen and Free People of Color. Victor Hugo was among those who sent letters to the paper. When after two years Jean-

Charles Houzeau, a Belgian, became coeditor, it became mostly a political sheet. At least one German paper existed as late as the 1870s, the *Gazette.*

L'Abeille began printing original poetry in 1827 when a reader remarked how little verse was published in New Orleans (though a newssheet from the Collège d'Orléans, *L'Ami des Lois*, had printed many short poems). This reader was, it was revealed, Jean Duperron, who subsequently provided a poem in praise of Andrew Jackson. Many little newssheets and magazines followed suit, printing narrative, quasi-epic, or lyrical verse; fiction followed, in the form of short pieces or serialized novels, on the French model. Some papers republished work from France; an early version of Stéphane Mallarmé's "Don du poème" appeared in *Le Meschacébé*.[17]

An important publication of later decades was the *Comptes Rendus* published by L'Athénée Louisianais, a society whose aim was to preserve French language and culture after the Reconstruction-era laws on English. The society was intended also for "assistance mutuelle" and helped displaced Alsatians settle in Louisiana. Much poetry appeared in the pages of its journal—including verse by the Creole of Color Lucien (Lolo) Mansion. Among the society's lecturers from France were poet Henri de Régnier and dramatist Eugène Brieux. In the postbellum period, the *Daily Picayune* printed fiction and poetry of high quality by such authors as Mark Twain, Joel Chandler Harris, and Bret Harte; another literary publication was *South*, edited by John W. Overall. *De Bow's Review*, which began publication in 1846, was published for decades, though it became less literary, more commercial.[18]

The *imaginaire* of Louisiana writers was and remains concerned often with landscapes and weather. (Yellow fever likewise had its role.) These features, not necessarily friendly—a mighty river, threatening, given to flooding; large lakes and the Gulf; dark bayous; forests, beautiful or strange; forbidding swamps; hurricanes—offered unusual settings for poetry and fiction, some of which could be called Romantic Gothic. There were destructive storms in the 1700s, especially in 1779 and 1794. The great hurricane of 1856, which destroyed L'Isle dernière, or Last Island, with enormous loss of life, inspired several literary treatments. (It carried away an entire hotel at which a large party was taking place.) It was followed in 1893 by a similarly destructive storm that demolished Chênière Caminada and left only Grand Isle.[19]

An early storm description—perhaps the first—dates from the colonial period: Jean-François-Benjamin Dumont de Montigny's "Poème en vers, touchant l'établissement de la Province de la Louisiane." The poem traces Louisiana history from 1716 to 1741 and relates the storm of September 1722 that struck the young settlement of New Orleans.[20]

La grêle se mettant d'une telle manière
Qu'elle fit craindre à tous en ce triste moment
Que l'on allait avoir le dernier jugement!
Et même les oiseaux tombaient sur le rivage.

[The hail was arriving in such a way
That it made everyone fear in this unfortunate moment
That the Last Judgment was to come!
And even the birds fell on the shore.]

Additional literary reflections of *ouragans* are found in Mercier's *L'Habitation Saint-Ybars* and François Tujague's "A travers l'océan," in which a ship must confront the tempest. Whereas in continental Romantic poetry the image of a storm is usually a metaphor for passion, in Louisiana literature such an image carries precise referents. Thus, in reading Thierry's poem "L'Amante du corsaire," the Louisianan has a clear correlative of hyperbolic emotion when the speaker says:

Pour lui parler encore, pour lui dire: Je t'aime!
 J'irais sur l'Océan;
Pour baiser ses cheveux, j'irais, oui, fût-ce même
 En un jour d'ouragan!

[To speak to her again, to tell her: I love you!
 I would go onto the ocean;
To kiss her hair, I would go, yes, even if it were
 On the day of a hurricane!][21]

Finally, a glance is necessary at the most featured Louisiana setting of all, the urban landscape of the French Quarter. Among the oldest of city centers in America, it was laid out in 1718 by the engineer Adrien de Pauger, in a rational grid. Three eighteenth-century fires (1778, 1788, 1794) nearly destroyed it; only the Ursulines Convent (now the oldest building in the Mississippi Valley) survived; but each time the city was rebuilt. Its moral and social centers were the Church of Saint Louis, King of France (destroyed by fire in 1788, rebuilt, raised to cathedral rank in 1793); the Place d'Armes, later Jackson Square; and two buildings flanking the cathedral, the Cabildo, once the seat of the Spanish government, similarly destroyed in 1788 but rebuilt in the 1790s, with a French mansard roof, and its companion, the Presbytère, erected at the same time. The French Market, where Indian women sold their sassafras and objects made of latanier, dark-skinned women peddled calas (rice cakes) and other items, and fruits and vegetables were piled up, was a commercial and social center and also an aesthetic delight. The Quarter was subject to flooding, though less than some portions of the great river crescent, and for decades had muddy, unpaved streets, over which the women trod sometimes on boards, lifting their skirt hems, or were carried.

Along with the Tremé, the French Quarter was the heart of the Louisiana Creole world, for both whites and some Free People of Color also. While plantations and other outlying areas were important in both fact and literature, as illustrated in *L'Habitation Saint-Ybars*, and some fiction by Creole authors, notably Mercier, is set abroad, much writing by and concerning Creoles is centered on the Vieux Carré, where characters live or to which they gravitate. The novels of Cable and Sidonie de la Houssaye would be radically different without this anchoring in what was, even for the time, a small area. As in Paris, street names have entered into the literary (as well as popular) imagination, and they, together with evocations of buildings, the great river that borders the Quarter, and human figures, created in the nineteenth century (as later) a colorful, dynamic urban poetry.

CHAPTER THREE

Père Rouquette and Other Early Francophone Poets

French language is one marker of the writers grouped in this chapter (though some wrote in English also). They were born in the eighteenth or early nineteenth century, were white and, to the degree their political and social views can be determined, generally conservative. Their conservatism is pertinent insofar as it affected their writing and its reception. They and many from later generations were fundamentally colonials, who, as it was observed earlier, visited France as the mother country (not the way Anglophone Americans went on the Grand Tour). They were not quite a diaspora; rather, they returned to the matrix of their culture. They used verse principally. Though most were born after the transfer of authority to the Americans, they remained French in many ways, corroborating Grace King's words: "Our city brought her entire character from France, her qualities, as in French good qualities are called, and her defects." The earliest among them may be the first colonial authors to publish in France.[1]

Their audience was composed of Louisianans and readers in France. Among sympathetic readers there were doubtless a few monarchists; nostalgia for the connection to throne and Church as well as traditional class structures remained strong. As Lafcadio Hearn noted, "Creole society in Louisiana was an aristocratic and feudal organization . . . Planters and merchants lived and reigned like princes." Though monarchists were widely viewed in nineteenth-century France as reactionaries, loathed and feared by Bonapartist sympathizers as well as republicans—just as avid republicans feared Bonapartism—among native Louisiana writers, political factionalism did yield somewhat to a common sense of Frenchness and loyalty to the fatherland.[2]

The earliest writers were travelers, some of whom came with the initial parties of French explorers and settlers. Their manuscripts and accounts, published in France, have primarily historical interest. Literary reflections of the early colony include Antoine-François Prévost's *Manon Lescaut* (1731), the final episodes of which take place in Louisiana, and François-René de Chateaubriand's famous tale set in the American wilderness, *Atala* (1801). The sympathetic attitude toward the Indians displayed by Antoine-Simon Le Page du Pratz and others contrasts with the attitude of many British in North America. In a passage that anticipates Jean-Jacques Rousseau's praise of *le bon sauvage* and echoes Michel de Montaigne's famous depiction of the Cannibals, Le Page commended the goodness and common sense of the local natives: "One would be quite wrong to name Savages men who know how to make very good use of their reason, who think well, who possess prudence, good faith, and generosity, much more than certain civilized nations . . ." Elsewhere Le Page added: "[The natives] have no regulations other than reason, because in following exactly the law of Nature, they have no discussion and thus have no need for judges. Similarly, avarice, ambition, and several other passions so well known in the old World do not stifle in the fathers the feeling of Nature, which makes us wish for our blood to be perpetuated . . ."[3]

Two very early works deserve a word. One is a neoclassical poem, "La Prise du morne du Baton Rouge par Monseigneur de Galvez" (printed 1779), sometimes called the first Louisiana literary work, by Julien Poydras de Lalande (or Lallande) (1746?–1824), a native of Nantes, said to be a Protestant, who arrived in New Orleans in 1768 and became a merchant and planter in Pointe Coupée Parish. (The Pointe Coupée slave rebellion began on his property.) The poem was in praise of the Spanish governor, Bernardo de Gálvez, and the successful attack he led on the British. A river nymph speaks: "Quel Mortel, ou quel Dieu vient ici dans sa rage / Troubler la douce paix de mon heureux rivage?" [What Mortal, or what god comes here in his anger / To trouble the sweet peace of my happy shore?] While these alexandrines are entirely conventional, the topic is noteworthy, as Alcée Fortier remarked.[4]

The first recorded Louisiana drama is a neoclassical tragedy, *La Fête du petit blé; ou, L'Héroïsme de Poucha-Houmma*, by Paul-Louis Le Blanc de Villeneufve (1734–1815), performed in New Orleans in 1809 and published in 1814. Born in France, Le Blanc had joined the army and had been assigned to Louisiana, where for six years he served among the Choctaws, whom he liked and whose language he learned. Along with Le Page's history, the tragedy was among the earliest writings to depict the indigenous inhabitants and recognize their humanity, and it is a prelude to subsequent writings criticizing the settlers' treatment of indigenous and black peoples. The author's view is, however, somewhat ambivalent. The play, based on actual events, is a drama of murder, revenge, and honor, with a Voltairean strain of both religious scepticism and deism. But, as Mathé Allain has observed, the language is wooden, there is no character development, and the absolute law that would justify dying for honor is somewhat undermined by skepticism. When Cala-bé, the son of Chief Poucha-Houmma, kills a Choctaw, he takes refuge among the Attakapas, where he is welcomed. He marries the chief's daughter and takes his bride home. But the Choctaws demand vengeance and will not be satisfied with gifts; his father then offers his own life, which is accepted, in place of his son's.[5]

The poems of Louis Allard (1777–1847) were published simultaneously in New Orleans and Paris, just after his death, under the title *Les Epaves* [Driftwood]. The author was identified only as "un Louisianais." The preface claimed that the poems were found in the wreckage of the steamboat *Hecla*. (He may have viewed himself as a piece of flotsam.) Allard studied in Paris and returned home to live on his father's plantation, pieces of which he sold off when he needed money; the property later became City Park. He knew Latin well and rendered some Latin epigrams of Martial into French with concision and a rather blasé wit. He wrote a charming poem to a mockingbird, a creature that clearly appealed to the colonists' imagination.

The most Romantic of nineteenth-century Louisiana authors, perhaps, and one of the most markedly Louisianan, Adrien-Emmanuel Rouquette (1813–87), known as Abbé or Père Rouquette, was a born poet. His writings combine in striking fashion French romantic tropes and diction with local materials. He was eccentric and picturesque; in Louisiana, only the peripatetic Irishman Hearn, his friend for two years or so, rivaled him in that respect. Rouquette's two brothers, François Dominique and Térence, were likewise active in letters; the latter was among white contributors to *L'Album Littéraire* (see chapter 6). In most respects, Adrien's writings illustrate French Romanticism in full-blown mode, including adoration of nature and a penchant for natural religion as it was imagined by Rousseau and then put into verse by Alphonse de Lamartine and other major poets. Rouquette's nature was that of forests—friendly but untamed—and the great river. Unlike Lamartine, but like Alfred de Vigny, whom he admired, Rouquette tended toward conservatism. He was also fundamentally orthodox in religion. There are no grounds to consider him merely a poseur exploiting the *mal du siècle*; his romanticism was genuine and well founded in a vision of God and nature, a vision that may be called mystical. Though he wrote of the brotherhood of all races, preached against slavery, and lived among and ministered to Louisiana Indians, whose treatment by whites he criticized, he was capable of demeaning remarks on blacks. He supported Charles Gayarré and, with him and King, attacked the liberal George Washington Cable. Unlike other Louisiana conservatives and even many liberals, however, he supported the Federals during the war—through loyalty to the Union as an idea.[6]

Rouquette, whose father was originally from the Gers in France, was born on Royal Street in the French Quarter. In 1819 the mother, widowed that year, purchased a property on Bayou St. John. Relatives on his mother's side had an estate in St. Tammany Parish, across Lake Pontchartrain. He learned black Creole speech from the servants. He also became well acquainted with the Chactas Indians, or Choctaws, of St. Tammany. Stories about his running away as a small boy to live with them are, however, probably apocryphal. He began his studies at the Collège d'Orléans, then was sent to Transylvania University in Kentucky, and later to Mantua, Pennsylvania (now a neighborhood in West Philadelphia). These studies enabled him to learn English well; he took advantage of that skill to enlarge his audience.[7]

In 1829, Rouquette was shipped to France. He spent time in Paris, then enrolled in the Collège Royal de Nantes (1830). In 1833 he obtained a baccalaureate degree from the Collège de Rennes. He would cross and recross the ocean on several occasions in the following years. During each stay in France, he missed Louisiana greatly, perhaps seeing it better from abroad; but in New Orleans he felt deprived of the intellectual stimulation offered by Paris. He was thus, at least at the time, a man of two countries. His writing does not, however, reveal anxiety concerning linguistic identity or other transatlantic and transnational questions. Having returned home, he was later persuaded to study law in Paris, but he broke off his studies, too practical, and devoted himself to literary occupations. When his family decided to bring him home again, he arrived with a large library in his trunks. He failed the bar examination in 1839. He sailed again for France in 1840 but shortly returned to Louisiana; a final crossing took place in 1846.

By age eighteen he had read Chateaubriand's *Atala*. It affected him greatly, like countless other readers. As John R. Williams wrote, "Chateaubriand's influence upon French literature cannot be overestimated." Rouquette read other Romantic poetry and fiction and the unorthodox theologians Blaise Pascal, Joseph de Maistre, and Félicité-Robert de Lammenais, though he recognized that the heterodoxy of Lammenais was dangerous.[8]

Rouquette was drawn to the Choctaws' forest haunts and what he saw, in a neo-Rousseauistic vision, as their unspoiled life. Once, apparently, he met on the Lake Pontchartrain schooner a lovely Indian maiden, who may have been the inspiration for Oushola (that is, The Bird Singer), around whose image he wove what he himself called (in biographic "Révélations" prepared by a secretary) a "legend," which cannot be entirely credited. While the early death of a maiden he might have courted is plausible, the scene in which he comes upon her funeral procession is obviously a Romantic set piece. What is significant is not his liberties with fact but his idealization of Indian culture and an imaginary love that remained platonic. He admitted to, or boasted of, having identified himself with Chateaubriand's character Chactas and of wishing to marry an Indian maiden.[9]

In late 1842 Rouquette entered a seminary in Assumption Parish; he took orders in 1845, allegedly the first Creole ordained after the Louisiana Purchase (other priests having come from France). In 1848 he was appointed an assistant at St. Louis Cathedral; he remained there for some fourteen years. He contributed to *Le Propagateur Catholique*, a religious weekly in French and English. Repeatedly, he asked permission to retire to a solitary life; whether or not it was formally granted, in 1854 he left New Orleans for Mandeville, in St. Tammany Parish, where his brother Dominique likewise spent much of his time. While Adrien's withdrawal took place within a Catholic and clerical context, it is not without resemblance to Henry David Thoreau's retreat to Walden Pond, since both emphasized the relationship between isolation and authenticity, personal and civic. By 1859, Rouquette was firmly established as a missionary among the Choctaws, where he remained, except for occasional visits to the city, until 1886, a beloved figure called "Chahta-Ima," that is, "like a Choctaw."[10]

He wore his hair long and sometimes adopted Indian dress. He erected five rustic chapels or hermitages, including one halfway between Mandeville and Bayou Lacombe (Notre-Dame de la Solitude); one to the west of Mandeville (Kildara, or Cabin of the Oak); another, destroyed in 1862, at Buchuwa, the largest Choctaw village, at the headwaters of Bayou Lacombe; and another on the bayou. Under Federal occupation in 1862, the Indians withdrew into swamps and bayous where Union soldiers could not pursue them; Rouquette followed, passing (with Federal protection) across enemy lines to get medicine and other supplies, including quinine.[11]

In addition to journalism and criticism, Rouquette turned his hand to three genres: tale, eloquence and polemic, and poetry. He favored French but wrote also in English and patois; his poem "Mokeur Shanteur" was set to music by W. T. Francis. Among influences on his poetry were *The Seasons* of James Thomson, who had influenced the French pre-Romantics earlier.

Rouquette's first collection, published in France and New Orleans, was *Les Savanes; poésies américaines* (1841). It includes "Saint Paphnuce and Sainte-Thaïs l'Egyptienne," which anticipates Anatole France's exotic tale *Thaïs* (1890). Thomas Moore called Rouquette "the Lamartine of America" and wrote that *Les Savanes* "breathed forth the perfume of the forest flowers." Others called him "Ossian the Younger," in reference to the popular epic poems published under that name, in fact composed by James Macpherson. Rouquette received praise also from William Cullen Bryant, Charles-Auguste Sainte-Beuve, Lamartine, and Chateaubriand, who doubtless saw that *Les Savanes* was full of references to his writings. To current tastes, Rouquette's verse is overblown; Paul Verlaine had not yet recommended, "Prends l'éloquence et tords-lui le cou" (Take eloquence and wring its neck). Enthusiasm was, for Rouquette, the hallmark of poetry, which he viewed as "the language of inspired reason"; he believed that one must feel in order to know.[12]

In the preface to *Les Savanes*, Rouquette claimed that, notwithstanding Chateaubriand (who traveled in America but whose accounts of seeing the Mississippi and Natchez were invented out of whole cloth), no European had succeeded in depicting the New World; only those born there could do so. (Rouquette mentions Charles Brockden Brown, Washington Irving, James Fenimore Cooper, and Bryant, and quotes a poem by an unidentified Brainard, "The Falls of Niagara." The name of Walt Whitman might have been added had he written later.) Rouquette was aware that Chateaubriand had stopped on the Ohio. "Ta prose n'a rien peint; elle a tout transformé" [Your prose depicted nothing; it transformed everything].[13]

Typical of Rouquette's Romantic lyricism are these lines:

Et là, tranquille enfin, donner libre carrière
A cet élan du coeur qu'on appelle prière;
Croire, prier, aimer; à toute heure, en tout lieu
Ne voir et n'adorer que l'image de Dieu.

[And there, calm at last, to give free rein
To the movement of the heart which is called prayer;
To believe, pray, love; at every moment, in all places
To see and love only the image of God.]

Another sample is equally eloquent:

J'ai rêvé l'infini de tes bois, ô Nature!

Et je viens au doux bruit de la forêt de pin,
Pour pleurer librement, me pencher sur ton sein!

[I have dreamed of the infiniteness of your woods, O Nature!
And I come to the soft sound of the pine forest,
To weep freely, to lean on your bosom!]

Another poem illustrates his devotion to trees:

Oh! comme il en tombait une étrange harmonie;
Un bruit semblable au bruit de la mer en furie;
Un grand bourdonnement de branchages touffus;
Je ne sais quoi de sourd, de vague et de confus
Qui roulait dans l'espace immense et magnifique,
Et que l'homme n'entend qu'aux déserts d'Amérique!

[Oh, what a strange harmony fell from it,
A sound like that of the ocean in fury,
A great buzzing of the dense branches,
A *je ne sais quoi*, dull, vague, confused
Which rolled over the immense and magnificent space,
And which can be heard only in the American wilderness.]

An avaricious American fells the tree; but he cannot destroy the tree of Eden nor the cross, to which the tree is assimilated. Despite the Romantic themes and motifs—the omnipresence of divinity in nature, the immensity of the wilderness—Rouquette's verses are generally classical alexandrines of twelve syllables, with a caesura after the sixth (as opposed to Victor Hugo's "Romantic line," with two caesuras).

In 1841 Rouquette also published in Paris *La Thébaïde en Amérique*, a mystical work on the contemplative life. In 1860 he brought out *L'Antoniade ou la Solitude avec Dieu*, called a "hermit poem," in four parts, combining works published earlier. (Another "poème érémitique" followed in 1869.) Both French and English are used. His characteristic didacticism informs *L'Antoniade*; he ascribed to poetry a holy mission, somewhat as Vigny did in a nonreligious sense. Rouquette later published in English a poem about the holy Mohawk girl Catherine Tekahkwitha (beatified in 1980); he translated the poem into French prose.[14]

Rouquette's attitude toward America was ambivalent, despite his loyalty to certain of its premises and love for its natural beauty. In part two of *L'Antoniade*, "Poèmes patriotiques," he criticized immigration. (The anti-immigrant Nativist movement had begun to take shape in the 1830s and 1840s; the American or "Know-Nothing" Party, founded in 1849, had many followers in Louisiana. But Rouquette could not have subscribed to its anti-Catholic bias.) In part three, "Le Conciliabule infernal," Satan and associated devils rejoice over how they have corrupted the modern world, especially America, which should have been a paradise but instead has become an anti-Eden. Rouquette's choice to have Satan speak may reflect the example of John Milton's *Paradise Lost* and the enthusiasm of certain French and English Romantics for the figure of Lucifer. Rouquette's Satan says:

> Banni du ciel natal, j'ai bâti sur la terre
> Avec l'autel brisé, mon trône populaire!
> Je suis maître du monde, établi dans la chair,
> J'y suis maître et j'y règne aussi bien qu'en Enfer!

> [Banished from my birthplace, heaven, I have built on earth,
> With the broken altar, my popular throne!
> There, I am master of the world, established in flesh,
> I'm the master and reign there as well as in Hell!]

The chorus of demons speaks in short *vers libérés* (irregular verses), some with uneven numbers of syllables—as if the poet wanted to suggest their disorderliness. He anathematizes both the eighteenth and nineteenth centuries and certain famous figures and developments (but not Rousseauesque pre-Romanticism). The Enlightenment, the Revolution of 1789, commercialism, industrialization, the bourgeoisie, Protestantism, the French government under Louis-Philippe, and American democracy, that is, demagoguery, in which the devils delight, all receive attention. "Le peuple règne ici; l'Amérique est à moi!" [The populace reigns here; America is mine!] The author is particularly hard on women. He singles out Mormons for attack and calls Protestants "Voltaire's apes." Little escapes his wrath; only those who flee into the wilderness or adopt monasticism are not the devil's disciples. Yet elsewhere he holds out hope for America, if it accepts the Church and becomes, as he wished, Roman Catholic:

> L'Eglise d'Amérique, en qui tant d'espoir brille,
> De l'Eglise Romaine est la plus jeune fille,

Rayonnante de gloire et pleine d'avenir.
Gloire aux Etats-Unis! Gloire à la République!

[The American Church, in which so much hope shines,
Is the youngest daughter of the Roman Church,
Radiant with glory and full of the future.
Glory to the United States! Glory to the Republic!]

New Orleans comes off as badly as Paris—full of evils such as theaters, parties, commerce, painted and perfumed women. Anti-Protestant as he was, he had Calvinistic, or Jansenistic, attitudes (perhaps from reading Pascal); he did not, apparently, believe that Creole, or Latin, culture excused laxity in moral matters. A demon speaks:

Le peuple Américain, peuple gynécolâtre,
Contre la chair n'a point d'armes pour me combattre.
. . . .
Des vénins de l'Europe infectant l'Amérique,
Je vois y refleurir le culte idolâtrique. . . .
Depuis Philadélphie, aux froids palais de marbres, . . .
Jusqu'aux bords où croupit la Nouvelle-Orléans,
Sentine de l'Europe et nid de mécréants.

[The American people, idolaters of women,
Have no arms to fight the flesh and me;
I see flourish there the idolatrous cult
Of European venom, infecting America.
From Philadelphia, with its cold marble palaces,
To the shores where New Orleans lies stagnant,
Bilgewater of Europe and nest of heathen.]

Rouquette's best-known work is the 1879 prose romance he called a "legend," *La Nouvelle Atala; ou, la fille de l'esprit. Légende indienne par Chahta-ima (de la Louisiane)*, a contribution to the Indian vein in American literature and art, perhaps reminding readers of the paintings of George Catlin and the novels of Cooper—the *Leatherstocking Tales*, which include *The Last of the Mohicans* (1826)—and anticipating *Ramona* by Helen Hunt Jackson (1884). It is useful here to set out the generic difference between the romance, as commonly understood, and the novel. Deriving its name from the vulgar

Roman-derived tongue in which it first appeared, the romance has traditionally been seen as a lengthy fictional tale involving elements of the marvelous or wondrous, or set in a former time or distant place, conveying a sense of the strange, and involving adventures and striking deeds by heroes (historical or otherwise) who are usually one-dimensional. The romance is thus not mimetic, that is, not set firmly in reality as understood by modern writers. Fantasy is not essential, but the genre always appears under the star of the strange or distant and may have epic proportions. The genre of the novel can likewise trace its origins to medieval tales and, more remotely, epic, but its hallmarks are a firm grounding in reality, psychological interest (usually), and social concerns. Adventures are not excluded, but they belong to the realm of the plausible, not the marvelous. Rouquette's tale involves the remoteness of a different culture and various improbabilities that contribute to a sense of strangeness and wonder.[15]

Rouquette's romance was publicized in *Le Propagateur Catholique*; Hearn called it "the most idyllic work in the literature of Louisiana." It purports to have been recounted to the author by an Indian woman 125 years old. With quotations from Chateaubriand, it is clearly intended as a parallel but also a corrective. The signature ("by Chahta-ima") emphasizes the purported authenticity of the tale. It has many pre-Romantic and Romantic clichés—including the pathetic fallacy (identification of human emotions with a natural setting)—and illustrates what Irving Babbitt famously did not like about Romanticism—its infantile and feminine character. The author displays belief in the noble savage, whose morals are naturally good, and praises the Indians' adoration of the Great Spirit. Such natural religion supposes innate ideas (in contradistinction to the position of most Enlightenment figures, for whom knowledge came through the senses). Rouquette's prose is florid and ornamental, as well as edifying, with long preachy passages, apostrophes to the Divinity, and innumerable exclamation points.[16]

After her convent education, Atala, the daughter of a New Orleans family, rejects society, anathematized as corrupt. She wishes only to live naturally and worship God in nature's temple. She gets herself "lost" in the wilderness and lives henceforth like a savage, isolated except for animals, an Indian friend, and the latter's brother. (Disguised, she attends mass at a chapel, however.) She speaks sometimes in patois and also invents a "natural" language. She renounces all worldly life and vows virginity (to which Rouquette gave great importance). "Everything spoke to her of God alone" (52).

Her former slave, Rosalie, comes to find her and builds herself a hut nearby. Closely echoing Chateaubriand's *René*, she asserts, "Les passions sont semblables à ces grands orages qui dévastent la terre" [Passions are like great storms which wreak devastation on the earth] (61). Thus she rejects the Indian's love. Yet, when he is about to kill himself in despair, she changes her mind and runs after him, "craignant que tu ne commisses quelque acte insensé," using erudite French [fearing lest you commit some insane act] (68). After the most improbable events (one involving a mesmerizing rattlesnake and a panther), Rosalie marries him; with his sister, he is converted and baptized in haste by Atala when he seems about to die. (Rouquette clearly believed Rosalie to be the moral equal of the white Atala.)

An older Frenchman appears; he belongs to the tribe. His Indian name means "Wise Man." A "true philosopher," he is Rouquette's political spokesman, a corrective to Chateaubriand, since he *stays* in the "desert" rather than returning to the degenerate France of Louis-Philippe, its "ignoble democracy," "prosaic shopkeeper bourgeoisie . . . vulgar aristocracy" (75–76). Seeing the resemblance between Atala and an Indian woman he once loved, he suggests marriage to Atala. She falls into a stupor, presumably shocked by even the *suggestion* of marriage. A great storm arises, showing heavenly displeasure; might he have offended God? Of course both stupor and storm are *la voix du sang*, warning against incest: Rosalie, the depository of secrets, informs everyone that Atala is the daughter of this Frenchman and a Chactas princess. Kidnapped by her own brother (in punishment for marrying a white), the princess lived in Tangipahoa Parish, then died in New Orleans, where a kindly family took in her child, little Atala. Furthermore, Atala's Indian friend and the brother are her stepbrother and stepsister. Her stupor, which includes religious ravings in erotic language, having turned to fever, she dies, but not without the last sacrament, administered by le père Emmanuel, who sometimes visits the forest. The work ends with a funeral oration, in which Rouquette deplores the oppression of the Indians and the servitude to which they have been subjected. "Happy he who is free and who does not seek to enslave his fellow man" (101).[17]

The third genre cultivated by Adrien Rouquette was eloquence and polemic. His 1846 speech at the cathedral commemorating the Battle of New Orleans illustrates his views on patriotism and liberty, as well as Creole support of the American cause in 1812; British rule would have been more unpopular than the American presence. In 1855 he published a two-part pamphlet, *La Question américaine*, concerning civil and political matters, which showed his general conservatism on taxation and voting. More important is his 1880 polemic, *Critical Dialogue Between Aboo and Caboo on a New Book*;

or, a Grandissime Ascension, a racist attack on Cable's novel *The Grandissimes* (to be considered below).[18]

Adrien's elder brother Dominique (1810–90), likewise a poet, published less. Adrien held his work in high esteem, however, and took him as the ideal type of poet. Born on Bayou Lacombe, Dominique studied at the Collège d'Orléans, then was sent to the Collège Royal de Nantes. He returned to the United States, studied law in Philadelphia but abandoned his studies, went back to his home city, then traveled again to France more than once. He ultimately died there. Like his brother, he spent time among the Choctaws. His fortunes fluctuated; he wandered a good deal. He married and had children, but they were ultimately reared by his nephew. Abroad, he apparently suffered from homesickness, perhaps because of the climate, which inspired the Baudelairean line "Quand un voile brumeux enveloppe Lutèce" [When a misty veil wraps Paris]. Auguste Viatte found in his verse both Lamartinian echoes and prefigurations of future poetry by Charles-René Leconte de Lisle, Charles Baudelaire, and Stéphane Mallarmé. Rouquette celebrated the ocean with the same devotion and acquaintance shown by Victor Hugo and, later, Jules Supervielle.[19]

Dominique Rouquette's 1839 collection of verse, *Les Meschacébéennes*, a volume of 162 pages, features outdoor scenes, in which Viatte identified "un sentiment profond de la nature," and other types of local color. One of the old spellings of *Mississippi*, so beloved of French Romantics, is used.

> Qu'un autre, ingrat enfant, vieux fleuve, te blasphème,
> Moi, je conterai, Michasippi—je t'aime.
> Je chanterai toujours, lorsque l'on te maudit,
> Tes savanes, tes bois, où le bison bondit.
> A toute âme, aspirant aux émotions neuves,
> Je dirai: "Venez voir le plus grand de nos fleuves,
> Ce vieux Nil des déserts où Chateaubriand but,
> Et les mille affluents qui lui portent tribut . . .
> . . . .
> Viens voir les Indiens, dans nos pinières vertes,
> En cercle, insoucieux, couchés sur les couvertes;
> Viens voir le nègre heureux pêchant au bord de l'eau . . .

> [Let another, an ungrateful child, blaspheme against you, old river;
> I shall tell of the Mississippi; I love you.

> I shall sing always, when you are cursed,
> Of your savannahs, your woods where bison leap.
> To each soul, aspiring after new emotions,
> I shall say, "Come see the greatest of our rivers,
> This old Nile of the wilderness where Chateaubriand drank,
> And the thousand streams that pay tribute to it . . .
> Come see the Indians, in our green pine groves,
> Lying in a circle on the ground cover, without care;
> Come see the black man, happy, fishing at the water's edge . . .][20]

The trope of the noble savage is woven into this ideal portrait, which shows bison leaping in the woods—not impossible, though generally bison were grassland animals and by mid-nineteenth century the huge herds had largely disappeared. Rouquette here takes at face value Chateaubriand's misleading account of seeing the river.

A nearly unknown author of the same generation, Amadeo Morel (1813–67), published a fifty-page poem in two parts, in rhymed alexandrines, *Récit sur l'Ouragan de la Dernière Ile*, which treats the great 1856 storm that destroyed L'Ile dernière, or Last Island (just to the west of Grand Isle). A third part was to be composed and published later, if subscriptions were sufficient; apparently Morel died before it could be completed. Morel begins on a melodramatic note of fatalism and features a well-known literary trope—a disclaimer saying that he is incapable of describing the event:

> Fatale Dernière Ile! oh! drame détesté,
> Qui plongea dans le deuil notre société!
> Pourrai-je retracer de si sombres images!
> Puis-je enfin embrasser tant d'illustres naufrages?
> La tâche est impossible, il n'est homme ici-bas,
> Capable d'esquisser les scènes du trépas;
> La nature en ce jour de son cours échappée
> Dans la nuit ténébreuse était enveloppée;
> Affligée en un mot de ses propres fureurs,
> Un voile impénétrable en cachait les horreurs;
> Mais il est quelques faits qu'avec beaucoup de peine
> J'essaierai cependant de mettre sur la scène,
> Car pour bien exprimer tout ce que je ressens,
> Il faudrait qu'Apollon accepte mon encens.

[Fatal Last Island! Oh, hated drama,
which plunged our society into mourning!
Can I retrace so many dark pictures!
Can I finally embrace so many illustrious shipwrecks?
The task is impossible; there is no man here below
Capable of sketching the scenes of death;
Nature on that day, escaped from her course,
Was enveloped in dark night;
Afflicted, in a word, by its own furor,
An impenetrable veil hid its horrors;
But there are a few facts that, with a great deal of trouble,
I will nevertheless try to dramatize,
For, in order to express well all that I feel,
It would be necessary for Apollo to accept my incense.]

Morel then depicts the joyous atmosphere of the vacationers on the island:

Voyez-vous ces hôtels, ayant un air de fête,
Dont la splendeur au loin sur la mer se reflète,
. . . .
C'est le séjour des ris, la lumière y ruisselle,
Ainsi qu'un diamant au loin il étincelle,
Et l'éclat qu'au dehors versent les bâtimens [sic]
Imprime à mille objets des reflets égayans [sic];
Dans les nombreux cafés, de jeunes fashionables
Se livrent aux plaisirs qui leur sont agréables . . .

[See those hotels, with a festive appearance,
Whose splendor is reflected in the distance on the sea.
It's the abode of laughter; light streams there;
Like a diamond it sparkles in the distance,
And the brilliance that its buildings shed
Prints on a thousand objects cheery reflections.
In the numerous cafés, young fashionable people
Indulge in the pleasures that are agreeable to them . . .]

The florid nineteenth-century rhetoric is to be expected, as are the *chevilles* (redundancies to fill out the line or rhyme, such as "agreeable pleasures").

What is unfortunate is that the prolixity does not produce a proportionate effect of awe or horror. Later passages dramatize the destruction better than the opening lines would suggest, but the effect of the whole is not felicitous.[21]

A minor literary figure of the same generation as the Rouquette brothers, Charles-Chauvin-Boisclair Deléry (1815–80), born in St. Charles Parish, is noteworthy for his archconservatism. He was sent to study at the Lycée Louis-le-Grand. He completed medical school in Paris and returned to New Orleans in 1842 to practice medicine. For years he carried on a quarrel with another physician over the susceptibility of native Louisianans to yellow fever. He wrote poetry, drama, and essays. After General Benjamin Butler and his troops occupied the city in 1862, Deléry expressed vitriolic criticism of the Union army; though unpublished, his views became known and Butler ordered his arrest. Deléry went to Cuba and then France for the rest of the war. During Reconstruction he was, as one annotator puts it, "the voice of the old social order refusing to concede defeat." Production of his 1877 drama *L'Ecole du peuple* (perhaps an echo of a Molière title), satirizing Lieutenant Governor P.B.S. Pinchback, a man of color, was prohibited. He wrote charming fables, including "L'Arbre et le mât."[22]

Slightly younger, the poet Charles-Oscar Dugué (1821–72), born in Jefferson Parish, was sent to the Collège Saint-Louis in Paris. Having returned home, he worked as a journalist, then studied and practiced law. For some years before the Civil War he served as director of Jefferson College. He published poetry in newspapers, and in 1847 his *Essais poétiques* appeared, with a long poem dedicated to Chateaubriand, still alive, whom he admired. Dugué died in Paris. His diction recalls that of the French master and the Rouquette brothers. Here, for instance, are the opening lines of "Souvenirs du désert":

O belle Louisiane, ô vastes cyprières,
Où m'égaraient jadis des courses solitaires;
Où j'allais, tout enfant, ainsi qu'un un saint lieu,
Ouïr, déjà rêveur, la grande voix de Dieu!

[O beautiful Louisiana, O vast cypress groves,
Where in the past lonely wanderings took me;
Where I went, as a small child, as to a holy place
To hear, a dreamer already, the great voice of God.]

The poem evokes a young Choctaw mother and the birds and trees that surround her. Other poems concern love, jealousy, and a girl glimpsed at a ball.[23]

A poet of the same generation is Alexandre Latil (1816–51). Born in New Orleans of a good family, he contracted leprosy at age fifteen, shortly, it is said, after his betrothal. Thenceforth he lived in the leper colony on the banks of Bayou St. John, founded under the Spanish, when leprosy "raged with violence." In this *terre aux lépreux*, the afflicted had provisions but others were forbidden to approach. His fiancée, declining his offer to break the engagement, agreed to marry him so that they could be together. Charles Testut wrote two tributes to him. In newspapers, Latil published poems, some of which were collected (with subscribers' assistance) as *Les Ephémères: essais poétiques* (1841). They display elegant diction and standard forms, usually regular alexandrines, sometimes shorter measures, varied within the stanza or uniform; they thus mirror established nineteenth-century versification in France. They bear the moving, if discreet, imprint of a man suffering unspeakable disfiguration (including loss of hands and feet and blindness). As the reprint puts it (translated here): "His best lines compete with the most beautiful creations of French romanticism. If France is endowed with Alfred [de] Musset, Louisiana can boast of Alexandre Latil, certain of whose *Ephémères* are in no way inferior to [Musset's] *Nights*."[24]

Latil introduced his collection by thanking his subscribers, observing that their support furnished refutation of the anonymous charge that literature languished in his "fatherland." He confessed that his poetry was by way of consolation, or compensation—a Romantic motif, here to be taken literally—and expressed the familiar hope that, despite the title, his work would survive. His models were, he wrote, Pierre-Jean de Béranger (to whom an ode is dedicated), Auguste-Marseille Barthélemy, and Casimir Delavigne—French figures who have barely remained on the literary horizon but whose stature was considerable at the time. All three wrote in a nationalist vein, whether dithyrambic or satiric. Latil was obviously familiar also with Victor Hugo and Lamartine (whose liberal political opinions he did not share, as his note to the twenty-first poem indicates). As for the "melancholy" character that some criticized in his writing, Latil, anticipating one strain of modern criticism, denied to commentators the right to blame or praise according to the emotional content of a work. Pronouncing the dichotomy of classicism and Romanticism to be false, he expressed his literary ideal as, simply, excellence. He praised the Rouquette brothers, who are quoted and alluded to obliquely. The "poète louisianais"—envied, calumniated—to whom "Le Talent et l'envie" is dedicated is probably Adrien Rouquette.

Among the topics treated is marriage, in an epithalamium for the wedding of Latil's sister. One poem is dedicated to her, with an epigraph from Lord Byron's "Stanzas to Augusta" (1816). (Latil was, presumably, unaware of their alleged incestuous relationship.) Other poems deal with love, loneliness, suffering, the need for resignation, and death, "the surest of ports"—all in Romantic tones and diction. Latil's complaint is not, however, a conventional one, but rather founded in genuine pain and loss of freedom. As the penultimate poem says:

> Triste dans ma retraite obscure
> Où le destin m'a confiné,
> Je me crois seul dans la nature
> Et de Dieu même abandonné.

> [Sad in my dark retreat
> Where destiny has confined me,
> I believe that I am alone in nature
> And abandoned even by God.]

The counterpart to loneliness is pleasant solitude; Latil imagines Mandeville, across Lake Pontchartrain, as an oasis, a respite from "le tourbillon du monde" [whirlwind of the world] (specifically New Orleans) and its "plaisirs trompeurs" [deceitful pleasures]. He alludes to his professors and studies at a school in the former Ursulines Convent, and praises Béranger for respecting the vanquished Napoleon while condemning his despotism. "Prière," a poem dated only "May," suggests heartache; the "elle" to whom it is addressed seems not to listen to the poet. An unusual poem is "Au Dr. P. A. Lambert"; it honors Hippocrates and all who follow him in dedication to curing others' ills or at least alleviating their suffering. Another homage poem is to Latil's grandfather, and in the final poem he praises his parents. In "Le Poète souffrant" he thinks of a woman friend, an "ange adoré," unidentifiable, who has gone away and left him without hope; he has cursed his fate. Yet, in a standard poetic commonplace, he hopes—doubtless genuinely—to meet her in heaven.

CHAPTER FOUR

Mercier and Other Novelists Born in the Early Nineteenth Century

Revolutions in America (1776) and France (1789, 1830, 1848) and new bodies of law, including the Napoleonic Code and American law after 1803, marked Louisiana, as it were, for nineteenth-century liberalism. Yet America remained the land of slavery also. While the grounds for liberalism vary, what is shared by most writers here and in chapter 5 is rejection of all rationales for slavery.

A French republican, Alexandre Barde (1816–68), is credited with the first Louisiana novel, *Mademoiselle de Montblancard* (1843) (which takes place in Languedoc, however), though Pierre-Louis Berquin-Duvallon had published a *Mélusine*, apparently in Louisiana, and *Eglantine ou le secret*, by Emilie Poullant Gelbois Evershed, was composed in Louisiana, though published in Paris (1843). Another early novel, reflecting the French fashion, was *Les Mystères des bords du Mississippi* (1843–44), by Charles de la Gracerie. Louis-Armand Garreau's historical novel *Louisiana* (1849), based on histories by Charles Gayarré and others, follows the formula as set primarily by Victor Hugo, Alfred de Vigny, and Alexandre Dumas père. The same events were depicted in English by T. Wharton Collens (1812–79) in *The Martyr Patriots; or, Louisiana in 1769* (1836) and in various other French-language works: the drama *Les Martyrs de la Louisiane* (1839) by Auguste Lussan; *France et Espagne, ou la Louisiane en 1768 et 1769* (1850), which follows Lussan's work closely, by Louis-Placide Canonge; and "La Frénière" (1894) by François Tujague.[1]

The writings of Gayarré (1805–95), a conservative, comprise political commentary and history, but also poetry, a comedy, and fiction, including the autobiographical and historical novels *Fernando de Lemos: Truth and Fiction* and *Aubert Dubayet*. Most of his work—including a four-volume history of Louisiana—is in English, a literary policy adopted doubtless to increase his audience among "Americans"; but he published a two-volume history in French. His father was of Spanish origin (his ancestor had arrived with Antonio de Ulloa in 1766) and, on his mother's side, Charles was the grandson of Etienne de Boré, a Frenchman of Norman descent who married into a family with Louisiana connections. What is now Audubon Park was the de Boré plantation. With the help of immigrants from Saint Domingue, Etienne became responsible, in the mid-1790s, after the indigo crops failed, for establishing the sugar industry by successfully and profitably granulating cane sugar. Charles, called by one literary historian "Louisiana's most picturesque historian and man of letters," spent some of his childhood in Spain. He studied English and law in Philadelphia—which had more cultural prestige than New York; he was admitted to the bar there and in Louisiana and was elected to the U.S. Senate but resigned his seat for reasons of ill health and went to France to consult French physicians (1835–43). He was later a prominent political figure on the Louisiana and national scene. He owned a sugar plantation on the Mississippi-Louisiana border. Before the war of 1861–65, he opposed a law intended to expel Free People of Color from Louisiana, but he supported the Confederacy passionately and was a white supremacist. Refusing to take the loyalty oath, he lost his fortune in "the great sad struggle that swept away the princely fortunes of the Gayarrés." In his old age he delivered a lecture on "The Latin Race in Louisiana." He died in straitened circumstances, leaving an unpublished manuscript on "The Quadroons of Louisiana," in which he expressed patronizing views. To his embarrassment, another Charles Gayarré was listed in the city directory—his own son, fathered by a woman of color who was his mistress.[2]

Fernando de Lemos begins with the young hero's studies at the Collège d'Orléans; the author provides a sketch of Joseph Lakanal, its last principal. Father Antonio de Sedella, or le père Antoine, who presided at St. Louis Cathedral, is likewise sketched. Lemos, something of an invalid, goes to Europe with his boyhood friend Trévigne, who, though poor, turns out to be a Spanish grandee. Among those Lemos meets is King Louis-Philippe, who had visited his grandfather in Louisiana. The author expresses clearly his disapproval of the 1789 Revolution and the "monsters" of the Terror (399–400). Back home, Lemos becomes a successful businessman, but loses his fortune in the "War of Secession." Attempting in vain to find employment, he has the good fortune to inherit a substantial legacy. Topics treated in passing include piracy, Andrew Jackson, atheism, blacks, and Jews. *Aubert Dubayet*, called a sequel, although its action precedes that of the previous novel, is labeled a romance, since it consists of semifictionalized history, with a long appendix on the republic of Rome. The action involves such historical figures as Washington, Talleyrand, Robespierre, Marat, and Charlotte Corday. The theme of incest arises: when the young Louisiana hero is told by his mother, in a melodramatic disclosure, that the woman he wishes to marry is really his illegitimate sister, he flees and fights in both the American and French revolutions.[3]

Alfred Mercier (1816–94) is the only white native-born liberal among the major Louisiana authors of his century; others of liberal outlook were immigrants or Creoles of Color. His views were surely shaped by his time in France as a member of the Creole diaspora. Had he written in English, his audience would have been much wider, perhaps rivaling that of George Washington Cable. Both he and his older brother Armand (1813–95) were well-known practicing physicians as well as authors. Armand, who, like his brother, studied in Paris, was among the founders of L'Athénée Louisianais and its first president.

They were both antiassimilationists (though Alfred came late to this position)—that is, they supported the French language and Creole culture in the struggle against Americanization. In other respects they were opposed politically, Armand being conservative. As Alfred's novel *La Fille du prêtre* (1877–78) and other works show, he was, contrary to Creole tradition, very anticlerical—probably he had no religious belief; that position and his other liberal views, especially on slavery, alienated many contemporaries. Réginald Hamel speaks even of his "socialist" ideas. Mercier was, however, a supporter of the Confederacy, which he saw as "Latin," in contrast to the Union, composed of Yankees and Protestants. Alfred wrote fiction, poetry, drama, biography, and miscellaneous texts, published in Paris and New Orleans. The fiction usually appeared serially. Worth noting, in addition to works discussed below, are his story "1878," a humorous treatment of death and the yellow fever epidemic, and *Fortunia: drame en cinq actes*, inspired by the sordid career of his brother-in-law, Pierre Soulé.[4]

Mercier's father, Jean-Baptiste, left France in 1793 in order to escape the guillotine; his mother's family was Canadian. Jean-Baptiste acquired a land concession and became a planter in Jefferson Parish. Alfred was educated first in New Orleans, under the tutelage of Soulé. The principal language on the plantation was Creole, which Mercier later promoted (he translated the fables of Aesop into Creole in 1890). In 1829 he was sent with Armand to the lycée Louis-le-Grand in Paris; he subsequently studied law but disliked it. He returned to New Orleans to work as a journalist, then crossed to France again. Back in America once more, he was sent to Boston to improve his English. Returning to France in 1842, he published his first book, then traveled through Europe as tutor to Soulé's son. He was active in liberal politics in France; among his associates was the socialist Louis Blanc. Mercier was friendly likewise with Alexandre Dumas père and worked briefly for his paper, *Dartagnan*. He undertook the study of medicine and subsequently married. One of his professors was Jean-Martin Charcot, an eminent neurologist and specialist in mental pathologies. In 1855 Mercier defended his thesis on the yellow fever epidemic of 1853. He returned to Louisiana briefly, left for France again before the Civil War began, but finally settled definitively in New Orleans in the late 1860s. He served at one time as the opera critic of the *Picayune*.[5]

La Rose de Smyrne et l'Ermite du Niagara, poèmes, "par A. Mercier, américain" (1842), is marked by a derivative Romanticism. Preceded by epigraphs drawn from the sixteenth-century poet Pierre de Malherbe and from Dominique Rouquette, it consists of an epic poem or "nouvelle poétique" in three cantos, concerning a slave in the sultan's harem in "Stamboul" at the approximate time of the struggle for Greek independence, and an unplayable drama, called "mystère," in five acts, set on the shores of Niagara Falls. Alexandrines are used primarily. French newspapers appear to bear no trace of the praise from French critics which New Orleans papers mentioned.[6]

L'Ermite du Niagara concerns the missionary le père Daniel, Indians, including a maiden, and a white man who, after disappointments, has become a recluse near the mighty falls. The prologue, "A Melpomène," reveals literary kinship to Jean-Jacques Rousseau and François-René de Chateaubriand. "Insoucieux enfant de la Louisiane, / Je poursuivais la chasse au fond de la savane" [Carefree child of Louisiana, / I carried on the hunt in the depths of the savannah]. The poet once thought of visiting Greece, but, blasé and world-weary like Chateaubriand's René, he rejects that nation and the rest of Europe in favor of the New World:

> Grèce, pour tes beautés j'eus un pieux amour,
> Et je voulus ... Mais non ... l'indépendant Créole
> Ne pouvait se courber au joug de leur école.
> J'avais déjà trop vu, trop senti, trop aimé,
> Pour demeurer longtemps sous leur grille enfermé.
> Un jour, comme Chactas à Lopez qui s'étonne
> Je remets au régent l'habit que j'abandonne
> Et je reprends dès lors, dégagé de mes fers,
> L'entière liberté de l'enfant des déserts.[7]

[Greece, for your beauties I had a pious love,
And I wanted . . . But no . . .the independent Creole
Could not bend to the yoke of their school.
I had already seen, felt, loved too much,
To remain long enclosed by their fencing.
One day, like Chactas to Lopez, who is astonished,
I give back to the regent the garb that I abandon,
And from that time I take back, freed from my irons,
The entire freedom of the child of the wilderness.]

The fourth line is an echo of Alfred de Musset's poem "Tristesse." The Chactas mentioned is an Indian whom Atala loves in Chateaubriand's tale of that title; Lopez is her father, and also turns out to be the adoptive father of Chactas (a fact that introduced a vaguely incestuous note into Chateaubriand's text but is not crucial to Mercier's passage).

Another work dating, in its first version, from Mercier's early period is *Hénoch Jédésias ou l'Avare de New-York*. First a play, it was rewritten as a novel, "Auri-Fames, ou l'Avare de New-York" and printed in Paris but not published, because, just as it was to appear, the publishers' offices were burnt in the Revolution of 1848. Perhaps recast, it appeared serially in *L'Epoque* in New Orleans (1869); only a few installments survive. It was republished serially in *Les Comptes Rendus de l'Athénée Louisianais* in 1892-93, then reprinted in 2004.[8]

Dumas would not have disavowed this novel, nor Eugène Sue, the author of the extremely popular *Les Mystères de Paris* (1842–43). A mixture of Romantic imagination and realist social depiction, it contains echoes of Victor Hugo and occasional pithy statements that recall Stendhal. "She knew that the human soul is a delicate instrument. It resounds under the hand that touches it to the degree that the hand approaches it suitably" (*Avare*, 166). Among the authentic elements is Voltaire's chateau at Ferney; Mercier, who lived there at one time, collected some of his materials there. In addition, Mercier puts himself into the novel, obliquely, as a young medical specialist, and also depicts Soulé and the latter's dog.

The narrator, who is also a participant, addresses his tale to "cher docteur," who might be taken as a stand-in for the author. But the narrator is likewise an authorial substitute, not by his origins (he is an Irishman from Boston) but his philosophical reflections and concern for social justice. True happiness, he avers, is based on noble thoughts and honorable sentiments; the treasures of Croesus are gone, whereas Socrates' name endures (*Avare*, 102). In typical nineteenth-century French fashion, the story relies on coincidence. There are numerous prolepses (forward-flashes or anticipation) and analepses (flashbacks); one relates the story of the miser Jédésias before he reached New York. The work explores one unusual, though not paranormal, psychic activity: somnambulism, on which the novelist published a study in *Les Comptes-rendus* (1889). The miser is powerfully conceived and portrayed, almost a Balzacian character, whose "energy in crime" (*Avare*, 83) is astounding. The assertion that great passions are "always tinged with a bit of insanity" (*Avare*, 343) is consonant with his extraordinary avarice. He pays dearly (by dying immured) for his obsession. "This gold that you count out is your life itself; each coin that falls into this black marble urn is a piece of your soul that flies away" (*Avare*, 71). Perhaps Mercier had in mind Balzac's hero in *La Peau de chagrin* (1831), whose life is shortened as each wish is fulfilled.

La Fille du prêtre: Récit social (1877–78), a long didactic tale (three parts, nearly four hundred pages), shows that Mercier's work was evolving towards realism. He asserted that all the action was founded on fact, though disguised. Given the lack of verisimilitude and the incredible coincidences, this claim is hard to honor, though some true events may be depicted. Certain remarks on history prefigure twentieth-century historical thought as illustrated in the Annales school: what is needed is not a history of those "whom their genius or ambition, or the chance of circumstances, placed on a stage seen by everyone . . . [but rather] another history . . . not less instructive . . . That of unknown souls . . . in the shadow of an existence unknown." The hero is Louisiana-born (his royalist family was in exile during the Revolution), but the tale is set chiefly in Europe, with some episodes elsewhere in the United States and in Siberia. One part takes place in Normandy near a factory where Mercier had served as a doctor. A long section concerns the Franco-Prussian War and the Commune of 1871, notably the street battles between the *insurgés* (insurgents) and the government troops, or *Versaillais*. Mercier, who did not witness the events, considered the revolutionaries' ideas as promising for the proletariat. The underlying thesis of the work is not, however, the desirability of revolution but the premise that clerical celibacy is against nature and leads to disaster. While the principal male character is a priest who impregnates a girl, the most noble and honorable character is his friend, a doctor; later, the latter's father, likewise a doctor, has *le beau rôle* also.[9]

More significant is *L'Habitation Saint-Ybars; ou, Maîtres et esclaves en Louisiane* (1881). It likewise is called a *récit social* and is both a historical novel—inspired by memories of the family plantation—and a naturalistic work in the vein of Emile Zola. The action begins in New Orleans in 1851 and goes through the Federal occupation. While, as the subtitle would suggest, there are numerous black characters, most very likeable, the point of view is that of whites. The novel is without literary genius and is excessively moralizing but shows skill at characterization and conveys well the mores, geography, and social structure of pre–Civil War Creole plantation life and the devastation of the war. The work seems based in reality; the author, or his persona within the text, rather, alludes to having been present at the hanging of one Stoval, a minor character. The plot is, however, melodramatic, with ill-fated loves, a father-son conflict, a devastating hurricane, a near-disaster on the stormy river, discovery of a foundling, a double suicide, two additional suicides, a murder, a fatal duel, a near-rape, consumption and a death-bed wedding— that is, what would later be called Southern Gothic. Many passages are in black Creole and provide useful documentation on this patois or "Gombo."[10]

A plantation visitor from France, Antony Pélasge, wounded in the uprising of June 1848 and deported, serves as an observer but becomes a principal actor also. In the opening scene he witnesses transactions at a slave market, as Saint-Ybars, a plantation owner, buys two slaves and accepts, at no cost, a third, old and deformed. He also hires Antony as tutor to his son; the tutor eventually becomes an advisor and almost a family member. Antony's ideas, typical of nineteenth-century progressivism, may stand for the author's: "For him, the indefinite progress of the human spirit was not in doubt; thus he contemplated . . . the general emancipation of peoples and their federation on the bases of universal rights. Reason was his religion . . ." (19).

The Saint-Ybars plantation is large, the house imposing and elegant, with its eight columns on each side, Doric below, Corinthian above. Generally, slaves are well treated; some are literate, and others are allowed firearms, contrary to general usage. There are even free workers. Saint-Ybars has a terrible temper, however, and turns it against anyone—a house slave, his own son—who dares to cross him. Mercier shows full awareness of both the illegitimacy and the strengths of this society. Pélasge and old Vieumaite—the patriarch—see that slavery is unjust. Thanks to his tutor's teaching, Démon, the youngest son (misnamed), agrees: "The social conditions in which I was born were based on a flagrant violation of human rights. They had to disappear, necessarily . . . I have blushed more than once when I thought of the source of the money I spent" (167). Before dying, Vieumaite predicts war. Yet the motives of northern abolitionists are not pure either. During and after the war, greed, brutality, and abuse of authority shown by Federals and carpetbaggers illustrate fully other impulses behind the invasion. The plantation, first attacked by Union troops, is then ruined by roving bands, both whites and blacks. Meanwhile, one family disaster follows upon another, until at the end almost everyone is dead, as in Elizabethan tragedy.

Racial matters, especially mixed-race liaisons, are the source of much strife. Whereas Salvador, a free mulatto carpenter who is the son of Vieumaite, is both strong and good (and doubtless a symbolic savior of the future), one of the patriarch's grandsons has fathered a son whose wickedness brings about tragedy. After the war, Démon and the beautiful pale-skinned foundling, Blanchette, wish to marry, but, owing to the wicked man's machinations, it is discovered that, though by arrangement she had "passed" as white, she has some African blood. (Cable developed this miscegenation theme in the contemporaneous *Madame Delphine*.) Old aunts and cousins—all that remains of the family—oppose the match, and neighbors turn hostile. Since the couple is without funds to go elsewhere, marriage becomes, practically speaking, impossible—whence the double suicide.

Pélasge's idealism is greatly affected thereby. Mercier cannot, however, let physical destruction, violence, dashed hopes, and other grounds for pessimism prevail. The tutor envisages a new South in which the abilities, attitudes, and adaptability of the blacks, whom he considers superior to the local Indians (ruined by alcoholism—an interesting judgment), allow them to be integrated as equals. A Russian governess who had been at Saint-Ybars before the war and with whom Pélasge had corresponded arrives to invite him, on behalf of her husband, a liberal activist, to join them in Switzerland and militate for reform throughout Europe. "It is always the struggle, the eternal struggle between light and darkness, between ignorance and progress, between freedom and servitude" (230). Pélasge leaves his property in the hands of energetic blacks.

A number of works by Mercier were inspired by his interest in pathological behavior. He had a physician's acquaintance with various pathologies and also saw cases in his own family. His sister Armantine, the wife of Soulé, may have killed herself, or perhaps was murdered by her husband, who later died insane from syphilis. His nephew Nelvil Soulé died of insanity; his sister Adèle died of dementia, as did a daughter-in-law. Another sister may have taken an opium overdose. Some madness appears incidentally in *L'Habitation Saint-Ybars*.

The novella *Le Fou de Palerme*, published in 1873, is strongly marked by insanity. Its action takes place in Sicily, which Mercier had visited. It is a frame story (one type of embedded tale)—that is, an outer, or frame, story told in one voice, first- or third-person, enclosing an inner story—often the principal one—presented by a different voice. Whether ostensibly factual or not, the inner story has a different status from the outer. (The term *metadiegetic*—beyond the principal diegesis, or time-space continuum—is sometimes used to characterize the inner story.) In the present instance, the outer frame is established by a prologue spoken by a visitor to Palermo; the story concludes in the same voice. The main narrative is an account given to him and his companions. The plot is melodramatic; the characters resemble the heroes and heroines of Romantic novels by Victor Hugo and Dumas père. It deals with the Romantic theme of illusion, that of a melancholy young painter whose beloved Zingara, a Gypsy, is stabbed by a jealous member of her traveling band. The lover believes thenceforth that he is married to Death. He is happy only in the garden where they sat together and where he believes she appears. Coincidence plays a large role; a powerful sense of fatality hangs over the hero, and Zingara has telltale signs on her face and neck. A masked ball, the central episode, foreshadows that in Cable's *The Grandissimes*. The evocative power of fragrance—that of an exotic plant—recalls olfactory evocations by Charles Baudelaire, whose *Les Fleurs du mal* (1857) Mercier must have known. "Its aroma evoked, as if by enchantment, a whole world of forgotten facts" (84).[11]

Mercier's story "L'Artiste amoureux," which appeared in *Le Courrier de la Louisiane* (1844), similarly concerns illusion, carried here to pathological intensity. The eponymous artist discovers a priceless portrait, done by Jacques-Louis David, with an attached letter (which constitutes another type of embedded story). The portrait is that of a beautiful Tuscan woman, who married a disciple of David. Like Pygmalion, the artist falls in love with the picture and believes the likeness is a woman, real but deaf. When the picture is mutilated by pranksters, his suffering is acute. "The common people are wrong to envy, on days of moral suffering, the happiness of the insane; this happiness does not exist; all insanity is pain, a horrible pain which leads to the tomb" (118). By coincidence or "Providence" (128), an acquaintance meets the woman's sister in Tuscany, takes her back to Paris, and sets up a scene that will be either "the cure or the consummation" of the man's misery.

In 1873, a productive year, Mercier published *Lidia* anonymously in *Le Carillon de la Nouvelle-Orléans*. This highly Romantic novel, an "idyll," set principally in Paris, reintroduces previous themes: love, fate, religious celibacy, mental illness, debilitating distress. Relying enormously on coincidence and marked by the pathetic fallacy, it revolves around Aurélien's love for the beautiful Lidia, whom he has seen and heard at night while, surreptitiously, she plays the piano and sings. Love appears to be the gift of a benevolent fate, which plans well; this fate is in harmony with, or is identical to, the will of a rather deistic Divinity.[12]

What seems to be congenital anticlericalism reappears, particularly with respect to religious celibacy, suitable only for those who need to retreat from the world, otherwise unnatural, leading to hypocrisy and other evils. A Mother Superior is not only petty but sadistic. A Jesuit, a glutton named Espiou (almost *Espion*, that is, *spy*), illustrates lust: after having plotted against Lidia and threatened violence against her, he attempts to seduce her. Liberal and learned readers would have recognized such as the stuff of Denis Diderot's posthumous novel *La Religieuse* (1796). The Jesuit, in order to cover himself, devises a nearly fatal lie, telling Aurélien that Lidia has left for Sicily. In fact, she is in seclusion, desperate. While she does not become insane, she does fall ill of typhoid and delirium. Only Aurélien's portrait, presented to her as an ultimate measure, brings her back from delusion and despair.[13]

L'Aventure de Johnelle (1891), another novella dealing with paranormal behavior, includes passages in Creole, translated in the reprint. The manuscript was deemed so offensive by its topics (suicide and abortion, especially planned stillbirths) that publishers refused it. It was finally printed by the goodwill of subscribers; then most of the copies were lost in a flood. Although liberal, Mercier deplored the practice of abortion as destructive of Creole society. The novel denounces the error by which life is assumed to start not at conception but when the child moves in his mother. Hamel views the work as an explanation of the "grandeur and decadence"—perhaps even mental derangement—of Louisiana Creoles. Despite Mercier's liberalism, the conceit—old but not abandoned by the time of publication—by which former slaves preferred to stay on with their masters in 1865 persists here.[14]

Self-destruction and other extreme behavior mark the novella. The father of the young hero, Tito, drowned himself before the story opens. Shortly, a sister, Johnelle, is stillborn. Some years later, Tito learns that his mother had recourse to an abortionist so that the child would be born dead; he also was to have been eliminated similarly. His devotion to the dead sister is a disease, cult-like; he sees her (or so he believes), talks with her, has her portrait painted as though she were alive, and, in short, lives in pathological ecstasy or delirium. An intelligent and devoted, though misanthropic, physician is summoned. Embedded tales and a letter reveal that he is the illegitimate son of an archbishop and a marquise; he expresses gratitude to them for his life. He devises a plan by which Dolorite, a lovely girl, pretends to be Johnelle, in order to wean Tito away from his hallucinations. Though Tito is not deceived, he does reacquire a taste for life and indeed falls in love with the girl. It is decided not to reveal to him that she is engaged to another. When finally she must tell him, he relapses into inertia and worse; he walks to the levee, calls out to Johnelle, and drowns himself in the Mississippi.

Strangely, the wisdom of such an experiment is not called into question. The doctor, to be sure, believes it may well work; and he views the case as desperate. Yet the likely consequences of failure—worse mental derangement and, given Tito's heredity, suicide—are not, apparently, weighed; nor does the doctor consider the morality of deceiving Dolorite (whose name alone should be a warning). While Dumas's influence on Mercier cannot be doubted, one wonders also whether Zola, with his theories of heredity and the "experimental novel," might not have served as a model here.

The journalist and fiction writer Charles de la Bretonne (d. 1878 or 1879), who wrote under the name Jacques de Rouquigny (or Roquigny), warrants inclusion in this chapter because of his depiction of Indians. In his long story, "Le Soulier rouge," published almost simultaneously (in 1849–50—well before *La Nouvelle Atala*) in two French-language publications, *La Violette: Revue musicale et littéraire*, and *Le Vigilant*, he paints a different picture of the Native Americans from those offered by Chateaubriand and Adrien Rouquette. In the mid-eighteenth century, on the Côte des Allemands and across Lake Pontchartrain, one group of Choctaws wars against the whites and other tribes. Far from acting like *le bon sauvage*, the Choctaws are hostile and cruel; they scalp and burn their enemies at the stake. Yet, like *La Nouvelle Atala*, this story also includes an idyll, featuring a French officer, an Indian maiden, and another European, a disciple of Rousseau. The latter, having forgone in France the frivolity of aristocratic society to become a practical man, served in the navy, then settled in Louisiana, where he lives in a forest hut and hunts. Because he travels on tree branches and vines, he is known to the Indians—friendly and hostile both—as The Squirrel. He is, in fact, the French officer's uncle, living incognito; his identity is revealed by documents in a buried chest. The familiar literary device fits the story well, with its emphasis on nature and its Romantic diction and style.[15]

Another Louisiana Francophone author can be treated here, an early feminist whose identity is unknown but who wrote under the name of "Petite Rose." While there is no proof of the author's sex, one concludes from the story "L'Histoire d'un domino" that it was a woman. The story, an explicit denunciation of servitude, whether in marriage or bondage, was published in *La Renaissance Louisianaise* in 1867, thus well before Kate Chopin's *The Awakening*. One would like to know whether "Petite Rose" had read the works of Germaine de Staël and George Sand, early French feminists.[16]

The story begins with a short position paper in the first person concerning the superiority of women and the injustice—indeed folly—of their submission to men, each "a director who imposes himself upon us with all his prejudices, whims, and ignorance" (79). The author then explains the title: disguised in a domino, with hood and mask, she can tell her story anonymously. (Masking, connected with Latin celebrations, is an important motif and plot device in works by Cable, Mercier, and others.) Her grandfather was nearly executed as a rebel against Spanish occupation; her father participated in a plot to prevent transfer of Louisiana to the United States. Spoiled and kept in ignorance by her family on its plantation, she knows nothing of the world, not even of New Orleans. Embarrassed by her gaucherie during a first experience in the city, she resolves to educate herself, but, notwithstanding her secret love for another, she must accept an arranged marriage to an "American," a union she terms "slavery" (87). Not only has happiness for *her* become impossible; the Creole, who returned her love but, being honorable, postponed his declaration until he was better established, has lost her and must also suffer. Her newfound consciousness leads her to sympathize with the plight of slaves—victims, like herself, of a cruel social system, the inhumanity of which erodes moral sensibility in all. The distress of any wife whose husband has taken a slave mistress is one illustration of the odious social relationships created by bondage; another is the jealousy of a mistress who is abandoned. That "Domino's" husband, upon learning of her love for another, lets her go at the price of his own happiness and, ultimately, blesses the couple before he dies and leaves them his fortune is a tribute to him; but the social evils remain.

CHAPTER FIVE

Mid-Nineteenth-Century Immigrant Francophone Authors

The careers sketched here show how French-born immigrants to Louisiana were often more radical than locals of liberal persuasion. The violent revolutionary tradition—begun in 1789, with its proclamation of the universal Rights of Man, and reaffirmed in 1848—and the early veins of French socialism constituted a line of radical thought that differed from American liberalism, even that of the abolitionists. The writings of these immigrants illustrate how literary Romanticism and liberal republicanism were often allied on both continents. Their adherents looked upon literature as an almost sacred undertaking, not mere self-expression or *l'art pour l'art* but enlightenment for the public and activism.

Tullius de Saint-Céran (1800–55), who abandoned the particle *de*, was born in Jamaica, but reared in New Orleans, where his family settled following an insurrection. He became a printer and edited the French section of the *Gazette de la Louisiane*. He was a prolific poet and wrote in French, Spanish, and English. In 1836 he published *Chansons et poésies diverses*, drawn from *L'Abeille*, and the following year another collection. In 1838 he brought out an epic poem on the Battle of New Orleans; his collection *Les Louisianaises* followed in 1840.[1]

Charles Testut (1816–92) left France as a young man and went to New York, where he started a French-language paper. He later worked in La Pointe-à-Pitre, Guadeloupe, until the extremely destructive earthquake and fire of 1843; he then settled in Louisiana, except for a brief, unfruitful stay in Mobile. He was married and had children. His main activities were literary and journalistic. He bought the weekly *La Chronique* in 1849 and as an associated project began a series devoted to Louisiana fiction, "Veillées louisianaises," in which he published his *Saint-Denis* (1849), a historical tale involving the founder of Natchitoches and his travels to New Mexico. Testut also composed the serial novels *Calisto* (1849) (with an important hurricane episode) and *Or et fange, ou les Mystères de la Nouvelle Orléans* (1852–54), the title of which reflects Eugène Sue's *Les Mystères de Paris*. Testut's novels are, in the words of *The Cambridge History of American Literature*, "long, loosely composed, and often forced in language and sentiment . . . [yet] eloquent, and rich in Louisiana lore." The length is not surprising, given their date. They are derivative, containing whole pages borrowed from Charles Gayarré. One paper for which Testut wrote in the 1860s was *La Tribune de la Nouvelle-Orléans*. It was noted earlier that his *Portraits littéraires de la Nouvelle-Orléans* (1850) is one of the earliest ventures into literary history and criticism in Louisiana. He was both a Freemason and an anticlerical, and was drawn into spiritualism. He became secretary of the New Orleans branch of The International.[2]

In 1849 Testut brought out a collection of poems, *Les Echos*, followed by *Les Fleurs d'été* (1851). Illustrating the connections among French and Louisiana authors, *Les Echos* includes dedicatory and adulatory verses to a French poet, Amable Testu (no relation), thanking her for counsel and encouragement, in addition to a poem in praise of George Washington, a "grand phare" (great beacon), and one dedicated to Alexandre Latil.

> Oh! de tes vers en pleurs que je sens l'harmonie . . .
> Oh! comme ta souffrance arrive et chante en moi . . .
> . . . .
> Poète des douleurs, qu'une douce croyance,
> Comme un baume divin, dore ton avenir!
>
> [Oh! how I feel the harmony of your lines, weeping . . .
> Oh! how your suffering reaches and sings in me . . .
> . . . .
> Poet of suffering, may a gentle belief,
> Like a divine balm, make your future golden!]

"Le Retour" features lines of four syllables, an unusual form for the date. "Sur la mort de l'auteur des *Ephémères*," from *Les Fleurs d'été*, dedicated to Latil's widow, is a long elegiac poem.[3]

In 1871 Testut published serially in a paper he had founded, *L'Equité*, his abolitionist novel *Le Vieux Salomon, ou une famille d'esclaves au XIXème siècle*, which has been called the first American Marxist novel (but its Marxism must be considerably qualified). Its similarity to Harriet Beecher Stowe's *Uncle Tom's Cabin, or, Life Among the Lowly* (1852) has been rightly noted. (Among other common features, they both have New Orleans as a major setting and Creole characters.) Testut's work is an eloquent, if sentimental, protest against the injustice of slavery in both principle and practice—no matter how kindly slaves are treated—but especially against abusive masters, including those who (violating the Code Noir) separate couples and families. According to a prefatory note, added in 1872, it was composed in New York in 1858. If this is true, then it was not influenced by the prose of Martin R. Delany, who published serially, starting in 1859, his novel *Blake: or the Huts of America; A Tale of the Mississippi Valley, the Southern United States, and Cuba* (partially reprinted, 1970). The question of contact arises because, in addition to the focus on the horrors of enslavement and what it does to the human person, Freemasonry or at least a secret society is featured in both novels, and a portion of each story is set on a Caribbean island, the rest largely in the South. (One of Delany's episodes takes place in New Orleans during Mardi Gras.)[4]

Testut's note stresses that his story is to have a broad application. By its antitheses and its concern with justice, injustice, and the trials of the good, it is not without resemblances to Victor Hugo's novels, especially *Bug-Jargal* (1826), which concerns the slave revolts in Saint Domingue; similar episodes and other features, including friendship between the black eponymous hero—the first black hero in a French novel—and a white man, lead one to conclude that Testut read that early Hugo work. The nineteenth-century credo of progress underlies Testut's entire work. Despite reference to the proletariat, the novel does not, however, feature crowd actions in which the proletariat appears as a single historical agent, unlike, for instance, Emile Zola's *La Débâcle* (1892).[5]

Testut should be considered a *Christian* socialist. Christ died, it is averred, to teach the three Revolutionary virtues. "Courage! brothers ... courage and patience! Corporal bondage has been abolished, the proletariat—monetary slavery—will be in its turn, and, once these two scourges are destroyed, True Liberty will be born in the bosom of order, between equality and fraternity, in the second stable of a second Bethlehem." In *Le Vieux Salomon*, a *camp de marrons*, or fugitive slave camp, near the volcano La Soufrière in Guadeloupe, is organized on socialist principles: there is no ownership of real property, no mercantile exchange, but residents are given land to cultivate, the amount being decided by the family size. Grand-Soleil, an imposing black man whose name suggests majesty as well as light, exercises authority generally. A council decides disputes. Unlike classical Marxism, however, Testut's socialism favors the singular over the collective or *corps social* (in Christian terms, the lost sheep is valued more than the flock); social disorder is turned into order by *individual* action on grounds of *individual* values.[6]

Le Vieux Salomon is coherent, its composition not so loose as suggested by the *Cambridge History* assessment. Given the elements of lore and strangeness, the work may be read as historical romance as well as a novel. The narrative rhetoric includes analepses and prolepses and, unsurprisingly for the date, a first-person plural omniscient authorial voice, *nous*, embracing readers ("We shall see . . .") and making judgments. There are further authorial interruptions—breaks in the diegetic line (time-space continuum), which call attention to the work qua work: reference to the novel itself, the date of its composition, and its moral lesson; and apostrophes to readers. Testut tells, ostensibly in his own voice, extraneous though thematically related stories, purportedly true, and uses the editorial *nous* in the singular, thus speaking outside of the plural that embraces narrator and narratee. He also reproduces in his own name the opening poem of *Les Echos*, "La Guadeloupe," thus interrupting the principal story line and introducing autotextuality (self-allusion or self-quotation).

Hyperbole, romantic antitheses, and exclamation marks are abundant. Scenes are vivid, with lively conversation; sometimes the narrative present is employed. In contrast, for instance, to *Uncle Tom's Cabin* and Ruth McEnery Stuart's stories, which attempt to reproduce by a rough phonetic spelling and other means the morphology, syntax, vocabulary, and pronunciation of slaves and unlettered whites, Testut uses excellent French throughout; occasional spelling errors in the reprint may be scribal or typographic. Thus, like that of the white planters, slaves' speech, though said to be "less than that of the Academy" (127), is correct, with no reflection of their condition; the imperfect subjunctive appears, and slaves often address each other as *vous*. Similarly, coarse overseers speak beautiful French. Such written language used to convey spoken discourse, however unlettered the ostensible speakers, was customary in France then. (Decades passed before popular speech appeared routinely in French-language fiction; it was not firmly established until Louis-Ferdinand Céline published his *Voyage au bout de la nuit* in 1933 and even then was considered shocking.)

Part one of *Le Vieux Salomon*, which bears the title "Splendeurs et misères," echoing Honoré de Balzac's *Splendeurs et misères des courtisanes*, alludes doubtless to the contrast between nature's splendor and man's misery; it also suggests the vicissitudes of human existence, including those of Old Salomon, a freed slave aged more than a hundred years, as wise as suggested by his name and his blindness (recalling Tiresias). He has a Terre Neuve dog—like the Newfoundland dog in *Uncle Tom's Cabin*. As in that novel, Christian faith underlies the entire belief system, especially the slaves'. Allusions to God, Christ's sacrifice, and Providence are frequent; all men are said to be God's children, and slavery is called an insult to the Divinity. But this faith is a broad, tolerant one, more a universal human impulse than a doctrine. Additionally, in contrast to Stowe's work, where references to sexuality are rare and understated—doubtless as a consequence of her New England morality—the faith of Testut's characters is not colored by Puritanism. Sexuality receives considerable attention: on the one hand, an appealing voluptuousness—seen, following views of the time, as natural to black women—as well as conjugal love and even one voluntary infidelity by the heroine; on the other, assaults by owners on slave women and near-rapes. Self-defense is a right; killing can be justified, especially when a man defends his wife against a brutal slave owner. Honor, yes; humility, much less, in view of the fundamental principle of human equality. Predication is not so prevalent as in *Uncle Tom's Cabin*, whether by the authorial voice or characters; wine and spirits are not banished, and the text is less lachrymose.

The story begins and ends in Guadeloupe, a natural paradise disfigured by the institution of slavery; blacks there live in bondage or else as fugitives from the law. Moreover, while certain whites are fundamentally good and treat their slaves fairly, others are brutal, thus morally dark, in contrast to the principal black characters, noble of character and morally light, such as Grand-Soleil. There are villainous blacks also, however—Testut does not imagine any society without evil. Gradually it becomes clear that Salomon is part of a spiritual association, somewhat like the Freemasons, to which many generous men of both races, encountered later in the novel, belong; the society will ultimately be identified as Frères de la Croyance Universelle. It is explicitly opposed to bigotry and the Roman Catholic Church, viewed as intolerant and tyrannical, and other "foolishness and mysteries of religions fabricated by men" (505). In contrast to Rouquette's anathemas, Protestantism is praised, but only as a tolerant, nondoctrinal position. There are even suggestions of mysterious spiritual insight and paranormal phenomena.[7]

Although Salomon gives his name to the novel, the chief male character is the slave Casimir, sold, with his wife, Rose, to an American, Captain Jackson, a spiritualist. The sale is part of an elaborate plot eventually to free Casimir and Rose. Jackson is in fact Casimir's half-brother, though the relationship is not known by the reader or Casimir until later—a typical nineteenth-century withholding of information. The great earthquake of 1843 and its aftermath delay the departure of Jackson's ship. Testut describes the disaster (despite his "plume défaillante" [failing pen]) in the detail that natural catastrophes called for in nineteenth-century accounts. Before Casimir and Rose depart, Old Salomon relates to them his story, as instructive. This embedded account, one among others, echoes Prosper Mérimée's famous tale "Tamango" (1829; collected in 1833), in which an African chief who sells other blacks to slavers is then himself sold. As in Mérimée's story—which shares with Testut's novel a humorous ironic tone, and in which both whites and blacks are subjected to criticism—Salomon, formerly a trader in men, acknowledges his own brutality. He too was tricked, by a slaver, Captain Lebon (the name echoes Mérimée's Ledoux), who separates him from his love, Aurore (another name suggesting light). Salomon was sold first to a good master in Guadeloupe, then an evil one, under whose mistreatment he learned the value of suffering, like Uncle Tom, and like Jean Valjean in Hugo's *Les Misérables*.

The title of part two, "L'Esclavage dans les pays libres," emphasizes the antithesis between freedom and bondage. The ship calls first in New York, then New Orleans, where the slaves' American adventures begin. Practiced on a huge scale, and with ample legal protection for owners, slavery corrupts and dehumanizes perpetrators, victims, and everyone in between: black women who consent (frequently under duress) to liaisons with owners; slaves to whom oversight is assigned and who become abusive (few men can be more brutal than a black overseer); officers of the law. Despite Jackson's goodwill, events, including his death, expose Casimir and Rose to terrible trials. First, they are under the control of a fanatic Catholic, called Madame L. (use of the initial suggests a real model) and her son, a would-be seducer of Rose, who, however, in a melodramatic reversal, changes his behavior entirely and becomes devoted to her. Later, the two become the property of a horrible Cane River planter—the sort Stowe described and Kate Chopin would later evoke briefly—named Roque. Roque forces himself on Rose and drives a slave to drown herself. Testut denounces not only slavery but also the nearly universal prejudice against a woman who has been assaulted, a prejudice shown to be unreasonable.

The title of part three, "La Terre et le Ciel" (Earth and Heaven), provides another antithesis but also suggests reconciliation in the Christian eschatological perspective. Structurally, the story circles around, as Casimir and Rose, assisted by members of the brotherhood, are repatriated, via Mobile, to Guadeloupe. (Casimir is saved at the last hour from death on the scaffold for the murder of Roque, and Rose, a runaway, is similarly rescued.) Old Salomon, still alive, evokes a great vision he has had of brotherhood and celestial happiness.

Secondary themes deriving from that of slavery are theodicy and literacy. Why does a just God allow evil? While no answer is provided, it is clear, following the Christian dialectic of *felix culpa*, that good can arise from evil, as if evil were its crucible. "Each day of great unhappiness has created for us in its wake better days" (488). It is not that the soul must be tried, though often it is; Testut does not have Stowe's apparent belief that suffering, fundamentally, is good for the spirit. Rather, events proceed by false steps and even wickedness; God "leads man well" out of his errors. History itself is a product of error (albeit without the intermediate syntheses conceived by Marxist dialectics) and thus a series of Hugoesque antitheses and reversals: "War with its barbarity will bring peace; slavery with its horrors will bring emancipation; tyranny with its abuses will bring freedom. Good always arises from an excess of evil . . ." (413). As for literacy, it is (as for Stowe) viewed as the great key to emancipation—from slavery, from ignorance, including the moral ignorance of slave owners. When slaves have a chance to acquire skill in reading, they take it, learn, and share their learning.[8]

Louis-Armand Garreau (1817–65), a printer by trade, was another figure of liberal, even radical, persuasion, as printers often have been. He was the son of a Creole from Martinique, with whom his father had founded a second family after divorcing his first wife. Born in La Charente, the youth was sent to Paris for his education but was obliged by lack of funds to return home. He married and had a large family. In 1841 he went to New Orleans, where he began teaching and wrote for newspapers, including *Le Démocrite*, a short-lived paper he founded. After nine years he returned to France, where he became a publisher, moved in political circles that included Victor Hugo, and was active in underground opposition to Louis-Napoleon after the latter's coup d'état (1851). Garreau went back to Louisiana in 1858. After war broke out, he joined the Confederate army; his son was killed at Vicksburg. His novel *Louisiana* (1849), published in France, relied on formulas developed by the great Romantic generation, and its features—political conspiracy, imprisonment, love, poison, revenge—made it attractive to French readers. But the background, setting, and characters (including Choctaws) mark it as distinctly Louisianan. Expanding upon the historical accounts, it depicts the rebellion against the Spanish in 1768 at the time of Alejandro O'Reilly and the project of forming an independent nation. Garreau portrays with enthusiasm the conspiracy and its heroes, representative of all who rise against illegitimate authority. As he wrote, he must have kept in mind the violent struggles of the 1848 Revolution, during which his brother died.[9]

The melodramatic plot includes a love story, a prison wedding, a duel on the dueling grounds near Bayou St. John, and poisoning of the villain by a faithful slave from Guinea (who speaks perfect French; Garreau, like Testut, eschewed writing the language as she would have spoken it). O'Reilly and other French (Gayarré's ancestor among them) appear under their true names. One, Nouan de Bienville, had recently married; he refused to dissociate himself from his companions and thus turned down a pardon offered on condition that he renounce them. The hangman is likewise based on a historical figure. It was forbidden in the French colony for an enslaved Negro to execute whites; and no white was willing to serve as executioner against the rebels. In Garreau's version, the Spanish authorities demand that Jeannot, a free black, perform the task; they attempt to blackmail him by threatening his beloved, Julia, who otherwise will be bought and mistreated by the horrible Spaniard don Manuel. In reply, he cuts off his right hand. The execution is carried out instead by a firing squad of Spanish soldiers.[10]

Garreau also published stories, six of which are collected in a modern edition. Under the title "Souvenirs d'outre-mer," four appeared in France (1856) in *Les Cinq Centimes Illustrées*, a popular publication featuring serial novels; others, one of which, posthumous, may be by his son, appeared in *La Renaissance Louisianaise*. The most striking stories, which would not have been well received locally, are devoted to plantation slaves and their mistreatment. Attached to melodramatic situations, Garreau's depictions are graphic and horrible, like those by Stowe, Testut, and George Washington Cable.[11]

The tales describe plantation, or "plantocratique," society. In "Un Nègre marron," a frame story, the account of the inner narrator (a newly hired overseer) constitutes almost the entire text, without the use of quotation marks; the effect is that the inner narrator's voice bleeds into the outer voice, which has narrative authority. Thus, when the reader sees, for instance, the comparison of a slave to a monkey, or reads that blacks are imbeciles and cannot control their passions, the point of view appears to be (but surely was not) the author's. D., a sadistic planter (based, implied Garreau, on a real figure), dominated by greed, castrates a slave who has run away repeatedly. Contrasted to D. is the new overseer, a decent fellow who attempts to alleviate the slaves' misery. Instead, he loses their respect and they become undisciplined—thus appearing to prove that one gets nowhere with blacks by being gentle. The fault, as Garreau surely believed, was in the system of bondage; unfortunately, the author gives voice to arguments for severe treatment of the enslaved. Many contemporary readers may have accepted these arguments; slavery had not long been completely abolished in French territories, and even abolitionist sympathizers often saw blacks as essentially inferior. Another figure, the apparently oversexed slave who cannot control his desire or think of the consequences of his lust, illustrates the widespread American fear of unbridled Negro sexuality.

Twentieth-century Marxist social analysis and particularly the Frankfort School's neo-Marxist social theory support (as Fabrice Leroy indicates in the introduction to the collected stories) what must have been Garreau's understanding. The plantation economy, in which the worker is alienated from both his labor and himself, distorts all human relationships. In a system founded on theft and violence, gentleness is ineffective; the principles of mercy and proportionality in justice are discarded. D. is the most corrupt of all; but the overseer, who takes the job out of need, must become a cog in the wheel of persecution or fail. The slaves themselves, being without autonomy and subject to tyrannical treatment, know nothing but brutality, and, as the foreman notes, "It is not unusual to see a black man, having other slaves under his control, be crueler than the most ferocious planters" (54). Seen in this light, Garreau's story is, under the guise of studies of manners, a denunciation of the plantation system.

In "Bras-coupé," which has conversation in black Creole, D. appears again. He forces a pregnant slave into a murky bayou and pushes her down until she drowns. He loses thereby valuable property, but gains, he asserts, by affirming his power and demonstrating to his other slaves that they should not threaten suicide. Others in the sphere of the plantation economy and on its edges are likewise guilty, whether unconsciously greedy (an Irish shopkeeper whose grasping and insensitivity make him accuse the slave of theft and ultimately contribute to her death) or simply willing to participate in the system. Bras-coupé, who loves the drowned slave, becomes a runaway and lives in the forests and swamps. Shot through the arm and caught, he is taken into custody but escapes. He continues to survive as an outlaw, killing without scruple those sent to track him. The offer of a huge reward inspires a Spaniard to go after him; the runaway is captured by chance and cunning. The story is to be compared with the Bras-coupé episode in Cable's *The Grandissimes*.[12]

"Naïda," a tragic idyll, takes places in the virgin forest as François-René de Chateaubriand and the Rouquettes evoked it. The narrator, disillusioned like Chateaubriand's René, comes upon an Indian maiden, an Atala figure. Echoes of the great Romantics come through: "Tout, à cette heure, révélait à l'intelligence des mystères qu'il n'est pas donné à la faiblesse humaine de pénétrer, tout enfin renfermait des flots de poésie dans lesquels l'âme aime à se bercer..." [At that hour, everything revealed to the intelligence mysteries that human weakness may not penetrate; everything enclosed waves of poetry in which the soul loves to rock itself] (102). Though she is in fact half-English and thus cross-cultural, the Indian girl is unspoiled by contact with civilization and its corruption; indeed, her tribe, the Seminoles, has struggled nobly against the white man to preserve its ways. In this Rousseauesque vision, social ills are viewed not as the result of an evil human nature; rather, they are the product of human customs and social organization.

Another topic in Garreau's stories is the immoral double standard according to which society disowns a woman who commits a fault and brands her child as illegitimate, whereas the man responsible for her seduction is free to marry properly and ignore his victim's claims. In "Un Jour de noces"—which illustrates feminine solidarity—the woman who has been seduced and abandoned appears on the seducer's wedding day to plead for her son. In despair, she has taken poison, but she lives long enough to confront the father and beg him to take the boy. The man refuses all responsibility. The bride, however, overhearing the conversation, promises that she will take care of the child; moreover, though, as a Catholic, she cannot leave her husband, she vows that the marriage will not be consummated.

"L'Idiote"—set in Les Landes—is an early example of what one may call Bordelais Gothic, a vein made famous in the twentieth century by François Mauriac but foreshadowed by Garreau (as by Balzac). A deranged woman, deprived of her just inheritance by a greedy half-brother, sets fire to his house on the evening that his daughter is to be married; the fiancé arrives in time to attempt a rescue of his betrothed, trapped, but, ironically, the body he carries down from the upper story as it collapses is not hers. Again, an initial injustice—not just the man's mistreatment of his sister but the legal and social system by which his theft of her legacy stands up—leads to death. The final story, "Une Créole," relates how a beautiful woman jilts her lover because his notion of success is not satisfactory; she requires wealth. Having taken orders, he officiates (unidentified) at her wedding to a wealthy man. But the latter wastes his fortune, and she is left poverty-stricken with two children. At her death, the priest, revealing his identity, promises to take care of the children.

Another radical writer, Joseph Déjacque (1822–65?), generally labeled an "anarcho-communist," was born in Paris. His mother, widowed, was a laundress; he adopted readily the socialist ideas of Karl Marx and Pierre-Joseph

Proudhon, though he criticized the latter for supporting individual ownership of the products of labor. After participating in the Revolution of 1848, Déjacque was banned from Paris. *Les Lazaréennes*, a collection of radical poetry (1851), led to his arrest. He fled to Belgium and England, then New York and finally New Orleans (1856–58), where he published an enlarged version of the volume. During his short stay, he composed his tract *L'Humanisphère, utopie anarchique*, later published in New York. In New Orleans he also founded *Le Libertaire*, an anarcho-communist journal. He published abolitionist pamphlets and called for armed insurrection against the South.[13]

Another French immigrant, François Tujague (1836–96), differs from those surveyed above; he was, as his work shows, a traditionalist and devout Catholic. He arrived in New Orleans in 1841. He may have attempted to live by writing, but shortly went into business. He served as president of L'Union Française and vice president of L'Athénée Louisianais. He published *Le Premier Pas: Essais littéraires* and contributed to periodicals his tender and well-crafted studies of character and mores, Acadian and Creole, a "race chevaleresque" (95). Many stories, he claimed, were based on facts and models. He likewise composed nature and historical sketches, including portraits of Jean Lafitte and Nicolas-Chauvin de la Frénière, who was executed in the plot against the Spanish. The great forests and Trembling Prairies of Louisiana are well evoked. In "Les Forêts de la Louisiane," he first recalls Chateaubriand's depictions of luxurious nature and the natural life as preached by Chactas; to this picture is opposed, however, the mortal danger a forest can present. "Les Chasseurs de crocodiles en Louisiane" evokes similar dangers in untamed nature, but humorously. These pages do not reflect the upheavals of the 1860s and beyond in Louisiana, nor social concerns; blacks are depicted as happy. His regret that Creole life had changed led him to treating dueling as an unfortunate but honorable tradition. On the Franco-Prussian War, he displayed strong patriotic sentiments comparable to those of Zola and Alphonse Daudet: in Tujague's story "Repentir," a Frenchman speaks candidly of his "hatred of the implacable invader" (37).[14]

CHAPTER SIX

Fiction and Drama by Mid-Nineteenth-Century Free People of Color

A substantial and significant body of French postcolonial literature in nineteenth-century Louisiana was produced by the Free People of Color, parallel to that produced by white authors but created out of very different personal concerns and within contrasting social circumstances. Thus, although they shared many interests, tastes, and literary skills with their white contemporaries, they deserve separate treatment. Almost all the *gens de couleur libres* who contributed to the extant corpus were male. Reasons for the absence of women's writing can only be surmised. Chris Michaelides has remarked that authors in the nonwhite community saw themselves as combatants in the struggle for racial justice, almost as warriors and prophets (an image fitting the Romantic understanding of poets as "phares" [beacons]). As Alfred de Vigny wrote, "The poet reads in the stars the route shown to us by the Lord." Girls, wives, and mothers would not have been viewed, or would not have viewed themselves, as fit for the task. Though Michaelides's observation has doubtless an element of truth, perhaps the explanation for the near-absence of writing by Free Women of Color should be sought in the different level and quality of education that they received; there were fewer schools for them, and, in particular, their families did not send them to Paris for schooling. Additionally, men may have assumed that publishing of any sort was unsuitable, or unimaginable, for them. Or women may have kept their writing to themselves. Even in France, with its much larger population, the number of women writers in the nineteenth century was not large.[1]

Like the poets treated in the following chapter (often the same persons) and journalists who founded their papers in 1862 and afterwards, prose writers examined here were serious devotees of their calling. Though they may be qualified as *amateurs*, the word must be taken in its French sense. They wrote first for their friends and others in their community. They wrote also, secondarily, for whites, a partly antagonistic class but one that could ratify their work by its approval—or possibly be moved by appeals for sympathy and justice. Michaelides emphasizes the good relationships between the elite People of Color and the white intellectual and literary elite (14). Frans Amelinckx notes that "the local press readily accepted the literary production of Creoles of Color, so long as it conformed to the norms—that is, no racial or social references." Their literary style, marked by elevated language, beautiful crafting of sentences, and routine use of the *passé simple* and imperfect subjunctive, illustrated their education and abilities. The Romantic and sentimental features of their writing, founded in nineteenth-century French literary practice, were also suited to their semialienation and their need to excel. Their local readership was matched in France, where some Creoles of Color published or had dramas produced. These writers could have agreed with Maryse Condé, speaking for herself and other West Indians, who asserted that "language . . . is the only way of shaping the future."[2]

Mixed-race Creole writers were not, however, simple propagandists, using writing only as a tool for change, as certain other nineteenth-century authors, white and African American, did in inflammatory tracts and thesis fiction directed toward overturning institutions or cultural uses and codes. Reimagining social order entirely after the fashion of European utopians and revolutionaries was not the vein of the colored Creoles—nor would they have been free to cultivate it, given the state law of 1830 restricting speech or writing deemed seditious or with a "tendency to produce discontent among the free coloured population . . ." Obtaining greater freedom and the removal of the stigma of race for themselves was certainly, however, their wish, and much of their writing can be considered *littérature engagée* (committed literature). Poetry was discreet, but fiction and drama—especially published in France or after 1862—served to make openly their points about restrictions on marriage and other unjust limitations on their caste. The sufferings and unhappiness of their heroes differ from the sentimental complaints of those depicted by early French Romantics—Benjamin Constant, François-René de Chateaubriand, and Etienne de Senancour. The Creoles of Color were genuine outcasts in some respects and were seen sometimes as repulsive. Suicide is more understandable if, for instance, one is being pushed into prostitution. Mixed-race Creole characters resemble more those genuine victims of society to whom Victor Hugo devoted eloquent fiction, from *Le Dernier Jour d'un condamné* (1829) through *Les Misérables* (1862) and beyond.[3]

Thus the primary axes of conflict in prose by Creoles of Color are not principally in the soul but in the social system, between races and castes. The social restrictions had, of course, moral and sentimental consequences; hence the frequent theme of the impossible love, or at least marriage, between a white and a Creole of Color. Since marriage was commonly viewed (in the bourgeois literature and culture of the time) as indispensable for happiness, the legal restriction had existential effects. A recurring figure is the quadroon or octoroon (dubbed by critics subsequently the "tragic octoroon"). Whereas admirers of later white authors such as George Washington Cable and Kate Chopin stress how they violated "taboos" by depicting such women sympathetically and as heroines, for the Creoles of Color there was no such taboo; they were writing about their own women, their own lives.[4]

Called the first prose piece published by a Louisiana Free Man of Color, and identified as the first short story by any African American, "Le Mulâtre," by Victor Séjour, appeared (1837) in Paris in *La Revue des Colonies,* an abolitionist review edited by Cyrille Bissette, a nonwhite from Martinique. Séjour (1817–74), born Juan Victor Séjour Marcou et Ferrand, had a successful literary career, especially as a dramatist. His father, Louis, was an octoroon immigrant from Saint Domingue, his mother a free octoroon. The family lived in the French Quarter, where Louis owned a small business. Earlier, he had been a promoter of a Quadroon Ball. Some sources say that the boy attended the Saint-Barbe Academy, and studied perhaps with Michel Séligny, the half-brother of Camille Thierry; on chronological grounds, J. John Perret disputes those claims. In 1834, at approximately age seventeen, the young man read a poem, called remarkable, at the opening session of a new black Creole club, the Société des Artisans. Encouraged by his father, he went to Paris in 1836 to study; there is, however, no record of his having matriculated anywhere. He was received in literary circles and had two plays presented at the Théâtre Français (Comédie-Française) and nearly a score more at other theaters, including the Porte Saint-Martin; these plays were also published, and he was viewed as a dramatic genius. Alexandre Dumas père, himself a man of mixed blood, and the playwright Emile Augier befriended him. Séjour was named to the Legion of Honor. According to one source, he became private secretary to Napoleon III, who was broad-minded about racial matters, as his policies toward Algerian natives demonstrated. (While Perret charges that Séjour's adulation of the emperor was a weakness, it is understandable that the playwright admired the emperor's tolerance and personal interest in other cultures.) Séjour had three common-law wives, who bore him three sons. He died in straitened circumstances and was buried in Père-Lachaise Cemetery in Paris.[5]

"Le Mulâtre," a frame story, is a pioneering protest piece. The principal tale is narrated by the inner speaker after an outer narrator has established one level of narration, but at the conclusion there is no return to the outer frame—an error of literary tactics, since readers would benefit from concluding comments or interpretation by the outer narrator. The story appeared in Paris; its criticism of racial laws could thus be open. Its Haitian setting emphasizes the close ties between that island and New Orleans. By its melodrama—hidden identity (the slave hero does not know he is his master's son)—and violence—flight from pursuers, ambushes—it resembles fiction by Dumas père and Victor Hugo. It also anticipates portions of Charles Testut's *Le Vieux Salomon* by its plot (which became a sterotype) and positions, especially the view that a slave has a right to avenge himself on a master who attempts to seduce or otherwise abuses his wife. The concluding revelation of the slave's identity, after he has poisoned the master's wife and is in the act of murdering his master—that is, his father—dispels the narrative irony, but tragically, since the mulatto shoots himself.[6]

In New Orleans, the first prose by a Creole of Color may have been "Souvenir de 1815," by Séligny (1807–67), which appeared in *L'Abeille* (1839). Séligny, who had gone in 1824 to Paris, where his father was a lawyer, and had studied there at the Collège Sainte-Barbe and the lycée Louis-le-Grand, returned to Louisiana in 1828 and shortly founded a school called Sainte-Barbe, after the Paris establishment; he served as its director until it closed in 1846. He returned to Paris about 1857, fleeing New Orleans with a white married woman after they had become outcasts. He settled permanently in Bordeaux in 1862, where he died, later. He was thus part of the Creole diaspora, but he felt also, like numerous compatriots, that he had two homelands; France appears explicitly as a "seconde patrie" (53). His short "Souvenir," an evocation of the Louisiana past, is replete with Romantic nostalgia and regret for times and places since changed. This nostalgia includes a heroic vein, as the author recalls the military feats of Andrew Jackson and his troops (including Free Creoles of Color) against the British. New Orleans is evoked with affection and without overt lament over the sufferings of Séligny's caste, although there is intimation of conflict in his phrase "Attristé du présent, inquiet de l'avenir" [saddened by the present, anxious about the future] (53). Another Séligny story, "Le Pêcheur de la Guadeloupe," similarly came out in *L'Abeille* (1858). Its classical references (to Homer, Ovid, Plutarch) illustrate the author's learning. The story, like various others, concerns the "absurd prejudices" of caste and illegitimate birth.[7]

"Un Mariage de conscience" (August 1843) is by Armand Lanusse (1812–67), who studied in Paris at the Ecole Polytechnique and later was professor of languages and headmaster (1852–67) at the Institut catholique des orphelins indigents (Couvent Institute). The piece appeared in *L'Album Littéraire: Journal des jeunes gens*, about which a further word is in order. An important though ephemeral publication, with just a few numbers, printed by J. L. Marciacq, it seems to have been the first journal of African American writing in the United States. As the manifestation of a remarkable literary nascence, it may be considered a foreshadowing of *The Double-Dealer*, a showcase of very able writers published in New Orleans in the 1920s. It included work by whites also, Térence Rouquette among them. It was bold for its period and place. For instance, an article protesting censure of writings by Creoles of Color appeared anonymously. Lanusse's short story concerns the practice whereby priests occasionally consented to marry a white and a Free Person of Color. The union was illegal and could have no value in law. In this case the husband subsequently abandons his wife in order to marry within his class. Desperate, she throws herself in front of his carriage and is killed.[8]

Another story, "Marie," written possibly by a woman and published anonymously in the same issue of *L'Album*, portrays a young girl of color who commits suicide rather than agree to be "placed" by her mother. The narrator's horror and indignation against the mother's unnatural venality convey the blame many put on *plaçage*, despite its advantages for the caste. It is noteworthy that Marie is buried from a church on Rampart Street, her suicide notwithstanding.

Published over the initials F. M. S. in *La Tribune de la Nouvelle-Orléans* in 1865, "Souvenirs de Bonfouca" is a short frame novella. The outer narrator encounters a fellow soldier in the Native Guards. The unhappiness of the narrator's new acquaintance is so obvious that he is asked to explain it; his tale constitutes the framed narrative. It illustrates poignantly the "préjugé barbare" that prevents Free Men of Color from marrying whites (166). Ironically, that law has just been superseded by Union codes, but it is too late for him. The novella includes a hurricane scene, in which the protagonist manages to evade whites who are pursuing him, believing him to have incited slaves to riot and disobedience. The white girl he loves, who has come to warn him, catches cold in the storm and dies of consumption; his life is irreparably saddened. Like Lyle Saxon's *Children of Strangers* and Anne Rice's *The Feast of All Saints*, it also depicts the social gulf between Creoles of Color and non-mixed-race blacks, especially slaves. In this case, the unhappy narrator seems to sympathize with the slaves, and his enlistment in the Native Guards points to a social conscience.[9]

"Simple Histoire" and "Trois amours" by Adolphe Duhart, which both appeared in 1865 in *La Tribune,* under the pseudonyms L. D. and Lélia D. (after his deceased daughter), show the inherent difficulties of a three-class system. Duhart, who was born sometime between 1835 and 1840 and died in 1909, was a teacher at the Couvent Institute and later its director, following Joanni Questy (discussed below). Duhart wrote fiction, poetry, and drama; *Lélia ou la victime du préjugé* was performed at the Théâtre d'Orléans in 1866. "Simple Histoire" relates succinctly a consummated love affair between a white girl and her playmate and "brother" (83), the mixed-blood son of her favorite slave. Past childhood, no normal life is possible for the two. Upon discovering the affair, her father sends away the slave and the young man; the young mother rears their child, a girl, within the household, under the pretext that it is the slave's. In later years, the daughter becomes the mother of a martyr for Haitian independence, the Free Man of Color Vincent Ogé, executed after the uprising of 1790 (28). This little morality tale may be read sympathetically, or ironically, if one notes that a black rebel leader comes from partly white stock—white blood being perhaps desirable for the energy and leadership needed in the occasion.[10]

Like "Souvenirs de Bonfouca," the novella "Trois amours" illustrates the damage done by the race barrier. It is not the author's sole concern, however; similar burdens are created by illegitimate birth, as Séligny showed also. For many pages, Duhart conceals carefully from readers—although they have grounds for suspicion—the precise origins of the heroine, Lydia, who has been adopted by the Duménil family. Her family members generally remain ignorant likewise. But Lydia herself knows that her real mother, who gave birth to her in Mexico (chronologically, the earliest "love," though perhaps not one meant by the title) after having been seduced by Duménil (now head of this family), was of mixed race. Lydia realizes that marriage with a white is impossible for her. The Duménil family circle also includes another orphan, Beaufort, taken in by M. Duménil after the death of the man's father, a close friend.

Lydia overcomes her own love for Beaufort to promote the cause of her all-white half-sister, Valentine, likewise enamored of him. Beaufort and Valentine, who is of fragile health—doubtless consumptive—are subsequently betrothed, over her possessive mother's objections. Valentine dies after waltzing at a celebration ball; though dancing is forbidden to her, she has insisted, to prevent Beaufort from waltzing with Lydia, of whose affections he is, significantly, jealous. Two years later, having overcome his grief by traveling in Europe, Beaufort realizes that he loves Lydia. Returning, he presses his suit, but she refuses him. Letters left by Duménil, now deceased, explain her origin and thus her refusal. While such turns of plot and features such as prematurely white hair and sacrificial women appear now as nineteenth-century literary clichés—as used by Alfred Mercier, for instance—they were accepted vehicles for conveying fictional and social truths. Convention, that is, prejudice, nearly prevails in "Trois amours"; but, unlike "Simple Histoire," the story ultimately ends well: Beaufort insists on marrying Lydia despite what she calls "le lâche préjugé de notre société" [the cowardly prejudice of our society] (140). (This "transgression" against color laws is, according to Michaelides, accompanied by another, against laws forbidding incest. But in fact there is no incest.) Where the lovers will marry and live is not specified; the story suffices as wish-fulfillment. Postbellum laws would allow them to settle elsewhere in America, but prejudice would still be against them; one can imagine them in Europe.

"Monsieur Paul," by Questy, was published in 1867 in *La Tribune*. Questy (1817–69) became a teacher of English, French, and Spanish at the Couvent Institute in 1845 and later its director. His tale begins with a "Post Scriptum," a short manifesto concerning bourgeois commercialism in the city. Reigning literary taste is criticized by implication: if writers abandoned a "sterile silence" and "vague empyrean," and descended into the street, they could please all classes of readers and at the same time bring about an "important reaction." The topics Questy lists as suitable for literary treatment include Romantic antitheses but also a tendency toward what would later be called Naturalism, by which infamy, hypocrisy, ingratitude would be depicted in "all their truth."

The action of the novella takes place just before the Civil War. The narrator is a Creole of Color; Monsieur Paul, in contrast, is a cultivated white. The awkwardness of color lines is illustrated when Monsieur Paul takes the narrator for white and solicits his friendship; the man's embarrassment is painful to witness. Paul's drama, subsequently related, is that he loved a colored Creole, to whom he was united in a "mariage de conscience"; she then left him, with their children, for an Anglo-Saxon (whose dishonorable seduction is perhaps to be seen as indicative of American character, the aggressive commercialism alluded to in the "Post Scriptum"). Like countless other nineteenth-century characters, Paul believes himself a victim of fate. Chance leads him to discover the Anglo-Saxon, whom he calls out. He kills his adversary but dies himself of wounds—perhaps symbolizing the end of a way of life. One consequence of his death is that his slave Georges learns he is the son of Paul's brother—and thus another artificial and secret relationship is brought to light, happily in this instance. The woman Paul had loved, gnawed by remorse, lives licentiously and finally poisons herself. The resemblance to Gustave Flaubert's *Madame Bovary* (1857) is worth noting, but poison was a frequent motif in Creole fiction.

Another genre cultivated by the Creole writers of color was drama. Although dramatist Dion Boucicault was Irish, he lived for a while in Louisiana, and his English-language play *The Octoroon; or, Life in Louisiana*, produced in New York and elsewhere, can be examined briefly. Like "Marie," "Monsieur Paul," and Chopin's "Désirée's Baby," the drama concerns the suicide of a woman of mixed race. The heroine, Zoe, who originally thought she was a free Creole, discovers she is a slave. Her white lover declares the prejudice against their marriage to be absurd. But it becomes clear that she will become the property of an unscrupulous overseer; her solution is to poison herself. In this version, the play was first performed in 1859 in New York. Two years later in London, the denouement was changed, because of different attitudes and public pressure, to a favorable one, by which she and the man will go marry in an unspecified land.[11]

It will be seen that Boucicault's plot was anticipated by Séjour, whose plays in Paris received often laudatory reviews from such critics as Théophile Gautier, Edmond and Jules Goncourt, and Jules Janin. The playwright listed Shakespeare and Victor Hugo as his masters; he borrowed frequently from them and used numerous Hugoesque antitheses. *Le Fils de la nuit* ran for six months, starting in July 1856. Napoleon III attended two of his premieres. Three plays of his were adapted into English and performed during his lifetime. Séjour also did a drawing room comedy, *Le Paletot brun*. In Louisiana, however, a proposal to award him a medal, after one drama was presented successfully, was not honored, because of his race. The fact that he did not treat American topics on the stage suggests his desire to cut himself off from the Louisiana class system and the painful sense of inferiority that resulted from it.[12]

Although Victor Hugo's last play, *Les Burgraves* (1843), had prefigured the ultimate end of melodramatic spectacles on the stage, the French theatergoing public of midcentury retained its taste for the "great spectacle" dramas of Hugo and Dumas père. It was likewise enthusiastic about new modes of staging based on improved stage machinery, thanks to which plays could become even more complicated, melodramatic, and spectacular. (*Le Fils de la nuit* showed on stage a moving ship and apparent waves.) Séjour's dramas, with large casts, suited these tastes. Some material was excised by the imperial censors for its political content. Yet as more realistic drama, provided by such playwrights as Augier and Eugène Scribe, came to dominate the stage, Séjour's work fell out of favor. *Henri de Lorraine* (1870) was panned by critics. Then with the defeat of France in the Franco-Prussian War and the end of the empire, he lost an important supporter and much of his audience. To present-day readers, his work seems "sterile and pompous." Not even the skill of Norman R. Shapiro can offset the melodrama of the two plays he translated, one in rhymed couplets; only the message can justify publication in an English version.[13]

Diégarias, Séjour's first drama, in classical alexandrines, opened in 1844 at the Théâtre Français and had eleven performances. Anticipating Somerset Maugham, who in *Of Human Bondage* dramatized by the disablement of the club-footed hero, Philip Carey, his own disabilities—homosexuality and a bad stammer—Séjour used Jewish characters as stand-ins to represent the colored Creoles' difficult existence. The choice of Jews for this role was apt, given that the Code Noir had excluded Jews from the colony of Louisiana (though of course they came to be tolerated). In France, Jewish characters and topics were current at the time, owing in part to Fromental Halévy's 1835 opera *La Juive*. The play is set in fifteenth-century Spain, when anti-Jewish measures were instituted, including a statute prohibiting converted Jews and Muslims from holding public office. Jews were then expelled in 1492 and Muslims in 1502.

The play turns on social and legal obstacles to love and marriage with a person of a different race or caste; it also shows the way parental choices are visited on mixed-race children. Diégarias, who is really the Jew Jacob Eliacin, eloped years before with a Christian girl when her uncle forbade their romance. Diégarias returned later, with a daughter, who is unaware of her origins, and he has become minister of the treasury. The girl, Inès, loves a Christian named, aptly, Don Juan, who has seduced her via a sham marriage. Diégarias attempts to make him marry her properly, but Don Juan reveals to the grandees that the man is half-Jewish and thus his daughter also is tainted; a Spanish grandee cannot marry someone of Hebrew origins. The elaborate revenge plotted by Diégarias on Don Juan and the king ends in her suicide by poison.

The drama is thus one of racial prejudice and its consequences. This subject can lead critics to overlook the fact that it also concerns reasons of state, which put the prejudice in a different light. By the logic of fifteenth-century

Spain—and even that of the various nineteenth-century French governments with respect to natives of Algeria (occupied first in 1830)—racial policies were simply part of statecraft; in the Iberian kingdoms of the time, Moors and Jews alike were seen as subversive and dangerous. The king and Spanish grandees of the play merely follow reasons of state—which, in Golden Age drama, the Elizabethan theater, and French classical drama, are often shown to offset legitimate personal concerns. To view the play as turning only on unfounded racial distinctions is simplistic.[14]

The 1850s were a productive decade for Séjour. His *Richard III*, a historical drama in prose dedicated to his father, appeared in 1852. The action, which is limited to a short period, following classical French dramatic rules, takes place in 1485, after Richard has been king for two years. Discontent surrounds him, and he suspects treason everywhere. One rebellion has been successfully put down, but the second Earl of Richmond, Henry Tudor (later Henry VII), plots against Richard from France. Poison, horoscopes, murder, and numerous deaths mark the play. Séjour chose not to stage scenes from the battle of Bosworth Field, in which the historical Richard died; instead, he is killed by conspirators. The style has nothing of Shakespeare's vigor and poetry, and the rhetoric is not the equal of Victor Hugo's, but the play is interesting and deserved its popularity.

Les Noces vénitiennes, a *drame*, premiered in 1855, and in 1858 Séjour wrote, with Jules Brésil, *Le Martyre du coeur*. Likewise called a *drame*, this prose work nevertheless has elements of comedy. The action takes place during the First Empire, with analepses to the Revolutionary period. Class divisions are emphasized. The plot is noteworthy because it anticipates Grace King's "Monsieur Motte." A former valet, Laborie, secretly pays school tuition for the daughter of the marquis de Nepteuil, his former master. The girl does not realize that he has disappeared, having been killed, presumably, by revolutionaries.

La Tireuse de cartes (1859), in prose, carries a message against racial prejudice and racial laws. It was written in collaboration with Jean-François Mocquard, then private secretary to Napoleon III, whose subsequent foreign policy regarding Italy may have been shaped by the issues raised in the drama; the emperor attended the premiere. Again, the prejudicial laws and attitudes in question are against Jews. Based on a true story called the Mortara case, modified, it comprises a long dramatized prologue and five acts. While the parents are away, a Christian nurse in a Hebrew family in Bologna baptizes secretly the small daughter, for whose salvation she fears in the child's illness. She then kidnaps the child, who is given to a loving couple. (Church law, as the Mortara case demonstrated, actually protected such transfers, since it required that Christian children be reared in Christian homes. The author surely had in mind also the antebellum practice of separating slave families, widespread in Louisiana despite the Code Noir.) Years later, the girl's true mother discovers her. The situation is Solomonic: two mothers (as well as two religions) in competition for a child, each unwilling to yield. Since the daughter is grown, the choice is finally hers; it drives her temporarily insane and nearly kills her. Her mad scene, in which she plucks petals from a flower, is not without resemblance to Ophelia's in *Hamlet*. Her ultimate choice, to return to her birth home but retain her Christian belief, is an almost untenable compromise. Owing doubtless to the notoriety of the Mortara case, Séjour's drama was translated into Italian and performed in Bologna, and adapted into English. In France, it was attacked as too pro-Semitic; Séjour argued that it was simply a critique of intolerance.[15]

Without, presumably, wishing to demean his Jewish characters, the dramatist attributes to them traits traditionally associated with their race, now known as stereotypes. The parents' absence, which makes the baptism and kidnapping possible, is occasioned by the Jewish father's greed: out of self-interest, he goes to the side of a dying uncle, in order to win his affection and fortune. For her part, the mother displays the fanaticism and hatred toward Christians of which Jews were often accused. She loathes them, accusing them of nothing but oppression, overlooking the tolerance shown by many; she vows terrible revenge; it is intimated that she would rather see her child dead than baptized. Later, in disguise, she becomes a moneylender (that is, a usurer) as well as a fortune-teller. After she finds her daughter, she is unwilling to agree to a rest cure for her; maternal love for an ill child is less powerful than hatred of the Christian adoptive mother. These were entirely stock images for the period; anti-Semitism had been strong in France and remained so, as the Dreyfus Affair would show at the end of the century. What is interesting is that Séjour used these characters as stand-ins, presumably, for those, like himself, with African blood.

Alice Dunbar-Nelson, née Moore (1875–1935), came from a middle-class New Orleans family. She attended Straight College, became a teacher, and published fiction, drama, poetry, history, and journalism, including a collection of local color tales, *The Goodness of St. Rocque and Other Stories* (1899), and *Masterpieces of Negro Eloquence* (1914). Though she is associated chiefly with the Northeast, where her career unfolded, she also wrote, usually discreetly, about the "color line" and the difficulty of being a mixed-race person in Louisiana. In stories from *The Goodness of St. Rocque* these themes are treated obliquely; in "The Pearl in the Oyster" and the unpublished "The Stones of the Village," she confronted them directly.[16]

Rodolphe-Lucien Desdunes (1849–1928) must be mentioned here, although his genre was literary history, and *Nos hommes et notre histoire*, the style of which was praised by Alcée Fortier, did not appear until the twentieth century (1911). His ancestry was Haitian on the paternal side and Cuban on the maternal. The family had a tobacco plantation and cigar factory. Desdunes preferred civil service; he worked for the U.S. Customs Service until an accident blinded him. He was proud of his French ascendancy, the language, and the achievements of his fellow Creoles; he took issue with the unfavorable light in which W. E. B. Du Bois presented them. An outspoken opponent of state-enforced segregation, Desdunes was among those who brought the legal challenge that culminated in the 1896 *Plessy v. Ferguson* Supreme Court decision, which upheld the "separate but equal" principle but evoked dissenting arguments that would be crucial later. The position of Desdunes was in direct opposition to many others' views, as represented, for instance, in the separatist tenet expressed just five years earlier by Joseph H. Choate, who praised "the maintenance of the integrity of the races, which, with the approval of both races, has formed the basis of Southern civilization."[17]

The term *Nos hommes* is used generically in Desdunes's title. Providing biographical sketches and historical summaries, the book pays homage to the New Orleans black Creole community from the early nineteenth century on. One chapter is devoted to women, especially the philanthropist Justine Couvent. Desdunes expresses repeatedly his sympathy with the difficulties under which his predecessors labored as they exercised their professions and his personal resentment of the white community, which put obstacles in their paths and, most hurtfully, humiliated them. He pleads their case with concern for their long-term reputation. He also reargues the case against the post-Reconstruction "separate but equal" laws.

The literary achievement of Creoles of Color in the mid-nineteenth century was remarkable, as the following chapter, devoted to their poetry, illustrates further. They wrote from a situation that was both similar to—in some ways identical to—that of Louisiana white authors and yet vastly different. In that difference lies their unique contribution.

CHAPTER SEVEN

Poetry by Mid-Nineteenth-Century Free People of Color

Poetry in nineteenth-century Louisiana by both *gens de couleur libres* and whites displayed "a quality inspired and polished by their sense of community." Using European forms to which they added local cultural elements—geographic, lexical, historical—Louisiana poets produced accomplished verse, often moving and striking.[1]

The most important collective work of the literary community formed by the *gens de couleur libres* was an anthology called *Les Cenelles: choix de poésies indigènes* (1845), prepared by Armand Lanusse. It has been called the first volume of Afro-American poetry and, by Charles Hamlin Good, "the first American Negro literary movement." The title refers to red holly berries, or, according to some, hawthorn berries. The word may be intended to suggest prickliness in the Creoles' situation. The term *indigenous* indicates simply that the contributors were of native stock. The volume consists of eighty-five poems. Biographical details for the authors are not abundant, and at least one is pseudonymous. The number of poets seventeen—does honor to them and their community; but it must be remembered that these were the times in which poetry was widely honored in civilized countries, and Alphonse de Lamartine could say to a detractor that his book would soon be in every cobbler's pocket. The anthology was an admirable expression of consciousness by a group representing the larger caste and should not be dismissed as an elitist publication by privileged authors. Whether it was an antagonistic gesture to the white literary community is doubtful; but it expressed pride.[2]

Authors include Lanusse (born in New Orleans in 1812 to Haitian refugees); his brother, Numa Lanusse, who died young; Joanni Questy; Victor Séjour; Valcour B. (probably a pseudonym for B. Valcour), who was educated in France and knew Latin and Greek; Camille Thierry; and Pierre Dalcour. Others are Mirtil-Ferdinand Liotau; Auguste Populus, a mason; Michel Saint-Pierre, a fencing master, called "le Bayard créole"; Bernard Désormes Dauphin; brothers Louis (a tailor) and Jean Boise; and Manuel Sylva, of Spanish origin. Saint-Pierre and Populus were friends; in the poem "Deux ans plus tard," Saint-Pierre thanked his friend for coming to his aid when he was contemplating suicide. Dauphin became a teacher in L'Isle Brevelle in north-central Louisiana. The anthology bears an epigraph from A[lfred] Mercier: "Et de ces fruits qu'un Dieu prodigue dans nos bois / Heureux si j'en ai su faire un aimable choix!" [And of these fruits that a god scatters abundantly in our woods / Fortunate am I, if I have been able to make a pleasing choice.] It should be noted that certain contributors—Questy especially, and Nelson Desbrosses—were spiritualists and acted as mediums in seances.[3]

Les Cenelles shows the influence of the French Romantics, especially Lamartine, from whom lines are frequently quoted as epigraphs. Many poems, such as Nicol Riquet's "Rondeau redoublé," a short song in praise of wine, display light lyrical touches. One reviewer called the poems "aimables" but derivative, and also repetitious, "monotonous"—features, he acknowledged, of Victor Hugo's and Lamartine's work also, but offset there by poetic virtues and frequent flashes of genius. For many poems, suitable tunes are mentioned, including some by Pierre-Jean de Béranger, who was very popular (though his fame has not lasted well) and particularly admired by the Creoles of Color. He was antiroyalist, anticlerical, and sympathized with the working classes. *Les Cenelles* is not, however, folk-like; the language and form illustrate standard nineteenth-century literary styles and display verbal beauty. Calvin Claudel, a folklorist, spoke of the "artificiality of this literary coterie in their imitation of the Classical French literary style." He is mistaken to call it *classical*. The alexandrine, though a classical marker, endured long into the nineteenth century and was the form of choice for most nineteenth-century poets; in other respects the poems are in the established Romantic mode. Claudel found their writing too derivative: "They lack the creative originality of the uneducated singers mentioned by [George Washington] Cable." The argument that what is learned or intellectual is necessarily inferior to what appears spontaneous or is produced by "folk" authors is old but fallacious. Authors' background, audience, and taste should be taken into account in such an assessment.[4]

Some poems in *Les Cenelles* are in the heroic vein of French Romanticism, well illustrated by Victor Hugo. Many are love poems. While it may be assumed that the beloved is generally a Creole of Color (even those who are blonde with blue eyes), this is by no means certain. Still others concern nature or death, often with Christian overtones. Régine Latortue and Gleason R. W. Adams assert that the poetry is "superficial and imitative since it lacks the subtext of revolution and liberty which existed in the works of the best French Romantics" (xiii). This statement is oversimplified; countless well-known poems by Lamartine and Hugo have no connection to politics. Furthermore, Alfred de Vigny was a conservative, and Alfred de Musset was apolitical. In any case, given official censorship after 1830 of anything seditious, and doubtless some self-censorship, the poems could not offer explicit criticism of the caste system, nor laments over the poets' ambivalent status. A few discreet allusions may be political, such as to "maux," or evils, suffered by the poet (Dalcour). In "Epigramme," Armand Lanusse treats, ironically but critically, *plaçage*, which he had criticized in "Un Mariage de conscience." He also alludes to it in "A Elora." Liotau (1800–47) expresses the wish that Christ might change the fate of the Creoles of Color and destroy social hatred and discord ("Une Impression").

Caryn Cossé Bell, who reads *Les Cenelles* in the light of subsequent writings by the same poets in the newspaper *L'Union*, has seen more political weight in the poems. Political figures do appear, including Napoleon, viewed as a liberator, not a tyrant; "Le Retour de Napoléon," by Séjour, originally published in Paris in 1841, celebrates the return of the emperor's remains to France. Toussaint L'Ouverture and the Haitian revolution are mentioned likewise. Lanusse in his introduction speaks of the "disdain" and "calumny" to which the authors are sometimes subjected. A quatrain by him runs thus:

> Le vice seul est bas, la vertu fait le rang;
> Et l'homme le plus juste est aussi le plus grand.
> Les richesses, l'orgueil, ne sont que des chimères;
> Enfants du même Dieu, tous les mortels sont frères.

> [Vice alone is base; virtue creates rank;
> And the man most just is also the greatest.
> Riches, pride are only chimera;
> Children of the same God, all mortals are brothers.]

Lanusse's "Le Prêtre et la jeune fille," dedicated to Mercier, expresses the latter's thesis in *La Fille du prêtre*—that clerical celibacy is against nature and horrible to endure.[5]

The fact that Dalcour's twelve poems begin and end the collection suggest that Lanusse held his verse in high regard. The son of two Free People of Color, Dalcour was sent abroad to study. He returned to New Orleans but chafed under the social restrictions and went back to France, where he moved in Paris literary circles frequented by Alexandre Dumas père. One of his poems was a "letter" dedicated to a white classical scholar, Constant Lépouzé, a native of France who taught in New Orleans. Dalcour's "Au bord du lac" may refer to Lake Pontchartrain, but the features of the setting are generic, as the first two stanzas show:

Viens, ô ma bien-aimée,
La brise est embaumée
    Quand le jour fuit;
Tout dort, tout est silence,
Au bord du lac immense;
    Viens, il fait nuit!

L'oiseau dans le feuillage
A cessé son ramage,
    Son chant joyeux;
Pas un léger murmure
Ne trouble la nature—
    Veillons tous deux.

[Come, oh my beloved;
The breeze is fragrant
    When daylight flees;
Everything sleeps, everything is silent,
On the shore of the immense lake;
    Come, it is night!

The bird in the foliage
Has ceased its warbling,
    Its joyous song;
Not even a light murmur
Disturbs nature—
    Let us both watch.]

The following stanzas from Thierry's "Adieu" can be compared to "L'Isolement" by Lamartine, whose influence is often perceptible:

Canal Carondelet, le vent du nord me chasse
   Aujourd'hui de tes bords.
Adieu, je vais chercher près de l'âtre une place
   Pour abriter mon corps.

Sur ton chemin poudreux plus de vertes cigales,
   Plus de beaux papillons,
Rien que le bruit du vent qui vient par intervalles
   Mourir dans les buissons.

Mais semblable à l'amant qui loin de son amante
   Pleure et gémit toujours,
Loin de toi je n'aurai qu'une voix gémissante,
   Et que de mauvais jours.

[Carondelet Canal, the north wind chases me
   Today from your banks.
Farewell; I am going to seek near the hearth a place
   In which to shelter my body.

On your dusty path no more green cicadas,
   No more beautiful butterflies;
Nothing but the sound of the wind which comes intermittently
   To die in the shrubbery.

But like the lover who far from his beloved
   Weeps and sighs constantly,
Far from you I will have only a moaning voice
   And dark days.]

In fact, despite the mention of the north wind, the speaker flees to get away from a "nymphe cruelle."[6]

Similarly, these lines, from "Une Impression" by Liotau, recall Lamartine's.

Eglise Saint-Louis, vieux temple, reliquaire,
Te voilà maintenant désert et solitaire!
Ceux qui furent commis ici-bas à tes soins,
Du tabernacle saint méprisant les besoins,
Ailleurs ont entraîné la phalange chrétienne.

[St. Louis Church, old temple, reliquary,
Here you are now, deserted and solitary.
Those who were charged here below with your care,
Scorning the needs of the holy tabernacle,
Have carried elsewhere the Christian phalanx.]

The mention of a *mandore* (a sort of lute) and the phrase "poète infortuné" recall Musset's poetry.

Poète infortuné, j'ai brisé la mandore
    Que j'avais sous les doigts—
A quoi bon de chanter, quand celle que j'adore
    Reste sourde à ma voix!

[Unfortunate poet, I have broken the lute
    That I had under my fingers—
What is the use of singing, when the one I adore
    Remains deaf to my voice!]

Thierry (1814–75), who contributed fourteen poems to *Les Cenelles* and published in France a collection of his own, *Les Vagabondes, poésies américaines*, deserves extensive treatment. He has been called by several literary historians the greatest New Orleans Francophone poet, though George Dessommes (treated in chapter 9) is a rival for that honor. A "Biographical Note" in *Les Vagabondes* speaks of Thierry's "stormy youth" (a Romantic cliché, recalling François-René de Chateaubriand's *René*), his "originality," his "somewhat eccentric character." This note was, according to present-day editors, written by Joseph Rousseau, a New Orleans native who later settled in Haiti, the author of *Souvenirs de la Louisiane*. Thierry alludes to the "orgies" in which he participated, to the "dark dens" of vice, and evokes them in "Hôpital." He was the illegitimate son of a Frenchman from Paris who became editor of *Le Courrier de la Louisiane*, and an *octavonne* (octaroon) from Saint Domingue who had a son already, the poet Michel Séligny. Thierry bore his mother's name until the 1850s. He was educated in New Orleans, probably at the Collège Sainte-Barbe. His father's death shortly before he was to depart for France prevented his leaving then. He practiced the trade of shoemaking but also had income, probably from his mother and from properties he acquired; he owned slaves. At the age of forty-one, he finally crossed to France and, for some time at least, lived in Bordeaux—another member of the Creole diaspora of the time.

His exile is an unfortunate reflection on the legal and social status of Creoles of Color. He had an unhappy love affair in France. It has been suggested that the beloved's father denied permission for the couple to marry not because of Thierry's race but because there was no verification of the Louisianan's financial, and perhaps social, status; at least one poem (see below) suggests otherwise. The poet returned once to New Orleans for business reasons (he had entrusted his wealth to a firm that went bankrupt). He is listed on the roll of the New Orleans Freedmen's Aid Association in 1865, formed by prosperous Creoles of Color and whites. A poem read in public by Armand Mercier spoke (erroneously) of Thierry's shooting himself and dying in poverty. In fact, he left a respectable legacy. The poem illustrates the ties between the elite Creoles of Color and liberal whites.[7]

Half of Thierry's poems from *Les Cenelles* were not collected in his 1874 volume; he may have found them unsuitable or inferior. According to the publisher's note, the poems of *Les Vagabondes* were written well before they appeared in print. Internal evidence supports this claim; the collection has features of full-blown Romanticism. While alexandrines are common, Thierry also uses the quatrain form used in four stanzas of Lamartine's "Le Lac" (12/ 6/ 12/ 6), octosyllabic verse and, elsewhere, other mixed forms (*vers libérés*). Among recurrent themes are suicide (at least three poems), love, storms (as noted earlier in connection with hurricanes), poetic inspiration (a "Muse"), suffering, fatality, death, exile (as in "La Chanson de l'exilé"), and wandering (suggested by the title). Here are lines from "Le Suicide":

> La vie est un affreux rivage;
> On craint trop d'en quitter le bord:
> Frêle esquif battu par l'orage,
> Dois-je pâlir devant la mort?
>
> [Life is a frightful shore;
> One is too fearful of leaving its edge.
> Frail skiff, beaten by the storm,
> Should I pale in the face of death?]

While each theme and motif can be found in countless other poems from the Romantic period, they also speak to the Creole heart. Edward Larocque Tinker noted "the bitterness characteristic of colored writers in those days." Thierry may well have thought of suicide himself; he lived in exile, loving his homeland (as the subtitle suggests), yet choosing France. "Regrets d'une vieille mulâtresse" [Regrets of an old mulatto woman], in patois, suggests nostalgia for his Louisiana past. Even in France, he may have feared racial rejection, as suggested by his early poem "Le Nautonier," which alludes to the "old man who refused me your hand / while cursing my race."[8]

Thierry himself is not the sole subject of his poetry, however; the book speaks of various figures from New Orleans. For instance, there is the eponymous "Eugène B . . . ," a friend who killed himself in his late teens in 1838. The first line of the poem concerning him, "Je suis le malheureux, le suicide Eugène," is, by its beat and word choice, reminiscent of "El Desdichado," by Gérard de Nerval, who hanged himself in 1855. Other poems evoke Diane de Poitiers, la Reine Margot, François I, and Abd-el-Kader, whose struggle against the French in Algeria may have appealed to Thierry as a parallel to the desire of his caste for full recognition. Elsewhere one encounters a Spanish woman, formerly a great beauty, who went mad; a French actress who died in New Orleans; and the poets Tullius Saint-Céran and Alexandre Latil, in the poem "Remercîment," dedicated to Charles Testut.[9]

A substantial body of protest poetry by Creoles of Color, unsuitable for open publication (given censorship), may have circulated in New Orleans before 1865. One poem, of uncertain date, on the final campaign of the War of 1812 was attributed to Hyppolyte Castra, about whom nothing is known. The piece reveals his bitterness regarding the scorn with which he and other black Creoles were treated after they had fought honorably for their nation. Another poet worth noting is Joseph Beaumont, who wrote a song on the notorious Toucoutou affair. It centered on Anastasie de Sarzant, known as Toucoutou, who in 1858 sued a neighbor for slander for stating she was a person of color. The trial revolved around her parentage; she lost her suit, since black ancestry was proven.[10]

Poems from the 1860s by black Creole authors (and a few sympathizers) that originally appeared in *L'Union* and *La Tribune de la Nouvelle-Orléans* were collected in 2001 in *La Marseillaise noire*. The title comes from a poem by Camille Naudin (perhaps a pseudonym), who may have borrowed the phrase from Lamartine's drama *Toussaint-Louverture*. Among the authors (arranged roughly alphabetically) are Armand Lanusse and Questy, called simply "Joanni" (but appearing as Q.). Several poems are anonymous; others appear under half-names or pseudonyms—"Antony," "Berthe D . . . t," "Lélia D.," the pseudonym of Adolphe Duhart, "Yacoub" (J. Mansion). Despite the signature "Berthe D . . . t," it is unlikely that a woman was the author of "L'Amour"; that poem also was probably composed by Duhart.[11] Most of the verse is in traditional forms; there is also freer verse. Lines by one poet sometimes answer another's. The clichés of French Romanticism and older literary tropes are found throughout, and local color is exploited. A poem by Duhart, "La Fleur blessée," embroiders on the Renaissance cliché by which a young girl's life (probably in reference to his deceased daughter) is compared to that of a flower.[12]

Several selections concern poetry itself. "La Poésie," by "Yacoub," begins thus:

> La poésie, ami, c'est le reflet de l'âme,
> Le sublime miroir de la Divinité,
> C'est le baiser brûlant que dépose une femme
> Sur le front d'un époux quelquefois attristé.
>
> Aux pieds de l'Eternel, c'est le rêve de l'ange,
> Le murmure du vent dans nos sombres forêts,
> Les doux propos d'amour que parfois on échange
> Avec les sylphes égarés. (83)
>
> [Poetry, friend, is the reflection of the soul,
> The sublime mirror of Divinity.
> It is the burning kiss that a woman places
> On the forehead of a husband sometimes saddened.
>
> At the feet of the Eternal, it is the dream of the angel,
> The murmur of the wind in our dark forests,
> The sweet words of love that one sometimes exchanges
> With sylphs who have gone astray.]

The raison d'être of the anthology is, however, political and social. As James L. Cowan asserted: "If literature is always the reflection of a collective identity in relation to the historical and social situation, that definition applies particularly well to the poetry by Gens de couleur libres of New Orleans" (10). The publishers call the selections "de brûlants appels à la liberté, à l'égalité, à l'émancipation des Noirs, aux droits civiques, un émouvant hommage à la France de la Révolution et du Romantisme" [burning appeals to liberty, equality, the freeing of the blacks, civil rights, a moving homage to the France of the Revolution and Romanticism]. Thanks to the changes in law brought by the Civil War, the racial disadvantage under which the poets had lived and continued to live even then could be addressed freely, even as they acknowledged how conditions had changed; these themes mark the anthology much more than *Les Cenelles*.

The title poem, crafted to be sung to the standard "Marseillaise" tune, recalls the diction of Rouget de Lisle: "sillons" (furrows), "sang" (blood,) "fers" (irons), "tristes victimes" (unfortunate victims), "Liberté." Fraternity of black and white is upheld as the ideal. The Louisiana poem differs from the original in one important respect, however: Jesus and the Gospel are cited here (and elsewhere) as the models of human brotherhood, whereas French revolutionary rhetoric was anticlerical and posited only a civil religion, based on an abstract, rational deity. Another poem by Naudin, "Ode aux martyrs," compares the martyrdom of the Louisiana blacks and certain supporters of theirs to the Saint-Bartholomew massacre of Protestants in France under Charles IX (the resemblance is noted elsewhere also). In particular, the martyrs John Brown, a white northern dentist named Dostie, and a certain Victor Lacroix (on whose name Naudin plays) are mentioned, along with others killed in the bloody Mechanics' Institute uprising of July 1866.[13]

Titles such as "Votre temps est passé!" (addressed to the exploiters of the past), "Les Tyrans au tribunal de l'histoire," "Le Triomphe des opprimés," "Combat de l'aigle républicain et du copperhead" are transparent. The respective poems are all anonymous (as if reprisals might be feared). The deceased Abraham Lincoln, called a regenerator and martyr, is celebrated by "Lélia." "E. H." celebrates André Caillou, a hero of the Creoles of Color, and evokes "Liberty, our mother" and the Union. "Le Droit de suffrage des noirs" (1866), preceded by a quotation from Jean-Baptiste Rousseau (an eighteenth-century French poet), is called an "imitation in French of Burns's style." The poet expresses the hope that in time blacks will be granted the right to vote; the white man "lui-mêm' s'accuse / D'avoir été si sot que ça" [accuses himself / of having been so stupid as that] (58).

One of the most interesting selections in *La Marseillaise noire* is the 1867 Masonic poem "Le Triangle sacré," attributed to one Schneitz. Racial equality, fraternity, and the divine law of love are proclaimed in connection with the Masonic emblem by the "gardiens du lumineux symbole" [guardians of the shining symbol] (119). Readers will recall the quasi-Masonic veins in Testut's *Le Vieux Salomon* and other indications of the growing importance of Masonic orders for those with African blood. Another Masonic poem is "La Tolérance," by Charles Potvin (1867). According to the note accompanying its original publication, Potvin read the text at the inauguration of a lodge named "La Liberté," in Ghent, Belgium (105). Potvin was Belgian himself ("our free Belgium ... our little nation"), but the poem was published in Louisiana.

Under the signature "Henry," "L'Ignorance" appeared first in September 1862 in *L'Union*, then was revised and republished 28 May 1865 in *La Tribune*. It deserves extensive quotation for its political statements. M. Lynn Weiss believes that "Henry" may be Henry Train, a white attorney who clearly had ties to the Creoles of Color and was among the white journalists who contributed to the paper. (In addition, Train is represented by name in *La Marseillaise noire* by a short poem on Washington and Lincoln and a lovely pastoral meditation, "Résignation.") Noteworthy are mentions of the nineteenth-century idol of progress and belief in reason, of which ignorance is the enemy, as well as allusions to Socrates, Jesus Christ, Joan of Arc, Galileo (persecuted for his use of reason), and eighteenth- and nineteenth-century visionaries and socialists.[14]

L'Ignorance

C'est le mal de l'humanité,
C'est le ver rongeur qui l'épuise,
Ce qui de tout temps la maîtrise
Et muselle la Liberté.

C'est par ses lois que Galilée
En instruisant est accusé,
Que la science est ravalée
Et l'absurde divinisé.

C'est par arrêt de l'ignorance
Que Jésus, l'apôtre divin,
Subit une ignoble sentence
En voulant le progrès humain;

Que Paul, Jeanne, Socrate, et d'autres,
Colomb, Fourier et Swedenborg,
De la vérité les apôtres,
Sont ou raillés ou mis à mort.
....
Mais ce grand siècle de lumière,
A sa barre veut juger tout
Et notre raison libre et fière
Pénètre maintenant partout.

De ses assises solonnelles
Sort l'arrêt de la vérité;
Liberté, paix universelle,
Bonheur humain, fraternité! (123)

[It is the evil of humanity,
The gnawing worm which exhausts it,
It's what in all times masters it,
And muzzles freedom.

It is by its laws that Galileo
While teaching is accused,
That science is reduced
And absurdity made divine.

It is by the judgment of ignorance
That Jesus, the divine apostle,
Suffers an ignoble sentence
While desiring human progress;

That Paul, Joan, Socrates, and others,
Columbus, Fourier and Swedenborg,
Apostles of truth,
Are either mocked or put to death.

But this great century of light
At its bar wishes to judge everything
And our reason, free and proud,
Now penetrates everywhere.

From its solemn court hearings
Comes the judgment of truth;
Freedom, universal peace,
Human happiness, fraternity!]

Like the anthology as a whole, this poem declares universal values, in accordance with the doctrine of the Revolution of 1789 and its universalist aspirations. "Henry" published in *La Tribune* another poem of note, not collected here, "La Rébellion du sud en permanence." It concerns his "muse," who has been silent, since, as he explains, poetry is not permitted to curse, to execrate, not even the oppressors of his race. The poet proceeds to list the wrongs visited by the South on slaves and now freedmen. These wrongs include an attempt by white supremacists to circumvent the 1864 constitution, whose machinations led to the Mechanics' Institute massacre.[15]

CHAPTER EIGHT

Cable and Hearn

The appearance of George Washington Cable (1844–1925) on the literary scene in Louisiana signaled a new vigor in Anglophone literature. Whereas French had been the principal literary language in previous decades, it would be quickly displaced. Cable, the most eminent Louisiana author of the period, was born in New Orleans of northern Puritan stock on the maternal side and, on the paternal, slave-owning Virginia planters. He served in the Confederate cavalry (he was wounded twice). He considered himself a Creole. He wrote to the editor of the *Boston Literary World,* "I am a Creole myself, living in sight of the house where I was born." Some contemporaries and others have considered him an outsider, however, "not really from New Orleans"—that is, by his attitudes.[1]

He began working at age fourteen, after his father's death, becoming a clerk and bookkeeper and then a newspaper reporter. In 1869 he married Louise Bartlett, from Louisiana, by whom he had seven children. The Puritan stock may be responsible for his deep Christian convictions. After a lecture tour with Cable, Mark Twain wrote: "Cable's gifts of mind are greater and higher than I suspected. But— . . . You will never, never know . . . how loathsome a thing the Christian religion can be made until you come to know and study Cable daily and hourly." Cable viewed gambling, dancing, and theaters as sinful; he gave up his job on the *Picayune* rather than edit the theatrical column. He then returned to accounting.[2]

Invited nevertheless to continue contributing to the paper, he wrote sketches under the title of "Drop Shots," which he developed into short stories, some published in *Scribner's.* The first was "'Sieur George," 1873. In 1879 Scribner's brought out *Old Creole Days,* which in the 1927 edition (one of several) bore the subtitle *A Story of Creole Life.* Local speech is featured, perhaps excessively, and there are strong Gothic veins (the threatening, the mysterious, the improbable). Cable asserted later that he wrote his first stories out of indignation at the Code Noir; many pages are correspondingly serious. Subsequently, though, he was asked by a visiting Scribner's editor to write a novel based on the same "delightful and comic characters" of his sketches. This invitation led to *The Grandissimes* (1880). While depicting white Creole society, the Free People of Color, and the blacks with keen insight and apparent accuracy, even fondness—as an anthropologist might write about a curious community—he was passionately against slavery and opposed to the racial divisions and the injustice on which they were founded, and he criticized openly the Creole society that preserved them; he is thus viewed by many critics as objective. He did not, however, favor mixing the races; like numerous liberal contemporaries, he seemed personally opposed to racial intermarriage, while acknowledging that it might improve the black race, which was "inferior to the white."[3]

In his home city, his writings were not well received, generally, although Lafcadio Hearn wrote no fewer than five laudatory reviews of *The Grandissimes*. The reviewer in *L'Abeille* was affronted by *Old Creole Days*. When Cable published "The Freedman's Case in Equity" (1885) and *The Negro Question* (1890), he was widely attacked, notably in the *Times-Democrat*. He was challenged to duels, which he declined, and threatened with horse-whipping and tar-and-feathering. Charles Gayarré denounced him in a public speech. According to Donald Demarest, the Creoles seemed offended as much by his mockery of their customs, seen as "quaint," and his exposure of their overweening pride as by his implication of miscegenation (so called after an inflammatory pamphlet of 1864) in the best families and appeals for racial justice. That is not, however, the prevailing view. As one historian wrote, "White Creole anger at the victories of proponents of black citizenship and suffrage during Reconstruction turned to rage when . . . *The Grandissimes* appeared . . . In 1890 the rage at Cable turned to hysteria when the author hinted broadly in the *Encyclopedia Britannica* that white Creoles might be less than pure white . . ."[4]

In the North Cable's stories sold well—he was accused even of writing to gain popularity there—and his best work was later praised, by Edmund Wilson, for instance, in *Patriotic Gore*. In 1884 Cable left Louisiana and the following year settled in New England, where he composed romantic fictions about Confederate soldiers and their chaste women. They include *The Cavalier* (1901), *Dr. Sevier* (1902), set in New Orleans before the Civil War, *Gideon's Band* (1914), which has a mixed-blood heroine, and *Lovers of Louisiana* (1918). Far less admired today than earlier writings, they were later called by one commentator "stilted romantic novels that might have been by another person." Another critic spoke of their "banality." Wilson considered that by the 1890s Cable was finished as an artist. Age may have been partly responsible for this decline, but it is due more, doubtless, to lessening conflict and ambivalence about his home city. His two-part study on Creole dances and slave songs, including the bamboula, and his *Strange True Stories of Louisiana* (1888) are noteworthy additions to his Louisiana writing.[5]

Cable's short fiction serves as an introduction to views on caste and race set out at length in his fictional masterpiece, especially concerning laws and customs regulating the Free People of Color. Until William Faulkner appeared, it was Cable, among white writers, who dealt best, and most dramatically, with the subject of miscegenation. Like two sides of a diptych, "'Tite Poulette" (1874) and the novella *Madame Delphine* (1881) both portray a quadroon mother and her daughter, alike caught in the trap, or "méchanique" of the law that forbade whites to marry anyone with black ancestry. The stories are reminiscent of the true case of Toucoutou. Both stories evoke, though in less detail than Sidonie de la Houssaye's works, the world of the quadroon balls in the 1820s. In "'Tite Poulette," the quadroon, known as Madame John (connected to "Madame John's Legacy," a house in New Orleans), has reared a white girl as her own—that is, as colored—after the girl's Spanish parents died of fever. The young woman loves and is loved by a Dutchman but will not break the law to marry him, though Madame John asserts that "the law is unjust." (The man's letter to his mother does acknowledge his "horror of mixed blood"—a revealing admission—but insists that the young woman's "blemish" is "hidden.") The couple's happiness is secured by the mother's revelation (at great emotional cost) that the girl is not her own, and that both parents were white. Readers may interpret the denouement as a risky but effective social lie; there is no verification. If that was the author's intention, he let a falsehood stand in his fictional world in order to make the point that light-skinned Creoles could, if they were willing to dissemble, "pass" and join white society. Cable himself called her *white* elsewhere, however.[6]

In *Madame Delphine*, the devoted quadroon mother similarly makes sacrifices for her daughter; in this case, she swears (again, a painful act) that her light-skinned daughter is really white and produces a portrait of her supposed white mother, whereas in fact, as Cable reveals, the girl is an octoroon. This plot conforms to what Grace King saw: "The great ambition of the unmarried quadroon mothers was to have their children pass for whites, and so gain access to the privileged class. To reach this end, there was nothing they would not attempt, no sacrifice they would not make." To Cable, the law is unjust, and perjury is warranted; all of society is responsible for the injustice of racial laws, and thus blame for concealing racial origins is general. The same thesis of collective responsibility is illustrated in "The 'Haunted House' in Royal Street" (1887). The latter story demonstrates that Cable was as concerned about black slaves as about Free People of Color; he relates with convincing indignation the story of vicious treatment of slaves by Madame Lalaurie as well as an unfortunate episode involving students of mixed race under Reconstruction, at the time of the White League (1874).[7]

The Grandissimes: A Story of Creole Life, published in 1880, frequently reprinted, depicts New Orleans in 1803–1804, just before and after the signing of the Louisiana Purchase agreement, when the Creoles—fearing for their land grants from France and Spain, their appointments, the slave trade, and their culture and language—are either incredulous (not believing that Louisiana will really be sold) or ready to revolt against the Americans, "a nation of parvenus," "the most clap-trap government in the universe." "If incredulity is dead, Non-participation reigns in its stead, and Discontent is prime minister!" The work is thus a historical novel and partakes of that genre's appeal. Without being solely responsible for creating the literary stereotype of the (white) Creole, the novel contributed greatly to that image, which now can be analyzed in terms of "The Other"—similar to other white Americans but exotic (Catholic and "Latin") and vaguely suspect, as well as threatening to the other castes. To whites elsewhere, this cultural strangeness was not so obvious as that of the black characters, always different and, in Louisiana writing, appearing particularly alien. The novel includes many short passages in French, black Creole patois (spoken also by some whites), a crude black English, and, unfortunately, a crude English (that of white French speakers), spelled somewhat phonetically. Certain local whites were incensed at having such speech attributed to their ancestors, though the use of black patois by whites at the time the novel is set was prompted by necessity, and the Creoles in general did not know English at the time either.[8]

Cable is interested, obviously, in showing the mores and attitudes of that period but also in holding up a mirror to his own time, since he believed that Creole attitudes had not changed, essentially, although he does write of the "sweetened" character of later generations. What newly arrived Governor Claiborne says about the Creoles' attitude toward the American government in 1804 was pertinent also during the postbellum regime: "All sympathy with it, all advocacy of its principles [is] odious—disreputable—infamous." The novel was "as plain a protest against the times in which it was written as against the earlier times in which its scenes were set." Whether Cable expected to change attitudes by conflating the two periods is doubtful, however.[9]

Cable uses various devices and plots and deals with all classes: Creoles, of course, of 1803–1804 and earlier (including settlers, cassette girls, correction girls, and a few Huguenots); white Americans; mulattoes; and "the quadroon caste"—"the shame of two races"—and Quadroon Balls. There are also blacks, sometimes servants to the quadroons; Indians; and those of mixed white and Indian blood. The outsider Joseph Frowenfeld, recently arrived in the city (and who barely survives the yellow fever that kills his family), acts as an observer. His perspective (like Cable's somewhat) is that of the foreigner and, inevitably, a judge. His request for explanations leads to analepses and other introduction of information, needed by the northern audience to which the novel must have been partly directed. Voodoo and hoodoo (folk magic, overlapping and often confused with the religious beliefs of voodoo) are featured prominently (certain whites fear hoodoo as much as blacks do); African dances and chants ("hideous discords," "wildest contortions") are evoked; the political corruption (of Americans) is underlined. The issues of mixed blood and racial injustice are treated in the plot of the two Honoré Grandissimes—the white son of Numa Grandissime and his half-brother of the same name, a Free Man of Color, whom caste separates, officially. In fact, the white Honoré, living up to the true sense of his name, violates custom by taking his half-brother as a business partner.

Cable was not indifferent to the charm of Creole society—the Creoles' joie de vivre, their fidelity to France, their good manners and skill at masking straitened circumstances, their impracticality, "all-or-nothing" attitude, and curious superstitions. He was, however, probably anti-Catholic—a reflection of his Protestant roots. In a scene with a Huguenot, a Catholic official pleads in favor of religious hypocrisy (one need not, really, believe; one simply goes through the motions); Cable could not have countenanced that principle. He was also, probably, anti-French; the authorial voice speaks of the pleasure of Anglicizing a French name. Use of French patois by the Creole white characters and their inferior English work against them (or in the hostile novelist's favor); they appear ignorant, as well as indolent. Cable may have intended this feature as instructive, leading his local readers to judge the white Creoles harshly. He was singularly unsuccessful. In connection with a family duel, he also denounces the code of honor. The story of Aurore Nancanou similarly illustrates how deplorable dueling is. She lost her husband and her fortune when he and Agricola Fusilier quarreled over a gambling debt; her pride prevented her from accepting the property back in restoration. It is later returned by Honoré, to whom it had fallen.

More importantly, Cable lays bare the graver flaws in Creole society, its "amiable, old-fashioned philosophy of conservatism" and its social code, notably the Creoles' pride, which, as Aurore's story shows, is destructive, even suicidal. This pride includes the conviction of racial superiority. "When we say 'we people,' we always mean . . . white people. The non-mention of color always implies pure white . . .." This is the evidence as well as the foundation of racial injustice—out of date in European intellectual circles, in view of new human rights principles of the Enlightenment and 1789 Revolution, but still entrenched in America. Speaking through Frowenfeld, Cable castigates, in the name of "one flesh" of which all are made, Creole racial attitudes and the violence to which they lead. Whereas "in a vague hope of preserving the old condition of things," they struggle against the historical fate that has made them Americans, their story points to the illegitimacy of their social order—not just racial inequality but caste divisions—and its inevitable failure. The quadroon caste is portrayed as especially vulnerable, illustrated by Honoré, the Free Man of Color—his misery and, ultimately, his drowned body.[10]

The intercalated story of Bras-Coupé, the African chieftain slave who, through a misunderstanding, when drunk, strikes his master and takes to the swamps, brings out dramatically the criminal nature of racial oppression and the social disorder it signifies. "All slavery is maiming." The story contains powerful evocations of the swamps and features a hurricane—its natural disorder accompanying, perhaps representing civil disorder. Bras-Coupé is subsequently recaptured and tortured; his death is a horrible waste of a strong, naturally superior man. The moral failure of racial policy is also a practical failure, since the ostracizing of blacks and others creates dissension, detracts from the economy, and will lead to disasters later in the century. However well-meant, Christian efforts to make their "poor brethren" content with their lot are "criminal benevolence." The view of Agricola—who, although he has some Tchoupitoulas Indian ancestry, is a member of the "Brahmin Mandarin Fusilier de Grandissime clan"—is not the author's: "If the different grades of race and society did not have corresponding moral and civil liberties . . . *this* community, at least, would go to pieces."[11]

King, who, like Cable, was of Protestant stock, was a supporter of the late nineteenth-century white Creoles and attacked the book. She later admitted that he did not deserve the treatment he received from his fellow citizens. She had wanted nothing to do with him, but when he returned to New Orleans as a visitor, he was invited to speak at a Historical Club meeting she attended and was well received. She wrote: "I am glad that at last he got that compliment from New Orleans. He deserved it, not only as a tribute to his genius. But as compensation for the way we had treated him. He is an old man, very picturesque, very sad, with beautiful manners."[12]

Another detractor was Adrien Rouquette in his pamphlet *Critical Dialogue Between Aboo and Caboo on a New Book* . . . The work is replete with hyperbole and fictions. The satire is blunt and direct, but it corresponds to the general principles of the genre, which "seeks to persuade an audience that something or someone is reprehensible or ridiculous . . . [and] engages in exaggeration and some sort of fiction."[13]

The title page specifies that it was edited by "E. Junius." This is a fiction to allow for the "Preface of the Editor," in which Junius pretends to have come by the anonymous manuscript after an unnamed person discovered it wrapped in a blue handkerchief at the foot of a willow tree at West-End. The status of such an element, called *paratextual*, is, like the outer level of a frame narrative, neither that of what it introduces nor of authorial statement outside the book; it may or may not correspond to facts but in either case has its own level of fictional validity, or diegesis (time-space continuum), and is intended to shed independent light on what follows. Tempted at first to destroy the manuscript, the discoverer decides otherwise, since the author must be "a representative Creole, a Franco-American, a vigorous offspring of the Latin race" (3). The editor, wandering in the same locale, learns of the manuscript and proposes to publish it, to appeal to "intelligent, candid and unbiased Readers, who are more fond of simple truth than of complicated and tortuous errors . . . more or less dramatized to impressionate literary coxcombs and blue-stockings." The "editor" goes on to say that the subject of the "critical dialogue" is George William Cable (rather than *Washington*), whose works have been taken as history. "The most historical and honorable creole families are therein pasquinaded." Asserting that those publications, like Molière's *Les Précieuses ridicules*, display a spiteful mood and pedantic phraseology, the "editor" observes that such ridicule can be corrected only by further ridicule. (Hence the "manuscript" is justified.) He compares Cable to the mendacious Choctaw Mingolabee, "Chef-Menteur," the "Great-Liar," who was banished by his fellow Sachems.[14]

The dialogue is introduced by still another paratextual element, an untitled note telling how Agricola Fusilier (the fictional character), or "Aboo," allowed to return to earth, discovers his "dear Louisiana" in ruins and desolation. Weeping, he is approached by "Caboo," a living descendant who recognizes "Aboo" by *la voix du sang*. The two then unburden themselves in conversation, which, recorded by a reporter, is the substance of the dialogue. While these devices—editor, found manuscript, returning ghost, recorded conversation—traditionally serve to suggest authenticity and distance the author from his text—perhaps conceal his identity—it was well known that Rouquette was the author.

The dialogue proper accuses the author of *The Grandissimes* of having written "for the prejudiced and inimical North, against the olden customs, habits, manners and idiosyncrasies of the Southern Creole population in Louisiana, thereby so slanderously misrepresented" (9). "It is the finical refinement of disguised puritanism, assuming the fanatical mission of radical reform..." The text contains such allusions as "despi-*cable*" (italics in the text) and "Grandissime, Mandarin ... Charlemagne Scribner." Cable is accused of being a High Priest of "Negro-Voudouism" (20), of betraying Louisiana, "so wildly beautiful and so beautifully wild," as portrayed by François-René de Chateaubriand and Henry Wadsworth Longfellow (11,16). Even Cable's prose is attacked as a "savage discord of sounds" (12). (Given the amount of patois and bad English conversation in *The Grandissimes*, this charge is not entirely groundless.) Cable is called "a venom-swollen, dust-covered insect," and his novel "an unnatural, Southern growth, a bastard sprout, *un digne pendant* [a worthy counterpart] of *Uncle Tom's Cabin*" (14, 18). Blacks are demeaned by allusions to Bras-Coupé: "What would you feel, what would you say, were you to see a buzzard, glutted with carrion, lighting heavily upon a consecrated shrine?" (15) The tract ends with two "choruses" of bullfrogs and "Weird Song by a Zombi-Frog." The latter, in black patois, intimates that Cable had sexual relations with "bel négrèsse" [*sic*] or Marie Laveau. Although the pamphlet is directed principally at Cable, mention of Marie Laveau and other details convey without doubt considerable hostility on Rouquette's part toward blacks, even though he had preached earlier against slavery.[15]

Newton Arvin, in his introduction to a 1957 edition of *The Grandissimes*, argued for the importance of Cable for Southern literature in general:

> In a quiet way the novel made a sharp break with the central tradition of Southern fiction, as it was then and was long to be; it pointed forward to the kind of thing that was to assert itself only after several decades. This is what led Hamilton Basso to say ... that Cable was the first writer to question the validity of the aristocratic tradition in Southern fiction—the "spiritual grandfather" ... of more recent writers such as Ellen Glasgow, Thomas Wolfe, and William Faulkner.

Similarly, Shirley Ann Grau considered him "the first writer of the modern South" and his work the best picture of New Orleans that has ever been done and "the first indication of the great southern literary renaissance."[16]

Cable's sometime friend and rival Lafcadio Hearn (1850–1904) was born on Santa Maura, an Ionian island, of Anglo-Irish and Greek parentage. He was sent back to Dublin at age two. Though not an orphan strictly, he was separated thenceforth from his parents and depended upon a stern great-aunt and others, among them her manipulative friend. After erratic schooling in France and England, in the course of which he was blinded in one eye during outdoor games, he was sent to New York, where he survived with difficulty. From there he went to Cincinnati. He worked as a reporter and contracted a pseudomarriage (real union was illegal because of Ohio miscegenation laws) with Althea Foley, a former slave, from whom he later separated. He arrived in New Orleans in 1877 and remained in the Crescent City for a decade. It was exotic enough to fascinate him, and he wrote to a friend that he loved it. In 1887 he left for New York; later he visited the West Indies and lived for a while in Martinique. Ultimately he traveled to Japan, where he taught English, married, wrote, and died.[17]

In New Orleans he worked as a journalist first for the *Daily City Item*, a reform paper, writing anonymous editorials, poems, vignettes, stories, translations, for some of which he furnished woodblock prints (some 175 in two years). In 1880 he moved to the *Democrat,* then the newly consolidated *Times-Democrat* (in 1881). His chief personal and journalistic interests were New Orleans and Creole culture in general. He also published in the *Cincinnati Commercial*; it printed his sketch "New Orleans in Wet Weather," which conveys brilliantly the very feel of dampness and describes the lovely ironwork fences of the city, including the famous cornstalk fences. In addition, he wrote for *Harper's Weekly,* which published his essay on Saint-Malo, a Malay fishing village on a Lake Borgne island. Another magazine brought out his fine essay on dueling and a Spanish fencing master in New Orleans. Some pieces were collected posthumously as *Creole Sketches.* These include journalistic sketches of street scenes and characters, quoted songs and conversations in French and black Creole or Gombo, numerous street cries (in French or black Creole), and illustrated remarks on architecture. (His acquaintance with Gombo French helped prepare him for his visits to the Caribbean.) His writing displays no single theme but has unity as a reflection of the times; some pieces are almost short stories.[18]

Hearn also was interested in local literature (he considered Gayarré, Alfred Mercier, and Cable as strong novelists), plus the Irish and American communities on the other side of Canal Street, as well as dress and food; he published a cookery book. Working sometimes with Cable, he collected black Creole songs, and also proverbs, which he published in *Ghombo Zhèbes*. He was indefatigable as a promoter of continental literature, especially major

French figures: Théophile Gautier, Gustave Flaubert, Anatole France, Emile Zola ("one of the greatest novelists who ever lived"), Guy de Maupassant, and the exotic writer Pierre Loti, whose prose he admired. He published translations from their works in New Orleans papers and ultimately a volume in New York and another in Boston. He also translated sections from foreign newspapers. He was a liberal but not an agitator, and, like Cable, criticized (sometimes obliquely, sometimes directly) the two-race, three-caste system.[19]

Hearn's main work connected to Louisiana is *Chita: A Memory of Last Island*, first published in *Harper's New Monthly Magazine*, concerning the hurricane of August 1856, which destroyed l'Ile dernière. At a dinner in 1883 Cable recounted the event to him; but Hearn also got information from others and help with the Spanish-language passages and descriptions of yellow fever from the prominent physician Dr. Rodolpho Matas. Hearn's interest in the scientific thought of Herbert Spencer is reflected in the theme of heredity. A Boston reviewer compared the work favorably to novels by Victor Hugo (from whom there is an epigraph); comparisons with Loti are more apt. There are Spanish-language passages and bits of black Creole patois.[20]

Hearn was a master colorist in prose. The first part of *Chita*, "The Legend of L'Ile Dernière," is beautifully written, with lush descriptions and rich diction. The Gulf waters are nearly personified, in pantheistic evocations that refer to Πνεύμα, or spirit ("eternally mystical and divine—eternally weird"). Hearn's pages are also a model of close observation, furnishing information on the setting, the storm, and the devastation. The account foreshadows and complements similar evocations of the Gulf by Kate Chopin and Adolphe du Quesnay in the following decade. Of swimming far out, Hearn writes: "As the water deepens beneath you, and you feel those ascending wave-currents of coldness arising which bespeak profundity, you will also begin to feel innumerable touches . . . The gulls fly lower about you, circling with sinister squeaking cries . . . Then the fear of the Abyss, the vast and voiceless Nightmare of the sea, will come upon you . . ." The storm begins with a tsunami-like windless heaving of the water; then come waves of enormous height. Meanwhile, and despite the warnings of nature, those vacationing on the island—nearly four hundred, mostly from New Orleans—are dancing in the hotel, its windows ablaze with light. Particularly dramatic are the passages in which a boat manages to come through the storm from St. Mary's Parish; the captain rescues from the sea two score of the nearly drowned. All others perish, and every building is destroyed. The only life remaining is that of scavengers—birds, Sicilians, Corsicans, and other plunderers.[21]

Part two, "Out of the Sea's Strength," recounts how a Catalan fisherman and his wife on a nearby island find a child, nearly dead, apparently without parents, who speaks only Creole patois (learned from servants). The couple, calling her Conchita or Chita, rears her as their own, in near-isolation—another Romantic foundling, a child of nature, a true creature of the island. In part three, "The Shadow of the Tide," set during the yellow fever epidemic of 1867, chance brings to the lonely spot a New Orleans doctor who is, in fact, her father; he had not drowned (though he had seen his own epitaph on a headstone) but did not know his daughter had been found. When he sees her, he is struck by her resemblance to his lost wife, yet cannot quite believe it might be his daughter. Ironically, he dies of the fever he has, unwittingly, contracted, before he can inquire and reveal himself as her father—a variation on the Romantic trope of recognition too late.

CHAPTER NINE

Late Francophone Figures: de la Houssaye, du Quesnay, Dessommes

Although Sidonie de la Houssaye (1820–94) belongs by birth date to an earlier period, she came late to publication and thus is treated here. Née Hélène Perret, sometimes called Louise, self-styled Sidonie, she wrote under her married name and also the names Louis and Louise Raymond. She is sometimes called "acadienne," but most of her ancestors were from the French colonial class. She was devoted to her French heritage and the language. One finds in her writings traces of sympathy for quadroons, caught between two other castes, and for slaves, "les pauvres noirs," treated like cattle to be sold; she acknowledged that many masters beat their bondsmen. In a letter, she accused her compatriots of being avaricious and racist. She wrote also, however (showing paternalism), of good owners who treated their slaves "as if they had been their children," and her writings do not call for radical social change. While one commentator calls her "anti-racist" and "proto-feminist," this is probably hyperbole, at least if the terms are taken in their twenty-first-century meaning. She does not need, however, the sort of rehabilitation that Clyde Wilson calls "presentistic redemption."[1]

She was born on her father's sugarcane plantation, in St. John the Baptist Parish. The family founder, Jean-Baptiste Perret, had come to New Orleans in 1723 from Grenoble. One great-grandfather, from St. James Parish, was named Bossié (now spelled Bossier—an important Louisiana name). After short periods in New Orleans and elsewhere, Sidonie's family settled in Franklin (St. Mary Parish), in 1828. She was probably not taught by a French governess, as she claimed, but studied briefly (perhaps only for religious training) at a convent.[2]

In 1833, at the age of thirteen, Sidonie married riverboat captain Louis Alexandre Le Pelletier de la Houssaye in St. Martinville, founded by aristocratic refugees from the French Revolution. She had six children, of whom three survived past childhood. In 1847 she sued her husband, who, in violation of Louisiana code, had sold some of her property (four slaves). She thereby regained her independence, but her circumstances were straitened. For a livelihood, she opened a French-language school (1849), which endured until the Civil War. Disputes with creditors continued in court, and some of her husband's properties were sold to pay his debts.

Widowed in 1863, she reopened the school in 1867, and ran it until 1875 or so. She also reared her daughter's children after the mother's death; she did not want their Anglophone father to have them. Her literary interests date from her youth, as early writings attest (Vidrine, 14). Although in the convent she would not have encountered the masterpieces of French Romantic fiction, since all novels were viewed as wicked, later she must have become familiar with the writings of Alexandre Dumas père, which her own resemble; she might have been interested in him especially because he was an Antillean Creole and a quadroon. She was acquainted with works by George Sand, another grandmother-author; she may have known her *Contes d'une grand-mère*. She also read Sir Walter Scott. De la Houssaye received a short letter of encouragement from Emile Zola in 1892; though she spoke of his "indécences," her characters, like his, are emphatically creatures of their heredity and milieu, bearing out Hippolyte Taine's thesis.[3]

Stricken repeatedly by misfortune, she endured, with her mother's assistance, and at age sixty-three published serially her first work, *Le Mari de Marguerite*, a free translation of a Canadian novel, in *L'Abeille*. The same year she published, in the same paper, *Chattanooga*. She also wrote for *Le Meschacébé*, *Le Franco-Louisianais*, and other periodicals, and pages of hers appeared in Paris. Additional publications include *Charles et Ella* (1892) and *Amis et fortune* (1893), both serialized prior to book publication, both set in the Bayou Tèche country of Iberia Parish. She sold her first story, "Voyage de ma grand-mère," in 1883 to James Birney Guthrie, without knowing he was George Washington Cable's literary agent. Cable purchased "Lettre de ma tante" (translated as "The Young Aunt with the White Hair") and "Alix de Morainville," and included all three stories in his *Strange True Stories of Louisiana* (1880). J. John Perret has demonstrated that, far from being true, these tales were invented, marked by errors of fact and additional misstatements.[4]

De la Houssaye attempted in vain to sell more stories to Cable, and Scribner turned down another piece, "Claire," dealing with adultery. But she published at least 116 short stories and six novels, some posthumously. She thus belongs in the company of other Francophone women writers of the nineteenth century—Germaine de Staël, Marceline Desbordes-Valmore, George Sand, and Rachilde—who made literary careers for themselves. In 1890 L'Athénée Louisianais awarded her a gold medal, and writings by her appeared in the *Comptes Rendus*; Perret concluded, however, that the prize-winning stories were by another hand.[5]

De la Houssaye's case illustrates the connections between the Cajun and Creole worlds, since her historical novel *Pouponne et Balthazar* (1888), which includes Acadian French, concerns the *grand dérangement* (the exile of the Acadians from Canada and the resettlement of many in Louisiana). The sources are said to be Acadian oral tradition from her grandmother and great-grandmother. It concerns two Acadian lovers, separated by the exile. They are not reunited until after six years have passed. The Cajuns are seen through the eyes of two Creole characters, based on the author's ancestors, the wealthy planter M. Bossier and his wife, who befriends the heroine, Pouponne, teaching her reading, embroidery, and social refinement. The episode where Balthazar's old Acadian father dies displays considerable sympathy toward the displaced French Canadians, but, as May Waggoner points out, the author clearly feels superior and deals rather condescendingly toward them. The account of the couple's Rabelaisian wedding feast shows the Acadians' vulgarity; Pouponne, who has grown accustomed to better manners, is shocked.[6]

It was as teaching materials that de la Houssaye published the stories (including the three questionable ones) collected as *Contes d'une grand-mère louisianaise*. The manuscripts reveal that some date from the 1850s. They include edifying sketches and tales intended to teach behavior. Plots depend considerably on coincidence, and sentimentality dominates, but one can admire their narrative skill and considerable charm. In "Les Petits Soldats" the young white boy playing at soldier learns that he must obey and treat slaves decently (but slavery is not pronounced unjust). In contrast, in "Une Poupée d'autrefois" [A Doll of Yesteryear] the young heroine is not punished for disobeying by climbing into the attic. Her fear of Indians, inspired by a book showing their savage violence (another indication of the author's conventional views), is only partly countered. In "Le Bonhomme Pistache" [Old Man Pistachio], the basic honesty of two street children contributes to a happy denouement by which one finds his grandfather and both find homes.

"La Fauvette et le poète" [The warbler and the poet], is a fable, or, as de la Houssaye wrote, an allegory, inspired by a real marriage. It honors poetry, to which the bird's song is allied. "L'Amour qui renferme en lui seul tous les amours" [The love that includes in itself all other loves], an "idyll," celebrates love (by implication, erotic) between a young man and a girl, an orphan—a love depicted as superseding paternal and fraternal love. While its diction and imagery are acceptable for children, the suggestion that love between man and woman replaces family love strikes one as a simplification. Here and elsewhere there is a strong bias in favor of blond hair, blue eyes, and fair skin, even among whites—a prima facie argument that de la Houssaye privileged the "white."

In the short novella "Les Petits Vagabonds," purportedly based on truth (perhaps a counter to readers' skepticism, or reassurance for children), misbehavior is, again, not clearly punished—although an orderly child, hearing the story, would be convinced that running away from home is wrong as well as frightening. The boldness of the elder "little vagabond," Henri—who fears no one and faces down adults with his lies—serves him well for three years, as he and his brother, having left home, perform in a traveling circus. Henri is finally captured and sent to an orphanage by his father, but he later becomes a lieutenant in the navy—perhaps an object lesson in rehabilitation of the young; the younger boy, teased as a circus brat, is so unhappy later that the family must move to Australia.

De la Houssaye's quadroon novels, or, more properly novellas, appear to be the last fiction in French serialized in Louisiana. Published under the name Louise Raymond, they were written to make money. The series was called by Auguste Viatte one of the three best works of fiction in Louisiana (with Alfred Mercier's *L'Habitation Saint-Ybars* and Charles Testut's *Le Vieux Salomon*). Perret notes that the author's use of family genealogy was viewed as scandalous. According to her introduction (really a preface, not to be confused with the lengthy introduction by the reprint editor), "Octavia la Quarteronne," first published in *Le Meschacébé* (1894), edited by Charles Lasseigne in Bonnet Carré, is the development of a narrative found in 1878 in her grandmother's trunk, "Les Quarteronnes de la Nouvelle-Orléans, de 1800 à 1830." The author did research, she claimed, to fill in the outline. (This paratextual authorial note, which creates a first diegesis, does not appear, however, in the manuscript.)[7]

This old fictional device of the "found manuscript" is, like the "fireside tale" claim, made elsewhere, intended to lend authenticity to the action, which she herself could not plausibly have witnessed, given the dates indicated. She stated elsewhere that she had found notes in her grandmother's papers—to which she alludes occasionally—and also remembered oral accounts from her mother. Either or both statements might be true; probably neither is.

The literary strategy of the found or dictated manuscript can be mocked as antiquated, but in fact it has not disappeared; it is used in *The Autobiography of Miss Jane Pittman* by Ernest J. Gaines (1971). The device is called into question by the feminist critic Alice Parker. It strikes her as false, not in itself—it is well-known and might have some factual basis—but because it serves as a screen behind which the author could hide. (Pseudonyms can serve a similar purpose.) That is, de la Houssaye can pretend not to be responsible for what is, to Parker, the heavy eroticism, racism, and class prejudices of the tales. Parker supposes that the author's defensive strategy was unconscious.[8]

This presentist interpretation, which assumes absence of self-knowledge, allows critics to blame authors for being themselves and writing according to the customs, views, and measures of their time, and thus offers an instance of changed reader-reception. According to Hans Robert Jauss's "aesthetics of reception," the work always exists in a triangular relationship with the author (in the original context of production) and the reading public; as the public changes, the writing appears different. "The literary work contains an ever unfolding potentiality of meaning, which can be seen as actualized in reception at various historical moments." Parker approaches nineteenth-century writing through a screen of guilt theories—repression (Freudianism) and oppression (as enunciated by Frantz Fanon and other race and gender critics). The "meaning" of de la Houssaye's pages cannot, however, be the racism and classism Parker identifies, since they did not exist at the time in their current conceptualizations. Like her contemporaries, de la Houssaye used the term *race* without inquiring into the legitimacy of the distinction on social or anthropological grounds.[9]

Whatever truth the paratextual claim may have, the narrative *je* in what follows must be taken primarily as that of the pseudograndmother-recorder, who speaks of having been a neighbor to families featured in the stories. But the authorial voice—the author's persona—occasionally intervenes, joining the outer to the inner diegetic plane. While "Octavia la Quarteronne" was at the printer's, she encountered an old gentleman who had attended Octavia's elegant midnight suppers and described them to her; thus while the original story had no such description, she is able to add it to a later tale, drawing also, she says, on old newspaper accounts the gentleman shared with her. (That the accounts are inventions is immaterial.) Elsewhere, she writes herself into the text as "Hélène Perret," claims she saw one principal character, and imbeds accounts related to this woman, ostensibly, by acquaintances who knew the principals and witnessed events. One account is dated 1870, after the period in question but before de la Houssaye's work appeared. She also includes portions of a diary, purportedly verbatim. Such "outside" sources, quoted material, author's notes, and other markers such as real names, eschewed by purists but used by Stendhal and others, contribute, paradoxically, to the fictional illusion, as André Gide's *Les Faux-Monnayeurs* (1925) and certain later metafictions illustrate. De la Houssaye also uses the narrative present frequently, another technique for creating a sense of immediacy.

Except that such unions were not legal, de la Houssaye's novellas (like Anne Rice's *The Feast of All Saints*) illustrate black novelist Frances E. W. Harper's allusions, at the conclusion of *Minnie's Sacrifice* (1869), to "stories about white men marrying beautiful quadroon girls, who, in so doing were lost to us socially . . ." The tales are Romantic by tone and style, topic, characters, and exotic setting (earlier New Orleans and the actual and moral space of the French Quarter); but the stories also tend toward the naturalistic in Zola's vein, especially "Violetta la Quarteronne," which records the destruction of a respected businessman, a worthy husband and father, who is bewitched by the heroine. The novellas depict quadroon women conventionally: exotically beautiful and enticing, the bodies "fetishicized," in today's terminology. The author underlines the Spanish features and sometimes Spanish names of her characters (possibly an attempt to diminish French responsibility, or to emphasize their eroticism, but also showing how they took on *noms de guerre*, constituting denial of the self). She stresses simultaneously their pale skin. Selective breeding had indeed produced very fair types. One English traveler wrote that they were the most beautiful women he had ever seen, "resembling the higher order of women among the high caste Hindoos, lovely countenances, full dark liquid eyes, lips of coral, teeth of pearl, sylph-like figures, and such beautifully rounded limbs and exquisite gait and manners that they might furnish models for a Venus." Exploitation of lovers by the quadroons is stressed. "It's not the man we consider; it's his pocketbook" (128).[10]

"Octavia la Quarteronne" begins with a secondary story related to the rest by plot and themes—an unusual, if not unique, opening. It concerns a planter's son, devoted to his parents but inexperienced with women. In New Orleans to sell his father's harvest, he sees at the opera a stunning quadroon who calls herself Adoréah. He falls victim to her enticements and agrees to buy her an expensive necklace she covets, said to be that of Marie Antoinette. The profits from the crop sales not being sufficient, he counterfeits his father's signature on a check. Once the necklace is hers, the seductress sends him away. The authorial voice, while recognizing that Adoréah and her sister had earlier been robbed by their own mother of a gift from their white family, blames the quadroon in plain terms, calling her a "vile courtesan" (68). While not the first Louisiana writing to stress disorder and immorality, it was also far from the last; it has been remarked that the state name was almost synonymous with lax morals, graft, pleasure, and vice. The tale foreshadows the following stories, in which disorders, even horrible, premeditated crimes, follow upon such liaisons. Grace King had observed concerning quadroon mothers, "Assuming as a merit and distinction what is universally considered in the civilized world as a shame and disgrace by their sex, their training of their daughters had but one end in view. Unscrupulous and pitiless, by nature or circumstance . . . and secretly still claiming the racial license of Africa, they were, . . . the most insidious and the deadliest foes a community ever possessed."[11]

De la Houssaye does not analyze the historical background of the Quadroon Balls, the tolerance of interracial liaisons, *plaçage*, nor the underlying question of miscegenation; nor does she condemn the society that favors such practices. Her view is closer to the portrait sketched by William Faulkner's character Charles Bon in *Absalom, Absalom!* (1936). She does, however, lay blame on men who frequent the quadroons—they are both enablers and exploiters of the system—and one character expresses pity for the women, while despising them. Writing to Cable, the author spoke of the quadroons as having, "like leprosy, afflicted New Orleans for so many years by their crazy luxury and their licentious conduct" (27). Distinguished throughout by their three-quarters white blood, they are depicted, more or less accurately, as despising full-blooded blacks, whom they call "black as the ace of spades." "This word 'negress' is the greatest insult to a quadroon" (195).

Fear of mixed-race Creole women runs through white society—their sexual magnetism, venality, indifference to social judgments, even their practices of hoodoo; their patois suggests that their veneer of European education is thin. To see this portrait as springing from repressed desire on the author's part for her own sexual freedom, or to suppose that she desired quadroon men, is to swallow whole the myth of frustrated white eroticism. It is not unfair, however, to suppose that the social situation of respected white women, dramatized by Kate Chopin in the same decade, displeased her. The nearly invisible wife in "Violetta la Quarteronne" is so meek, from early training and from living in the shadow of her husband, a wealthy merchant, that she would not even ask him for a gift—an especially beautiful cashmere shawl from his store—nor would he offer it. The condition of proper women is thus depicted as a kind of bondage, akin to institutionalized slavery.

The main story of "Octavia la Quarteronne" is highly melodramatic, involving passion, wealth, the social and legal code, and vengeance wrought after the courtesan's lover, Alfred D., leaves her and marries. She resembles Stendhal's criminal heroines (de la Houssaye might have read his posthumous *Chroniques italiennes*, 1855). The author condemns both her and the general immorality (not just amorality) of quadroon society. Nineteenth-century types populate the scenes: an avaricious Jewish moneylender, a hot-blooded Cuban who becomes the quadroon's lover, a weak and indulgent grandfather, corrupt young white men, suborned servants, and criminal accomplices. The writing is lively, and the work has not aged entirely, though readers cannot be unaware that the social conditions depicted are completely out of date.

While Octavia is helped by chance—chiefly the fact that Alfred and his wife produce both a son and daughter—it is her own energy and inventiveness that enable her to exact an extraordinary vengeance. Nothing devised against the guilty in *Le Comte de Monte Cristo* by Alexandre Dumas père (whose works she must have known) surpasses her elaborate plan. With help, she kidnaps the baby daughter, renames her Mary and rears her in Cuba and Europe as her own, then brings her back to New Orleans, turns her into a child courtesan, utterly corrupted, and arranges for her to seduce her own brother. The attraction that the latter feels for the girl is doubtless partly *la voix du sang*—not as warning, however, but as the pull of similarity—but the attraction has also been cultivated cleverly by Octavia, with the unwitting Mary's cooperation. After Octavia arranges successfully for the brother and sister to commit incest, she sends a servant to Alfred, the father (the mother died of grief), with a letter revealing all and a chest containing the baby's clothing. He rushes to the house of assignation. Finding his two children in bed, he kills the girl and himself; the son is struck witless by the discovery and must be confined in a lunatic asylum. Octavia is already on shipboard, with a new lover, en route to a foreign port.[12]

De la Houssaye offers no excuse for Octavia, who, according to custom, should have expected her lover to leave eventually; he is not blamed. But no punishment is meted out to the courtesan, whereas in countless French Romantic novels the wicked meet a bad end. Despite the extravagance of the society depicted and the expansive style, the author is thus closer in her judgment to the French realists. That is, the disturbed moral order is not restored. She does not argue, however, as some would, that moral order is fundamentally lacking in any society where rights are not shared by all.[13]

"Violetta la Quarteronne" appeared serially in 1894. The action, which takes place prior to that of "Octavia," features recurring characters and familiar plot elements. This Balzacian technique is justified by the subject matter, since quadroon society was a small one. Violetta, who is blonde, is another abusive courtesan; the authorial voice shows no sympathy for her. While she does not devise an elaborate scheme of revenge, her pettiness, venality, and vanity destroy several lives. Pierre Saulvé, her lover, is vulgar, foolish, cruel to his wife and children—a source of social disorder, as the authorial language indicates. Before he repents, he loses much of his fortune, and his wife and elder children suffer from his liaison. Even when he leaves Violetta, he remains violently jealous. A young man, fascinated by her, subsequently leaps to his death from her balcony. Another, who works in Pierre's business and is engaged to his elder daughter, is destroyed. The tale includes a description of the bamboula.

The posthumous *Gina* and *Dahlia*, written before the other tales and published serially in 1897 and 1898, have inordinately complicated plots. The former (which involves the character Adoréah) is noteworthy for its parallel and connected family lineages, one white, the other of mixed race, contrasted to each other, as in Cable's *The Grandissimes*. Readers of Faulkner's *Absalom, Absalom!* and Shirley Ann Grau's *The Keepers of the House* recognize the compositional advantages of this opposition and its potential for social commentary. The following statement from a quadroon about white responsibility is noteworthy:

> You reproach me for my conduct.... You white grandes dames, you get married; you can choose a husband among your equals; we 'place' ourselves in order to enjoy life. If there is a difference between us, it escapes me. But you, who accuse me, aren't you in part the cause of the crime I committed in picking myself a rich lover? Scarcely were we born, my sister and I, when you brought us into your bedroom. You raised us as your children; you had us given an education.... You instilled in us a taste for luxury....[14]

The tales emphasize what many Creoles of color believed: that they belonged in Europe, not Louisiana; in *Dahlia*, numerous characters flee, some to return and find misery, others to remain. De la Houssaye concluded the last tale with an apostrophe to the reader expressing her sympathy for certain characters, despite her own censures: "When a voice is raised to condemn women like Octavia, Violetta, and Adoréah, be indulgent to those sweet creatures ... Gina and Dahlia, pushed by fate into the path of evil, and more worthy of pity than scorn." While one cannot think of Octavia and Violetta as "sweet"—the contrary evidence is too abundant—the authorial voice indicates that deep social disorder is partly to blame. Such sympathy can be compared to that expressed by the anonymous author of "Marie" (chapter

6 above), who castigates those who exploit young quadroons for mercenary reasons—the exploiters being not only white men but the girls' mothers.

Adolphe Lemercier du Quesnay (1839–1901), Romantic in his literary tastes, a traditionalist in his religious views and apparently in social outlook also, published in Paris *Essais littéraires et dramatiques* (1892), comprising "Le Mal d'Oreste, poème dramatique," "Sursum corda!, nouvelle" (first published in *L'Abeille*, 1891), "Chant d'Ipomoea, Légende créole," and "Un Eté à la Grand'Isle," a novella. The du Quesnay family had settled in New Orleans about 1869, coming from Jamaica, where Adolphe was born, and, before that, Saint Domingue and Paris. The family included musicians, men of letters, and men of the church. Adolphe was educated in Versailles and Paris.[15]

While the poem concerning Orestes and his murder of Aegisthus and Clytemnestra is unrelated to du Quesnay's Creole writing (except, perhaps, in its fatalism and themes of exile and wandering), it should be noted as a late nineteenth-century revival of a classical subject—anticipating the wave in the next century of ingenious French dramatic and fictional works on classical topics. A modern tone of disabused philosophy marks the poem, which includes long passages of dramatic dialogue but also narrative summaries. At its best, the style, by turns severe and lush, conveys the author's literary kinship to the great classical writers, especially Jean Racine, and to his fellow nineteenth-century authors.[16]

Du Quesnay's prose tales are somber, in contrast to the beauty of their setting: Martinique and Louisiana. In "Sursum corda!" a prosperous merchant's son is sent at age eleven from his home island to Paris for his education in a Catholic *collège*. There, like Robinson Crusoe in Saint-John Perse's *Eloges* (1911) and like the Rouquette brothers and du Quesnay, probably, he suffers from homesickness, keen enough to undermine his health: "The young wild boy withered quickly" (170). He then falls victim to the smallpox epidemic. As he dies, he gazes at an image of the Virgin, which is transformed into that of his mother; he himself is "already almost an angel" (173). In Martinique, his father is informed by telegram but keeps the news to himself; but the mother, without news, dies from anxiety and exhaustion. She perceives an angel holding her son, transfigured but recognizable. When the father dies in turn, he and they are reunited in a vast cloud of spirits rising before the Queen of Heaven. Following Christian logic and especially the vision of St. John the Divine, earthly suffering has been turned into happiness.

In "Chant d'Ipomoea," the waters of the Gulf and the Caribbean Sea are depicted as beautiful but fierce and destructive. The descriptions recall Victor Hugo's powerful evocations of the ocean. Du Quesnay acknowledges the destruction wrought by Europeans on foreign shores, but he does not condemn colonialism as such nor the plantation economy of Louisiana. The tale is simple. A young couple, radiant with happiness, leaves their sugar plantation and sets off by sea to visit an old relative in Mexico; a storm arises; and the boat is never seen again, except by sailors who claim to glimpse a ruin in the depths. Subsequently, the old Mexican, who has lost his fortune, often lingers on the shore, imagining the sea as an expression of divine power. His last moments bring a vision of light descending over the water and Christ calling him to follow. His body is found the next day by fishermen.

"Un Eté à la Grand'Isle" is set partly on that island, south of New Orleans—a spot that Lafcadio Hearn called "an old-fashioned, drowsy, free-and-easy Creole watering place"; the rest of the action takes place in the city. It has a well-handled frame structure. The tale displays, unfortunately, late-Romantic rhetoric and tone, unilateral understanding of psychology, and abundant moral conclusions. A major theme is devastation wrought by violent weather. The outer narrator, a Frenchman named Marcel, who has come to Louisiana, tells of meeting his friend Olivier, also from France, one winter evening the previous year in the French Quarter. Olivier is about to leave New Orleans forever. As inner narrator, he recounts to Marcel the tragic end to his stay; Marcel then relays it to a friend back in Paris, in the form of a letter, written from New Orleans. This information is furnished by a subtitle, "Lettre de Marcel B. . . à une connaissance, à Paris," which the publishers of the translated version omitted, unfortunately.[17]

The story, a tragic one, is told appropriately in five parts. Creole mores, weather, features of the French Quarter, the particular flora and fauna of the bayous and rivers, and especially the natural and human features of Grand Isle are evoked with attention to detail and accuracy; perhaps only Hearn rivals or surpasses du Quesnay in describing weather in New Orleans. The characters are well depicted but lack psychological complexity. Local color is exploited, as well as the pathetic fallacy, focussing on the ocean and its moods—"this prodigious giant, this unique and mysterious force." The plot is melodramatic and the question of fate—or theodicy—is predominant. As an embedded story within the inner narrative, providing foreshadowing, du Quesnay includes an account of the 1856 hurricane.

Olivier, married to a beautiful Creole woman, Diane, and with a lovely child, goes to spend the summer at Grand Isle. While described lyrically elsewhere as beautiful and serene, the Gulf of Mexico is also forbidding: "One has a painful feeling of isolation; it is as if one were at the ends of the earth." The ocean fills Diane with "admiration and horror." During a storm, the family is thoroughly soaked and must take refuge in the woods. The disorderly waters constitute "the most awful attack on the blessed work of the Creator." The child becomes feverish and dies. The wife grieves, but a new pregnancy returns hope to the family. At the end of the season, however, for unstated reasons, Diane swims out far into the Gulf and is drowned. Olivier has lost all: wife, child, child-to-be; nature or fate has deprived him of everything he had striven for. He returns to France, leaving the paradise of Louisiana that had turned against him. "I have heard nothing more about Olivier," writes Marcel to conclude his letter.

Louise Augustin Fortier (1850–1924), who married into the Fortier family, was born in New Orleans; her family had fled Saint Domingue. She taught French for thirty-five years and contributed to *Les Comptes Rendus de l'Athénée Louisianais*. In 1924 she received the society's Gold Medal. Three reprinted stories of hers illustrate her politics—conservative, pro-Confederacy—and her social outlook. The repetition of the phrase "Le bon vieux temps" (the good old days) in titles and texts can be taken partly at face value, indicating that antebellum social structures and manners were superior to what followed. The phrase must be read as partly ironic also, however. In the story of that title, which takes place at the time of slave revolts, the loyal old slave Pierre saves his young mistress and her husband from the predations of outlaw slaves, but cannot save his old master, who is murdered and mutilated; and though the slave is freed in an act of gratitude, the old man's death is too much to bear, and he dies trying to lift him. In "La Folie aux roses," which is set during the "confederate war," a woman manages to frighten off a Yankee officer who is despoiling the house, but her invalid son is captured and, presumably, killed. "Chronique du vieux temps" recounts another incident of the Civil War, in which a Rebel officer sent onto occupied territory as a spy barely manages to escape captivity, after blacks denounce him, but then dies in the battle of Pleasant Hill. Only a rare phrase in these stories suggests that nostalgia for the Confederacy might be replaced by loyalty to the Union.[18]

George Washington Dessommes (1855–1929) was born in New Orleans of a wealthy Creole family. In 1860, the family settled in Paris so that he could attend the lycée Louis-le-Grand, where he won a Latin prize. His elder brother Edouard was already in Paris, studying art and writing. Perhaps another family motive was to flee the United States before the looming war. When Dessommes was fifteen—that is, during the Franco-Prussian War, some episodes of which he may have witnessed, according to the poem "La Revanche!"—the family returned to New Orleans. He became an office clerk. Three years later he started writing for *Le Carillon*, in which he published prose and twenty-two poems; contributions were commended in other newspapers. Subsequently, he served as secretary to L'Athénée Louisianais and contributed more than a score of poems to its journal. He wrote two articles on Zola, one praising *Nana*, and a piece on Alfred Mercier's *Lidia*. Doubtless owing to their devotion to French language and culture, he and Mercier were friends, although Dessommes, unlike Mercier, wrote only about whites and was not socially liberal, according to the evidence. He was also a painter of seascapes. He ceased writing after Mercier's death (1894) and devoted himself to the cotton business. Financial constraints later obliged him to move to Montreal, thence to California.

The unsigned cover comment on *Vendanges*, a collection of Dessommes's poems (2007), alleges that Louisiana French poetry was too derivative ("une francité usée et rebattue"); the poets felt French, not American, and, presumably, let that tie stifle their originality. Rouquette, though recognized as describing well the vast cypress forests and trembling prairies of Louisiana, is criticized for his Chateaubriand-like tone. A nod is given to the Creole of Color Camille Thierry, but since he lived in Bordeaux, Dessommes is claimed as the greatest local Creole poet. (Yet Thierry was still Louisianan and his verse is often superior and range of topics greater.) Viatte similarly asserted that Dessommes was the most modern and original of Francophone poets in Louisiana and that his verse "would have opened the possibility of a renaissance in Louisiana if talent sufficed to save a disappearing language."[19]

The diction in *Vendanges* (the title comes from a drinking-song poem) is, however, largely conventional, with numerous exclamation points and awkward inversions, as in "La lune à resplendir commence" [The moon to shine begins] (65). The influence of Victor Hugo, Alfred de Musset, Alphonse de Lamartine, and other great Romantics is felt everywhere—for instance, in the appeal to isolation, the refuge of nature, and the dying past; Musset is called "adored master," and the "medodious lute" may be his (83). While mention of "spleen," a certain grimness, and glimpses of the poor suggest the writing of Charles Baudelaire, numerous poems are entirely conventional; at age eighteen years, Dessommes says "Adieu to poetry," and writes of white hair and advanced age.

There are highlights in *Vendanges*, however. Though most poems are not localized, a few are clearly connected to Louisiana. "Mandeville" (a town in St. Tammany Parish and a popular watering spot), "Un Soir au Jackson Square," "L'Orage" (a hurricane poem), and "Afternoon" (in French), which evokes Canal Street, impart a local flavor, as do mentions of Louisiana trees and birds. The Jackson Square poem, in which the former Place d'Armes is depicted as a corner of France, is noteworthy for its complaint about the Anglicization of New Orleans; it echoes distantly Baudelaire's urban poetry, with its evocations of crowds and complaint against modernization. Dessommes's control of form (especially the sonnet) and range of versification are noteworthy. He uses the alexandrine well (whether 6/6 or 4/4/4), as in "Geoffroy le troubadour" and "Sténio." In addition, there are octosyllabic and hexasyllabic lines, often in the same poem, and also decasyllabics, an unusual form for the nineteenth century. Among the best work are "Coucher de soleil," a sonnet, and "L'Orage," in which great oaks and pines confront the storm majestically. (Their resistance to the storm might symbolize the Creoles' resistance to Americanization.) "Afternoon" is marked by modernity, enjambments, and the rhyme "oda-" (from the enjambed word *odalisque*) and "soda." The title and numerous English words suggest the unfortunate invasion of French culture by American usage; aesthetically speaking, however, the poem is a success.[20]

A story by Dessommes, "Mon Premier Amour à la Nouvelle-Orléans," published in *Le Carillon* in 1875, illustrates the disabused wit and self-irony characteristic of the younger French Romantics—Musset, Baudelaire, Théophile Gautier. The first-person narrator sets himself up for disappointment by imagining that a woman glimpsed at a facing window is in love with him. His illusions are destroyed when he discovers that the figure is a man rehearsing his theatrical role as a woman; only mockery and self-chastisement are possible.[21]

The only known novel by Dessommes, *Tante Cydette*, first published serially in *Le Franco-Louisianais* in 1888, part of the last wave of Francophone fiction in Louisiana, is short and displays restraint; in France, it would be called a *récit* (a tightly focused form, with few characters and emphasis on psychology as well as mores). Dessommes skillfully uses indirect style (pronouns in quotations constituting first-person thought but in the third person) to suggest characters' views.[22]

The action takes place in the French Quarter during the 1870s. Stress is laid on the climate, its "intoxicating waves of heat," its *ardeurs*, which "embrace" one's being, physically and sentimentally, and thus "where nature has so much influence on energy and passions" (47, 68). Dessommes's understanding of the climate and its effects must spring from his own observations but also echoes French writings (starting as early as the eighteenth century) that explore the differences between septentrional and meridional peoples. It reflects also, doubtless, the views of Zola and Taine concerning the influence of milieu on character formation. George Reinecke argues that the work reflects the influence of Henry James's *Daisy Miller*. In addition, Dessommes emphasizes, albeit discreetly, the erotic charms of young New Orleans women, their light gowns that "allow to be seen what one dares not show"—a certain Latin daringness in erotic matters (70).

The story begins with an Easter scene at St. Louis Cathedral and ends with a marriage there, followed by a ball. The impressionistic and dynamic Easter episode, full of movement, evocations of sound, and graphic touches, illustrates the Creoles' frivolity and the shallowness of their faith (by indirect style, the Gospel according to St. John is characterized as "cette longue élucubration sans queue ni tête" [this long lucubration without either tail or head]) (40). The Americanization of Creole society is not passed over, particularly the newfound obsession of Creole men with making money in business ("notre société positive") and the "laisser-aller tout américain," or what Viatte called "la liberté des moeurs américaines" [the freedom of American mores]—for instance, "the quite American freedom of these tête-à-tête meetings" between young people (50, 68, 77). Because of their losses in the recent war, or because the American elements have largely prevailed, the Creoles, except for the "positive" ones, are nearly poverty-stricken.[23]

The title character, Aunt Cydette, is an embittered and malicious spinster who excels as a matchmaker. She is even called Carabosse, after an evil fairy in French lore. She succeeds in marrying her niece Ermence to Henry, a very proper young man newly arrived from France, who is not only well-off but also automatically endowed with the prestige of the mother country and has the *particule* (de) in his name. Another niece, Louise, a kind of failed Cinderella, whose father has died and who lives with her sickly mother in genteel poverty, loves the man; but, citing the girl's poverty and maneuvering skillfully, Cydette manages to push her aside in favor of Ermence. Her strategy is to have the three young people and another cousin put on a drawing-room play, a romantic comedy. The strategy nearly fails: Henry is quite taken with his dramatic partner, Louise, and there are rumors of a wedding between them; but Cydette triumphs at the end, and even the death of Louise's mother on the wedding eve is no obstacle. As the languor and passions of the Creoles are explained, if not excused, by the climate, Cydette's malice is attributed likewise not just to disappointments as a young woman—that is, to her failure to catch a suitable beau—but to the "burning nature" around her, which "dissolves" resolution and encourages bile (47). Her malicious meddling might be seen as a function of Creole mores—for instance, the quasi-obligation for a girl to marry before the age of twenty-five and the artificiality of marriage arrangements. This is not, however, Dessommes's position, though a certain critical irony suggests that he might sympathize with it. At a farther remove, a Marxist critic—even a socialist such as Charles Testut—might cite the falsity of all human relationships in a society governed by nineteenth-century capitalist codes.

Alcée Fortier (1856–1914), an eminent educator, critic, and historian, was a defender of his class. Reinecke called him "a sincere Catholic conservative." Born in St. James Parish, he was the son of Florent Fortier (1811–86), who composed a poem on Robert Cavelier de La Salle. The family, originally from Brittany, settled in Louisiana in 1720, and Alcée was of the sixth generation there. His maternal grandfather, the wealthy Gabriel (Valcour) Aimé, owner of Le Petit Versailles, a plantation in St. James, contributed to the improvement of the sugar-refining process, experimented with other crops and breeding, and had luxurious gardens. (The mansion on the plantation was destroyed by fire around 1920.) Alcée studied in New Orleans and at the University of Virginia and taught at Tulane University. A well-rounded man of letters of the period, he was the chief founder of L'Athénée Louisianais and from 1893 to 1914 served as its president. He was also the first president of the Modern Language Association. He produced school editions of French masterpieces such as Pierre Corneille's *Polyeucte* and Molière's *Les Femmes savantes*; he also published literary biographies of nineteenth-century French writers, and did research on local history, biography, and speech (including Acadian language).[24]

In addition, as an early folklorist he was a founder of the American Folklore Society. From Laura Plantation in St. James Parish and elsewhere he collected Afro-Creole tales, proverbs, and songs, which he published in *Bits of Louisiana Folklore* (1888) and *Louisiana Folktales in French Dialect and English* (1895). He called blacks "a crude and ignorant" race. The tales include the Compair Lapin or Brer Rabbit stories, spread by slaves in the Americas, from the South through the Antilles and to northern Brazil. These animal fables are based on a West African folk hero, Leuk, known in Louisiana as early as 1722. Fortier collected and published these tales after Joel Chandler Harris began publishing similar tales in the *Atlanta Constitution*; his *Uncle Remus and Brer Rabbit* first appeared in 1880. Fortier criticized publicly Hearn's *Gombo Zhèbes*; Hearn retaliated by challenging certain statements by Fortier.[25]

A sometime friend of Hearn's, Léona Queyrouze (1861–1938), deserves inclusion in this chapter. Her father, who came to Louisiana at age twelve, was the son of a Napoleonic soldier. The father was cultivated and broad-minded; his house became a sort of Creole salon. Her mother was a Louisiana white

Creole. Léona was tutored at home in classical subjects, became a woman of learning, taste, and accomplishment, and maintained her own salon. According to one specialist, who reads her career in today's terms, she "called for egalitarian reform and suffrage even as she struggled with her own elitism and assumptions of racial hierarchy." Seeing Hearn in a French Quarter bookshop, Queyrouze expressed her admiration for his articles in the *Times-Democrat*. Hearn called on her and gave her literary advice; he praised her article on Racine. She helped him with patois and his research into songs and proverbs. Perhaps some feeling warmer than friendship developed between them; he described her as "all fire and nerves and scintillation; a tropical being in mind and physique." They quarreled, however, as he had quarreled with Cable and various others. In 1933, *The Idyl: My Personal Reminiscences of Lafcadio Hearn* appeared in Japan. She corresponded, at least briefly, with Zola.[26]

In 1901, Queyrouze married Pierre Barel, under whose name she is sometimes listed. She published poems in magazines and newspapers, including *Les Comptes Rendus de l'Athénée Louisianais* and *L'Abeille*, where two poems in French, discreet but almost surely alluding to Hearn, appeared under a pseudonym. "A Magda" (1891) is a group of three elegiac sonnets of high quality marking the death of a child; one alludes also to a notorious incident when a mob of citizens attacked the prison and murdered eleven Italians held there in connection with the murder of the police chief David Hennessey. The prosody is refreshingly modern; Queyrouze uses bold enjambments ("'Viens,' dit / Une invisible bouche" [Come, says / An invisible mouth]); she even includes enjambment from one stanza to another. One sonnet ends with a comma; linked thus, the following one begins with the direct object of the previous verb. While purists may have deplored such liberties, it is clear that she had moved away from late-Romantic rhetoric (except for a few holdovers such as "ma lyre") and was on the threshold of modern poetics.

CHAPTER TEN

Kate Chopin

Among writers who dealt with Louisiana Creoles, Kate Chopin (1850–1904) is certainly the one whose pages are read now most widely. This currency is due to the remaking of her reputation by feminist scholars; criticism on Chopin has become an industry. In one writer's view, feminists "recognized in [her writings] their own revolt against socially prescribed roles and especially definitions of female sexual behavior." Emily Toth has published several books and various essays dealing with her; in addition, no less a figure than Sandra Gilbert, among the leading American feminist critics, edited a one-volume collection of all Chopin's fiction and has published on her elsewhere. Interest is added to Chopin's case by the charges, since disputed, that upon publication of *The Awakening* (1899) she became persona non grata in her home city, St. Louis, was blackballed from the Fine Arts Club, and saw her books banned there. She is widely honored, consequently, as a rebel and pioneer in radical women's writing. As one commentator put it, succinctly, "Chopin's *Awakening* is a major text of literary realism and a precursor of a century of feminist fiction to follow." Library readers can be sure they will find copies of her best-known works marked up, often in ink. In the twenty-first century she has been taken up likewise by postcolonial critics, but in a less friendly fashion. Her name is useful to commentators hostile to modern feminism, who know it will be recognized and can use it, abusively, as a kind of shorthand in writing of what one observer calls "the 10,000 feminist exercises in bad prose and false sentiment."[1]

The woman who has become a heroine of women's studies was born Katherine O'Flaherty in St. Louis, the daughter of Thomas O'Flaherty, an Irish immigrant, and Eliza Faris, of French ascendance. The household, a large one, included slaves. Her father died in a railroad accident when she was five. She attended Catholic schools and made her debut in St. Louis society.

In 1870 she married Oscar Chopin, a New Orleans cotton broker, the son of a Creole family (his father was French-born) living near the small settlement of Cloutierville, in Natchitoches Parish in the Cane River area. Natchitoches, founded in 1714, is the oldest settlement in the Louisiana Purchase, and the Creole heritage there was dominant and remains important.[2]

After a honeymoon in Europe, the couple settled in New Orleans, which she had previously visited once (1869). Her husband's father initially displayed typical prejudice toward her, annoyed that she was half-Irish and that the couple settled in the American sector of the city. Their last house was at 1413 Louisiana Avenue. Oscar was associated with the White League. In 1879, after his business ceased to prosper, the couple—with five sons—moved to Cloutierville, where a daughter, Lélia (named for a George Sand heroine), was born; the husband ran a store. Three years later he died. In 1884 Kate returned to St. Louis. Except for apprenticeship work, all her writing was done thereafter. Occasionally she visited Louisiana. Her experience in New Orleans was "exceptionally beneficial to her as a writer," according to one commentator, who suggests that her depiction of the city is a principal reason for the endurance of her work. However, once the wave of feminist criticism has ebbed, she may last principally because of her depiction of Cane River characters and mores.[3]

Her first publications were in the *St. Louis Post-Dispatch*, other newspapers, and minor journals. Some then appeared nationally, including a story in *Vogue* (1891). Her collected stories, which Willa Cather is said to have called "incandescent," are marked by local color and revealing scenes of the past but are not attempts at depicting an entire period. As Per Seyersted writes: "Discreetly, yet forcefully, [Chopin] evokes her particular locality with the enchanting Cane River atmosphere . . . But . . . she never emphasized the strange or remote; and though, like George W. Cable and Grace King, she commanded a wealth of local material, she did not join them in focusing on old Creole days." The charge of regional writer or "local colorist," frequent at one time and still applied selectively, is unfortunate, since, in practice, it is pejorative. Wise critics know that narrowness of scope in characters, settings, and time does not necessarily entail narrow understanding; the local is the nexus of the universal, as William Faulkner's novels illustrate brilliantly. In fact, the charge often reflects prejudice (though not under Seyersted's pen).[4]

While Chopin's stories are built around social and personal difficulties, most are not thesis fiction, with plots arranged to produce an edifying outcome. "When Kate Chopin dealt with such problems as slavery, miscegenation, and integration, she concentrated on the psychology of the individual rather than the social issue as such." The story "Désirée's Baby," discussed below, illustrates this authorial posture. One of her models was Guy de Maupassant, a volume-length selection of whose stories she translated (but did not get published). This influence may have, ultimately, taught her authorial objectivity; he had learned from Gustave Flaubert to eschew didacticism, to *show* rather than rely on rhetoric. Flaubert himself may have been a model for Chopin; critics, Cather included, mention *Madame Bovary* in connection with *The Awakening*—both being novels of romantic illusion and escape, though the differences between the two heroines are considerable. Flaubert did not adopt for Emma Bovary, his romantic heroine, the sympathetic narrative tone that Chopin used for hers; he maintained his distance. The well-known phrase "Madame Bovary, c'est moi" suggested that his novel was an exercise in self-punishment, inflicted after he had composed *Salammbô* and other arch-romantic tales. Chopin knew some of Emile Zola's work likewise; she reviewed *Lourdes* (1894), but in its concern with religious belief and doubt it is very different from *L'Assommoir* (1877) and other novels of Naturalistic social analysis. Her charges that he was sentimental and that his aim was to instruct his readers may have arisen from incomplete acquaintance with his oeuvre.[5]

In comparison with various Continental and British women of roughly the same period or much earlier, Chopin was not bold and was never revolutionary. Sand, Mary Wollstonecraft, Germaine de Staël, Flora Tristan, Marie d'Agoult, Charlotte Brontë, George Eliot, Rachilde, and others not only led unconventional lives, but expressed views that were socially and politically daring, even radical; some waged public campaigns connected to women's and workers' status. Male authors such as Stendhal, Lev Tolstoy, Flaubert, and Theodore Fontane had written about adultery. Even in America Chopin was not a pioneer; Louisa May Alcott attempted to publish a feminist novel, and Margaret Fuller, likewise of New England, editor of *The Dial*, argued for reforms in prisons, women's rights (including education and employment rights), and emancipation of slaves. She admired Sand for taking "rank in society like a man" and for leaving her husband, "a stupid, brutal man," as she wrote to Ralph Waldo Emerson around midcentury. To state that is in no way to discredit Chopin, a very accomplished author with a fine ear for dialogue and eye for setting, but simply to put her and her writing in perspective and note that it is closer to that of her contemporary King, known as a conservative, than is generally acknowledged.[6]

Like countless Continental novels of the mid- and late nineteenth century, Chopin's fiction features many miserable women and unhappy unions, of which feminist and biographic critics often make much. "The Dream of an Hour," for instance, suggests conjugal dissatisfaction pointedly. It is not demonstrated whether her own marriage was happy or otherwise. At least, while independent of mind, she adhered to traditional roles, and her attitude toward class and caste distinctions was that of her time, not pioneering—so much so that *At Fault* (1890), her first novel, is said "almost to embarrass Chopin scholars."[7]

The action of *At Fault* is set in the Cane River country; railroad history shows that the time is 1881 or so. In the background are, on the one hand, the Civil War and the destruction of property and families, and, on the other, the spread of industry into the South. It has been observed that the novel "is weakened by shifts of tone and the awkward intrusion of an authorial voice"—the sort of defects Chopin learned to avoid later. The heroine, originally from New Orleans, and her country nephew are Creoles. The main concern—it is a "problem novel"—is the feminine situation. While Thérèse, the heroine, manages her plantation competently and sees to her business affairs after her husband's death, she is still the epitome of gracious femininity, and marriage with the man she loves—a liberal northerner who settles in the area—would be her true fulfillment. He is, however, divorced. A principled Catholic, she views divorce as unacceptable and must abide by her conscience. Whether imposing one's moral views on others is appropriate remains, however, open to question, in principle and in practice. When she successfully urges the man to return to his alcoholic wife, the results are terrible, bringing suffering to three people. The theme of broken marriage had been treated previously in America, by William Dean Howells (*A Modern Instance*, 1882) and, of course, by innumerable French authors Chopin might have read; she herself treats it elsewhere, rather lightly, in "Madame Célestin's Divorce" (from *Bayou Folk*, 1894). Since in *At Fault* she arranges the matter by having the man's wife, desperate for liquor, die in a bayou-bank collapse, marriage becomes possible. The union may be considered, if one wishes, as the reuniting of North and South. The matters of principle are not entirely worked out, however.[8]

The novel includes black and Cajun characters, toward whom Chopin's attitude is conventional. Nothing here or elsewhere in her oeuvre corresponds to Cable's "The Freedman's Case in Equity," and certain critics who read her only as a feminist overlook the fact that she did not extend her liberalism fully here or elsewhere, though some have discerned this limitation. The heroine's pursuit of autonomy is, according to one, a colonial enterprise that "erases and dispossesses" the characters of color. Another speaks of the "unacceptable political caricatures of Reconstruction and the southern black," and calls Chopin not only politically conservative but "deeply racist." Chopin does not criticize, even by implication, the blacks' status as laborers and sharecroppers. Their ignorant speech, as she records it, has so many missing consonants and mispronounced vowels that the unwary reader *must* see the blacks as primitive. The contrast between this speech and the beautiful French used by writers among the Creoles of Color indicates an enormous difference in caste. Chopin's blacks are superstitious and childlike. She even refers to the "ape-like" appearance of a black man. After Grégoire, the heroine's nephew, takes a visitor to see the grave of the plantation owner whom he identifies as the model for Simon Legree in the novel by "Mrs. W'at's her name" (that is, *Uncle Tom's Cabin*), there is no further comment on slavery. (It is averred that this plantation owner was based on Robert McAlpin, from whose estate Chopin's father-in-law bought his plantation. Each was said to be notoriously cruel to his slaves. Chopin alludes twice to McAlpin.)[9]

At the same time, Chopin attributes to blacks—called, explicitly, a *race* (122)—a wholesome fear of the Lord and good judgment in moral matters, better than that of some whites. Similarly, an old black woman who had been the heroine's nurse is shown as devoted and wise. This depiction conforms to the long-enduring conventional image, presented by King and Ruth McEnery Stuart, of good, wise, blacks, whose understanding comes from labor and long-suffering. Chopin's picture, here and elsewhere, thus shows traditional racial co-dependency—in what is basically a simplified biracial system without nuances (except for Creoles of Color in the city) where mulattoes (Chopin's term) have the same status as other blacks, and Cajuns, though viewed as inferior, are classed with whites. "Ole Marse" or old Missus and faithful Negroes need and respect each other; the loyal retainer figure is common. Elsewhere Chopin speaks, in connection with an old servant, of "the patience of the savage" (420). Close contact between the races is expected, as long as the one remains in the capacity of servant to the other. An ill-starred character in *At Fault* is part Indian; perhaps because of his heritage in the wilds, he has more difficulty adjusting to changing times than do the blacks; or maybe he is simply inferior in moral terms. He is shot in the act of committing arson.

The stories and vignettes—some very short—in *Bayou Folk* are likewise set mainly in the Cane River area. The focus, as the title makes clear, is on people; mores are secondary. Whether typical or eccentric, the characters clearly fit their setting on or near the bayous, the way Maupassant's figures, whether in Normandy, Paris, or elsewhere, belong to theirs. The economical presentation proceeds by deftly chosen gestures, words, and details of settings. Recurring surnames in various stories, as well as some recurring characters (following the Balzacian and Zolaesque technique) provide cohesion as well as ties with *At Fault* and other fiction. The stories and sketches also illustrate the cultural connections and ethnic and linguistic spillover among various groups: French-speaking or bilingual Creoles of the Cane River or New Orleans; 'Cadians, as Chopin calls them; blacks and mulattoes speaking French or patois. One character with Spanish blood is called by Chopin (following other characters' image of her) a "vixen" (302); one woman speaks Choctaw and English. There are samples of Cajun English and French. Many of the portraits are indulgent; Chopin does not disdain a warm sentimentality, as in "A Gentleman of Bayou Têche" [sic].

A few representative stories give a sense of the collection. In "Ma'ame Pélagie," the authorial tone adopted toward two spinsters whose plantation house was set aflame during the war is that of sympathetic comprehension; the legitimacy of the antebellum plantation culture is not questioned, even by implication. Of Laballière, a character from "In and Out of Old Natchitoches," Chopin writes, "People said he was entirely too much at home with the free mulattoes. It seems a dreadful thing to say, and it would be a shocking thing to think of . . ." (192). He is, in fact, shunned by his fellow whites. The author concentrates her attention, however, not on his ostracism but on relations among him, the schoolteacher, and her distant cousin, a New Orleans gambler.

"La Belle Zoraïde," a frame story set in New Orleans, concerns marriage obstacles for quadroons. It depicts a beautiful woman of color (a slave owner), who acts as house servant and companion to a white woman. Declining her mistress's offer of a splendid wedding if she marries a manservant of her acquaintance, Zoraïde falls in love with "a column of ebony" who dances the bamboula in Congo Square (213). The manipulative white mistress conspires to have the man sent far away; when a child is born, it too is placed elsewhere and the quadroon is informed that it is dead. Her mind is destroyed; she believes a coarse rag doll is the child. While the story illustrates an aspect of racial and class oppression—the mistress manipulating cruelly another life—it also brings home the strong and frustrated maternal feelings of the quadroon, a reminder of how many black lives were disrupted before, during, and after the war by separation of families.

The abundance of commentary on "Désirée's Baby," another story, frequently anthologized, from *Bayou Folk*, shows critics' concern with miscegenation, which plays no role elsewhere in Chopin's fiction. The heroine, Désirée, now married, was an orphan—abandoned, it is thought, by people en route to Texas; her ascendency is not known. When her husband, Armand, detects traces of black blood in their child, he drives them both from the house. She drowns herself and the child. It has been made clear already that he is swarthy. Subsequently, he discovers, in papers he is about to destroy, a letter from his mother alluding to her own small fraction of black blood. Thus what he viewed as the child's contamination came from him as well, or him alone (quite likely—his skin is said to be darker than his wife's). The attitude displayed by Désirée's adoptive mother and the husband was that of the nineteenth century, and Chopin's own narrative voice does not denounce it, explicitly, nor the social system; but the irony of the situation may be read as qualifying the attitude, though the intention is not certain. Chopin's stories include numerous other examples of ironic turns of events, or twists, that affect characters without carrying any implied judgment.[10]

Chopin's second collection of stories, *A Night in Acadie* (1897), has much in common with its predecessor, though the settings range more widely, including Grand Isle and nearby Chênière Caminada (depicted as they were before the destructive hurricanes). The title comes from the initial story, "Athénaïse," a multipart story dealing with an unhappy bride. Chopin treats the topic with reserve, alluding only once to the husband's having made love to her "passionately, rudely, offensively" (379). The bride runs to her parents on the "rigolet de Bon Dieu" (rapids on a bayou), then, with her brother's help—his role should be noted—leaves for New Orleans. Her dissatisfaction vanishes with the discovery that she will have a child.

Whether the story should be read as an accusation of nature, an indictment of men, a bow (perhaps ambivalent or reluctant) to conventionality, a testimony to the power of motherhood to bring true happiness to women—reproductive sex being, in one view, their only genuine fulfillment—and thereby overcome their assumed distaste for sexual intercourse, or as simply the portrait of a very silly woman, perhaps blind to her own attraction, is a function of readers' attitudes. In any case, the denouement and authorial tone go against current feminist dogma; upon her return, the heroine kisses her husband warmly, for the first time. One critic confessed disappointment with the ending, presumably finding the solution of marriage dull in comparison with possibilities Chopin sketches out in the New Orleans scenes. Moreover, since the tale ends with the sound of a black child crying, readers are invited to imagine, beyond the bounds of the story, the drudgery of motherhood (for women of all races) and curse of the feminine condition. In a simpler story,

"The Going Away of Liza," the wife similarly returns to her husband. Yet in other tales, such as "Regret" and "Wiser than a God," the women at the center choose not to marry or are pleased they did not. As a variation on conjugal dramas, the story "In Sabine" presents an unusual case in which two men—one white, one black—cooperate to get an ill-treated wife permanently away from her husband.[11]

Other stories depict the pull of affection and the magnetism of children. "After the Winter" illustrates the change in a misanthropic war veteran when he hears the glorious Easter music at church. In "A Matter of Prejudice," a narrow-minded Creole woman of the French Quarter who disdains Americans and their children in particular nevertheless nurses a little American girl, who turns out, by one of Chopin's characteristic plot twists, to be her granddaughter, the offspring of a son whom she had banished because he did not marry a Creole.

The Awakening is the story of a dissatisfied wife, who deliberately swims into deep water and does not return, thus ending the novel. What else the work may be depends on readers. It is the preeminent Chopin text for recent critics, who almost all give it a feminist reading. Harold Bloom furnishes an exception, writing that "many of them weakly misread the book, which is anything but feminist in its stance." It is likely that numerous commentators and teachers of the novel have read few of Chopin's other works and thereby have deprived themselves of a useful context for understanding; Bloom himself admits he did not read *At Fault*, but at least he does not blindly follow the feminist line of interpretation. Instead, he sees *The Awakening* (less good at second reading than first, he asserts) as a flawed but noteworthy Whitmanesque experiment in the "ecstatic rebirth of self." (It should be noted that in "A Respectable Woman," from *A Night in Acadie,* one character quotes from "Song of Myself.") Bloom suggests that the work draws part of its power from the attempted negation of "its own deepest knowledge" (that is, an ineffectual auto-censorship of an existential dimension). Certain contemporaneous reviewers similarly saw through to what he views as this "lust" after the inner person (not a male lover), lust which could be expressed only in a veiled form. (He rightly notes that contemporaneous reviewers were not stupid or shallow—as some recent commentators assume.) Whether the author had indeed such incomplete self-awareness is, however, a valid question.[12]

Biographic, psychological, and sexual readings of *The Awakening* are common. Edna Pontellier is viewed not as oversexed but undersexed (that is, not "awakened" to her own sexual drives). Toth's research showed that Chopin, after her husband's death, was very friendly with a married planter, a neighbor. Toth believes she probably had an affair with him. The author herself might be the model, thus, for the dissatisfied and adulterous woman. Seyersted judged that Chopin identified strongly with Edna; other critics speak of the author as "schizoid." Readers who know "Athénaïse" can see Edna as a woman displeased with her husband's embraces, which may leave her sexually unfulfilled. Or she can be viewed as someone looking, on physical grounds or on principle, for sexual freedom or social emancipation, the latter to be obtained by defying the religious and civil prohibition against adultery. Toth points out that Chopin had fallen away from the Church years before.[13]

Donald Demarest, borrowing T. S. Eliot's term from his *Hamlet* essay, spoke of Chopin's "brilliant use of the objective correlative . . . especially the scarcely-recognized awakening of long-dormant emotions" and her "extraordinary insights into female psychology." Edmond Wilson pointed out Edna as the precursor of D. H. Lawrence's Lady Chatterley, and certain passages are indeed Laurentian. Edna's swimming in the Gulf constitutes a rejection of the Creole society summering on Grand Isle, just as her decision to leave her husband's house and settle in a cottage is a rejection of her condition as chattel. Her suicide need not be interpreted *principally* as a social act, but the role of Creole society in producing the suicide is not insignificant. One critic has gone farther and read the novel as "a sustained attack on the insularity of the Creole community and its inability to communicate with a wider Anglophone world." In that light, the writer appears as another Cable.[14]

The most fanciful interpretation may be that of Gilbert, who views the novel in mythological terms. In "The Second Coming of Aphrodite" (a title crafted to challenge so-called patriarchal thinking by putting the goddess on a plane with Christ), she sees Edna's swimming experience as a rebirth in the sea, that archfeminine element, a "birth of Venus"; she also views Edna as a myth herself, a new figure for a new womanhood. The death to which her final swim leads must be interpreted, according to Gilbert, as transcendence. The heroine's fantasies and the imaginative tableaux Chopin creates, notably the hedonistic banquet (chapter 30), scarcely justify such fantasy in criticism; more sober approaches are suitable.[15]

Clearly, Chopin's design is to examine and assess the feminine condition realistically in its social, economic, sentimental, and physical dimensions. Through sexuality and childbirth, nature has provided for the continuation of the race, but childbirth is torture; hence, by Edna's reasoning (remembering her own experience and seeing her friend Adèle give birth), being born female is a curse. Nature and society have both afforded compensation for the torture: sexual pleasure, the thrill of romantic love, the satisfactions of maternity, the ostensibly privileged status of receiving the protection of a stronger, superior figure. But in the heroine's view, ultimately, this status is merely enslavement. The story "Athénaïse" may well have prefigured this discovery.

While femaleness is universal, it varies, of course, and is weighted differently according to time, place, and circumstances. Chopin seems to accept the central tenet of Naturalism: mores grow from the environment; individuals and groups are a product of their environment as well as heredity. She shows the relationships between the heroine's situation and the white Creole milieu in New Orleans, which she contrasts explicitly to Protestant America. This Creole world is characterized by isolation, self-conscious pride, and sense of its past. There is a veneer of culture, and artistic undertakings appear to be valued; yet the one person who is genuinely artistic, Mlle Reitz, is condemned to live on the periphery in poverty and solitude. Women have considerable freedom of action; this is not Puritan America. Card-playing, betting at the race track, smoking, walking by oneself are all acceptable conduct. But appearances are crucial; decorum is all.

The Awakening, albeit greatly admired, is not necessarily superior to other writings by Chopin. The depiction of the seashore and Gulf waters is lyrical—she departs in this respect from Maupassant—but is marked by abstractions, without the precision and color Lafcadio Hearn brought to bear. "The voice of the sea is seductive, never ceasing, whispering, clamoring, murmuring, inviting the soul to wander in abysses of solitude" (654). While self-flagellation on her part is implausible, she may have put herself into the work as a warning, or as an experiment—life without consequences—that she could not afford in reality. Edna's story was that of disorder; and, as the author believed, moral and social disorder are, ultimately, threats to civilization itself.

CHAPTER ELEVEN

King, Stuart, and Others

Born in New Orleans, Grace Elizabeth King (1852–1932), a fiction writer and popular historian, was not of French or Spanish Creole stock. Her father was born in Georgia and educated at the University of Virginia; her mother was likewise of Georgian stock. Though she was not Catholic, Grace attended French Catholic schools, including the Institut Saint-Louis (disguised, it seems, as the Institut Saint-Denis in her stories), and she learned to move easily in Creole circles as well as appreciate Continental French culture. Before the war her family owned a sugar plantation. Her father practiced law and served in the legislature but lost his fortune with the defeat of the Confederacy and struggled to reestablish his practice while the family lived in straitened circumstances. Though only a girl at the time, she later remembered well the occupation of New Orleans by General Benjamin Butler's troops and the Reconstruction years, and she suffered from the family's losses, which are the background to her 1916 novel, *The Pleasant Ways of St. Médard*. Like Sidonie de la Houssaye, she needed to make money from her writing. (Her father died in 1881.) It was not until 1904 that she was able to purchase a house on Coliseum Square in the Lower Garden District, and she was chagrined that both her parents were deceased by that time. This home, where she lived with her sisters (who relieved her of certain household tasks) and brother, acted somewhat as a salon. She did not marry.[1]

The family was well acquainted with Charles Gayarré, her literary mentor, whose house, filled with French paintings and furniture, charmed her; she remained devoted to him. In 1891–92, she spent several months in Paris, where she wrote, did research at the Bibliothèque Nationale, and was welcomed into certain salons; much later, she returned for a lengthier stay. She was a member of the Quarante Club, a woman's book circle. She wrote on prominent French patronesses of the arts and socialites for *Harper's Bazaar*. It was noted earlier that she criticized George Washington Cable for his description of the treatment of blacks and mixed races in New Orleans, a portrayal that was, to her, a betrayal of the city. She wrote, she said, "from the standpoint of a white lady." While she acknowledged that he had given "a true picture of the Creoles as he knew them (mostly quadroons)," she added, "I have always considered his works a libel on the Creoles I knew. However, he pleased the audience he wrote for . . . ." She asserted elsewhere that he "proclaimed his preference for colored people over white."[2]

At a dinner party in 1885, King heard fellow New Orleanians criticize Cable in the presence of Richard Watson Gilder, the editor of *Century Magazine*. According to her account, he asked her why the Creoles did not produce something truer; the next morning she started writing. She acknowledged the influence of Gayarré and Lafcadio Hearn (Bush, 398). She met Hearn at a luncheon, but Hearn, whose social skills were inadequate, fled after the meal. The two writers were unlikely anyhow to become friends, given their differences. King may have learned literary skill from Guy de Maupassant also (she called herself a realist; she has been called a "pioneer of psychological realism"). "Monsieur Motte," a long story, was published in English in the *New Princeton Review* in 1886 through the good offices of Charles Dudley Warner of *Harper's Magazine*. The story was translated into French and later enlarged and published as a novella, *Monsieur Motte* (1888). She quickly brought out two additional collections of short fiction. Her friendship with Warner furnished occasions to spend summers in Hartford, Connecticut, where she became well acquainted with Mark Twain and his wife.[3]

King's stories are a mirror of her time as historians have described it—mores, racial relations, speech (except that she eschewed generally the use of bad English and quasi-phonetic spellings). William Dean Howells was among those who praised her writing (Bush, 53). While not a bigot, she held attitudes conventional for her time and class, her attitude toward blacks being, as one commentator put it, "both kindly and paternalistic, patronizing and apprehensive" (Bush, 6). A harsher critic, adopting a presentist position, applied to her the same terms as to Kate Chopin, writing of her "unacceptable political caricatures of Reconstruction and the southern black" and calling her not only conservative but racist. Another labeled her a "white-apologist." More than one commentator has intimated that Presbyterianism was significant in shaping her attitude (referring, presumably, to the deterministic doctrine of predestination). She is not, however, accused of defending slavery on biblical principles, as Richard Weaver did later. Her sympathy for the South and general conservatism have doubtless helped relegate her to the literary shadows, despite her merits. If, like Chopin, she had portrayed a sort of Madame Bovary, with adulterous impulses, King would doubtless be better known and more admired now. She was, at least, honored during her lifetime in the Northeast and at home; Tulane University awarded her an honorary degree.[4]

While commentators recognize King's "aristocratic" conservatism and sometimes attack her for being too close to patriarchal attitudes—or deplore that she could not find a way out—she has also been read as a feminist or sort of maternalist, since women are shown as responsible for much good in the antebellum and postbellum worlds. (Their particular achievements in the postwar period, as she saw them, are not surprising, given the vacuum created by the death or wounding of many fighting men.) This view of women's contributions was widely shared; woman's "gentle nature and ennobling spirit" were seen by blacks and whites alike as forces for good in society. Yet she appreciated strong and unorthodox women. In "Heroines of Novels," which contrasts German and French authors' treatment of women characters, she recognized the greater interest of French heroines (whether proper or not) and displayed impatience with the formulaic Victorian female (including fictional Americans) who lived only for her family and social roles. King read and admired George Sand and translated letters attributed to her. She likewise appreciated Charlotte Brontë and George Eliot.

King remarked, moreover, that the contributions and circumstances of black women were generally ignored, whereas "negro men have had their wrongs & rights blazoned from one end of the country to the other." She wrote that her aim in "Monsieur Motte" was to give a fair portrait of women, black and white, noting that the "holy passion" of Negro women served "to cancel those other grosser ones, with which they are really victimized by their blood." (The mention of "blood" underlines the role played by race in her determinism.) She added that it spoke well for southern women that they could be "so served and loved by slaves" (Bush, 14). Recent critics have rejected her views. Violet Harrington Bryan, for instance, asserted that "King would slander all women of color with the charge of excessive sensuality." According to Bryan, King and Chopin both looked "askant" at quadroons, "portraying them in the most positive sense as neat landladies and conscientious nurses and hairdressers, but more negatively as prostitutes."[5]

Some tendentious observers even consider King to be a critic of the racial system, despite herself—that is, unaware, like Kate Chopin. "It is hardly surprising that King was largely unconscious of or confused about the symbiotic relationship between racism and sexism in the society she renders with such detail," writes Anna Shannon Elfenbein. Illustrated here is the supposition, fed by Marxist analysis and race-class-gender theory, that conservative positions cannot be genuine and those who hold them must be in bad faith, though unconsciously so. Thus women writers, like the bourgeoisie for Marxists, can be denounced, yet claimed also for radical theory. Criticism of this sort is necessarily skewed.[6]

"Monsieur Motte," the story, may be viewed a classic tale of selfless devotion on the part of a quadroon—the extreme opposite of de la Houssaye's exploiting, greedy quadroons—and thus as portraying one workable and socially honored form of race relations as King saw them. She remains, according to this reading, vulnerable to the charge of racism. Or the story may be read as subtly and intentionally subversive, following some present-day critics. The quadroon, Marcélite, was rescued as a child (according to information confirmed in the novella) by a young white couple when her slave mother was sold; she became a devoted companion to their daughter, Marie Modeste. The man was killed in the war; the woman, not strong, died shortly. Marcélite enrolled the child in a year-round boarding school on behalf of an invented uncle and used her earnings as a hairdresser to pay the expenses. The crisis comes when, after graduation, the girl has no uncle to go home to. Marcélite must then confess that he never existed and that it was she who provided for the girl's education. Elfenbein (94) explains this devotion by suggesting that Marie is the quadroon's daughter; Marcélite's devotion is thus not disinterested. But, since Marcélite, unlike many quadroons, has African features, a dark-brown face, and wooly hair, and since no one at the school—where sensitivity to features and skin shading would be highly developed—questions the girl's breeding, this explanation does not seem plausible.[7]

However one reads the story, it is clear that the hairdresser has accepted and worked within the social conventions of the time—the separation of castes—and yet has violated them, at emotional risk to herself (obviously to Marie Modeste also) and, unfortunately, without steeling herself for the inevitable day of reckoning. After the truth comes out, she fears the girl is humiliated, and she even apologizes: "To be supported by a nigger! . . . Pardon me, my little mistress! Pardon me! I did not know what I was doing; I am only a fool nigger anyhow. I wanted you to go to the finest school . . ." (97). When the orphan protests (without making her motive clear) that she wants to go live with Marcélite, the latter exclaims: "What! You don't think you ain't white! Oh, God! Strike me dead!" (101). The favorable reception the story received in New York and Boston papers suggests that northeastern readers saw some aspects of white-black relationships in the same light as southerners.[8]

Monsieur Motte, the novella, begins with "On the Plantation," as Marie Modeste and Marcélite are guests on a St. Charles Parish sugarcane plantation. The hospitality is due to the schoolmistress, a friend of that family, who becomes betrothed to a New Orleans notary. The girl, reserved and child-like, and obliged to participate in countless religious services, warms to the lovely scenes and intimacy with nature. "The Drama of an Evening" describes an elaborate coming-out party in New Orleans, in which Marie is presented as the foster daughter of the notary and the schoolmistress, now married. The straitened circumstances of the postbellum whites are visible, especially among the chaperones, dressed in old, if distinguished, attire; yet manners remain exquisite, and money (likely borrowed) has been spent on the debutantes' dresses and the elaborate supper. Contrasted to the Creoles is the vulgar Madame Montyon, a Parisian, there with her stepson, the handsome Charles; she has come to claim an inheritance from an old uncle.

King's portraits are telling. Of an old gentleman glimpsing a lovely girl and thinking of how her grandmother had enchanted him: "'Aïe! It hurts me still!' and the old victim laid his wrinkled hand over the sepulchre of his defunct heart." Food and drink remain honored: "Who says Creole says gastronome." The Parisian spends her time buttonholing the notary and others who may owe her money. "Her conversation rolled on uninterruptedly, exhaling rent-bills, due-bills, promissory notes, mortgages, and every other variety of debt which had been used to procure money out of her or old Arvil. . . . 'Extravagant as Creoles, no wonder they cannot pay their debts.'" King adds: "Her voice took the suavity out of the truffles and the bouquet from the champagne" (208, 240). Creole snobbery remains keen. People are shocked to learn that one man at the soirée (who reappears in the following tale) is the son of a German plantation overseer. The German worked, in fact, on the Motte plantation; now his son is the owner. The arrangement by which he came to it is suspect.

The final story, "Marriage of Marie Modeste," offers confirmation of Marie's story and also indicates that the fiction of the uncle was never exposed to her; rather, he is said to have died. Marie mourned him, duly, but is thankful now for new happiness, as the handsome Parisian has asked for her hand, over the strong objections of his stepmother, unable to think of anything but money. Repeating her earlier generosity, the devoted Marcélite offers as a wedding present gold coins she has saved. It is a matter of pride for the quadroon and will enable the bride, without a dowry, not to be empty-handed. Yet Marie is unwilling to proceed with the wedding; taking money from a social inferior, even a cherished one, is not possible. The two women, Marie and Marcélite, quarrel. Reading the scene and indeed the entire novel in sexually symbolic terms, Helen Taylor asserts that "Marcélite is offering her symbolically her own life, her own sexual freedom, and it is the alliance between black and white women overriding proprieties of race and class (with its disturbing anarchic sexual implications) that Marie feels she must refuse." The word *proprieties* is revealing; the critic sees them only as oppressive.⁹

The notary, meanwhile, has verified that the plantation cannot legally belong to the German if it was known that an heir (the child Marie) was alive. Whether her statement is true or false, Marcélite affirms that she herself had announced the child's death, fearful of Yankee determination to kill all the family. Thus the German's deceased father and he are relieved of the onus of unlawful possession. Restoration to Marie of the Motte property, which constitutes a dowry, allows her to consent to marriage at last. Much has been made of the fact that at the wedding, it is Marcélite, not the schoolmistress, who walks behind the bride and fulfills other motherly functions. This is morally due: she has been the agent of Marie's welfare from the beginning, and her testimony is crucial in establishing the respectability of the Germans and thus permitting Marie to accept restoration of the plantation. If participation of a quadroon in a white wedding strikes readers as implausible, the extraordinary circumstances can well justify departure from custom. It will be recalled that King wished to give a fair portrait of women of her time and place, black and white; no subversive motive need be supposed, although Taylor adds that "Marcélite is the bride's mother because she has suppressed and then conquered her race's particular claims and desire for revolt." Certain mocking remarks about men (especially by Madame Montyon) do not constitute an antipatriarchal statement; male characters are generally respected and efficacious. Anne Goodwyn Jones speaks with some scorn of the "heart" illustrated by the characters—"the androgynous values that King would like so much to see prevail"—and regrets that the novelist did not pursue "the implications of the racial, sexual, social, and economic conflicts" in the work.¹⁰

Tales of a Time and Place (1892) comprises five long stories. Occasional use of indirect style marks them as of their time, but the narrative technique—switching between scenic presentation and summary—is modern. The three-caste system is featured, as well as relations between slaves and owners. "Bayou l'Ombre: An Incident of the War" takes place on a plantation in spring 1865, before the surrender has been publicized. The story is based on King's recollections. (After New Orleans was occupied, her father was obliged to flee; her mother succeeded in taking the children to the family plantation behind the Confederate lines, near New Iberia.) Names of plantation slaves are used, and the guerilla leader was probably based on King's uncle (Bush, 97). Three plucky white girls, left to the care of Mammy and old "Uncle John," the black retainer, are surprised by soldiers they take to be Yankees and their Confederate prisoners. Though King mocks the girls gently for their romantic loyalty to the southern ethos of glory and chivalry, she ascribes to them energy and determination, like traits displayed in Constance Fenimore Woolson's stories about the defeated South, which became standard in Civil War fiction. King's sympathy for the South and her basic conservatism are revealed in additional ways. The captain appears ridiculous, not heroic or forward-looking, when he asks sarcastically whether "Uncle John" and Mammy are blood kin to the girls, explaining that different skin hues are "just trifling distinctions of color" (*Tales*, 32). The Saturday-night pandemonium of drunken slaves is excused by atavism or custom: "But they were Negroes, ignorant, uneducated, barbarous, excited; they could not help it; they could not be expected to resist all at once the momentum of centuries of ancestral ferocity" (*Tales*, 48). The girls are outraged when they discover that most of the slaves have simply run away upon seeing men in blue, believing that deliverance has come.

"Bonne Maman" takes place in "back of town," one term for the mixed New Orleans neighborhood beyond Rampart Street, including the Tremé. In the war, the French grandmother of the title, heiress to a plantation, lost everything, land and fortune: "They came in a royal grant; they went in a royal cause" (*Tales*, 86). Having moved to the city, she lives in poverty, tended only by a devoted granddaughter and an ignorant black servant, Betsy, who has recently attached herself to the pair. The old woman recalls another servant she had, a quadroon slave named Aza, who as a mere babe was given to her. Bonne Maman had freed her before the war, presumably through exasperation: "She would have died for me—ah, yes!—but she could not be good for me" (*Tales*, 83). The quadroon's life that Aza has led since is suggested subtly by evocation of music from neighboring houses. When Bonne Maman dies, Aza, not knowing the old neighbor's identity or her race, goes to the wake out of curiosity. King's limning of the quadroon conforms to conventional models:

> She bent over the coffin with its emaciated, pitiful contents, and her eyes dilated with fascination.
> "White!" she whispered in surprise, with a contemptuous smile on her voluptuous lips. What exquisite flattery to her own rich, exuberant, sumptuous flesh. She raised herself with complacent comeliness.... (*Tales*, 104)

Having recognized the deceased, Aza curses the servant Betsy as unworthy and attempts to drive her away. But the servant defends herself, accusing Aza of "devilment" and indifference, "throwing away in the streets the money you stole out of the pockets of them white men!" (*Tales*, 108). "Nigger!" shouts Betsy. Whether the subsequent repentance of Aza is in character remains for readers to judge.

"Madrilène; Or, The Festival of the Dead" dramatizes aspects of the racial system. In its enduring, haunting concern with whiteness and, more generally, the theme of appearance versus being, it can be compared to Toni Morrison's first novel, *The Bluest Eye* (1970). King's title character, a white orphan taken by nearly everyone, including herself, for a Creole of Color, serves and is exploited by a spiteful quadroon who runs a boardinghouse and has evening "visitors." On the eve of All Saints' Day, Madilrène visits both a white and a colored cemetery. In each, families are cleaning and decorating tombs and "ovens" (mural sepulchres), and there is one white funeral. Allusions to Italian statues and "dagoes" indicate the New Orleans of the late nineteenth century. (In the fourth tale, "The Christmas Story of a Little Church," a Sicilian family appears, speaking Sicilian patois.) At the burial ground for Creoles of Color, most faces are yellow. "Differences of feature and expression, height and figure, were all lost in one monotonous hue—the hue of a race creeping down, or is it a race creeping up the scale? A *patois* race" (*Tales*, 144). Quadroons are not depicted favorably. An angry woman is described as having "white scum . . . around her lips—large, full, pampered, pulpy lips—with their inevitable subtle suggestions of immodesties." Before a white man, "she glided miraculously into the obsequious civility of her class . . . and sought to please, by voice and demeanor, and a deft flattery of prejudice" (*Tales*, 140). A colored Creole boy shouts at Madrilène, "Mulâtresse! nigger! nigger! 'coon!'"; the street violence is said to be characteristic of the colored, as is craven fear (*Tales*, 128). Speaking of the quadroon, who is terrified of voudoo [sic], King writes, "In her assurance she was white; in her fear she was all negro" (*Tales*, 172).

Madrilène supposes she will resurrect as white, the default pigmentation. Black blood is said to have "muddied the depths of so many clear eyes" (*Tales*, 146). As King wrote elsewhere, "It was not a day of advanced science or morality . . . To the black Christian, God was a white man, the devil black; the Virgin Mary, the Saviour, the saints and angels, all belonged to the race of the master and mistress; white, divinized; black, diabolized." The attitude of the narrative voice is not celebratory; rather, such racial hierarchy is shown as responsible for misery. Whether black or of mixed race, nonwhites "in their secret hearts... never disputed that the white are born above the black." "Did the whites want to change their whiteness for blackness?" (*Tales*, 151). In the ironic denouement, it is revealed that the girl really is white; the quadroon had concealed her origins but her old enemy, the voodoo practitioner, proclaims them.[11]

The final story of *Tales of a Time and Place*, "In the French Quarter. 1870," concerns the fall of Sedan in September of that year. It illustrates the suitability of short fiction for conveying snapshots of wartime. As in Maupassant's stories set during the Franco-Prussian War, the narrative tone is wryly humorous, rather than serious, unlike François Tujague's tale. Upon learning the news of the debacle, the chauvinistic French shopkeepers in the Quarter are astounded and aggrieved; one cannot bring himself to utter the word *defeat*, saying, rather, that France has been "eclipsed." As though they were in Europe, they turn indignantly upon Wilhelm Müller, a neighbor, theretofore respected, from the land of "Bice Marque" and "Molque"; the girl he loves shuns him. When an old blind Frenchman, who idolized the first Napoleon, demands to know the news, "Villem" volunteers to read aloud the dispatches. As he tells the old man about French triumphs and Prussian defeats, the neighbors recognize his goodness (this prevarication, if misguided, is not questioned by the authorial voice), and the girl, who realizes that his nationality made no difference after all, embraces him.[12]

Balcony Stories are briefer. As King defines them in a short opening piece, they are specifically women's narratives—the sort exchanged on a warm evening on the balcony—friendly reminiscences, bits of gossip. Some are just sketches, others developed. The narrative voices can be identified as women's—either an omniscient voice or a woman observer's. The plotting, use of tone and voice, and style show artistic control, not quite that of twentieth-century masters but well beyond Romantic and Balzacian models. King uses indirection and suggestion, and, rather than explaining characters, lets them reveal themselves. While she includes one O. Henry-like ending, like some of Chopin's, other pieces have more subtle conclusions.

King is at her best in these stories. Though there are echos of prewar days, they deal largely with members of old white Creole families in the postbellum period. These are the families who sent their sons to Paris for schooling, who retain manners dating from *avant le déluge*. Numerous characters are old—relics of the Creole past and their former selves; fortunes have been lost. King evokes the antiques and finery in Royal and Chartres street shops: "Old furniture, cut glass, pictures, jewelry, lace, china—the fleece (sometimes the flesh still sticking to it) left on the brambles by the driven herd. If there should some day be a trump of resurrection for defunct fortunes, those shops would be emptied in the same twinkling of the eye allowed to tombs for their rendition of property."

The author's sympathetic understanding of the white Creoles is obvious; but she mocks them, gently, for such foibles as the inability to pronounce *H* in English, and less gently for their stubborn snobbery and unkindness to those who lost their fortunes, the "nouveaux pauvres." In "Grandmama," a fine story, she depicts with gentle humor the Creole concern for honor. She stresses the dolce far niente of their life, speaking of the "easy sociabilities" of Mandeville, adding: "In New Orleans . . . there was some pretense of business. In Mandeville even this slight imputation of restraint upon the men was removed."[13]

In "La Grande Demoiselle," the destruction and ruin brought about by war are viewed as deplorable, and black soldiers and other Unionists are portrayed unfavorably. "Joe" (from the enlarged edition) concerns a devoted slave. He and others are well treated by their masters. The system of slavery is not questioned; the Presbyterian minister himself buys Joe. "The Story of a Day," set in St. Martin Parish, is a touching Cajun tale. "A Crippled Hope" concerns a deformed black girl, "Little Mammy," whom no one buys at the slave market but who becomes invaluable as a child-minder and nurse for ill slaves; eventually she is hired by whites. The story has been criticized as condescending and racist. One commentator acknowledged the optimistic quality of its vision, yet placed the author among women writers who "debunked and exposed the falsities for post Civil War America of the sentimentalist tradition they inherited."[14]

"The Little Convent Girl"—which presents the reverse situation of "Madrilène" (the two stories can be compared to Cable's "'Tite Poulette" and *Madame Delphine*)—depicts a Cincinnati girl reared in innocence in a convent. She is not quoted, and neither free indirect style nor close third-person discourse, either of which would open up her consciousness, is employed; the viewpoint is that of an observer. The conventual code of deportment is obliquely criticized, as the novelist shows the nuns' lack of emotional connection with their charge and the confining stiffness of the young woman's garments. The authorial term "black code of deportment" for rules of conduct in the convent recalls the Code Noir, though the code in this case is applied not to slaves but to young victims of a harsh, inhibiting education that prepares them for nothing. The terms "little" and "girl" suggest infantilism. Black garments suggest evil and sin (and are connected to dark skin also).

The girl's father, who had rejected her earlier but paid for her care, having died, she travels to New Orleans by riverboat to meet the mother she does not remember. Her deportment remains stiff, despite friendliness from the captain and others; she is afraid of herself and her sins. At the wharf, people whisper "Colored!" upon seeing the mother. (Readers recall then that the girl brushed her hair in order to take out its curliness.) One month later, when the same ship docks, the mother takes her daughter to greet it; the girl leaps into the river. (The act seems self-willed, though according to some commentators she falls accidentally). As in "Désirée's Baby," self-destruction affords a conclusion to a social dilemma that seems unresolvable and intolerable. While the death may be considered melodramatic, it takes place so quickly that melodrama is not possible. As the anonymous reprint editor observed in the foreword, "This tale is told so tactfully and objectively ... that the author's personal feelings about miscegenation could never be divined from it."[15]

The Pleasant Ways of St. Médard languished on an editor's desk for ten years, apparently because it was not conventionally pleasant enough, despite the title. It was finally brought out in 1916 in a small printing. It is set in New Orleans right after the Civil War, with analepses going back to the war. St. Médard is a fictitious parish downriver, between New Orleans and the real St. Bernard. The characters and neighborhood setting are based closely on what the Kings (called Talbots) experienced. They are the only "Americans" (non-Creoles); their neighbors are Gascons (many settlers had come from the Bordelais region).

In addition to indicating the practical difficulties faced by those returning, King offers excellent portraits of period types—the governess who, when the Federals arrived, was left behind to close the house and stole as much as several trunks could hold; the Ursuline sisters; the good priest who gives away produce from his garden; an Italian tavern owner who before the war had used his skills to enrich himself and then exploits his fellow citizens under the occupation; his arriviste daughters and cunning wife. "He bought Confederate money from the timid for gold, and sold it for gold to the confident; trading on the passion for patriotism as he had traded on the passion for drink" (Bush, 259). Under Reconstruction, he profits enormously and buys a mansion, though continues to live as he did before—a genuine miser, not a nouveau riche.

There is particular stress on racial matters. Whereas "Bayou l'Ombre" shows how, prior to the defeat, the racial situation was stable and racial questions were, for the white privileged class, in the shadows, after the war the situation is not only transformed but made central in political and civil life. The alliance, unholy to the returning whites, of blacks, carpetbaggers, and the unscrupulous whites who join them, is denounced by a local doctor: "You know who the public administrator is! A negro! And if he were only a negro, no more than that! But in addition there is a politician, a white carpet-bagger behind the negro . . . That is what our government is from governor down. Negro in front; carpet-bagger behind" (Bush, 286–87).

The chapter "Jerry" dramatizes difficulties faced by the newly freed, whatever their character. While King does not envision a reborn society rising from the ashes of war and the new regime of emancipation, she shows concern for former slaves and is not unaware of the responsibility that whites must bear for the unruly conduct of many newly enfranchised. Ragged and dirty bands struggle along the roads; elsewhere, a crowd of "lazy Negroes" loiters (Bush, 245). The freedmen are at liberty to go where they please, work or not work, and pay no mind to authority.

> They . . . had been freed and exalted . . . their owners conquered and abased. . . . To them belonged the spoils . . . There was nothing now but political equality to obtain, which, on account of their numbers and the disfranchisement of the whites, meant political superiority. And white men, from the victorious side's political party that had brought on and won the war, were even now forming parties in the State, to gain this last triumph for them, and with it their vote. (Bush, 247)

Some freedmen cut all ties with their past; others, older or less courageous, or grateful and farsighted, reforge the ties, whether of affection or otherwise, that held them to their masters.

Pointing out that the freed Negroes, formerly cared for, are now their own masters, Mr. Talbot takes pains to see that Jerry, who is portrayed favorably, finds work as a carpenter. What no one can prevent, unfortunately, is the misconduct of Jerry's daughters. Though he procures good jobs for them, the girls do not stay, and there is thievery, to which the mother closes her eyes. Eventually they settle among undesirable men. Jerry's resolve fails: he sets out to find his lost wife and daughters, though he cannot countenance their behavior. The moral problem he delineates is a racial one. Why, he asks Mr. Talbot, cannot blacks "keep themselves straight"—govern themselves. (In "Monsieur Motte," King had written of Marcélite's "untamed African blood," in rebellion against "civilization which had tampered with her brain, had enervated her will, and had duped her with false assurances of her own capability.") Jerry suggests that the African nature is wild, but then expresses the matter in religious terms: all men are sinners and God pardons all who repent (Bush, 51, 253–54).

Taylor calls the chapter on Jerry King's "most reactionary and racist story," and labels him "a virtuous, loyal, and obsequious Uncle Tom." Historians have often agreed with King's common-sense position, however. "Negroes had been enslaved for so long . . . that their efforts to build a meaningful life in freedom were hampered. . . . Blacks could not be expected to make many advances in the first decades following emancipation." Taylor, who observes accusingly that King wrote for the "(white) implied reader" or the "affluent white female New Orleanian," affirms that the loyal black "existed almost exclusively in the imaginations of . . . southern whites." This inaccurate charge may be connected to the fact that Taylor is British.[16]

The historical novel *La Dame de Sainte Hermine* (1924) shows few traces of post-1900 changes in literary taste. The action takes place at the time of the settlement of New Orleans by Jean-Baptiste Le Moyne de Bienville, who is portrayed favorably. Early buildings are carried away by a tremendous September storm, perhaps based on the 1722 hurricane. The cast of characters includes numerous historical figures, chiefly men; but the work is a woman's novel, emphasizing love, charity, and maternity. In France, an innocent girl of noble birth, Marie Alorge Sainte Hermine, married against her will, is shortly exiled by a lettre de cachet and sent to Louisiana; meanwhile, her fortune is at the mercy of unscrupulous relatives. She adapts to wilderness ways and rough manners; she is good to a poor convent girl sent to the colony as a chattel-like bride. While respect is shown for Christian belief, one senses anticlericalism or at least anti-Catholicism on the author's part: the Mother Superior knows to what fate she has delivered the girl; a Capuchin priest is depicted unfavorably; merry-making is accepted; and the lord high councillor shows disdain for a meaningless and imposed church marriage. La Dame de Sainte Hermine comes to agree with him: "It is the Church that does not understand."[17]

King evokes the romance of the forest, and shows the value of Indian medicine, but she depicts the natives as unscrupulous, capable of betrayal. The Ft. Rosalie massacre is summarized, then the senseless killing of peaceable tribes by Negroes on the order of Etienne de Périer, the new governor. Acknowledging that the Natchez were "the noblest and most civilized of all the Southern Indians," the novel shows nevertheless their gluttony and drunkenness, which kept them from carrying out plans to attack other white settlements, including New Orleans.

Historical writings by King are not scholarly by nineteenth-century historiographical principles, but they have a solid factual foundation and rich detail. She used French and local sources and unpublished materials from Gayarré. She is given credit for correcting a persistent historical error concerning a certain Sauvolle, said to be a brother of Bienville and Iberville. With her novelist's skills, she excels at scenes, the most extended being the Battle of New Orleans. Her style displays her grasp and keen appreciation of her topic, as in this passage reporting the entertainment offered by the privateer Jean Lafitte to British officers: "The host displayed as lavishly all the incomparable grace and charm of manner and brilliancy of conversation which, among the appreciative people of Louisiana, had been accepted as legal tender for moral dues."[18]

The journalist Sallie Rhett Roman (1844–1921) was born into a genteel South Carolina family that owned a plantation and a Charleston house. Her father, a senator, was a partisan of secession well before 1861; at one time he owned 190 slaves. Her mother was of Huguenot ancestry. Sallie was thus not a Louisianan, but her adult life was spent in white Creole society. She was well educated; she spoke French. During the war, she met a widower from St. James Parish, Alfred Roman, in South Carolina then as a Confederate official after having served as a lieutenant colonel in the Louisiana infantry. He was Creole on both sides. His father, André Roman, served two terms as governor in the 1840s and 1850s. He was the brother-in-law of Valcour Aimé. André owned a large plantation and at one time 369 slaves. After Alfred and Sallie, who had converted to Roman Catholicism, married in 1863, she went to live on his plantation near Vacherie. The family lost some of its fortune in the war, and by the mid-1870s the plantation no longer supplied a living for the couple and their numerous children, including a stepson. Alfred returned to law, which had been his first calling. In 1877, as the state emerged from Reconstruction, the family moved to New Orleans when Alfred was named clerk of the Supreme Court. Sallie became a member of the Quarante Club.[19]

She had journalistic connections also; her husband and stepson had worked for *L'Abeille*, and the stepson became editor of *Le Courrier de la Louisiane*. By 1891, a year before her husband's death, she began writing editorials (anonymous) for the *Times-Democrat*, owned by a powerful politician who was state treasurer and closely connected to the corrupt Louisiana Lottery. This was during the so-called "Bourbon" rule—an imprecise term referring to the dominant white oligarchy, whose control over government lasted well into the twentieth century. Roman's editorial positions were, like her father's and brothers' in South Carolina, conservative; she supported the principle of white supremacy, the lottery, tax advantages for the white ownership class, and home rule. She approved of immigration but only of Caucasians from northern Europe. Though her editorials were unsigned, she apparently had no reservations about pursuing political journalism as a woman. She began contributing fiction to the paper (using her maiden or married name), and in the course of eighteen years published hundreds of short stories and serialized longer pieces of fiction. A few stories appeared in national publications. The sheer number of these pieces and length of her journalistic career (and the fact that she made money) point to the avidity of the public for well-written, though sentimental, fiction.[20]

Roman's fiction seems older, less psychologically subtle, than King's, published in the same decade. Roman was familiar with Emile Zola's novels and was flattered, she wrote, to have her work compared to his, but specified, significantly, that she wished to do more than describe characters and situations. Indeed, while her fiction shares traits with that of the French Naturalists, the values set forth are generally southern and Victorian; the style is appropriately didactic and flowery, the tone sometimes Southern Gothic. Views on women's place are generally conventional, though she was not inattentive to issues of the day such as the proper role of a superior woman. Customs and mores, such as Comus ball usages and the Christmas Eve atmosphere in the cathedral and Jackson Square, are well suggested, but there is melodrama, with exaggeration.[21]

A noteworthy character sketch is "La Misère," concerning an impecunious Sicilian fruit and meat vendor on Esplanade Avenue. He once owned a schooner in Barataria Bay. His comely wife sailed out one day, with the mate; the schooner came back but not the woman. The mate died (with the captain's assistance); the boat was sold; and "La Misère" took up his new name and trade. His repeated call—"des poulets, des dindes, me–lons"—reminds readers how picturesque Lafcadio Hearn found the street vendors' calls in New Orleans. A similar sketch, "La Fortune," concerning a lottery-ticket vendor, is tender but melodramatic. "A Wedding in Spring," a sentimental story, asks a great deal of readers, since the observing consciousness, who thinks, remembers, and judges, is a dog. The novella "Tonie," published serially, is similarly sentimental (and there is weak motivation), but episodes that take place on the bayous and marshes near Lake Maurepas afford good details about the area and its inhabitants. Like Adolphe du Quesnay and others, Roman uses to good effect the pathetic fallacy.

The name of Ruth McEnery Stuart (1849?–1917), another conservative New Orleanian, a member of the Quarante Club, is often linked with King's, with whom she had much in common; King expressed admiration for her, though they may have considered themselves rivals. Little-known now, Stuart was born into a genteel family, of Scots and Irish ancestry, in Marksville, Avoyelles Parish. When she was still a child, her family settled New Orleans, where she was educated. The war brought impoverishment. Two of her cousins were governors of Louisiana. In 1879 she married a much older Arkansas cotton grower and lived on his plantation. After his death, she returned to New Orleans. Her first story, "Uncle Mingo's 'Speculatioms,'" appeared in 1888. A story set mostly in New Orleans, "Blink," collected in her first volume, may reflect this initial literary success. Around 1890 she moved to New York, where she continued publishing regionalist fiction, which sold well and gained for her a national following and an admiring readership, since it generally fit expectations about the postbellum and post-Reconstruction South. Reviewers in England as well as America praised her highly. Tulane University awarded her an honorary doctorate (1915). Her conservatism appears in her acceptance of the social status quo into which she was born. Yet with respect to women's situation in general she was forward-thinking—a postbellum southern woman who could be viewed as "womanly" (not feminist), as Chopin put it, but with an unusually open mind.[22]

Stuart wrote chiefly of plantation life and plantation blacks, creating humorous, sentimental pictures; she also depicted whites of straitened means in small towns, some in or near New Orleans. "Gascons" and "Dagoes" are mentioned. The stories have a solid historical foundation. She was a keen observer and turned a phrase well, using clever, pointed ways of expression often characteristic of women authors. "The domestic landscape needs its clouds to give value to the blue"; "If the living came as a perquisite in his lordly pursuit of pleasure, so much the better." Unlike de la Houssaye and King, she did not generally feature quadroons (occasionally one is mentioned, however, as "yellow" or having Indian blood). As in Joel Chandler Harris's writing, her characters are treated with sympathy and understanding by the authorial voice and by white observers.[23]

For numerous speakers—blacks, rural whites, and Sicilian Americans—Stuart used colloquial language, spelled roughly phonetically. Malapropisms, suggested inflections and pronunciations, and other speech features represented what she heard. Many present critics, neglecting the indicative functions of language, dismiss as demeaning such ethnic speech and anything that ties ethnicity with humor. Taylor alleges that Stuart was "exceptionally patronizing and racist"; she is accused of creating "reactionary and racist constructions of blacks of both sexes." Another commentator speaks of her "gross caricatures" and "ironic condescension." Stuart was conventional, however, and saw fiction as mimetic, not reforming. Her figures are not unduly exoticized; illiteracy and ignorance are indicated without sarcasm. To take such speech as intentional mockery is to misunderstand the function of literary (not social) criticism. In other stories, though blacks are the actors, the near-poverty, the ingeniousness displayed are those of all sorts of working people in the United States at the time—black, brown, white, foreigner. As Harris said of his works, they are not simply regional depictions; the truths belong to all.[24]

Among Stuart's characters are blacks who, after the war, choose to remain with their former owners, out of loyalty, habit, a sense of duty. Yet Stuart understood the wrenching pain when slave couples were separated in antebellum days and was not indifferent to blacks' need for freedom, whether by manumission or purchased by their own labor. The long story "Egypt," set before the war, tells how the slave Egypt, helped by a generous master, obtains leave from a plantation outside New Orleans in order to work for her man's freedom. By dint of ingenuity, keen sense, and effort, she saves nearly the entire sum. Her prudence and energy are depicted with delicate brush strokes. She comes to realize that the man nevertheless needs a master; freed, he would be worthless. Having been freed herself, she buys him as her slave—the right solution.[25]

A work featuring New Orleans Creoles is *The Story of Babette, A Little Creole Girl* (1894), representative of Stuart's storytelling craft, her humor and rosy sentimentalism, and her depiction of ethnic groups, which both relied on and popularized stereotypes. The novella begins by a Carnival episode depicting the streets, balconies, and parade of Comus on Mardi Gras evening and presenting a prosperous, upper-class Creole family, speaking mixed French and English. In the crowd, Babette, their three-year-old child, is stolen by an old gypsy woman from the Mississippi coast, who hopes to collect a reward but in fact is afraid to claim it. The gypsy is driven by the extreme poverty of the family with whom she lives, Sicilians. The father is an idle drunkard; the mother cares for a swarm of children. Three years later, in a rainstorm in the city, the gypsy is able to abandon Babette anonymously, leaving her in the house of a charitable couple whose children had died of yellow fever; they rear her as their niece. After their death, and with the help of her high principles and of coincidence, she finds her blood family. Identification is made by a conventional Romantic device: discovery of a message, left in the tassels of a dress she had worn that Carnival evening.

While childhood play on the Gulf Coast is depicted as idyllic—sand, waves, trees—the Sicilian family's penury and the father's worthlessness reflect badly on them. Blacks are portrayed more favorably, but their role is essentially what it was before emancipation. Babette's childhood nurse is a loving black woman, devoted to the family; she dies from exhaustion after having tried to trace the missing girl. Her position is made clear in the very first pages: "Befo de war I used to blongs to you all wie folks, now you all blongs to me." In the house of Babette's adoptive "uncle" and "aunt," two old retainers, a woman and a man called "Uncle Tom," furnish similar examples of devotion to their masters; the household is an image in miniature of a stable hierarchical society where interdependence of the races and peaceful intercourse are compatible with strict caste distinctions, illustrated by speech differences and manners. Another character, said to be Caucasian, a deaf-mute and half-idiot, afflicted with strange pigmentation and an unsettling gaze, is similarly in a subordinate position, almost an outcast. His devotion to Babette redeems him. Her suitor, a young doctor, restores his hearing and speech. Babette and the doctor marry, following perhaps the model offered by Charlotte Brontë's novels. Stuart's traditional sense of social and racial distinctions comes through, reinforced perhaps by her readers' expectations.

CHAPTER TWELVE

Some Twentieth-Century Louisiana Prose Writers

Although many fiction writers of the twentieth and twenty-first centuries, whether Louisianans or visitors, have dealt with New Orleans, relatively few have emphasized the Creole background, traditions, or their remnants; fewer still call themselves Creole or are of mainly Creole extraction. The Creoles of Color, who preserve and cultivate their *créolité*, form a more cohesive group than do the descendants of white Creoles, whose community is barely identifiable at the present. What visitors and many residents are likely to identify now as "Creole" would generally be bits of recalled history or incidental features—cooking, a few customs, the architecture of the French Quarter (mostly of Spanish design), and certain plantations.

Whereas during much of the nineteenth century isolationism characterized the white Creole community, confined largely to the Vieux Carré, it was ultimately driven across Canal Street, as the Quarter became dilapidated and business moved. This urban displacement reduced cohesion. Intermarriage of Creole whites (despite their prejudices) with local whites of Irish, Italian, Anglo-Saxon, and other origin, and with those who settled in Louisiana from elsewhere, has diluted the early Creole stock. In 1950 one commentator wrote of the changing names in New Orleans: "Not that there are not many that are still Creole, but for the past half century enough have been Anglo-Saxon to make the Creole the exception rather than the rule." Assimilation has been the effect, if not the intention—whereas by the 1960s blacks had learned that "you don't have to assimilate. You could do your own thing, get into your own background, your own history, your own tradition, and your own culture." Among Catholic church parishes in New Orleans populated by whites, the old ethnic identifications (Irish, German, French, Italian) are largely gone.

The "French" church, Notre-Dame de Bon Secours, was destroyed by fire, though the congregation continues under another name. The French language is widely studied in private schools but is no longer a part of everyday life. (In 1883 Alfred Mercier had predicted the extinction of the Creoles if French was no longer spoken in Louisiana.) Jazz is appreciated by whites as well as blacks, but Dixieland jazz remains a black creation, and white Creoles have no other special art or medium; nor, despite calling themselves Creole, do they identify so much with their legacy as in the past.[1]

With few exceptions, late twentieth-century white writers have been critical of the Creole legacy, especially in what can be termed its "Uptown" element (complacent, snobbish, traditionalist, racist). There is thus more agreement about the shortcomings of Creoles than their qualities and the importance of their heritage. Literary ridicule of such institutions as Carnival krewes, snobbish schools and churches, elite clubs (the Boston Club, Pickwick Club, Lawn Tennis Club), among the oldest such in the nation and populated chiefly by descendants of Creole families, is tempting and, indeed, facile; it has contributed to what is essentially an anti-Creole literature, or, more broadly, a satire of older social values. Changed social attitudes and broad public opinion have supported this negative approach, which makes the older ways seem not only antediluvian but immoral, so that to be alienated from them is to inhabit truth (akin to the alienation of nineteenth-century artists from the bourgeoisie and an illustration of what may be called a paradigm shift toward valorization of dark skin). The transformation of the French Quarter into a sort of theme park and its literary treatment by outsiders have occulted its Creole past. Contemporary fiction writers who illustrate this tendency include Ellen Gilchrist, Sheila Bosworth, Patty Friedmann, and Nancy Lemann. Broadly speaking, the situation of white authors in Louisiana illustrates the challenge facing southern writers in general, the confrontation "with the painful question of regional identity," as described by Kate Daniels: "The struggle of much recent southern literature has been to overcome . . . fragmentation . . . and to forge a new vision of wholeness that will reflect the changes the twentieth century has brought to bear on the region."[2]

Walt Whitman, Mark Twain, O. Henry, and others who visited or lived in New Orleans in the nineteenth or early twentieth century and are thereby associated with it used the city as background for some of their writing, though not always faithfully and successfully, and they often they saw Creole society only peripherally. Many less famous visitors felt the need to celebrate the characteristically old and picturesque aspects of Creole New Orleans. But even as early as the 1920s it was difficult to write about the city without falling into sentiment or clichés. As Helen Taylor observed, by the 1890s the "national construction of Louisiana as a mythic and romantic site" was well under way. Cleanth Brooks remarked in 1977 that "New Orleans has become one of the cities of the mind, and is therefore immortal." In the recent words of John Lowe, "New Orleans, in the works of poet Brenda Marie Osbey, novelist John Kennedy Toole, or short story writer [Ellen] Gilchrist, seems eternal and unique." Yet south Louisiana, whether Cajun or Creole, has proven resilient by lending itself to new writing and being reassessed and redesigned socially, even as it preserves tradition.[3]

A few Francophone fiction writers continued to publish well into the twentieth century. Among them is Ulisse Marinoni (1869–1930). Born in New Orleans, he took his degree in law from Tulane University in 1890 and practiced in the city. By its nineteenth-century style and nostalgic tone, his writing looks backward one or two generations. He treats reverently his ancestors; there is no critical vein, no suggestion that their way of life was unjustifiably patriarchal or predicated on others' misfortune. His vignette, "Ma Tante Louise," which recounts a visit to the cemetery on All Saints' Day, illustrates once again the devotion of Creole families to their dead and laments the death of white Creole men on the Confederate side and the difficult postbellum years. In "Mon Oncle Jacques," the title character similarly thinks of the Federal troops with bitterness and the Confederates with devotion. The decrepit Mississippi River plantation house near where he was reared and where he goes to cultivate his nostalgic reflections stands for "les ruines d'antan" [the ruins of yesteryear] and "les grands actes d'héroïsme." The scene recalls landscape paintings: "Des tumulus de gazon accusaient un ancien parterre, les barrières défoncées donnaient passage aux bêtes qui s'installaient sous les vestiges des galeries; un paysage de Paul Potter avec la mélancolie de Claude Lorrain" [Grassy mounds showed where a garden had been formerly; the broken-down fences let in animals, who settled under what remained of the porches; it was a Paul Potter landscape with the melancholy of Claude Lorrain]. Marinoni's description of plantation life furnishes valuable details for historians.[4]

The remainder of the authors treated in this chapter (roughly chronologically) are Anglophone. Considered a popular writer, and certainly prolific, Frances Parkinson Keyes (1885–1970) deserves respect as an excellent observer of white Creole mores and institutions as they survived in the mid-twentieth century. Moreover, she was a skilled storyteller. Born in Virginia, she married young and spent most of her life in Washington, D.C., and New Hampshire. She was a convert to Catholicism. After her husband's death, she became interested in New Orleans and south Louisiana. In 1945 she rented a French Quarter house where General P. G. T. Beauregard and Paul Morphy, a chess champion, had lived; in the 1950s she purchased the house. She published many other books—fiction, autobiography—before composing *Crescent Carnival* (1942), which deals with two related families, Protestant and Catholic; *The River Road* (1945), concerning old plantations along the Mississippi River; and her most famous novel, *Dinner at Antoine's* (1948), set in the French Quarter and nearby, published when she was in her sixties.

Although *Dinner at Antoine's* concerns a crime, it is also a novel of contemporaneous manners. The recent world war and its effects are not forgotten. Yet many habits and attitudes date from well before. Ruth, a young visitor from the East, whose observations serve to highlight local mores, remarks that Jackson Square "must look exactly tonight as it did a hundred years ago, and, while we were crossing it, I could imagine all sorts of ghosts wandering around under the palm trees.... I could just see those old-time French brides getting off a sailing ship with their little dowry trunks ... and the Ursuline nuns shepherding them along" (106–107). The white Creole characters preserve customs that seem timeless—elaborate Carnival traditions, refinement of home life, complicated mourning arrangements, burials in the ornate vaults above ground. Their places of pleasure reveal their caste: the Boston Club, the Sazerac Bar and Blue Room at the Roosevelt Hotel, the eponymous restaurant, weekend properties near Lacombe, in St. Tammany Parish.[5]

Keyes's attitudes are as conventional as her characters': without authorial qualification or irony, they speak in terms dating from the previous century. Dislike of Yankees and Cajuns is open. Blacks are present as butlers, cooks, and other servants; a faithful mammy-turned-ladies'-maid-and-hairdresser corresponds to the established type. (Keyes's choice to record the black woman's speech in an imitation phonetic system and to maintain grammatical irregularities, as Ruth McEnery Stuart had done, reinforces the inherited stereotype, set against the speech of the white, privileged patricians.) Snobbery is of varying sorts: the black maid looks down on "Yankees, tradespeople, and pass-for-whites"; a journalist of Italian descent is termed a "wop"; one haughty Creole woman remarks, "I don't want my only daughter to have an Irishwoman for a boon companion and a bosom friend" (39, 124, 240).

Katherine Anne Porter (1890–1980), a native of Texas who spent time in Louisiana, touched on the topic of Creoles, white and black, in stories such as "Magic" (1924) and "Old Mortality" (1937). As one commentator noted, "It is the exotic, aristocratic but decaying, moral-law-breaking life imputed to the Creole . . . that most arrested the attention of American readers, and of Katherine Anne Porter." Scenes in a restaurant, at a convent school, and at the racetrack suggest, without heavy-handedness, the uptown Creole milieu and character.[6]

A historian, preservationist, and cultural commentator, as well as director of the Federal Writers' Project *WPA Guide to New Orleans*, Lyle Saxon (1891–1946) was also a fiction writer. Though born in Bellingham, Washington, he was reared in Baton Rouge, attended LSU, and then moved to New Orleans to work as a journalist. He was a familiar figure of the French Quarter; he became friends with a half-dozen other Quarter figures who were famous then or later. The story "Cane River" (published in *The Dial*, 1926) is among his best fiction. He knew the area well from having spent weeks as a guest of Cammie Garrett Henry, the owner of Melrose Plantation, where he lived in Yucca House. This Isle Brevelle estate, which served somewhat as an artists' colony and research library, was built in 1833 by Augustin Métoyer, a wealthy, slave-holding Free Man of Color, descended from an important mixed-race family, whose more recent descendants continue to live in the area. With Kate Chopin and Ada Jack Carver (1890–1972), a native of Natchitoches and sometimes a fellow guest, Saxon is an important recorder of mores and characters from the area.[7]

Saxon's fine novel *Children of Strangers* (1937) takes its title from Leviticus 25:45 but also from the common local term for those of mixed race. He calls them *mulattoes*, but the term is not to be taken strictly (as one-half white); most Melrose Creoles of Color had many white forebears, mostly French; the language is still heard (the action begins in 1905), and the mulattoes' "Latin" character is stressed. One character, the boy Joel, is literally the child of a stranger—a white murderer from Texas who camps secretly in the woods. The author's tone is respectful toward all groups. Langston Hughes wrote to Saxon of "the great sympathy which you have shown for the Negro peoples and the beauty you have given them in your writing." Today's critics are not necessarily so generous.[8]

The caste system is firmly in place in Isle Brevelle: whites (very few), those of mixed race (numerous), and Negroes or blacks. Members of the latter two groups do field work on sharecropped lands; Saxon observes the drawbacks of the system. Socially, however, Creoles of Color and blacks are separate; the mulattoes despise the inferior caste, whose members in turn resent them. By the strict codes of employment on Yucca plantation and its "big house," only blacks tend the house, not mulattoes, partly because the latter refuse to eat with the former. When Joel's mother, Famie, through need and fatigue, breaks the code by working and eating with blacks, she loses standing. There is some aspiration among the mixed-race group toward whitening. "It's almost as though they were scheming to make the race lighter" (229). Joel's departure for Chicago, ultimately for California, with the proceeds from the sale of his mother's land, signals the ultimate rejection of his heritage and another step in the destruction of tradition.

William Faulkner (1897–1962), who wrote his first significant fiction in New Orleans, used the term *Creole* loosely, as illustrated in the volume he put out with William Spratling, *Sherwood Anderson and Other Creoles* (1926). Faulkner's *Mosquitoes* (1927) is concerned mostly with French Quarter artists and hangers-on, not true Creole descendants. He writes that the "vieux carré brooded in a faintly tarnished languor like an aging yet still beautiful courtesan in a smoke-filled room, avid yet weary too of ardent ways." Two years earlier, in a sketch published in the *Times-Picayune*, he had described New Orleans as "a courtesan, not old and yet no longer young, who shuns the sunlight that the illusion of her former glory be preserved." Such descriptions were less commonplace in the 1920s than later; the evocation was not perceived as a cliché to the degree it has become. *The Wild Palms* contains some fine vignettes of the city, and *Absalom, Absalom!*, with its scenes of antebellum Creole New Orleans, called a "worldly and even foreign city," and especially the French Quarter, also takes up again the nineteenth-century theme of miscegenation, with its portraits of mixed-race women and the Creole of Color Charles Bon.[9]

Tennessee Williams (1911–1983) left his native St. Louis for New Orleans in 1938. He found there, according to his mother, "wild drinking, sexual promiscuity [no comma] and abnormality." He depicted the city and its inhabitants, some with Creole connections, in minor plays such as *Vieux Carré* (1979) and in *A Streetcar Named Desire* (1947), surely the most famous mid-twentieth century work set in New Orleans. Its connection to Creole culture is tenuous at best; the French Quarter was no longer French, the old families gone. It may be supposed that Blanche DuBois and her sister, Stella, come from Creole antecedents, given the name and that of their plantation, Belle Reve, near Laurel, Mississippi (it was the French who explored the area and founded Biloxi, in 1699). It may then be suggested that Williams wanted to show the decadence of what few white Creole families remained; certainly Blanche's drinking and sexual promiscuity, along with the loss of the property—as well as Stella's choice of husband, with its implications of rather brutal sexuality—suggest decline. But the play has no further connection to the Creole past or present. Stanley Kowalski is, obviously, neither an ethnic Creole nor a member of any elitist class.[10]

Suddenly Last Summer, in contrast, features members of the Garden District set, connected to old wealth. ("Garden District" was the title of the double bill on which the play appeared in its original production in 1958.) While the drama was inspired by non-Louisiana figures (his mother and sister, Hart Crane), it suggests also the decadence of the Uptown aristocracy, if one agrees that, even to Williams (given his audience at the time), homosexuality (over which he felt guilt) was deviancy, as was insanity.

A brief look at certain other figures is in order. The philosopher and poet James K. Feibleman (1904–1987), who was born in uptown New Orleans and knew the city well, continued the tradition of hurricane fiction in his superb novel *The Long Habit* (1948), which takes place at Isle Chênière. The last section, "Escape from the Wheel" (based partly on newspaper accounts of the Ilse Dernière and Chênière Caminada storms), recounts a terrific hurricane that kills almost everyone. Hamilton Basso's *Relics and Angels* (1929) includes a summary of a storm inspired probably by the same hurricanes. Harnett T. Kane's *The Bayous of Louisiana* (1943), which deals with both great storms, provides nonfictional accounts.[11]

Walker Percy (1916–1990), born in Alabama but with antecedents in the Mississippi Delta, is considered by numerous critics and readers as a quintessential Louisiana novelist. He lived for a while in the Garden District and then moved across Lake Pontchartrain. He is not, however, a Creole himself. While *The Moviegoer* (1961), a tedious tale of existential malaise, is set in New Orleans, the characters are not generally Creoles (a French-named man is in fact Cajun, though, implausibly, he was king of Carnival); and, except for some general snobbery, there is little associated specifically with the city's heritage. *Lancelot* (1977), highly praised in the *New York Times* and elsewhere despite carelessness in execution and unoriginal form (used previously in Albert Camus's *La Chute*), alludes to Creole families and mores, but only secondarily, as a way of setting off the main character, with his old-planter roots (Anglo-Saxon, Episcopalian). The role played by hurricanes—an artificial storm set up by a Hollywood studio across Lake Pontchartrain and then a genuine one—is noteworthy; storms, artificial and real, are perceived as part of the landscape and the culture of southeast Louisiana.[12]

Fabulous Ancestor (1954), by Donald Demarest (1919–99), depicts late white Creole society around 1930 (thus some years before *Dinner at Antoine's* takes place), with constant reference to the previous century. Roughly, it can be considered a rewriting of *The Grandissimes*. When it was first published, it sold only eight thousand copies but received favorable comments from Kane, Keyes, and Robert Tallant. Kane wrote in the *New York Herald Tribune*, "It's as delightful a book as I have read about New Orleans in a long,

long time. It has spirit and charm and a true New Orleans flavor." Keyes observed, "The book rings true from start to finish." Lucy Templeton, a transplanted New Orleanian, began her review in the *Louisville Courier* by asserting (with some inaccuracy because she ignored numerous counterexamples): "Quite rightly we assume that the cultural background of New Orleans is both Catholic and French, but most of those who have written about the city have been Protestants of Anglo-Saxon heritage. Not only have the Creoles been silent; they have resented having others write about them, as witness the well-known case of George Washington Cable."[13]

In fact, as she divined easily, Demarest was both Catholic and Creole. Born in New Orleans, he was on his mother's side a sixth-generation descendant of the Bouligny family, established in New Iberia in the eighteenth century. On his father's side, Demarest had New England roots. Because of his father's army career, he spent much of his childhood elsewhere, including the Philippines, and was likewise away from the city during most of his adulthood. He believed that this distance, as well as his Yankee inheritance (like Cable's), allowed him to see Creole society more clearly than those in its midst.[14]

Fabulous Ancestor is both a novel of manners and a bildungsroman. Maurice duQuesnay termed it "a brilliant account of Creole culture," in which a sense of duration and permanence is apprehended in a "textured world of ritual, legend, custom, and religion" (iii). The action takes place after passage of the Volstead Act; federal liquor laws are violated openly. The tale, told in the third person, is centered around "the house on Felicity Street" (based in fact on a respectable residence at 1225 Milan Street, where the author's grandmother lived and where he was born). The eponymous ancestor—the animating spirit of the house—is "Mamoo" or Granny; the other principal character, autobiographical, is Sonny, her ten-year-old grandson, sent from the Philippines to be brought up in New Orleans. As he discovers Creole traditions, so do readers.[15]

Mamoo was based in part on Demarest's great-grandmother, Octavie Bouligny, who with her twin sister, Septima, formed a celebrated pair of belles. The family survived the Yankee occupation but lost everything under Reconstruction. Octavie married "Jack O'Diamonds" Wood—a Yankee, in fact—and reared her granddaughter—Demarest's mother—after the girl's mother, who found Creole life too daunting, left New Orleans. Granny, "bearing on her back the antebellum past, the plantation, the whole weight of France," stands as a representative of her society and her generation, but also of an idealized and fabulous past, "le beau temps d'antan" [the good times of yesteryear], which the author calls a myth (92, 110, 169). She also stands for the entire Creole cultural inheritance, which 1920s–30s white society wishes to preserve, like the past to which old Agricola Fusilier clings in *The Grandissimes*.[16]

Demarest uses various motifs and allusions—the Breviary, the Arthurian corpus, and even Tarot cards—to organize the story and show connections between present and past. He emphasizes liturgical time, which is circular and recurring, not progressive, and the Creoles' ritualism and other traditions, as well as the figure of the southern gentleman, incarnated (rather childishly) by Uncle Bob (110). Daily at the house on Felicity Street, however, there are complaints over changes: first, those wrought by the Civil War, especially emancipation and the presence, economic power, and pernicious Protestantism of Yankees. The Creoles dislike particularly what Kane called "crass New England money-pinchers." The Creoles have nothing but disdain for "those poor heretics" the Protestants, their ostensible moral superiority, which purchases rather than gives, and their "shopkeeper's religion" (57, 96). "Why, these people treat their servants . . . with a contempt based on the mere passing of money . . . The War was nothing but a business proposition for them all the way" (98–99). New social changes after 1900 and 1918 and further decline in the Creoles' prosperity are exemplified by the peeling paint of the house. "The old Creole families haven't two picayunes they can rub together" (225).[17]

One part of their inheritance is their attachment to things French—the language, the customs—although Louisiana has not been French for more than a century. As Tante Bébé—a delightful and revealing character—observes, "All Creoles are in exile from Paris" (108). Another element is religious pride. "Going to mass is part of our Creole superiority" (190). Illustrating the peculiar strain of Catholicism in New Orleans is All Saints' Day. The picture Demarest draws should be compared with similar episodes in Marinoni's "Ma Tante Louise," Grace King's "Madrilène; Or, The Festival of the Dead," and Anne Rice's *The Feast of All Saints*. The streetcar ride to the cemetery (the "Marble Orchard"), the stroll through the grounds, Granny's and Tante Bébé's conversations about and with the dead, the festive picnic with champagne and fancy victuals—all these scenes emphasize the Creoles' connection to their past and their distinctiveness.[18]

Creole society is seen also through the eyes of Yankee visitors, who appear to delight in the local prejudice against them—interiorizing others' judgment. Without irony, the author shows how Granny takes advantage of a northern woman's prying questions to state the case for Creole antebellum social structure:

> You malign us when you believe that our servants were ever the chattels, the chained and whipped beasts, of your Mrs. Beecher Stowe's libel. They were just like members of our family and bore our names and held a tyrannical sway over the youngsters and often the older people too.... They had their privileges and idiosyncrasies. We nursed them ourselves when they were sick and frequently they were buried in the family plot when they died.
> ... As a Catholic I reject servitude in any shape or form.... I hire a cook because I have no culinary talent, but I hire her as a cook and don't expect her to double as a maid.... (87)

Granny dramatizes her own difficulties as a child of Federal occupation: "I've humbled myself in a way that your Northern servants wouldn't dream of; I've robbed garbage pails and stolen vegetables and fruit from the Army of Occupation's stores . . . And my colored servants have come with me because I wouldn't have considered sending them out to do it alone" (88). Lest readers suppose that there is no corrective to these positions, it must be observed that Sonny displays a somewhat reformed view, and, unlike Granny, never uses the term *niggras*. Moreover, a Breton priest, who serves seamen and the destitute on Rampart Street, criticizes Mamoo obliquely by suggesting that she might appreciate the hardworking people in the neighborhood "if she could forget the color of their skins" (231).

It is given to Mr. Ligurno, the immigrant Italian tailor across the street who is not received by Granny, to summarize the unhappiness of the Creoles. Noting that their lost rank and prosperity were not their fault, he acknowledges that it might be the sins of their ancestors, visited on the fifth generation (a possible authorial allusion to collective guilt over slavery). But, he adds sympathetically, "They couldn't become good Americans and work for the future because they were still living in the past—trying to find out what went wrong. Instead of blaming their ancestors, they blamed the Northerners, or Negroes, progress or politics . . ." (105–106). Thus, as Granny had observed, using a metaphor that had served Cable and others: "New Orleans has become a perpetual bal masqué or a carefully preserved museum . . ." (88). The house represents imprisonment in the past: "That old house is mighty hard to get out of," says Uncle Bob, half blaming, half regretting (191). That Uncle Bob falls in love with the daughter of the Yankees who were the family's guests and subsequently joins her father's business in Boston shows that change is not impossible—is, indeed, inevitable.

Shirley Ann Grau (born 1929) is not of Creole ancestry but was born in New Orleans and knows the city well. In her early years, she lived with her grandfather, who appreciated literature ("a Southern gentleman with Unitarian leanings") and grandmother ("a genteel Southern lady who had Calvinistic leanings"). She was educated in Montgomery, Alabama, and New Orleans, where she graduated from Ursuline Academy and Newcomb College of Tulane University. She remained in the city and married Feibleman. She is particularly sensitive to place and blood. While her most celebrated novel, *The Keepers of the House* (1964), which won a Pulitzer Prize, is clearly set in the South, she scrambled the geography. Though some locales really exist (the Honey Island Swamp and Lexington, Virginia), others are invented, and clues to their identity are unclear or contradictory. Creole elements are peripheral in this work, but it is possible that in Grau's literary imagination, what have been identified as "repressive male constructs" that marginalize women are connected to Creole attitudes.[19]

Grau wrote about Creole New Orleans in early short stories and especially *The House on Coliseum Street* (1961). The house in her fiction has been interpreted as a metaphor for the female body. While this story of Joan, a rather jejune, perhaps neurotic young woman, could have been set elsewhere, white Creole attitudes (dislike of Protestantism, family pride, and a certain moral laxity, joined to a punctilious concern for appearances and finesse in maintaining them) are illustrated throughout and play a role in the plot. Grau evokes well the setting and displays sensitivity to its particularities, especially atmospheric and weather patterns—skies, winds, trees, temperature, heat, smells, storms—and what she depicts as the eroticism of the city. She provides local color in the description of architecture, streets, cooking, and streetcars. The title house plays a role as the sign of prominence past and present: "The memory of wealth is still a kind of power in New Orleans." This complex of gentility and propriety is supported by Joan's aunt, whose summer home on the Gulf Coast is another locus of the action. When Joan rebels, it is through sexual spite, but ultimately she is rejecting caste and maternal figures, that is, the whole Creole complex of ancestry, tradition, and appearances.[20]

Questioned about the place of blacks in her fiction, Grau expressed disagreement with extreme multiculturalist positions, denying that only those who have had the direct experience of being black (or a woman, a cripple, and so on) can write about it and are authorized to do so. Such a position "would turn fiction into nothing more than autobiography. And it would completely remove from fiction its basic, essential element: imagination." She went on to quote from "The World According to Grau," by Douglas Allen-Taylor, a black commentator. He wrote that she "can probably reveal more to us about the true nature of relations between blacks and whites in America than we will learn from a hundred finger-pointing hearings by President Clinton's Advisory Board on Race . . . Grau has written some of the most accurate portrayals of African-American life ever produced in American literature." Allen-Taylor observed additionally that Grau's early works were ahead of their time in the treatment of race (she agrees), and that she was superior to Carson McCullars and Eudora Welty, ahead "even of most African-American writers" by "her insight into a cornerstone of the souls of black folk: African spirituality." She is at her best when she creates "black characters who are not caricatures"—an unusual skill among white novelists. "Grau walks around quietly in unlighted black closets, with deep respect and without breaking a thing."[21]

Various other authors active after 1950 illustrate a range of modes for treating Creole society. The fact that most are women is consistent with the feminization of much American literature in recent decades but may reflect a particular trend also, an unspoken sense that what is (white) Creole is no longer manly. If there is such a fear, the conservative John William Corrington (1932–88), a poet and fiction writer from north Louisiana, did not yield to it. Corrington, whose writing was praised by Mel Bradford, is one of the keenest observers and best writers that the state produced in the twentieth century. While his stories and novels, often set in Caddo Parish, are concerned generally with politics and law and with "country" people (outside New Orleans), he does depict Creole characters also. An early story, "If Time Were Not / A Moving Thing," portrays a Creole woman of the immediate antebellum period. "Pleadings," "Nothing Succeeds," and the long story "Every Act Whatever of Man" present Creoles from New Orleans as well as other south Louisianans.[22]

The prize-winning novelist Ernest J. Gaines (born 1933) comes from a sharecropper's family on River Lake Plantation near Oscar, Louisiana, in Pointe Coupée Parish, where, until recently, black Creole French dialect was used, though chiefly by the elderly, and four racial, cultural, and language groups met: what he calls Creoles—that is, those blacks with French ancestry, who are nevertheless relegated to inferior status because of the "one drop of blood" rule; plantation whites; other blacks, sometimes labeled mulattoes; and Cajuns, whose dealings with the Creoles are hostile. Indians constitute a fifth, peripheral group. Names in Gaines's family suggest Creole ancestry. The fact that his Creoles belong to a rural setting rather than the city does not preclude connections, since many city Creoles have roots, some of them recent, in the countryside. Gaines depicts well the effects of the race and caste system, by which Creoles serve not only as a buffer between blacks and whites—effectively keeping the former down and enhancing the prestige of the latter—but also as a permanent scapegoat in what amounts to ongoing sacrifice.[23]

What may be Gaines's best-known novel, *The Autobiography of Miss Jane Pittman* (1971), deals incidentally with Creoles (other French-surnamed characters are Cajun); its chief burden is the long odyssey out of slavery (the Civil War and its displacements are particularly well rendered) and through other trials of the black race to mid-twentieth century. There are black Creole speakers (their words rendered in English). Miss Jane consults a Creole hoodoo practitioner from New Orleans, said to be rival of Marie Laveau. Then there is a teacher, Mary Agnes Lefabre, called "high yellow." She has left New Orleans because of its awkward, inhumane racial caste system; she prefers to teach black children in the country. But the racial system of "either/or" and its strict rules have come to apply there also; whereas a hundred years before, a white man could set up his colored mistress and acknowledge her children, any union is now impossible between her and the white man who falls in love with her. He ultimately kills himself.

The less-known *Catherine Carmier* (1964), Gaines's first published novel, is more directly concerned with the four-race caste system, based on origins and skin colors. Though its genesis was difficult (he started its first draft at age sixteen) and it is less often discussed than *The Autobiography of Miss Jane Pittman*, *A Gathering of Old Men* (1983), and *A Lesson Before Dying* (1993), which won the National Book Critics Circle Award, *Catherine Carmier* is admirably executed. The noticeable resemblance to William Faulkner's narrative models, in *Absalom, Absalom!* for instance, does not detract from its worth, nor do the similarities between it and Saxon's *Children of Strangers*.[24]

The heroine is a light-skinned woman of partly Indian blood, it appears; her sister, Lillian (Lily), is even lighter. Sent to be reared in New Orleans—protection and escape from the past—Catherine finds herself between two worlds. Her dilemma cannot be resolved unless she moves to the North. The women's father, Raoul Carmier, is a proud light-skinned Creole; he and his family constitute almost a race unto themselves, and skin tone is of utmost importance to him. He killed his wife's dark-skinned son; he is opposed to Catherine's love for Jackson, an educated man with dark skin. An earlier black lover, by whom she had a child, left her—knowing, perhaps, that he would not be accepted by the father. But Raoul does not wish her to marry a white either; he resents whites. Similarly, the blacks resent Jackson's attempt to enter the light-skinned Creole society that disdains them. As for

Cajuns, they are the enemy, having taken over (with the white owners' help) vast tracts of sharecropped land formerly worked by black Creoles. But the caste lines are hard to defend, and their consequence, illustrated especially by Raoul and Lillian, is as much self-loathing as self-confidence.[25]

Gilchrist (born 1935), a native of Vicksburg, Mississippi, spent part of her childhood on her maternal grandparents' plantation. She attended Millsaps College and, later, the University of Arkansas. Her collections of short fiction *In the Land of Dreamy Dreams* and *Victory over Japan* (National Book Award) include stories set in New Orleans. The social circles and manners are those of the Garden District and other Uptown blue bloods, mostly Creole. French names appear, some current; the characters are largely Roman Catholic; they belong to the prestigious clubs and Carnival krewes that remain bastions of tradition, helping preserve the caste system. Mardi Gras is accurately depicted, with the King's Toast and the large green, purple, and gold flags displayed during Carnival season by former kings of Carnival.[26]

The intention is, apparently, to demean this society; the members are shallow, snooty, anti-Semitic, sometimes drunken, often nasty to black servants, and without redeeming qualities. The author seems to view the Creoles as essentially, not incidentally, at fault. As Margaret Bauer put it, the characters continue to support the "still extant caste system and patriarchal rule of the New Orleans aristocracy" and "do not recognize the inherent depravity of their dream world." A husband, originally from Tennessee but married to a Creole descendant, is driven to murder and suicide in part by nasty rumors about his adopted daughter and the burden of social disapproval. Or is his weakness to be interpreted as springing from his being an outsider? Gilchrist's style is mediocre, and the character studies are superficial, almost trite; the reader may conclude that the shallowness comes less from the Creoles' absence of depth than the author's failure of human imagination. Yet *In the Land of Dreamy Dreams* was critically acclaimed and, it is reported, sold more than ten thousand copies in the first ten months. Perhaps that was because New Orleans still had its exotic appeal.[27]

John Kennedy Toole (1937–69), the author of *A Confederacy of Dunces* (1981), which won a Pulitzer Prize, was born in New Orleans. "No other writer, native or otherwise," asserted Kenneth Holditch, "seems to have known the city as well nor to have been able to evoke its sights and sounds and smells as powerfully as he." Toole's mother, nee Thelma Ducoing, was of French Creole and Irish descent. One ancestor fought in the Battle of New Orleans. Thelma's childhood home was on Elysian Fields, a boundary of the Faubourg Marigny, once "an exclusive suburb for the Creole aristocracy of

New Orleans" but by the time of her childhood inhabited by Sicilian immigrants. Only a few relics of Creole society are depicted in the novel. The hero, Ignatius Reilly, is based on Bobby Byrne, a New Orleanian, apparently of Welsh heritage. When Thelma Toole and her son amused themselves by inventing dialogues, they imitated not Creoles but "low-class New Orleans types," in her words.[28]

Rice is of Irish descent but writes about Creole customs and society (black and white). Born in New Orleans in 1941, she attended Catholic schools there until the family moved to Texas. Her husband of four decades, the late Stan Rice, a visual artist and poet, was a high school classmate. They went to California; Anne ultimately got a master's degree in creative writing from San Francisco State, where Stan taught that subject. In 1989, they went back to New Orleans. In 1998 she returned to her childhood Catholicism. But two years later she announced her second departure, not from Catholicism only but from all Christianity. The move was made in the name of liberal thinking: "I refuse to be anti-gay. I refuse to be anti-feminist. . . . I refuse to be anti-Democrat." Her first novel, *Interview with the Vampire*, appeared in 1973. There and elsewhere she portrays old Creole families decadent enough to practice vampirism and witchcraft. Subsequent titles, including the words *vampire, witches, devil, damned,* and *mummy,* suggest exploitation of public credulity and ghoulishness. Wikipedia calls her one of the most widely read authors of modern times. Three motion pictures, a miniseries, and comic books have been drawn from her work. She wrote the text of a vampire musical, starring Elton John. She also composed pornography, under pseudonyms. Her vampire books may in fact be viewed as pornographic, revealing "a degree of spiritual corruption that makes hard-core pornography look like a wholesome exercise."[29]

The Feast of All Saints (1979), a 570-page novel, has no vampire element; it returns to the world of plausibility, depicting the life of the New Orleans Free People of Color in the 1840s. Excepting a few whites, the entire story is concerned with that caste. Whether Rice's interest was due to true appreciation or rather a desire to milk the topic for exotic value, thumb her nose at white New Orleans, or profit from current multicultural fashion is unclear. Her work as a whole is unquestionably based on exploitation of readers and topics. Yet issues of justice that arise suggest genuine sympathy with the Creoles of Color—women's vulnerability, enforced inferiority, and legal restrictions on both sexes.

Echoing *The Grandissimes* and using invented characters and minor historical figures, the novel explores the system of three castes, all French-speaking. She highlights restrictions on the *gens de couleur libres*—the limitations on exercising professions; the prohibition against dueling, that is, defending one's honor, in a city where *affaires d'honneur* were socially crucial; and the law against marrying whites—a ban that affected the whites also, obviously. (Unfortunately, Rice writes of *gens de couleur libre*, rather than *libres*—making the color, not the people, free.) She does not draw explicit lessons for her readers but makes it clear that losses to one group constitute losses to the entire society. She expresses the historical dilemma of the Free People of Color as that of "a dying people . . . flowers of the French and the Spanish and the African." "The Americans have put their boot in our face" (470). Their choice is to be crushed directly by the whites, or to pass into white society and thereby similarly lose self-identity.[30]

The title looks backward and forward to the term "All Saints" in others' writing. There is no major episode concerned with that holy day, however. The word *saints* suggests the sacrificial charity, even the martyrdom of certain nonwhite Creoles. There are echoes of the Saint Domingue rebellion and the martyr's death of Vincent Ogé. Sybil Kein gives credit to Rice for restoring the term *Creole* and the Creoles of Color "to that degree of dignity demonstrated in Cable's nineteenth-century work." Rice's novel may indeed have been influential because it sold widely, owing to her reputation. By 1979, however, other factors—including political and civic success of Creoles of Color and Kein's own publications—likewise had helped attract attention to their achievements.[31]

While the novel is readable and is based on considerable research, it is mediocre. Fiction that draws one hundred million readers (with elements of soft pornography and homosexual desire in the present case) is unlikely to be fine. Basic grammar, punctuation, and diction errors, sentence fragments, lack of parallelism, dangling phrases, and other improprieties mark the novel. The portrayal of the French Quarter is unimaginative, relying on clichés and terms such as *banquette* (sidewalk—a frequent Creole marker). There are echoes of Quadroon Balls and a brief scene at a slave auction; patois appears in a song; yellow fever and voodoo play a role. Certain episodes take place on a Cane River plantation belonging to Creoles of Color. The language is frequently hyperbolic, and emotions are conveyed without shading and subtlety. Though minor, a few puzzles in the exposition are annoying. Rice does, however, demonstrate basic skill in plotting and creating dramatic scenes.

The tensions among the castes are dramatized within families. Marcel Sainte-Marie is a male quadroon—a type that appears infrequently in Louisiana fiction, although there are such figures in *Uncle Tom's Cabin*. Marcel, whose mother is of Haitian origin, has blue eyes and honey-colored skin (made darker by contrast with the eyes), but his hair texture shows his mixed blood, while his sister Marie passes easily for white. Another young man, Richard, has brothers who have settled in Bordeaux and married white women; their departure has broken his grandfather's heart. A third youth, Christophe, has made a name for himself as an author in Paris. The Free People both despise and fear white rabble as well as low-class blacks. The attitudes are mutual: "The country whites are afraid of the free negro" (66). "All things African frightened him and put him off," the author remarks about Richard (143), who would not consider marrying someone with more black blood than he. One man, who would not "set foot in the shabby waterfront cabarets that served the common black man" (153), observes proudly that "this family was the Famille Lermontant" when other blacks were "packed in the convict ships landing off the coast of Georgia" (66).[32]

The father of Marcel and Marie supports them and their free mother, until the son and father quarrel violently; the father flogs the boy. Marcel's plan to go to France with his father's promised support is then dashed. The father drinks himself to death. Marie's hope to marry Richard is challenged by her mother, who wants her to take a white protector. Marie is subsequently raped by five men, led to them by her slave, Lisette, an ugly, manipulating woman (though a victim in her own way) who is in fact her half-sister (the child of their white father from a plantation slave). Marie's expectations of being well placed are thereby ruined. (The slave hangs herself.) This sort of relationship was treated briefly by Kein in "Siblings: The Mulatto Slave" (from *An American South*); the slave gets revenge and vows to rip apart the lips of her whip-wielding sister. In Rice's novel, a white man named Vincent, connected to the family, challenges three of the rapists to duels, as he may legally, and kills them (if a man of color did so, it would be murder). Marie and Richard are finally able to marry; they sail to France. Marcel, who has shown talent for photography, takes it up as a career. Vincent, who has himself fathered a child from a Creole of Color, comes to realize that keeping such a mistress is a gravely immoral choice with consequences stretching far into the future—and the more he loves the woman, the more immoral the relationship is. He can be taken to represent white guilt.

Almost Innocent (1984), the first novel by Bosworth (born 1948), a skilled literary craftsman, is an evocation of latter-day white Creole society (approximately the 1950s). Thanks to her acquaintance with New Orleans (she is a native) and her attention to detail, the novel is so faithful that it has documentary value. Nearly all the central characters are of French or Spanish Creole ancestry, and this heritage counts. Most are Roman Catholic. Allowing for some changes in circumstances, their attitudes do not differ greatly from those in Demarest's *Fabulous Ancestor* (with which *Almost Innocent* shares a comic vein as well as a powerful sense of human vulnerability and cultural loss). Details are not only generally accurate but telling. There are allusions to General Benjamin Butler and the losses that the "Creole aristocracy" sustained, especially the silver; to old furniture, the Garden District, and a house designed by James Gallier; to paintings by local masters; to Carnival season, the Pickwick Club, "rank according to skin color," and a family "long on name but short on money." (Masking for Comus recalls previous authors' use of the masked ball, even as the unmasking of one man suggests change to come.) A judge is described as "the sort of gentleman the South is crying out for right now." A devoted black cook and a manservant care for their employers and especially a motherless girl. Miscegenation, still illegal, brings shame; the encroachment on former all-white neighborhoods by people of color is called "black river"; and the appearance of an octoroon at a fashionable Mardi Gras Creole open house (a well-observed scene) causes a stir.[33]

That the characters, both white and black, labor under inherited burdens is clear. The blacks continue to work in white people's kitchens, drive, or do menial tasks. Among the whites, the adults drink too much; some are so impractical as to be indifferent to money; they think constantly of family and names; adults and children alike seem accident-prone and given to fainting and vomiting. At best, they appear vaguely culpable; often, they are plainly guilty (of white-collar crime or general snobbery and condescending attitudes toward blacks and Irish). The narrative tone is not, however, explicitly critical; traditions are not denounced, the blacks' servitude is taken as a matter of course, and the Creole descendants remain so childlike that they are "almost innocent." Clay-Lee, a child narrator, knows too much (as child narrators usually do). She reads Thomas de Quincey's *Confessions of an English Opium Eater* and Kane's book about Huey P. Long, *Louisiana Hayride*; yet she listens patiently as an old great-aunt reads aloud *Lives of the Saints for Little People*. It is Clay-Lee who, through negligence and mental anguish, is the most proximate cause of her mother's death, the sins of the fathers being visited upon the children. Unlike *Dinner at Antoine's*, the novel can be viewed as a subversion of the Creole heritage; yet a note of indulgent understanding constantly undermines the critical implications.

A somewhat similar but inferior novel, *Lives of the Saints*, by Lemann (born 1956), was first published by Knopf (1985); Walker Percy praised it.

The title, referring to brothers named "Saint," echoes the word used elsewhere concerning the old Creole, Roman Catholic society (and the hagiographic tradition). The work deserves mention not for its art and style (it is artistically mediocre and tedious) but its settings, character types, and implied judgments. There are no chapter divisions; it consists of scenes and other passages separated by spaces. This "chain of free association" reveals no "larger pattern." The time is contemporaneous; the settings are antebellum Garden District mansions, the racetrack, and other neighborhoods (though with needlessly scrambled geography); characters bear such Creole names as Legendre and Sully (the family of architects); there is a faithful butler who speaks of "the boy he raised"; mores are those of the decadent or at least idle aristocracy and its "buffoonish hedonism." A younger brother, accident-prone, falls to his death; the elder, ineffectual if charming, disappears into a French Quarter crowd.[34]

Whereas Bosworth speaks of "tragedy" in reference to the breakup of a marriage and loss of investments—not that money is the only god (far from it), but that the disorder introduced when one is without resources creates vulnerability and may lead to further disaster—Lehmann depicts a fatal weakness in an otherwise honorable character (or a family, a society). She does not concentrate on the value of tradition and what has been lost. Similarly, while Sonny and others in Demarest's *Fabulous Ancestor* who see the flaws in Creole society nevertheless recognize its value and—what is more important—know that in any well-functioning collectivity there must be *some* structure, some order (and orders), Lemann's *Lives of the Saints* does not acknowledge the value, practical or moral, in such tradition. Instead, there is almost hatred for the heritage.

This authorial attitude, symptomatic of a wider malaise concerning Creole society, also fits a change in critical attitude. Commentators can no longer be satisfied to note a writer's skill in rendering the tone, the flavor of what is left of Creole society; adversarial positions are expected on the author's part, and they reappear in reviewers' and critics' quotations and observations. What is called "codependency" among men and women, for instance—"the protagonists' concern with taking care of helpless men"—has been noted by some reviewers with a feminist bent. Critics likewise emphasize the destructiveness and nightmarish quality of Lemann's novel and others—in other words, the curse of being Creole.[35]

CHAPTER THIRTEEN

Louisiana Creole Poets of the Twentieth and Twenty-First Centuries

Dealing critically with present-day literary products is different from investigating and assessing work of earlier periods, since, obviously, the past, that is, the original context and intervening developments, can be known and understood (as well as misunderstood) in ways that the present cannot (though the inverse is true likewise). Products of the present have not yet gone through the sieve of evaluation over time. "Contemporary judgment is notoriously fickle and tends to be impassioned." The past has factual fixity. Yet, though it can no longer evolve, it is subject to expansion and correction (if new materials are unearthed) and reinterpretation. It was noted earlier that, according to Hans Robert Jauss's aesthetics of reception, the work always exists in a triangular relationship with the author (in the original context of production) and the reading public; as the public changes, the writing appears different. Similarly, M. M. Bakhtin argued that recorded utterances, while taking shape and acquiring meaning in a specific social situation, belong to a wider dialogue and continue to participate in this dialogue.[1]

Whereas not all authors previously treated have been the object of changing views—some are too obscure for that—the fact that many reprints have been issued recently and thus works have been rediscovered and reassessed establishes and demonstrates a changed context, a continuing dialogic relationship. Kate Chopin is the prime example of a nineteenth-century Louisiana author whose reception has been nearly revolutionized; additionally, numerous Creoles of Color have been brought back from obscurity, deservedly. A vertical (time) dimension is thus added to the earlier context. In the case of certain authors treated in chapter 12 and poets introduced here, there has been little time for evaluation and less for reevaluation. What appears important at the time of writing may lose its significance later in a context provided by posterior developments. In short, one cannot treat the present as one treats the past. This is true now especially because of the abundance of literary production, as yet unwinnowed. What follows here is, thus, only a tentative assessment; for that reason and the sake of convenience, the organization is not solely chronological.

For practical as well as aesthetic reasons, the nineteenth-century authors from the *gens de couleur libres* were especially drawn to poetry; this is true for their literary descendants. While prose has generally served American blacks well as a medium for writing family history, depicting struggle, and protesting the oppression of their race—as in work by Ralph Ellison and Richard Wright, for instance—poetry is just as suitable for highlighting social and racial injustice, exploring the experience of belonging to a minority ethnic group, and searching for identity and purpose. The flexibility of free verse, which is, with few exceptions, the medium of poets considered here, allows (as Langston Hughes illustrated) for a wide range of voices, tones, emotions, like fiction but with greater immediacy; contemporary free verse is particularly accessible to broad audiences. In a condensed, efficient form, narrative verse can achieve much the same ends as fiction; lyrical poetry can speak directly of the poet's feeling and in his voice; verse satire is often effective. As Patricia Smith wrote in connection with her preference for verse over prose, "I think I turn to poetry almost exclusively because it incorporates the challenge of telling a story in a small, defined space." Poetry also lends itself to public presentation before audiences who might not purchase books or read extended texts. When, after the civil rights movement, southern blacks were freer to participate in the larger literary and cultural life, while still working in their own cultural idiom, those in south Louisiana, at least, found poetry to be the most magnetizing of written expressions and the most accessible, and they have flourished. They have achieved national recognition far beyond what the nineteenth-century Creoles of Color gained, and their products are often close to the mainstream of American protest literature.[2]

Perhaps the model of jazz suggests why poetry has been so effective as a means of expression for black Creoles and certain white writers. Poems may be explicitly inspired by jazz; and the associated rituals (jazz funerals, the customs of solo passages and improvisation), as well as the music itself, with its themes and variations, can be considered as distant models. Several poets treated here have recorded music as well as words, and jazz is a recurrent motif and theme among Louisiana writers both black and white. Blues are another parallel and perhaps a source of inspiration. Jazz and blues were both connected to minstrelsy, now viewed as a disguised form of political activism—an "assertion of black nationhood and critique of the racism that perpetuated stereotypical imagery." Poetry similarly can be directed to affecting change, openly or subversively. Another source of the poetic impulse among black Creoles is the churches, the influence of which is enormous, exercised through social ties, pastoral rhetoric, and sacred music; this presence may have encouraged the development of poetry in their community, and certainly the rhetoric and singing have parallels in many poems.[3]

While poetry circles and supporting institutions—reading venues, magazines—have for the last hundred years generally been more numerous and more prestigious in New York and San Francisco, New Orleans likewise has had a lively literary scene, starting with *The Double-Dealer* (1921–26), an outstanding literary magazine. More recently, universities, both large and small, in the city and its surroundings have provided opportunities for readings as well as teaching of poetry and have supported literary magazines, such as *Louisiana Literature*, the *New Orleans Review*, and the *Xavier Review*, and associated presses. The Louisiana State University Press and the *Southern Review* (now under one administration), both nationally recognized literary institutions, often favored Louisiana authors, especially under the editorship of Lewis P. Simpson at the review.

The Free Southern Theatre, which was located in New Orleans starting in 1966, provided literary fellowship and support for black authors. (Its leader was the late Thomas C. Dent, with the assistance of poetry activist Kalamu ya Salaam.) Long-enduring poetry societies have offered encouragement to young writers as well as opportunities for seasoned authors to display their work. Among them formerly were the New Orleans Poetry Forum and First Backyard Poetry Theater, long directed by Lee Meitzen Grue (the Forum was subsequently directed by Andrea Gereighty). Another forum was NOOMO, founded by Salaam. His anthology *From a Bend in the River*, an eclectic collection, can serve as a guide to the New Orleans black poetry scene—loosely viewed, a modern counterpart of *Les Cenelles*. The *New Laurel Review*, edited by Grue since 1982, has likewise been significant. Poet Everette Maddox, from Alabama but long a local figure, served as a godfather to various poets new to the city. The Maple Leaf Bar, on Oak Street, was a major venue for presentations; Julie Kane has emphasized how important it was for her, and the Sunday afternoon readings are said to be the longest-running poetry series in America. Bookstores have afforded space for literary gatherings that bring together members of the poetry community; the Garden District Book Shop, Octavia Books, and Faulkner House Books in the French Quarter, sponsors of numerous literary events, deserve particular mention.[4]

Certain poets whose names may appear in connection with Louisiana are not treated here because they neither are of Creole heritage nor make it important in their work; or else they have not attained the stature that would warrant inclusion. A bilingual poet, Beverly Matherne (b. 1946) comes from a German family that settled around 1721 on the Côte des Allemands, and thus can be considered Creole; in fact, however, she writes in and translates from Cajun French, as some of her poems indicate by their titles or lexicon. Yusef Komunyakaa (b. 1947), a Pulitzer Prize winner, is from Bogalusa; while he had connections to poetry circles in New Orleans, evidence does not show him to be of Louisiana Creole antecedents, and his writing deals generally with other topics. Similarly, Pinkie Gordon Lane (1923–2008), often associated with Louisiana, is not of Creole heritage. Though she has been called an "unmistakably Southern writer," she was born in Philadelphia, and her first degrees were from Atlanta schools. Malaika Favorite is chiefly a visual artist, though she won the 2005 Louisiana Literature Prize for Poetry. Stella Nesanovich is partly of New Orleans Yugoslavian heritage but does not consider herself a Creole. Darrell Bourque is of Cajun ancestry, as are Jean Arceneaux (the pseudonym of Barry Jean Ancelet), Jack Bedell, John Doucet, and Beau Boudreaux. (Arceneaux's verse is in Cajun French, nonstandard.)[5]

Others not to be treated include David Middleton, the late John William Corrington, and Julie Kane, who are connected to the north of the state (although Middleton lives in Thibodaux, and Corrington and Kane spent some years in New Orleans and used it as a backdrop for poems). John Biguenet is chiefly a dramatist, essayist, and anthologist. His post-Katrina reports and exposés were widely read, but they are beyond the purview of this book, as is other prose writing on the storm. While New Orleans poet Peter Cooley, a native of Detroit, has spoken of how the characteristic light of New Orleans has inspired him, the historical and cultural background of the city has played little role in his work. After Katrina (2005), however, he composed poems on the storm, marked by immediacy of experience, and published them later in an essay called "How Hurricane Katrina Made Me into a New Orleanian." The present writer, long a resident there, has dealt often in her poetry (and prose) with what might be termed the refined legacy of New Orleans and the historical background, as in "Chrétien Point," but this is borrowed subject matter.[6]

The body of work examined here is in English, a fact that illustrates the failure of Alfred Mercier and other antiassimilationists. Additionally, one finds occasional black Creole and French elements, especially in the writing of Sybil Kein and Brenda Marie Osbey. These authors, albeit Anglophone, can be considered heirs of earlier writers who were determined to defend and illustrate their cultural inheritance. They display a wide range of voices—those of others or the poet's own, whether explicit, tacit, or ventriloquized.

A figure from the Beat generation, Bob Kaufman (1925–86), born in the Seventh Ward of New Orleans, is too important to be omitted from this survey despite his having cut many ties to his Creole background. His work was well known in the past and remains so not only in America but in France. One commentator compared his "Golden Sardine" to Victor Hugo's powerful poem "Ce que dit la Bouche d'ombre." His writing must have inspired other Creoles of Color. In 1984 Mona Lisa Saloy met him in San Francisco and he attended readings of hers; their work differs considerably, however.[7]

Erroneous biographical claims about him were, apparently, self-initiated—a choice that suggests denial of his true background. Both his parents were from the black community of the city. An ancestor (grandfather or great-grandfather) was probably Jewish. His father was a Pullman porter on the New Orleans–Chicago route. Contrary to the claim, his mother was not from Martinique. The poet's claim that a grandmother practiced voodoo may have been intended to highlight African connections. The mother was keen on literature, though the claim that she had the works of Proust along with those of James and Dickens is surprising. Kaufman, said to be fluent in Creole patois, left the city at age eighteen to join the Merchant Marine, in which he served for a score of years; he was active in its left-leaning union and had strong Popular Front–Marxist sympathies. After his service at sea, he met (by chance, it is said) Jack Kerouac in Los Angeles; the two went to San Francisco, where they joined Allen Ginsburg, Gregory Corso, and others in developing a new aesthetics. He lived marginally in North Beach and was imprisoned on occasion (see his "Jail Poems" in *Solitudes Crowded with Loneliness*). Herb Caen may have coined the word "beatnik" for Kaufman; it is claimed also that the poet invented it. Some have called him the best poet of the group and the American Rimbaud. He left San Francisco for New York in 1960 and may have studied briefly at the New School. He returned to the San Francisco area in 1963 and, having taken a vow of silence, neither spoke nor wrote for ten years. He was married twice and had two children.[8]

His choice not to return to the South after his time at sea is understandable, given his age: the civil rights legislation of the 1960s had not yet changed laws and practices (if not attitudes). The literary community among the Creoles of Color was fledgling, and segregation would have made it impossible for him to join white literary circles. It is thus not clear that he knew "what it means / To miss New Orleans." Although he mentions Louisiana, bayous, and Creoles occasionally, the major influences on his writing are not connected to the city; jazz composers and performers who apparently inspired him were not Dixieland greats but Charlie Parker, Charlie Byrd, Miles Davis, and Dizzy Gillespie.

Kaufman's writing is resolutely irrational. French surrealism influenced him—most of the major figures were Communist sympathizers—and he doubtless relied also on drugs. He found his material largely in American popular culture as a whole, particularly in California, but he drew also on a vast and miscellaneous fund of figures and motifs from around the world, including Africa. Federico García Lorca and Hart Crane are iconic figures. Kaufman used either prose or free verse, ranging widely in its vocabulary and focus, often dispersed across the page, with typographical markings such as capitals and boldface. Some poems consist of enumerations, without finite verbs but on occasion divided by slashes; the effect is incantatory.

> New York altar city / black tears / secret disciples
> Hammer horn pounding soul marks on unswinging gates
> Culture gods / mob sounds / visions of spikes
> Panic excursions to tribal Jazz wombs and transfusions
> Heroin nights of birth / and soaring / over bobby new ground

He favored improvisational or extemporaneous poetry, mixing in street talk and jazz; bebop was an influence also. He uses terms from the cinema as well as from music. Though not without moments of tenderness in soft tones, his work is more often violent in its imprecations. Loathing and contempt for America—not just the South—and the American experience, as he saw it, is omnipresent, as in his evocation of Caryl Chessman, arrested on multiple counts of rape and kidnapping as well as other crimes and put to death after twelve years on death row. Kaufman treats him as a suffering figure among the "universities of death."[9]

Dent (1932–98), grew up on South Rampart Street. His father was a longtime president of Dillard University. From 1959 until 1965 he lived in New York and was a member of the Umbra Workshop, connected to the Black Arts Movement, a consciousness-raising endeavor. He is known for his leadership in the Free Southern Theater and BLKARTSOUTH and for inspiring other black writers; Quo Vadis Gex-Breaux praised his role as a mentor. For some while he was executive director of the New Orleans Jazz and Heritage Foundation. In addition to a play (*Ritual Murder*, 1978) and documentary volumes, he published two collections of poetry, *Magnolia Street* (1976) and *Blue Lights and River Songs* (1982), which has strong connections to the world of jazz.[10]

Modeled perhaps on Hughes's writing, Dent's poetic practice is very free—not formless, since it is in verse lines, not prose, but without rhyme and much discernable or developed rhythm. He writes, for instance, without punctuation or capitalization:

> & soon all along this winding
> road
> plantations thrive
> . . . .
> the boats slipping up and down this
> muddy snake

As the late Donald Stanford observed,"Powerful yet sensitive rhythm is the heartbeat of good poetry. Without rhythm the poem is dead."[11]

The best-known Louisiana Black Creole writer currently active is Osbey, who was state poet laureate (2005–2007). She was born in New Orleans in 1957, the daughter of Lawrence Osbey, a boxer (whom she calls "Red Man"), and Lois Emelda Hamilton. Her neighborhood was Pailet-land, in the Seventh Ward. She grew up in Faubourg Tremé, with which she identifies strongly and whose older character she celebrates. Faubourg Marigny also figures in her work. She received a B.A. from Dillard University in New Orleans (1978) and an M.A. from the University of Kentucky (1986), where she studied with Charles Rowell, the editor of *Callaloo*. (A poem of hers is entitled "For Charles H. Rowell, on the Death of His Father.") She attended also the Université Paul Valéry in Montpellier (France). She thus belonged briefly to the Creole diaspora. Further personal information is scarce, but it is known that she has been associated with James B. Borders IV (a former actor with the Free Southern Theater and briefly connected to the Contemporary Arts Center in New Orleans), to whom she has dedicated poems and to whom her most recent volume, *History and Other Poems*, is dedicated in terms that echo her poetic diction. She has received numerous awards from various entities, including the Associated Writing Programs (1984), National Endowment for the Arts (1990), and the Louisiana Division of the Arts. She has been a fellow at the Bunting Institute of Radcliffe College and the MacDowell Colony, and has taught or been writer-in-residence at Dillard University (French and English), the University of California at Los Angeles, Loyola University, Tulane University, Louisiana State University, and elsewhere. In 2012 she was appointed Distinguished Visiting Professor of Africana Studies at Brown University. She excels at reading aloud her poems, well suited to oral presentation, especially lengthy and dramatic ones. The present author has witnessed her impressive performances in New Orleans, Baton Rouge, and elsewhere. Osbey is also a strong prose writer.[12]

Her first collection, *Ceremony for Minneconjoux*, assembled with Rowell's help, appeared under the Calaloo imprint (1983). *In These Houses* (1988) and *Desperate Circumstance, Dangerous Woman* (1991)—a single long narrative—followed. The former is dedicated to her mother, "in whose house my bones were cast and called by name." (Bones are an important motif in her verse.) *All Saints: New and Selected Poems* (1997) received an American Book Award. Her stature is not yet that of such high-profile African American women writers as Toni Morrison, Rita Dove, and Ntozake Shange (Paulette Williams), but by her interests and commitments she belongs in their company.[13]

Like Kaufman's, Osbey's importance is cultural. She is a poet of communities; she is a voice, or, better, many voices. The felt presence of the past is a major strength, perhaps the essence, of her writing. Repeatedly, she invokes her Creole ancestors and their context. "The place that I write about is a New Orleans that has not existed during any of my childhood except for vestiges of it." "I'm always writing about New Orleans; it's the true spiritual core of everything that I do . . . New Orleans is a place that gets its identity from its mixture. . . ." The glue of the mixture for her is a Creolism or *créolité* that is black in spirit, connected ultimately to Africa. Later writing suggests how important African languages, traditions, peoples are to her. She indicated that she wished not a Christian burial but one based on African traditions. In addition to local historical and social matters, she likewise addresses the sort of existential questions asked since the Greeks. Why is one born here and now? Why is she born black, and a woman?[14]

Osbey is not concerned primarily with aesthetic values of style and beauty or, like Kaufman, determined to challenge and overturn them. Like his, however, her medium is very free verse, often of short lines with little rationality in line breaks and other arrangements. Punctuation and capitalization, including the capital on the first-person singular pronoun, are generally eliminated, though some titles are in all capitals and others written normally; the spelling is standard, in contrast to Shange's texts. (The disconcerting lower-case *i* might be viewed as an attempt to minimize the subject—the self-conscious, rational self of European tradition—were it not for the presence of strong individual figures and voices.) There is no steady meter, and an occasional rhyme seems coincidental, though assonance is clearly deliberate. Almost no line, no image is memorable by itself. The texts rely on imprecise evocation and indirection—allusion, vague suggestion—which play the role in Osbey's verse that formal requirements, which may create aesthetic distancing, play in the work of traditional poets. Narrative dimensions are often vague; story lines are difficult to follow. Apostrophes to past figures are common; a speaker may call upon gods, or recount experiences of the past. As in Kaufman's writing, frequent repetitions create an incantatory quality. Creole terms and unusual words—some identified as African—are sprinkled liberally (glossaries in some volumes are useful). Much of the writing is dark; one could call it *poésie noire*. A strength of the work—as in that of many other Louisiana authors—is identification, or osmosis, between the poetic voice and place. "the geography I am learning / has me place myself / at simultaneous points / of celebration."[15]

Ceremony for Minneconjoux presents vignettes of African American women's lives, "the old ones / the mothers and grandmothers / wearing silk scarves / and hooped earrings" (83). Minneconjoux appears to be the offspring of a Choctaw Indian on Bayou Lafourche (spelled, reflecting local pronunciation, "lafouche") and a black girl, whose mother has sold or given her away. The ceremony is, presumably, that of "child-having" (21). Minneconjoux later lives with her grandmother in New Orleans, where the Mardi Gras Indians remind her of the past. She is, perhaps, interned in Charity Hospital, or Jackson (a state insane asylum); she then returns to the bayou to look for her parents. Back on St. Claude Avenue in New Orleans, she watches the Indians at Carnival time. The poems are frequently well-grounded in recognizable details; elsewhere they are almost visionary, even eerie and a bit mad. Hoodoo—the body of African American folk magic—is featured, along with numerous additional suggestions of spiritualism. "my voice is an okono drum / for sacred rituals" (48). The first-person singular prevails, to be identified variously with the narrating poet or a feminine figure.[16]

Certain pages clearly reflect the earlier black Creole experience and black neighborhoods—for instance, in evocations of slave memories and "madhouses." (The house motif returns powerfully in the next collection.) Other pages could, if separated from their context, be mistaken for women's writing by or on unhappy women of late nineteenth-century Vienna, the Victorian age, or mid-twentieth-century America. The sexual constrictions are not identical, but a strong bass note of hysteria (with suggestions of imprisonment) is reminiscent of earlier women's writing, and sexual possession appears as violation, even a form of slavery. Other manifestations of violence are frequent: murders (perhaps fantasy killings), suicide. Whether Osbey wishes the poems to be relevant to women's experiences generally, or whether she is an essentialist, believing in the uniqueness of the black female situation, is unclear. In any case, poetry is for her a defense mechanism as well as an attack, implicit or explicit, on men and whites. "do you think / i have spent all this time / sheltering myself / building this outer hull / only to be drawn in / like the rest of them?" (76).[17]

In These Houses (1988) was compiled in part from poems not selected for the first book. It is similarly focused on women, some insane or nearly so, and on violence. Men also appear, such as "Diamond," who hangs himself from love of a woman, and those unnamed who "get lost / in a house such as this" (3). One "Thelma Picou" resolves to kill the man who drove her mad; "Little Eugenia's Lover" ends up in the Jackson asylum after having killed her. In "augustine," Osbey evokes a legend according to which a woman used a meat cleaver to cut out her lover's heart; the blood stained the fireplace. The eponymous augustine, not quite right in her mind, tries to wash away the stain, then takes rat poison. Elsewhere, blues are a motif, as in "How I Became the Blues"; singing is emphasized, the song standing perhaps for a personal essence: "if you give them your song . . . / you pass on your soul" (36). In "The Old Women on Bourbon Street," one of the best poems by reason of its focus and tone, Osbey writes: "some of them i have seen / braiding songs into their hair . . . / their songs have an air / of learned resignation" (39); elsewhere the singing is the sign and last act of dying. The collection ends with the image of a house, in this case an *interior* one, carried inside, which nothing can tear down—akin to the house of poetry, of dreams, as described by Gaston Bachelard.[18]

The "saints" of *All Saints* in 1997 include "Hoodoo saints and their little Catholic cousins"—and canonic saints are mentioned ("Invocation"); but it appears that Osbey had in mind chiefly the women of her community. The title underlines also the deification of musicians and other figures. Among them are San Martín de Porres, a mulatto saint from Lima, and his sister, Sor Juana, whose lives seem in part expiatory. The tone is often elegiac; many poems feature dead figures, including Luís Congo, a Louisiana free black man employed in 1726 as executioner of escaping slaves, and Juan San Malo, the rebel leader of a maroon colony. Anger is felt throughout, though to whom or at what it is directed may be unclear. The lines tend to be longer than in earlier collections—though short lines still are found—and the poems are lengthier (some multipart) and more developed, while still dependent largely upon allusions, many obscure. Names as well as motifs from earlier volumes—houses, a factory, a "chamy" (chamois) bag, singing—reappear, as if in homage to a major theme: "memory is everything," that is, "cultural memory" (23, 63). Blues are a frequent motif: "this year / I interrogate the blues," says one speaker (63). The autobiographical element seems considerable, in "The Evening News," for instance, in which Osbey writes of her expatriate years.[19]

Osbey's most recent collection, *History and Other Poems*, consists of six moderately long sequences of free-verse poems. Formal and rhetorical features of her previous writing reappear, some seeming arbitrary, others carrying expressive weight. Among these features are absence of standard capitalization and punctuation, very short lines and some unconventional spacing, many enumerations without verbs (which substitute for discursive phrasing that might be more searching), words and names borrowed from other languages (French, Portuguese, Spanish, Creole, African, and West Indian tongues), and notes, with a glossary of terms. Many voices are heard: those of present-day heirs of the historically oppressed, imagined black and West Indian figures of the past, white traders, and fort-builders. The general tone swings between anger and lamentation.[20]

The burden of the collection—suffering, resentment, and culture as a life raft—is similar to that of earlier books but more explicitly and methodically so, with much less attention paid to New Orleans and its background and more to the history of black oppression as practiced from the fifteenth century onward. The premises on which the slave trade was based are challenged on nearly every page; the very notion of civilization, in the name of which colonies were established and developed, is undercut by Osbey's rhetoric, which stresses the hypocrisy of the colonizers as well as their cruelty and exploitation of the colonized. Sexual violation, emphasized, stands for rape of land and resources. France, with its Antillean and African territories, is singled out for blame, tagged by phrases such as "le monde créole." Even farther back, the entire European enterprise of exploring and developing the New World (as represented by Columbus and others) is condemned; "development" consists of ethnic abuse by extermination and enslavement. Attempts by anthropologists and historians to explain, if not justify, the past on grounds of human progress are nothing but lies, to which, implicitly, the truth value of legend and myth is contrasted. The historical spectacle inhabits and poisons the present, as the opening poem (which may refer obliquely to Hurricane Katrina), shows: "the city, the life / that slavery built, / tales altogether invented / . . . but we are sick of tales and of historians / sick of indigo, tobacco, rice and rum / . . . and can only wish hard-hard-hard / that the lakes, the bayous, swamps large and small / will have swallowed it all." The poet concludes that "there's always the chance" of a hurricane.

Born in 1950, Saloy, another poet of traditions and community, grew up in the Seventh Ward; she has lived on the same property nearly all her life. The house, destroyed by Hurricane Katrina, is being rebuilt as of 2013. She identifies with the neighborhood and the church of St. Raymond and St. Leo the Great, a historic parish. She is the descendant of Creoles on her father's side. He was light-skinned; she describes him as "high yellow," with blue eyes—not rare in New Orleans; he spoke some French and Creole (he was reared partly by his Uncle Henri, a Creole). She writes that her father would wake up saying, "Ahhhhhhhhhhh! Ya ya. Me Di parlé mais ça, d'ici là mon ya" [This day is good. My God tells me He is with us from now on]. He agreed sometimes to "functional passing"—acting as white in order to feed the family. He was once a preacher. Her mother was "dark chocolate." Her maternal grandfather, Frank Fitch, was born into slavery. She often mentions her elder sister. She was named for the famous figure in the Louvre; her father, who at the time hoped to have one more child, saw the portrait in the museum when he was in Paris with the liberation army. Saloy was married briefly as a young woman.[21]

Saloy took a B.A. at the University of Washington and also spent the post-Katrina year 2005–2006 there as a visiting professor. She has an M.A. in literature and writing from San Francisco State University; in 1984 she was poet-in-residence at the African American Historical & Cultural Society there. She returned, however, to Louisiana, and in 2005, just before Katrina hit, received a Ph.D. from Louisiana State University, with a dissertation on Kaufman. She presently teaches at Dillard University and considers herself a folklorist as well as poet and essayist. Her publications include literary history and studies of children's games under slavery. Her poetry collection *Red Beans and Ricely Yours* (2005) won the T. S. Eliot Prize. The title phrase is a common saying among Creoles of Color; her grandmother used it. It was popularized by Louis Armstrong but not invented by him. Saloy also won the PEN/Oakland Josephine Miles Award in Poetry in 2006. As of this writing (2013), she has completed a post-Katrina collection called "Second Lines: Handling Disasters & Hurricanes with Heart."[22]

Voices are important for Saloy, as for most poets treated here. In San Francisco, she was struck by Kaufman's raspy, booming voice. "His work spoke New Orleans to me," though it was different. She has stated that she wants to hear, and make heard, her own voice and that of her Seventh Ward community. Music and its rhythm and joyfulness, as New Orleans people have it—joie de vivre—inform her writing. Similarly, the pleasures of food and of beauty in the city have contributed to what she is. She points out that the Creole skilled craftsmen who worked in building trades from the eighteenth century on "knew how to make things beautiful." The New Orleans way of life is genuine, "though at some point it became a caricature [of] a tourist culture. They don't really understand the culture..."[23]

Saloy has read her verse in numerous settings and has published widely in anthologies and magazines. Her writing is friendlier in tone and more accessible, that is, less dependent upon obscure allusions, than Osbey's. She uses only free verse. As "Word Works" puts it, "I'm about how words / work up a gumbo of culture, / stamped and certified African, / delivered on southern American soil" (3).

Her collection is packed with local color and vignettes of New Orleans, mostly from the black neighborhoods but not exclusively. "This, my birthright / gives a sense of place . . . / The region gives you toast or beignets with jam. / The R&B, blues, jazz, and reggae rhythms spice / Saturday-night suppers / and street parades . . ." (3). The judge for the T. S. Eliot Prize, Ishmael Reed, noted that she "captures the street idioms and culture of New Orleans that challenge the tourist misconceptions about that fabulous city. She also succeeds where many performance poets fail. These poems are music to the ear . . ." (cover comment). Another endorser commented that "her poems are as richly evocative as the taste of homemade gumbo and the sound of a second line band." Dave Smith wrote: "The language is lively, the life is palpable, the observing eye is accurate and selective in distinctive ways, and the heart here is both true to the self and honest in its presentation."

Not to be overlooked is "The 'N' Word," which appeared in a brochure, a periodical, an anthology, and then *Red Beans and Ricely Yours*. This free-verse disquisition concerning and using the injurious appellation could fit, of course, into many social and geographic contexts, but Saloy puts it in a Creole setting, which emphasizes the skin color yellow. The burden of the poem is to reclaim the pejorative term as a genuinely popular and therefore legitimate word with a wide range of applications. As Clarence Major wrote, when the word is used by black people among themselves, it is "a racial term with undertones of warmth and good will—reflecting . . . a tragicomic sensibility that is aware of black history." When Saloy read the poem at the Lakeside School in Seattle, she was criticized for reading the offending text and having printed it. It was banned in Virginia after a high school teacher used it. But an anthology in which it was included appeared at the University of Virginia Press.[24]

Contemporary elements of popular culture in *Red Beans and Ricely Yours* include foodstuffs, made iconic in the title; chicory coffee and local alcoholic drinks; second-line parades; music types and beats, including gospel; Creole musicians such as King Floyd, Allen Toussaint, and Irma Thomas; shotgun houses and other neighborhood features; Jim Crow laws and "passing"; Mardi Gras and other celebrations; Catholic schools. Nineteenth-century motifs include voodoo (that is, hoodoo) as practiced by Marie Laveau. These numerous motifs may suggest that Saloy forces into her lines as many references as possible; a glossary of terms underlines the exoticism of her discourse. In fact, however, the allusions seem neither too numerous nor forced; they reflect the way she lived and the traditions around her, and their abundance proclaims a rich heritage and a vibrant present as well as the verbal facility and expansiveness of Louisianans.[25]

An extract from "Roots, 200 Years, Louisiana Purchase" in her "Shotgun Life" series is illustrative.

> It was 1803, New Orleans, world port,
> . . . .
> Third largest U.S. city, best land deal
> for four cents an acre, American,
> but France plus Spain, Latin roots now Creole
> when baked African spice spills in Vieux Carré
> Faubourgs, below Canal, downtown music,
> shotgun homes, brick walkways, lamb's ear gardens . . . (30)

Lines from "Louisiana Log" invite comparisons with Walt Whitman's for their accumulations of details. The alliterations and rich diction are striking.

> Land of Creoles, Cajuns, Black Indians, *cawains*, mudbugs, catfish,
>   and bayou crooners
> . . . .
> Land of Black-faced Zulus, Louis Armstrong, river dragons, and
>   griots, grits, and gris-gris with loup-garou sunsets
> . . . .
> The U.S. precinct of Mardi Gras and street parades with great
>   flambeaux and marching bands . . .
> . . . .
> Meridian of courbouillon and hush puppies, gumbo and deathless
>   days, everyday hallelujahs, crayfish bisque, praying in tongues,
>   novenas and graveyard gifts of lilies . . . and *bamboula*. (17)[26]

Consuela Marie Provost, née Moore, writes under the pen name Sybil Kein (which she construes as "not a prophet," based on German *kein* "no, none"). Born in 1939 in the Seventh Ward, she has a partly Creole, partly Acadian family background. She spoke Creole as a child. Her great-grandfather Jean Boudreaux was a Cajun landowner; his branch of the Boudreaux family was in Pointe Coupée Parish. A musician (singer and violinist) as well as a poet and dramatist, she received a bachelor's degree in music from Xavier University, a master's from the University of New Orleans, and a Ph.D. at the University of Michigan, where she studied under Robert Hayden. Long a member of the diaspora, she taught at the University of Michigan at Flint from 1972 until 2000. She returned to New Orleans and then, after Katrina, settled in Natchitoches. She is the author of *Gombo People: Poésie créole de la Nouvelle Orléans/New Orleans Creole Poetry* (1981; revised and enlarged in 1999 as *Gumbo People*), *Delta Dancer: New and Selected Poems* (1984), *Des gardénias et des roses* (1986), and *An American South* (1996). It was noted earlier that she also writes in gombo, or Creole French patois. Free verse is the norm, but some poems are formal. She has made recordings of folk songs in five languages (French, Spanish, English, Haitian Creole, Louisiana black Creole). Her brother Charles Moore has joined her in recorded performances of her poetry. When the levees broke in the aftermath of Katrina, her collection of hundreds of Creole songs was flooded.[27]

An American South begins with historical poems, with a focus on the black Creole experience but others' also, such as "Père Duveny Ruminates Among the Natchez." Subsequent poems are set either in the past (such as "Fiddler's Song: After a Flogging") or the present. Kein is a more self-conscious historian than Osbey, providing historically accurate portraits of antebellum black and Creole figures and differentiating between Cajuns and Creoles. Like Saloy, she pays homage, in "Legacy," to her father. The violence and cruelty that marked slavery are presented by discreet allusions and rapid sketches; vignettes such as "Spells" evoke the particular mores of the Free Blacks and other groups. "On Watching Zelime Being Sold" is a moving scene at an 1804 slave auction. "Apartheid," the opening section of "The Diaspora and the Revolution," notes that "blue eyes" will allow a person of color to "pass"; the passing theme appears also in "L'Enfant perdue." Though many figures are anonymous, others are recognizable: John McDonogh, a New Orleans philanthropist, and his Creole mistress; the Colored warriors of the Battle of New Orleans; Lafcadio Hearn (to whom an erotic dream of love with a quadroon is attributed).

The opening piece, "1724," celebrates the marriage that year of Jean-Baptiste Raphaël and Marie Gaspard. "Zalli" concerns the Creole woman known as "Madame Jean" (or John) and her inheritance, which kept her from poverty and allowed her daughter to live similarly, through "careful caring." "Thibodaux" commemorates the massacre of striking cane workers (mostly black and Creole) in 1887; the incident is called the second-bloodiest labor dispute in U.S. history. "From the French Market" treats the theme of class inequality: "Madame" buys pralines, flowers, or *calas* (rice cakes) from a slave "Mammy" vendor—the sort caricatured in dolls—without reflecting that each sale brings the woman closer to buying her freedom. "La Chaudrière pélé la grègue" ("The Pot Calls the Coffeepot") is a light lyric concerning Louisiana culture and the "melting pot." "But my friend, do not throw away the spice / Because it is too light or too dark. / If you do that you will not have Gombo / ever again . . ."[28]

Arthur Pfister, also known as "Professor Arturo," a native New Orleanian born in 1949, grew up in the Sixth Ward (a narrow strip comprising portions of the French Quarter and Tremé). He attended St. Peter Claver and, for a while, St. Augustine High School. He speaks with admiration of his "great father" and praises his mother. He went to Johns Hopkins for a master's degree in creative writing and then took a B. A. from the State University of New York, New Paltz. He returned to New Orleans in 1988, was active in the poetry scene, and taught in various programs. A Katrina refugee, part of "a new diaspora of displaced souls," he is on the faculty of Norwalk Community College in Connecticut. His work, somewhat Whitmanesque and influenced obviously by the Beat and Black Arts movements, illustrates the close connections between poetry and jazz (Duke Ellington, Charlie Parker, Miles Davis appear, but also Louis Armstrong, Aaron Neville, and the Marsalis family). It shows as well connections to homiletics as practiced in African American churches, featuring repetition and echoes, as in "Poem for Our Fathers." "I am a poet of the people." Pfister cites Amiri Baraka (LeRoi Jones) as a major influence.[29]

Pfister has a remarkable verbal gift and stands out in performance, reading rhythmically in a soft, mellow voice, deep on occasion, "preaching," "celebrating," accompanied by a percussion beat. His poems, which he calls incantations and even improvisations, are dependent upon ephemera. They move fast, with little punctuation, informal language (pronounced, when he reads, in the local fashion), even phonetically spelled distorted words (such as "chirrens"), but the presence of end-rhyme gives some structure and pacing to the free verse, as in "Stagolee and Billy." He celebrates family, his native city and its neighborhoods ("Pilette land" or Pallet or Pailet Land among them), food, picturesque figures (Marie Laveau, Satchmo, "The Special Man," a staple in local furniture advertisements), and features of local speech. Humor is a major vein; he rivals John Kennedy Toole in that respect. He occasionally writes in Spanish. In some poems he uses imaginative spatial arrangements and varied typography; they suggest the tonal variations introduced vocally at readings. "Whipped," a sequence (presumably autobiographical), marked by New Orleans colloquialisms and using the "N-word," is centered on love and its unsmooth course. Anger and resentment against intolerance and the sufferings of his people are visible also. Jim Crow and other markers of racial divides (including skin colors) are numerous; soldiers are honored but war deplored; there is a homage to Martin Luther King, Jr.

Sheryl St. Germain, born 1954, is descended from French Creoles (who arrived in the eighteenth century) and Acadians, with a few additional European ancestors. Whereas she does not feel closely connected to the Cajuns, she describes herself as "strongly connected to what I understand to be the fundamental sense of Creole in New Orleans." She was born there and grew up (in a loving but trouble-ridden family) in Kenner, a suburb. Her father's first language was French. She graduated from Southeastern Louisiana State University, and took two graduate degrees at the University of Texas at Dallas. She has spent time in Paris (where she studied at the Sorbonne for a year) and southern France; both are occasionally reflected in her poems. She was married briefly, then divorced, when she resided in Texas in the mid-eighties and has one son from that marriage; she subsequently traveled in Latin America. She later wed a Dutchman. Her teaching career has taken her to campuses in Lafayette (Louisiana), Iowa, and Pittsburgh, where she is professor at Chatham University and currently directs the MFA program in creative writing. She has won National Endowment for the Arts and NEH fellowships and additional prizes and awards. She has translated poems from the Cajun French. Her publications include several collections of verse and two volumes of personal, often poignant essays, *Swamp Songs* and *Navigating Disaster*.[30]

Like her contemporaries, St. Germain favors free verse, unrhymed and loosely structured, sometimes with erratic syntax and punctuation and lines of varying length. Erotic scenes and motifs are frequent. As in earlier Louisiana writing, eroticism is connected to the climate; its major role here reflects also changed standards in literary propriety. Foods (especially seafood), fishing, trees, and skies of the Crescent City, along with family dramas, are major motifs and themes. The Day of the Dead (All Saints' Day) makes an appearance. The effects of personal and family dramas (including alcoholism and drug addiction) occupy somewhat the place that racial dramas occupy in the writings of Creoles of Color, leaving scars (a motif) but begging to be expressed for cathartic purposes. ("A poem is a scar, not the wound / itself but the knowledge of the wound, the flag / of the wound . . .")[31]

St. Germain's essays provide poetic insights in a different mode and thus parallel her poetry well. In both genres she speaks of water—the Mississippi and other rivers, Lake Pontchartrain, swamps, destructive flooding, drownings, storms. "Eye of the Storm," concerning Hurricane Betsy (1965) in *Swamp Songs*, is a touching rendition of the event as experienced by a child. She connects water explicitly to woman's embodiment, and thus the watery features of New Orleans assume an erotic value as well as a deadly one.[32]

Katherine Soniat, who was born in New Orleans and attended Tulane University, has old Louisiana roots. She has taught poetry at Virginia State and elsewhere, and is presently at the University of North Carolina at Asheville; she is thus another exile from Louisiana. Her verse has won numerous awards. While certain collections are unrelated to Creole matters, in *Alluvial* (2001) she writes of New Orleans riverine life, weather, flowers, greenery, the cemetery "ovens." She also depicts curious characters and stresses the low elevation of the city. The title poem evokes briefly levees, battures, and oil refineries. In "Toppled Columns, Blue Sky and Sea," which has historical and mythic connections, she depicts Decatur Street, in the French Quarter, an old sign advertising the Acropolis Bar, and the Greek sailors who roam about, talking to women. "Our Lady of the Acropolis" stands for Eros, connected to the sea, an "Aegean sky," and thus the past (even Plato is mentioned, doubtless for contrast). The city's decadent side is evoked by the mention of ruins. "The House on Royal Street" portrays Madame Lalaurie and her murderous treatment of slaves; "Gens de Couleur Libres" depicts movingly men and women from the Free People of Color and their unique destinies.[33]

Born in Plaquemine, Louisiana, Grue has lived in New Orleans since the age of fourteen. As a young woman, she resided in the French Quarter; her residence for decades thereafter has been a West Indian–style house in the Bywater, farther downriver. She married a riverboat captain and reared children. Through her publishing and leadership she has fostered poetry in the city and has encouraged numerous young poets. From the 1960s on she became acquainted and worked with jazz musicians, mostly Creoles of Color. Like Pfister, she often reads to the accompaniment of jazz. Her poems, in free verse, are informal and conversational.

Downtown (2011), dedicated to the people of New Orleans who suffered (during Katrina), especially in the Ninth Ward, illustrates her interest in urban New Orleans and the Creole heritage. The book is divided into parts that, like the title, bear neighborhood designations: "Tremé," "Way Downtown," "Bywater," and so forth. The "downtown" orientation emphasizes Creoles of Color, contrasted to Uptown descendants of white Creoles. St. Louis Cathedral, streets, shops, contemporary and historical characters, musicians (Walter "Wolfman" Washington, Kermit Ruffin, Ernie K Doe, Fats Domino) all lend their presence to the dynamic scene. The first lines of "In the House of Marie Laveau the Palmist Reads Her Own Hand" illustrate Grue's manner:

sees the lifeline is deep but not long.

Here, in the back room
with the green lamp shade,
the reader sits alone, lays out the tarot,
writes in a yellow book. Expectancy
is the center of the room.

For a price, advice.[34]

The television documentary producer Danella P. Hero deserves brief mention. She is a native New Orleanian, from old Louisiana roots, one ancestor having immigrated from Bordeaux as a wine merchant, another having marched with Gálvez against the British. Her free-verse poem "now are we intruders?" is a direct but tasteful evocation of cultural blending, which she sees as rich. She depicts Uptown New Orleans and St. Charles Avenue as they had been (largely white) and as they became during her adulthood, that is, mixed. Not only that; in another variety of paradigm shift, her grown children have adopted and valorized black traditions, such as stuffed mirlitons and black music. "The things that bring them home . . . / are Black."[35]

The authors treated in this study, whether minor or major, from the eighteenth century until the present, all contributed to the literary culture of the Louisiana Creole community and sometimes the nation. Thereby they upheld, albeit in various ways, even antithetical or hostile in some cases, Western civilization—two of its illustrious literary languages, many of its aesthetic values, and its moral concerns. Dozens of other writers whose creative work belongs to this corpus but, for reasons of substance or practicality, are not treated here extended and enriched the work of their fellows. Louisiana Creole literature stands apart from the French and American traditions and yet has enriched them uniquely. Witnesses to a time and a place (or more than one), and to a cultural inheritance, these authors, whether Creoles themselves or simply concerned with the Creole heritage and its recent avatars, deserve attention and commendation for their literary energies, insights, critical positions, craftsmanship, stylistic achievements—in sum, for the dynamic body of writing that they created. May this tradition not be neglected.

NOTES

PREFACE

1. Bennett H. Wall, ed., *Louisiana: A History* (Arlington Heights, IL: Forum Press, 1984), vii; Barthes, *Le Plaisir du texte* (Paris: Editions du Seuil, 1973), trans. by Richard Miller as *The Pleasure of the Text* (New York: Hill and Wang, 1975).

2. Weaver, *Ideas Have Consequences* (Chicago: University of Chicago Press, 1964), 67.

3. Fruman, quoted by David J. Rothman, "Rescuing Literature," *Academic Questions*, 24, 1 (Spring 2011), 116; Eagleton, "Moll's Footwear," *London Review of Books*, 33, 21 (3 November 2011), 24; Jullien, *Richard Wagner*, trans. Florence Percival Hall (Neptune, NJ.: Paganiniana Publications, c. 1981), xxviii; Arturo Arias, *Taking Their Word* (Minneapolis: University of Minnesota Press, 2007), 86, 106; Debra L. Anderson, *Decolonizing the Text: Glissantian Readings in Caribbean and African-American Literatures* (New York: Peter Lang, 1995). Anderson illustrates the approach eschewed here; she does not, in fact, treat Louisiana Creoles of Color.

4. Caulfeild's autograph shows that the name is not Caulfield, as printed sometimes.

5. Kane, Keynote Address, *Louisiana Fictions: Proceedings of the Third Annual Louisiana Studies Conference* (Natchitoches: Northwestern State University/Cane River National Heritage Area, © 2011), 7. Auguste Viatte's two-volume *Histoire littéraire de l'Amérique française* (1954) is a useful survey but obviously leaves out English-language writers.

6. Chase, "The Decline of the English Department," *The American Scholar*, 78, 4 (Autumn 2009).

7. www.centenary.edu/french/louisiana/html; *Creole Echoes: The Francophone Poetry of Nineteenth-Century Louisiana*, trans. Norman Shapiro, introduction and notes by Weiss (Urbana: University of Illinois Press, 2004); Mathé Allain, ed., *Louisiana Literature and Literary Figures* (Lafayette: Center for Louisiana Studies, University of Louisiana at Lafayette, 2004). Where reprints exist, references will generally be

made to them, for readers' convenience. Some have typographical or scribal errors, and not all the Tintamarre reprints are critical editions.

8. Among those who group Cajun and Creole writing are Gérard Labarre St. Martin and Jacqueline Voorhies, *Ecrits louisianais du dix-neuvième siècle: nouvelles, contes, fables* (Baton Rouge: LSU Press, 1979). Their volume includes Acadian folk tales and fables in French that ranges from almost standard to Creole patois. The author of the "Breaux manuscript" (1901) called all Louisianans of French (or other "Latin" origin) *Creoles*; the word *Acadien* was still viewed as pejorative. See Jay K. Ditchy, *Les Acadiens louisianais et leur parler* (Paris: Droz, 1932); trans. in part by George Reinecke in *Louisiana Folklore Miscellany*, II (1966). See also Lyle Saxon, Edward Dreyer, and Robert Tallant, *Gumbo Ya-Ya* (Boston: Houghton Mifflin, 1945), 182; Waggoner, "Sidonie de la Houssaye's *Pouponne et Balthazar*: The Other Side of the Escalin," *Louisiana Literature*, 5 (1988), 61–70, republished in Allain, 97–103 (the quotation is on p. 97); Barry, "A French Literary Renaissance in Louisiana: Cultural Reflections," *Journal of Popular Culture* 23 (1989), 47–63; rpt. in Allain, 145–60 (the quotation is on p. 145); James L. Cowan, ed., *La Marseillaise noire et autres poèmes français des Créoles de couleur de la Nouvelle-Orléans (1862–1869)* (Lyons: Eds. du Cosmogone, 2001); Barry Jean Ancelet, Jay D. Edwards, and Glen Pitre, eds., *Cajun Country* (Jackson: University Press of Mississippi, 1991); Cheramie, *Julie Choufleur ou les preuves d'amour* (Shreveport: Editions Tintamarre, 2008); James L. Cowan, ed., *La Marseillaise noire et autres poèmes français des Créoles de couleur de la Nouvelle-Orléans (1862–1869)* (Lyons: Editions du Cosmogone, 2001), 41; Ancelet, ed., *Cris sur le bayou: Naissance d'une poésie acadienne en Louisiane* (Montreal: Editions Intermède, 1980). See also Ancelet, *Cajun and Creole Folk Tales: The French Oral Tradition of South Louisiana* (Jackson: University Press of Mississippi, 1994; New York: Garland, 1994).

9. Jambon, *L'Ecole Gombo* (Shreveport: Editions Tintamarre, 2006); de Pues, *Baron Rouge 19–59* (Shreveport: Editions Tintamarre, 2006). Jambon's writing is a dreadful mixture of English and French. See, e.g., "Chiac attack, Jack (un peuple en deux actes)," a text which, in addition to being linguistically appalling, is extremely coarse. Bourque, who was poet laureate of Louisiana, is a serious, learned poet; his work is in an entirely different category. See Allain for essays on Cajun writing in the 1980s and thereafter.

CHAPTER ONE

1. Taine set forth this critical insight in his *Histoire de la littérature anglaise* (1863). The word *nation*, from Lat. *natio* < *nasci*, to be born, itself suggests ethnicity. The "ethnicity" in Louisiana is, of course, multiple, but the cultural formation—*le milieu*,

le moment—was shared widely. See Charles L. Dufour, *Ten Flags in the Wind: The Story of Louisiana* (New York: Harper & Row, 1967), 2; Carl A. Brasseaux, *French, Cajun, Creole, Houma: A Primer on Francophone Louisiana* (Baton Rouge: LSU Press, 2005), 2; Ruth Salvaggio, *Hearing Sappho in New Orleans* (Baton Rouge: LSU Press, 2012), 53. Dufour is among countless observers who have used the term *unique* in connection with Louisiana; another is Bennett H. Wall. See Wall, ed., *Louisiana: A History* (Arlington Heights, IL: Forum Press, 1984), vii. The temporary fort and shrine built by the French in Lake Champlain (1666) and other short-lived settlements by the French in New England cannot be considered true colonies. Louisiana's bilingual tradition and its products are entirely different from—and superior to—the new English-Spanish bilingual culture and Chicano writing; moreover, self-conscious and highly literate products cannot be placed in the same category as Native American oral poetry, early Spanish writings about the New World, and other non-English texts.

2. *Nouvel*-Orléans is mentioned by some as the form. See Jacques de Rouquigny, "Le Soulier rouge," in *Contes et récits de la Louisiane créole* (Shreveport: Tintamarre, 2006), 35. On Law, see Janet Gleeson, *Millionaire* (New York: Simon & Schuster, 1999). An early account of the Ursulines' arrival is by mère Marie St. Augustin de Tranchepain (d. 1733), *Relation du voyage des premières Ursulines à la Nouvelle-Orléans* (published in "Nouvelle York" in 1859). Grace King's *La Dame de Sainte-Hermine* (New York: Macmillan, 1924) is a fictionalized version of the founding of New Orleans. See also Emily J. Clark, ed., *Voices from an Early American Convent: Marie Madeleine Hachard and the New Orleans Ursulines, 1727–1760* (Baton Rouge: LSU Press, 2007); Clark, *Masterless Mistresses: The New Orleans Ursulines and the Development of a New World Society, 1727–1834* (Chapel Hill: University of North Carolina Press, 2007).

3. Le Page du Pratz, *Histoire de la Louisiane*. 3 vols. (Paris, 1758), II, 309; Chaudenson, *Creolization of Language and Culture*, rev. with Salikoko S. Mufwene, trans. Sheri Pargman et al. (London and New York: Routledge, 2001), 3–4, 5; Sylvie Dubois, ed., *Une Histoire épistolaire de la Louisiane* (Quebec: Presses Universitaires de LaVal, 2011). Le Page arrived in 1718 and served as a doctor. See Grace King, *New Orleans: The Place and the People* (New York: Macmillan, 1895), 43, 45. On lexical development, see Vaugine de Nuisement, *Journal*, ed. Steve Canac-Marquis and Pierre Rézeau (Laval: Presses de l'Université de Laval, 2005), 72 ff. For further information and speculation on the term *Creole*, see Berrndt Ostendorf, "Creole Cultures and the Process of Creolization," in John Lowe, ed., *Louisiana Culture from the Colonial Era to Katrina* (Baton Rouge: LSU Press, 2008), 103–35. The term *culture* is used in this study, first, in its ordinary anthropological sense: the ensemble of arts, skills, attitudes, customs, language, rituals, and other mores of a people or subgroup, as transmitted normally from one generation to another, the adjective *cultural* referring

what is related to these products and ways of living; next, in the sense of *high culture*: arts that do not have a practical intent, and which aim at style and truth. T. S. Eliot provides a definition comparable to the first one: "all the characteristic activities and interests of a people." This definition, though decades old, remains valid. See his *Notes towards the Definition of Culture* (New York: Harcourt Brace Jovanovich, 1949), 30.

4. Robert Tallant, *The Romantic New Orleanians* (New York: Dutton, 1950), 38; Lyle Saxon, Edward Dreyer, and Robert Tallant, *Gumbo Ya-Ya* (Boston: Houghton Mifflin, 1945), 139; Chaudenson, 5, 6. For another example, see M. H. Herrin, *The Creole Aristocracy* (New York: Exposition, 1952), an unscholarly work despite citing of sources. The British used the term *Creole* for English born in the islands.

5. F. J. Woods, cited by Chaudenson, 7. See Albert Valdman, *Le Créole: Structure, statut et origine* (Paris: Klincksieck, 1978); Marilyn J. Conwell and Alphonse Juilland, *Louisiana French Grammar* (The Hague: Mouton, 1963); Valdman, senior editor, et al., *Dictionary of Louisiana French* (Jackson: University Press of Mississippi, 2010); Sylvie Dubois and Barbara M. Horvath, "The English Vernacular of the Creoles of Louisiana," *Language Variation and Change*, 15 (2003), 261. See also Raphaël Confiant, *Les Maîtres de la parole créole* (Paris: Gallimard, 1995), 9–10; Saloy, "Native Daughter: Growing Up Black in New Orleans," *Designer/Builder*, 12, 4 (Nov.–Dec. 2005), 8.

6. Dubois and Horvath, 257, 261; Murdoch, *Creole Identity in the French Caribbean Novel* (Gainesville: University Press of Florida, 2001), 4–5. On black Creoles west of New Orleans, see Carl A. Brasseaux and Claude F. Oubre, *Creoles of Color in the Bayou Country* (Jackson: University Press of Mississippi, 1994).

7. Chaudenson, 55, 135; Brasseaux, *French, Cajun, Creole, Houma*, 24. For a list of eighteen distinct groups of French speakers in Louisiana, from the earliest arrivals to the present, see 2. For information on "prairie Creoles," see 103–104.

8. Osbey, *Ceremony for Minneconjoux* (Lexington: Callaloo Poetry Series, University of Kentucky, 1983; reissued by the University Press of Virginia). Approximately five thousand American Indians lived in the Orleans Territory in 1803. There were intertribal massacres during the colonial period; and though the Indians generally received the whites well, clashes occurred, especially the Fort Rosalie massacre by Natchez (1729), which made the New Orleans Creoles fearful. By approximately 1850, only fifteen hundred indigenous residents remained, largely because many were relocated outside the state; by 1910, only about eight hundred appeared in the census, but they were doubtless undercounted. See Baron Marc de Villiers, *Histoire de la fondation de la Nouvelle-Orléans (1717–1722)*, preface by Gabriel Hanotaux (Paris: Imprimerie Nationale, 1917), 122; *Romance and Reality: American Indians in 19th-Century New Orleans*. Exhibit catalogue of the Historic New Orleans Collection, 20 July–16 Oct. 1999. Geary Hobson's novel *The Last of the Ofos* (Tucson: University of

Arizona Press, 2000) treats the topic of Indian and mixed identity in Louisiana via twentieth-century characters. See also Andrew Jolivétte, *Louisiana Creoles: Cultural Recovery and Mixed-Race Native American Identity* (Lanham, MD: Lexington, 2007).

9. See William A. Read, *Louisiana French* (Baton Rouge: LSU Press [1931]); Brasseaux, *French, Cajun, Creole, Houma*, 37–84, 88–115, 142–44. See the preface of the present study regarding the absence of a Cajun literary tradition.

10. See William C. Davis, *The Rogue Republic: How Would-Be Patriots Waged the Shortest Revolution in American History* (Boston & New York: Houghton Mifflin Harcourt, 2011). Voltaire's opinion is quoted by James L. Cowan, ed., *La Marseillaise noire et autres poèmes français des Créoles de couleur de la Nouvelle-Orléans (1862–1869)* (Lyons: Eds. du Cosmogone, 2001), 13. The "Isle of Orleans" was bounded by the Mississippi River, the small Manchac River, Lakes Maurepas and Pontchartrain, and Lake Borgne.

11. Lyle Saxon, *Fabulous New Orleans* (New York: Century, 1929; new ed., New York: Appleton-Century, 1947), 138–39; Brasseaux, *French, Cajun, Creole, Houma*, 121. As late as 1973 John W. Blassingame considered Saxon's volume, along with King's *New Orleans: The Place and the People* and Henry C. Castellanos's *New Orleans As It Was* (1905), to be among four most exhaustive general histories of New Orleans. See Blassingame, *Black New Orleans 1860–1880* (Chicago: University of Chicago Press), 275–76.

12. Ellen C. Merrill, *Germans of Louisiana* (Gretna: Pelican, 2005); Reinhart Kondert, *Charles Frederick D'Arensbourg and the Germans of Colonial Louisiana* (Lafayette: Center for Louisiana Studies, University of Louisiana at Lafayette, 2008); Gilbert C. Din, *The Canary Islanders of Louisiana* (Baton Rouge: LSU Press, 1988); "Saint-Malo," in Christopher Benfey, ed., *Lafcadio Hearn: American Writings* (New York: Library of America, 2009), 730–43. See the archives of the Swiss Society in the Louisiana Research Collection at Tulane University. For a depiction of Italians in New Orleans in the twentieth century, see Mary King O'Donnell, *Those Other People* (Boston: Houghton Mifflin, 1946). Between 1820 and 1860, 101,000 Irish immigrants arrived; many embarked at Liverpool. In 1850 one in five New Orleanians was Irish. Irish laborers were considered cheaper and thus more expendable than slaves, and there were hard feelings between the two groups. They were employed in canal-digging and on the docks, which they had taken over by the mid-1850s. They succumbed to yellow fever in great numbers; almost a fifth of them died during the 1853 epidemic. In literature of the time and later writing, little attention is paid to them and their sufferings.

13. Saxon, Dreyer, and Tallant, 139.

14. Dufour, 231; Brasseaux, *French, Cajun, Creole, Houma*, 24; Caryn Cossé Bell, *Revolution, Romanticism, and the Afro-Creole Protest Tradition in Louisiana 1718–*

1868 (Baton Rouge: LSU Press, 1997), 13; Blassingame, 201. On *plaçage*, see Joan M. Martin, "*Plaçage* and the Louisiana *Gens de Couleur Libre*" [sic] in Sybil Kein, ed., *Creole: The History and Legacy of Louisiana's Free People of Color* (Baton Rouge: LSU Press, 2000), 57–70. See also Judith Kelleher Schafer, *Becoming Free, Remaining Free: Manumission and Enslavement in New Orleans, 1846–1862* (Baton Rouge: LSU Press, 2003).

15. On the Code Noir and the status of blacks under the French and Spanish respectively, see Daniel C. Littlefield, "Slavery in French Louisiana: From Gallic Colony to American Territory," in Lowe, 75–99. As governor, Baron François de Carondelet introduced into the Code clauses for more humane treatment.

16. Emily Clark disputes assertions about marriage between persons of color and whites, affirming that native Louisiana women of color married at the same rate as white women in the early 1800s. The situation was different for those arriving from Haiti. Emily Clark, *The Strange History of the American Quadroon: Free Women of Color in the Revolutionary Atlantic World* (Chapel Hill: University of North Carolina Press, 2013).

17. Chaudenson, 135; Brasseaux, *French, Cajun, Creole, Houma*, 98; Wall, 71; Cable, *Creoles and Cajuns*, ed. Arlin Turner (Garden City, NY: Doubleday, 1959), 148–70. On terminology for mixed-race persons, see Gary B. Mills, *The Forgotten People: Cane River's Creoles of Color* (Baton Rouge: LSU Press, 1977), xiii–iv.

18. Kadish, "Contextualizing the Canon," in Dean de la Motte and Stirling Haig, eds., *Approaches to Teaching Stendhal's "The Red and the Black"* (New York: Modern Language Association, 1999), 110. There had been attempts under the Spanish to regulate dancing, at the same time that the *tignon* (kerchief) was imposed on free black women. See Bell, 19. Slavery was abolished in France in 1794—an important milestone for French colonials—but was reinstated by Napoleon in 1802; it endured in the colonies until the Second Republic (1848). The *tignon* persisted until the mid-twentieth century in some circles at least. Quo Vadis Gex-Breaux speaks of "Mama Goldie" and her "ever-present head-rag." See "Wisdom Is," in Joanne V. Gabbin, ed., *Furious Flower: African American Poetry from the Black Arts Movement to the Present* (Charlottesville: University of Virginia Press, 2004), 174.

19. Wall, 71; Chaudenson, 56 (he gives this racial breakdown: 23,574 slaves; 3,355 Creoles of Color; 26,059 whites); A. N. Yiannopoulos, "The Civil Codes of Louisiana," *Civil Law Commentaries*, I, 1 (Winter 2008), 5; Saxon, Dreyer, and Tallant, 139; Tallant, 62.

20. King, *New Orleans: The Place and the People*; King, *The Pleasant Ways of St. Médard*, both quoted in Robert Bush, ed., *Grace King of New Orleans: A Selection of Her Work* (Baton Rouge: LSU Press, 1973), 21, 318; Demarest, "Creole Days and Ways" (unpublished paper); Cable, 134.

21. See Tallant, 28, 59, 190–92; Wall, 171; Dufour, 246–55. Cities larger than New Orleans in 1837 were New York, Baltimore, and Philadelphia.

22. There is disagreement on which language was dominant. The Mandatory Education Act of 1916 specified that English be the principal teaching language in all schools.

23. David McCullough, *The Greater Journey: Americans in Paris* (New York: Simon & Schuster, 2011), 306. The Barrie statement is quoted in Rodolphe-Lucien Desdunes, *Nos hommes et notre histoire: notices biographiques accompagnées de réflexions . . .* (Montreal: Arbour &] Dupont, 1911), trans. and ed., with notes, by Dorothea Olga McCants as *Our People, Our History* (Baton Rouge: LSU Press, 1973), xxii. For the French original of the consul's statement, see the introduction to Georges Dessommes, *Tante Cydette*; rpt. ed. Ida Eve Heckenbach (Gretna, LA: Pelican, 2001), 19.

24. Bell, 2; M. Lynn Weiss, introduction to Victor Séjour, *The Jew of Seville*, trans. Norman R. Shapiro (Urbana: University of Illinois Press, 2002), xviii.

25. See Cable, *Creoles and Cajuns*, 87; Mills, 196–97; King, *New Orleans*, 346 (citing Gayarré); Patricia Brady Schmit, "Cultural Treasure Acquired," *The Historic New Orleans Collection Newsletter*, v, 4 (Fall 1987), 2. One count reports 165 Free Blacks in 1763. The New Orleans directory for 1788 listed 1,701 free persons of color in Louisiana and West Florida; by 1803 the number in New Orleans was 1,335 (contrasted to the slave population of 2,775). By 1810, the group composed 29 percent of the city population, a figure unmatched elsewhere in the United States. By 1812, the population in Louisiana had grown to 8,000. Some participated in battles against the British during the American war of independence, and a Battalion of Free Men of Color, with its own officers, fought at the Battle of New Orleans. By 1850 the free nonwhite community of New Orleans numbered 10,000 or more. (There were more than 15,000 enslaved persons.) See Alice Moore Dunbar-Nelson, "People of Color in Louisiana," in Kein, 3–41; Charles E. O'Neill, S.J., foreword to Desdunes, x–xiii; Brasseaux, *French, Cajun, Creole, Houma*, 107; "Identity, History, Legacy" (Sixteenth Annual Williams Research Center Symposium, Historic New Orleans Collection, 2011).

26. *Faubourg Tremé: The Untold Story of Black New Orleans*, by Lolis Eric Elie et al., video recording, 2008, Amistad Center, Tulane University (Osbey is interviewed in the film); "Tremé: People and Places," Southeastern Architectural Archive, Tulane University, 10 Dec. 2010–4 Nov. 2011. Note also "Tremé," a series that premiered on HBO in 2010 and was renewed for the 2011–12 and 2012–13 seasons. See also Osbey, "One More Last Chance: Ritual and the Jazz Funeral," in Lowe, 284–93. On Creolism and Africanism, see Lowe, 102.

27. Michel Fabre, "New Orleans Creole Expatriates in France," in Kein, 179–95; Mary Gehman, "Visible Means of Support: Businesses, Professions, and Trades of Free People of Color," in Kein, 209; Bell, 15; W. Darrell Overdyke, *Louisiana Plan-*

tation Homes (New York: American Legacy Press, 1965), 77. Much music by black Creoles remained in obscurity; recently, Givonna Joseph discovered in the archives of Tulane and Xavier universities and the Amistad Research Center forgotten vocal and operatic scores. See Chris Waddington, "Could Satchmo Have Sung Opera?" *New Orleans Times-Picayune* 16 Aug. 2011, Section C.

28. Littlefield, 76, 83; Bell, chap. 7; Blassingame, 33–35; Mills, 233; Lanusse, ed., *Les Cenelles* (1845), trans. and ed. Régine Latortue and Gleason R. W. Adams (Boston: G. K. Hall, 1979), xxv; Desdunes, 122. The *gens de couleur libres* were not drafted into the regular Confederate army, law prohibiting such service. On 9 April 1863, the 74th United States Colored Troops, known as the Louisiana Native Guards, stationed on Ship Island off the Mississippi Gulf Coast, engaged the Confederates in a successful skirmish in East Pascagoula. It was the first documented combat by U.S. African American troops. Natasha Trethewey (b. 1966) published a collection of verse that gives poetic voice to the Guards; it won the Pulitzer Prize. In June 2012 she was named poet laureate of the United States. See Trethewey, *Native Guard* (Boston: Houghton, Mifflin, 2006).

29. Blassingame, 153; Arthé A. Anthony, "Lost Boundaries," in Kein, 301; Rice, *The Feast of All Saints* (New York: Simon and Schuster, 1979), 7; Anthony G. Barthelemy, "Light, Bright, Damn *Near* White," in Kein, 253 ff.

30. Mills, 247–48; Cable, 323.

CHAPTER TWO

1. C. S. Brosman, "Interview with Shirley Ann Grau," *Louisiana English Journal*, n. s., 5, 2 (1998), 32–33.

2. Putnam's phrase, cited with permission, comes from a paper delivered at Denison University in June 2012.

3. Tinker, *Les Ecrits de langue française en Louisiane au XIXe siècle* (Paris: Honoré Champion, 1932), 1; Reinecke, "Alfred Mercier, French Novelist of New Orleans," *Southern Quarterly*, 20 (1982), 145–76; republished in Kenneth Holditch, ed., *In Old New Orleans* (Jackson: University Press of Mississippi, 1983); republished in Mathé Allain, ed., *Louisiana Literature and Literary Figures* (Lafayette: Center for Louisiana Studies, University of Louisiana at Lafayette, 2004).

4. See Auguste Viatte, *Histoire littéraire de l'Amérique française*, 2 vols. (Paris: Presses Universitaires de France, 1954), 251, quoting Thomas Théard; Dugué, "L'Importance du culte des souvenirs," *Le Courrier de la Louisiane*, 22 Aug. 1843, quoted by Jonathan Vidrine in his edition of Sidonie de la Houssaye, *Contes d'une grand-mère louisianaise* (Shreveport: Tintamarre, 2007), 13.

5. Le Page du Pratz, *Histoire de la Louisiane*. 3 vols. (Paris, 1758), I, 263; Germain

Bienvenu, "The Beginnings of Louisiana Literature," in John Lowe, ed., *Louisiana Culture from the Colonial Era to Katrina* (Baton Rouge: LSU Press, 2008), 26; Berry, "The Poetry of William Carlos Williams," *Sewanee Review*, 119, 1 (Winter 2011), 32.

6. Faulkner, *Absalom, Absalom!* (1936; rpt., New York: Modern Library, 1951), 74.

7. Robert Tallant, *The Romantic New Orleanians* (New York: Dutton, 1950), 20; King, 55–67; Brannan, quoted by Hennig Cohen and William B. Dillingham, eds., *Humor of the Old Southwest* (Boston: Houghton Mifflin, 1964), 358; Cable, *Creoles and Cajuns* (Garden City, NY: Doubleday, 1959), 189; Basso, *Days Before Lent* (New York: Scribner's, 1939), 29; Saxon, *Fabulous New Orleans* (1928; new ed., New York: Appleton-Century, 1943), 91. John Kennedy Toole, in *A Confederacy of Dunces* (Baton Rouge: LSU Press, 1980), called the French Quarter "the vice capital of the world."

8. See Robert Tallant, *The Romantic New Orleanians* (New York: Dutton, 1950), 289; Armand Lanusse, ed., *Les Cenelles: Choix de poésies indigènes* (New Orleans: H. Lauve, 1845); rpt., Edward Maceo Coleman, ed., foreword by H. Carrington Lancaster (Washington, D.C.: Associated Publishers, 1945); rpt. with English translations and preface by Régine Latortue and Gleason R.W. Adams (Boston: G.K. Hall, 1979), xvii. On black literature, see John Ernest, *Resistance and Reformation in Nineteenth-Century African-American Literature* (Jackson: University Press of Mississippi, 1995).

9. Johann Gottfried von Herder, *Philosophical Writings*, trans. and ed. Michael N. Forster (Cambridge: Cambridge University Press, 2002), 50. On these two poets, see Gérard Labarre St. Martin and Jacqueline Voorhies, *Ecrits louisianais du dix-neuvième siècle: nouvelles, contes, fables* (Baton Rouge: LSU Press, 1979), 187, 213–22.

10. See Marshall, "New Orleans, Nodal Point of the French Atlantic," https://dspace.stir.ac.uk/bitstream/1893/1746/1/NewOrleansart.

11. See Saxon, 280–83; King, 182–88; Dagmar Renshaw LeBreton, *Chahta-Ima: The Life of Adrien-Emmanuel Rouquette* (Baton Rouge: LSU Pess, 1947), 16–17.

12. Berquin-Duvallon is quoted in Viatte, *Histoire littéraire*, II, 222. A doctoral candidate at Tulane, Rien Fertel, is presently studying white Creole print culture and literature. The sort of literary portraiture and history that Gayarré and Testut produced conforms to the French model of the period, as illustrated by Charles-Augustin Sainte-Beuve in his famous *Lundis*.

13. See King, *New Orleans: The Place and the People* (New York: Macmillan, 1895), 150; Charles L. Dufour, *Ten Flags in the Wind* (New York: Harper and Row, 1967), 158–59; Alfred Mercier, *L'Habitation Saint-Ybars*, ed. and introduction by Réginald Hamel (Montreal: Guérin, 1989), 40; Starr, "Young Louis Moreaux Gottschalk and the Multicultural Musical Milieu of New Orleans," *Explorations*, 7 (1993), 1–23. Canoge (1822–1893), a segregationist, also composed poetry and reviewed drama. See Bernard Lavoie, "Louis-Placide Canonge (1822–1893): Un Américain de France, du sud de la Louisiane," in Allain, 132–37. At one time he was, according to some authorities,

director of the French Opera House. He is sometimes identified as a Creole of Color, perhaps because there was a homonym. See John W. Blassingame, *Black New Orleans 1860–1880* (Chicago: University of Chicago Press, 1973), 187; Rodolphe-Lucien Desdunes, *Nos hommes et notre histoire: notices biographiques accompagnées de réflexions* . . . (Montreal: Arbour & Dupont, 1911), trans. as *Our People, Our History*, with notes, by Dorothea Olga McCants (Baton Rouge: LSU Press, 1973), 109, n. 1.

14. Blassingame, xvi, 11. It would be erroneous to assume that there was no color prejudice in France; it was widespread and persisted past mid-twentieth century.

15. See "Après le Bal du Cordon bleu," in Sybil Kein, *An American South* (East Lansing: Michigan State University Press, 1996), 6–7, for a modern treatment of quadroon balls. See also in that collection the poem "Les Vagabonds," set in 1855, which depicts reveries of expatriation by Creoles of Color. In 1985 a revived *Tribune*, founded by Dwight McKenna, Beverly Stanton McKenna, James Borders, and others appeared. On literacy, see Desdunes, 104, n.

16. Gildea, *Children of the Revolution: The French, 1799–1914* (Cambridge: Harvard University Press, 2008), 174.

17. See Ruby Allen Caulfeild, *The French Literature of Louisiana* (New York: Institute of French Studies, Columbia University, 1929; rpt., Gretna: Pelican, 1998), 72–75; Viatte, *Histoire littéraire*, II, 284. J. John Perret's work on Francophone newspapers in Louisiana has not, unfortunately, been published.

18. The title of the publication varied. The journal was "couronné par l'Académie Française." Mansion and his son Numa E. Mansion are mentioned in Desdunes, 61–62.

19. See various authors in this study, especially in chapters 3, 8, and 13, and Harnett T. Kane, *The Bayous of Louisiana* (New York: Morrow, 1943), 55–60, 63–67. Mercier was among the authors who described yellow fever. Another was Mollie Moore Davis; see M. E. M. Davis, *The Queen's Garden* (Boston: Houghton, Mifflin, 1900).

20. The poem was not published until 1931. See Tallant, 292; Bienvenu, 40; *Journal des Américainistes*, 1914, 47; Marc de Villiers du Terrage, *Histoire de la fondation de la Nouvelle-Orléans (1717–1722)*, preface by Gabriel Hanotaux (Paris: Imprimerie Nationale, 1917), 105.

21. Tujague, *Chroniques louisianaises* (Shreveport: Tintamarre, 2003), 122–25; Thierry, *Les Vagabondes*, ed. Frans C. Amelinckx and May Rush Gwin Waggoner (Shreveport: Tintamarre, 2004), 55.

CHAPTER THREE

1. King, *New Orleans: The Place and the People* (New York: Macmillan, 1895), xix. Louisiana writing in French did not develop earlier than Canadian letters, if one in-

cludes histories and travel accounts published in France by French visitors; but the destruction wrought by the Seven Years' War and the transfer of Canada to Great Britain in 1763 caused disruption in learning and set back the development of Francophone writing there. Thus literature in Louisiana flourished more broadly, in more genres; it is the premier French colonial literature.

2. Hearn, "The Last of the Fencing-Masters," in *Lafcadio Hearn: American Writings*, ed. Christopher Benfey (New York: Library of America, 2009), 762.

3. Le Page du Pratz, I, 88, 263; II, 314, 388; Montaigne, *Essais*. In most French editions, this essay appears in Book I as chapter 31—e.g., edited by Pierre Villey (Paris: Quadrige/PUF, 2004); see also *The Essays of Michel de Montaigne*, trans. M. A. Screech (London: Allen Lane/Penguin, 2004). In certain editions, e.g., Bibliothèque de la Pléiade, it appears as Book I, chapter 30. Le Page's lines antedate Voltaire's famous tale *L'Ingénu* (1767) concerning the goodness of the Huron Indians. This view of the noble savage, likewise seen in *The Tempest* (1613) by Shakespeare and John Dryden's *The Conquest of Granada* (1669–70), remains a staple of both the popular and the literary imagination. (*Conquest*, Part I, I, i : "I am as free as nature first made man / . . . / When wild in woods the noble savage ran.") One need think only of the 1990 film *Dances with Wolves*, with its favorable portrait of American Indians, contrasted to crude whites, and of writings on early Mexicans by French Nobel laureate J. M. G. Le Clézio.

4. See Germain Bienvenu, "The Beginnings of Louisiana Literature," in John Lowe, ed., *Louisiana Culture from the Colonial Era to Katrina* (Baton Rouge: LSU Press, 2008), 40; Charles E. O'Neill, "French Literature in Colonial Louisiana," in Mathé Allain, ed., *Louisiana Literature and Literary Figures* (Lafayette: Center for Louisiana Studies, University of Louisiana at Lafayette, 2004), 24–29; D. A. Kress, Margaret E. Mahoney, and Rebecca Skelton, eds., *Anthologie de poésie louisianaise du XIXe siècle* (Shreveport: Tintamarre, 2010).

5. The drama was republished 1909–10 by *Les Comptes rendus de l'Athénée Louisianais*. It was translated and edited by Allain as *The Festival of the Young Corn; or, The Heroism of Poucha-Houmma* (Lafayette: University of Southwestern Louisiana, 1964). Her good scholarly introduction to this volume is republished in Allain, ed., 30–45. See also Auguste Viatte, *Anthologie littéraire de l'Amérique francophone* (Sherbrooke: University of Sherbrooke, 1971), 251; O'Neill, 27. Le Blanc de Villeneufve also published *Recueil de poiesies* [sic] *d'un colon de Saint-Domingue*.

6. See S[usan] B[lanchard] Elder, *Life of the Abbé Adrien Rouquette, Poet Missionary of Louisiana* (New Orleans: L. Graham, 1913); Dagmar Renshaw LeBreton, *Chahta-Ima: The Life of Adrien-Emmanuel Rouquette* (Baton Rouge, LSU Press, 1947). As LeBreton points out, Elder's study is "inaccurate and unreliable" (xvii). LeBreton's, while based on extensive research, is practically hagiographic. Some of Rouquette's

papers are held privately; others are at the Louisiana Research Collection at Tulane University and the Archdiocesan Archives of New Orleans; for the latter, a catalogue is available. See also Jackie Valabrègue-Landreaux, *Chata-Ima, la voix des Indiens* (Paris: Hachette,1999).

7. Stanley Clisby Arthur and George Campbell Huchet de Kernion, *Old Families of Louisiana* (New Orleans: Harmanson, 1931; rpt., New Orleans: Pelican), 120–22.

8. John R. Williams, "Francois-Rene de Chateaubriand," *Dictionary of Literary Biography* 119, ed. C.S. Brosman (Detroit: Gale Research, 1992), 74.

9. LeBreton, 7, 48–52, 379.

10. LeBreton, 94, 254, 344. Rouquette is called "the last of the Black Robe Fathers." Donald Demarest confirms the accuracy of the label. Rouquette wrote to Thoreau and sent some of his writings. See LeBreton, 334.

11. See LeBreton, 25, 223–24; Edward Larocque Tinker, *Les Ecrits en langue française en Louisiane au XIX siècle* (Paris: Honoré Champion, 1932), 138–43.

12. See LeBreton, 288, 337, 355, on Bryant and Rouquette's conception of poetry. The Moore statements are quoted in Tinker, 141. An example of Rouquette's criticism is the preface to Charles-Oscar Dugué's *Essais poétiques*, in which Rouquette writes of the holiness of poetic inspiration. The term *savane* was highly evocative to the French. In 1846 Louis Moreau Gottschalk premiered in Paris his piece "La Savane," which became famous. The 1840s was a decade of flourishing for Louisiana poetry, by both whites and Creoles of color. In addition to the authors treated here, one can mention Eugène Leblanc (1817–?), whose *Essais poétiques* appeared in Paris in 1842.

13. Adrien Rouquette, *Les Savanes* (Paris, J. Labitte; New Orleans: A. Moret, 1841), 2, 33–35. See also his English verse in *Wild Flowers: Sacred Poetry* (New Orleans: T. O'Donnell, 1848).

14. *La Thébaïde en Amérique; ou, Apologie de la vie solitaire et contemplative* (Paris, 1841; rpt., New Orleans; Imprimerie Méridier, 1852); *L'Antoniade ou la solitude avec Dieu (Trois âges), poème érémitique* (New Orleans: L. Marchand, 1860); *Trois âges; suite et fin de l'Antoniade. Poème érémitique* (New Orleans: L. Marchand, 1869); *Catherine Tegahkwitha, the Saint of Caughnawaga* (New Orleans, 1873).

15. *La Nouvelle Atala; ou, la fille de l'esprit. Légende indienne par Chahta-ima (de la Louisiane)* (New Orleans: Imprimerie du Propagateur, 1879); critical edition by Elizabeth B. Landry (Shreveport: Editions Tintamarre, 2003), to which page numbers refer.

16. See Hearn's review in the Landry edition. See also Babbitt, *Rousseau and Romanticism* (Boston and New York: Houghton Mifflin, 1919). Chateaubriand was influenced by Le Page du Pratz; see *Romance and Reality: American Indians in 19th-Century New Orleans* (exhibit catalogue of the Historic New Orleans Collection, 20 July–16 October 1999). Rouquette's work is not to be confused with Bernard Alciator's *La Nouvelle Atala* (Paris: Dentu, 1865).

17. The danger of incest was a frequent topic in nineteenth-century Francophone literature, as subsequent chapters indicate. An early instance is "The Quadroon of New Orleans: A Tale," by Joseph Holt Ingraham, in his *The American Lounger: or, Tales, Sketches, and Legends* (Philadelphia: Lea & Blanchard, 1839).

18. Rouquette, *Discours prononcé a la cathédrale de St.-Louis (la Nouvelle-Orléans)*... (Paris, Librairie de Sauvaignat, 1846); Auguste Viatte, *Anthologie littéraire de l'Amérique francophone* (Sherbrooke: Université de Sherbrooke, 1971), 273–74.

19. LeBreton, 252; Viatte, *Anthologie littéraire*, 266–67.

20. Dominique Rouquette, *Les Meschacébéennes* (Paris: Librairie du Sauvaignat, 1839). His other collection is *Fleurs d'Amérique: Poésies nouvelles* (New Orleans: Imprimerie H. Méridier, 1856).

21. Morel, *Récit sur l'Ouragan de la Dernière Ile* (Napoleonville: Imprimerie du Pionnier de l'Assomption, 1858); ms. letter 24 May 1901 from Mrs. Oscar Dugas (Louisiana Research Collection, Tulane University). In the 1860 census for Napoleonville, Morel's occupation was listed as recorder; a handwritten note calls him a notary.

22. See *Creole Echoes: The Francophone Poetry of Nineteenth-Century Louisiana*, trans. Norman R. Shapiro, introduction and notes by M. Lynn Weiss (Urbana: University of Illinois Press, 2004), 47; Gérard Labarre St. Martin and Jacqueline Voorhies, *Ecrits louisianais du dix-neuvième siècle* (Baton Rouge: LSU Press, 1979), 181–85. Deléry published posthumously in *Les Comptes Rendus de l'Athénée Louisianais* in 1911. On Deléry's quarrel with Jean-Charles Faget and another doctor, see Harnett T. Kane, *Gentlemen, Swords and Pistols* (New York: Morrow, 1951), 25–26; Charles L. Dufour, *Ten Flags in the Wind* (New York: Harper, 1967), 252.

23. See *Creole Echoes*, 56–65.

24. New Orleans: A. Moret, dated 1841, although the final poem bears the date 1842. Rpt., ed. Kelsey A. Bellamy (Shreveport: Tintamarre, 2003), cover 4. See Viatte, *Anthologie littéraire*, 262, and *Creole Echoes*, 98–107. On leprosy, see Henry C. Castellanos, *New Orleans As It Was: Episodes of Louisiana Life* (1895); rpt. introduction by Judith Kelleher Schafer (Baton Rouge: LSU Press, 2006), 333. Cable's story "Jeanah Poquelin," in *Creoles and Cajuns*, ed. Arlin Turner (Garden City, NY: Doubleday, 1959), deals with a leper, who eventually is taken to the refuge. Latil's situation anticipates that of the blind Creole of Color Victor-Ernest Rillieux (1842–98), and, later still, of Joë Bousquet (1897–1950), who, paralyzed in the Great War, spent his life thereafter writing in withdrawal and pain. On Rillieux, see chapter 7, note 2.

CHAPTER FOUR

1. On Barde, see Auguste Viatte, *Anthologie littéraire de l'Amérique francophone* (Sherbrooke: Université de Sherbrooke, 1971), 276–84. Louis-Armand Garreau introduced him in the *Revue Louisianaise* of 6 August 1848. During the Civil War, however,

Barde wrote fiery poems in favor of the South. On Evershed, see *Creole Echoes: The Francophone Poetry of Nineteenth-Century Louisiana*, trans. Norman R. Shapiro, introduction and notes by M. Lynn Weiss (Urbana: University of Illinois Press, 2004), 75. In addition to Gayarré, Garreau (treated in chapter 5) could have consulted Victor Debouchel, *Histoire de la Louisiane* (New Orleans: J. F. Leleivre, 1841). On Lussan, see Ruby Van Allen Caulfeild, *French Literature in Louisiana* (New York: Institute of French Studies, Columbia University, 1929; rpt., Gretna: Pelican, 1998), 31–32, 96–98. Lussan published also *La Famille créole*, a play (1837), and *Les Impériales* (1841), a collection of verse that included four poems on Napoleon.

2. Gayarré's *Essai historique sur la Louisiane* (2 vols; New Orleans, B. Levy, 1830–31) is, according to authorities, including the *Dictionary of American Biography*, largely a translation of François-Xavier Martin's two-volume *History of Louisiana, from the Earliest Period* (New Orleans: Lyman and Beardslee, 1827, 1829). See Edward Larocque Tinker, *Lafcadio Hearn's American Days* (New York: Dodd, Mead, 1925), 112; J. John Perret, "S. de la Houssaye's Quadroon Tetrology," *Louisiana Literature*, 2, 2 (1994), 14. I am grateful to Keli E. Rylance of Tulane University for information about Gayarré and the quotation on "the great sad struggle," from an interview he gave, printed in the *Daily Picayune*, 10 January 1894. The Seventh Ward house where he died in poverty still stands. On Gayarré's "passionate white supremacist views," see Helen Taylor, *Gender, Race, and Region in the Writings of Grace King, Ruth McEnery Stuart, and Kate Chopin* (Baton Rouge: LSU Press, 1989), 34.

3. Gayarré, *Fernando de Lemos: Truth and Fiction* (New York: Fenno, 1872); *Aubert Dubayet, or The Two Sister Republics* (Boston: Osgood,1882).

4. On socialist ideas and the opposition between the brothers, see Hamel, ed., *L'Aventure de Johnelle (roman d'Alfred Mercier)* (Quebec: Humanitas, 2004), xiv, xv; henceforth indicated by short title. On disbelief in heavenly rewards, see 85. Mercier's polemic for the "Latin" Confederacy was *Du panlatinisme* (Paris: Librairie Centrale, n.d.). The yellow fever story appeared in *Les Comptes-rendus de l'Athénée Louisianais*,1883, and is reprinted in *Contes et récits de la Louisiane créole* (Shreveport: Tintamarre, 2006); *Fortunia* was published in New Orleans by the Imprimerie Franco-Américaine, 1888. A biographical summary, chronology, and bibliography of Mercier's works by Hamel are included in *Johnelle*.

5. On medical studies, see *Johnelle*, xxvii, 41.

6. Mercier, *Hénoch Jédésias ou l'Avare de New-York*, ed. Hamel (Quebec and Paris: Editions Stanké, 2004), 348. Henceforth indicated by the short title *Avare*.

7. *La Rose de Smyrne et l'Ermite du Niagara, poèmes* (Paris: Jules Labitte, 1842), 84.

8. See George Reinecke, "Alfred Mercier, French Novelist of New Orleans," *Southern Quarterly*, 20 (1982), 145–76; republished in W. Kenneth Holditch, ed., *In Old New Orleans* (Jackson: University Press of Mississippi, 1983), 145–76. Might Mercier have been inspired by the strange case of one Foscue, a *fermier-général* in the Languedoc,

who became trapped in his cellar amid piles of gold and died there? See Edith Sitwell, *English Eccentrics* (Boston: Houghton Mifflin, 1933).

9. Mercier, *La Fille du prêtre: Récit social* (New Orleans: Imprimerie Cosmopolite, 1877–78), vii.

10. Mercier, *L'Habitation Saint-Ybars; ou, Maîtres et esclaves en Louisiane* (New Orleans: Imprimerie Franco-Américaine, 1881). Rpt., Montreal, 1982, 1989 (with footnotes and chronology). Rpt., Shreveport: Tintamarre, 2003 (minimal notes by D. A. Kress). Page numbers refer to the original printing. See Reinecke; S. D. Dickinson, "Creole Patois in the Novels of Dr. Alfred Mercier," *Louisiana Literature*, 8, 1 (Spring 1991), 69–80. At the deathbed wedding, a judge, not a priest, presides. This violation of verisimilitude underlines Mercier's anticlericalism.

11. Mercier, *Le Fou de Palerme: Nouvelle sicilienne* (New Orleans: Imprimerie du Carillon,1873); rpt., with *L'Artiste amoureux* (Shreveport: Tintamarre, 2006). Page numbers refer to the reprint.

12. *Lidia* was republished with *Emile des Ormiers* and *L'Anémique* (3 vols.) (New Orleans, 1891). *Lidia* was reprinted (Shreveport: Tintamarre, 2007).

13. Reinecke (155) attributes Mercier's anticlericalism to republicanism; republicans were strongly anticlerical.

14. See *Johnelle*, xxvi; cover 4 comment; 43, 47. Hamel calls Mercier "the greatest Louisiana author of the nineteenth century." Hamel's choice of title for the reprint is odd, attributing an "adventure" to the stillborn child. Reinecke, 170, suggests that the model for the central character may be Edward Dessommes, a novelist and painter, the brother of George Dessommes (perhaps also the model for the doctor-suicide in George Dessommes's *Tante Cydette*, discussed in chapter 9).

15. See *Contes et récits de la Louisiane créole* (Shreveport: Tintamarre, 2006), 35–76. Soulier-rouge was a historical figure; he was assassinated by the French around 1748. He is mentioned in *La Nouvelle Atala* (107, 136, n. 46). See also Caulfeild, 28–29. It is unclear whether Rouquigny is connected to the Free Man of Color Jean-Baptiste Roquigny (son of a white father). See Mary Gehman, "Visible Means of Support," in Sybil Kein, ed., *Creole: The History and Legacy of Louisiana's Free People of Color* (Baton Rouge: LSU Press, 2000), 215. *Le Vigilant* was published in Donaldsonville by J. L. Marciacq, who had arrived from France in 1842, started a school for children of color, and become a publisher.

16. See *Contes et récits . . .* , 77–94. References are in parentheses.

CHAPTER FIVE

1. See *Creole Echoes: The Francophone Poetry of Nineteenth-Century Louisiana*, trans. Norman R. Shapiro, introduction and notes by M. Lynn Weiss (Urbana: University of Illinois Press, 2004), 3.

2. Testut, *Saint-Denis* (rpt., Shreveport: Tintamarre, 2003); William P. Trent et al., eds., *The Cambridge History of American Literature* (New York: Putnam's, 1921) and subsequent editions. See also Camille Thierry, *Les Vagabondes*, ed. and trans. Frans Amelinckx and May Rush Gwin Waggoner (Shreveport: Tintamarre, 2004), 170–71.

3. *Creole Echoes*, 198–209; *French Women Poets of Nine Centuries*, trans. Shapiro, ed. with notes by Weiss (Baltimore: Johns Hopkins University Press, 2008), 604.

4. For information on Delany's work and an assessment, see John Ernest, *Resistance and Reformation in Nineteenth-Century African-American Literature* (Jackson: University Press of Mississippi, 1995), 109–39.

5. *Le Vieux Salomon* also resembles (partly by the theme of redemption) Hugo's *Les Misérables* (1862), which Jules Barbey d'Aurevilly denounced for its "socialism."

6. Testut, *Le Vieux Salomon, ou une famille d'esclaves au XIXème siècle* (New Orleans, 1872; rpt., Shreveport: Editions Tintamarre, 2003), 6, 9, 165. Other references are given parenthetically. See Sheri Lyn Abel, *Charles Testut's 'Le Vieux Salomon': Race, Religion, Socialism, and Freemasonry* (Lanham, MD: Lexington Books, 2009).

7. Spiritualism and paranormal phenomena, and the associations that favored and investigated them, played an enormous role in nineteenth-century thought and letters in France, England, and America, as positive phenomena, not the delusions displayed by Mercier's characters. Victor Hugo and his Turning Tables, the "Sâr" Joséphin Péladan and other Rosicrucians, the British Psychic Society, and William James can be cited. In Louisiana, certain authors among the Free Men of Color cultivated spiritualism (see chapter 7). On Freemasonry and spiritualism, see Abel, and also Caryn Cossé Bell, *Revolution, Romanticism, and the Afro-Creole Protest Tradition in Louisiana 1718–1868* (Baton Rouge: LSU Press, 1997), chapters 5 and 6; Chris Michaelides, *Paroles d'honneur: Ecrits de Creoles de couleur néo-orléanais* (Shreveport: Tintamarre, 2004), 189–210, 235 n. 28. Concerning a Freemason publication in French in Louisiana, see James L. Cowan, ed., *La Marseillaise noire et autres poèmes français des Créoles de couleur de la Nouvelle-Orléans (1862–1869)* (Lyons: Eds. du Cosmogone, 2001), 109 n. 99. Cowan avers that Testut's father was a knight of the Rosicrucians (108).

8. This outcome differs strikingly from that in Constance Fenimore Woolson's story "King David," in which emancipated slaves after the war turn to drink and become indolent, giving up any effort at learning. See Woolson, *Rodman the Keeper: Southern Sketches* (New York: Appleton,1880; rpt., New York: Garrett Press, 1969).

9. Garreau, *Louisiana*, ed. D. A. Kress (Shreveport: Tintamarre, 2003), 10.

10. Grace King, *New Orleans: The Place and the People* (New York: Macmillan, 1895), 80, 113. King says that the model for the hangman was connected to the Company des Indes; she also mentions as background the governorship of Vaudreuil and

Kerlérec (1740s and '50s) before the rebellion. See the section on Brenda Marie Osbey in chapter 13 for another mention of an executioner, probably the same.

11. Garreau, *Bras coupé et autres récits louisianais*, introduction by Fabrice Leroy (Shreveport: Tintamarre, 2007).

12. On the historical figure, see chapter 8. Twentieth-century writers who have mentioned him include Marcus Christian and Tom Dent. See Violet Harrington Bryan, *The Myth of New Orleans in Literature: Dialogues of Race and Gender* (Knoxville: University of Tennessee Press, 1993), 113, 138, 162.

13. See *Creole Echoes*, 32–33, 186–91.

14. *Le Premier Pas: Essais littéraires* (New Orleans: Marchand, 1863). See *Chroniques louisianaises* (Shreveport: Tintamarre, 2003). Page references are to this collection.

CHAPTER SIX

1. Michaelides, ed., *Paroles d'honneur: Ecrits de Créoles de couleur néo-orléanais* (Shreveport: Tintamarre, 2004), 33; Vigny, *Chatterton*, iii, 6, in *OEuvres complètes* (Paris: Gallimard/Bibliothèque de la Pléiade, 1950), I, 836. *Paroles d'honneur* contains almost all the extant corpus; references are in the text. The longer stories were published serially. See Frans C. Amelinckx, "Forgotten People, Forgotten Literature: The Case of Creole Authors of Color," *Louisiana Literature*, 11 (1994), 45–54, republished in Mathé Allain, *Louisiana Literature and Literary Figures* (Lafayette: Center for Louisiana Studies, University of Louisiana at Lafayette, 2004), 51–58. Two exceptional women authors from the Creoles of Color were Alice Dunbar-Nelson (treated below) and Louisa R. Lamotte (died 1907), born in New Orleans, who contributed to *L'Abeille* but spent her career largely in France, as a teacher and director of a school in Abbeville. See also Rodolphe-Lucien Desdunes, *Nos hommes et notre histoire: notices biographiques accompagnées de réflexions . . .* (Montreal: Arbour & Dupont, 1911), trans. and ed., with notes, Dorothea Olga McCants (Baton Rouge: LSU Press, 1973) (discussed below); John W. Blassingame, *Black New Orleans, 1860–1880* (Chicago: University of Chicago Press, 1973).

2. Amelinckx, "Forgotten People," 52; Condé, "Order, Disorder, Freedom, and the West Indian Writer," *Yale French Studies*, 83 (1993).

3. On the law, see Caryn Cossé Bell, *Revolution, Romanticism, and the Afro-Creole Protest Tradition in Louisiana 1718–1868* (Baton Rouge: LSU Press, 1997), 92–94.

4. See Anna Shannon Elfenbein, *Women on the Color Line: Evolving Stereotypes and the Writings of George Washington Cable, Grace King, Kate Chopin* (Charlottesville: University Press of Virginia, 1989), chapter 1. For other depictions of quadroons, see chapter 9 below.

5. On Séjour, see David O'Connell, "Victor Séjour: Ecrivain américain de langue française," *Revue de la Louisiane/Louisiana Review*, #1, 2 (Winter 1972), 60–75 (includes the story "Le Mulâtre"); Régine Latortue and Gleanson R. W. Adams, eds., *Les Cenelles* (Boston: G. K. Hall, 1979), xxviii–xxix; Perret, "Victor Séjour, Black French Playwright from Louisiana," *French Review*, 57, 2 (Dec. 1983), 187–93; Thomas Bonner, "Victor Séjour," in Trudier Harris, ed., *Afro-American Writers Before the Harlem Renaissance, Dictionary of Literary Biography* 50 (1986), 237–41; Charles Edward O'Neil, *Séjour: Parisian Playwright from Louisiana* (Lafayette: Center for Louisiana Studies, University of Southwestern Louisiana, 1995); M. Lynn Weiss, introduction to Séjour, *The Fortune Teller*, trans. Norman R Shapiro (Urbana: University of Illinois Press, 2002), xv; Weiss, introduction to Séjour, *The Jew of Seville*, trans. Shapiro (Urbana: University of Illinois Press, 2002). William Wells Brown could lay claim to publishing the first novel by any African American: *Clotel; or, The President's Daughter* (1853). See John Ernest, *Resistance and Reformation in Nineteenth-Century African-American Literature* (Jackson: University Press of Mississippi, 1995), 30.

6. The story, translated by Andre Lee, appeared in Mark Shell and Werner Sollors, eds., *The Multilingual Anthology of American Literature* (New York: New York University Press, 2000).

7. On Séligny, see Amelinckx, "Intersection France/Louisiane au XIXe siècle: La Littérature populaire dans les récits et nouvelles de Michel Séligny," *Francophonies d'Amérique*, 2 (1992), 169–82; Séligny, *Homme libre de couleur de la Nouvelle-Orléans: nouvelles et récits*, ed. Amelinckx (Quebec: Laval, 1998). See Michel Fabre, "New Orleans Creole Expatriates in France," in Sybil Kein, ed., *Creole: The History and Legacy of Louisiana's Free People of Color* (Baton Rouge: LSU Press, 2000), 180.

8. On *The Double-Dealer*, see Violet Harrington Bryan, *The Myth of New Orleans in Literature: Dialogues of Race and Gender* (Knoxville: University of Tennessee Press, 1993), chapter 4.

9. On *La Tribune* and especially the poems it published, see chapter 7 and Caroline Senter, "Creole Poets on the Verge of a Nation," in Kein, 276–94. Bonfouca is a bayou in St. Tammany Parish.

10. On Duhart, see *Creole Echoes: The Francophone Poetry of Nineteenth-Century Louisiana*, trans. Norman R. Shapiro, introduction and notes by M. Lynn Weiss (Urbana: University of Illinois Press, 2004), 67. Weiss gives Duhart's birth date between 1835 and 1840; Michaelides gives the date 1830 (38). He stresses the white father's severity; at the time, however, the latter's reaction was unsurprising. On Ogé, see Bell, 2–3, 20–21.

11. See Jennifer DeVere Brody, "The Yankee Hugging the Creole: Reading Dion Boucicault's *The Octaroon*," in Kein, 102–16.

12. Perret, 188; Fabre, in Kein, 187.

13. O'Connell, 60. No copy of *Henri de Lorraine* seems available. See Perret, 190.

14. Other historical examples of prejudicial policies based on what is perceived as national interest include the well-founded Germanophobia of the French before 1914 and during the ensuing war and American policies toward Japanese residents during World War II. These cases show how perceived racial differences can become the grounds for what is viewed as rational, indeed indispensable, state policy. The rationale is seen even in enmity between one royal house and another; one thinks of dramas by Pierre Corneille and, much later, Henry de Montherlant's 1942 play *La Reine morte*, similarly set on the Iberian peninsula, and not without similarities to *Diégarias*.

15. See Weiss's introduction to the Séjour translation, xviii–xxii.

16. See Dorothy H. Brown and Barbara C. Ewell, eds., *Louisiana Women Writers* (Baton Rouge: LSU Press, 1992), 260, and, in the same volume, Violet Harrington Bryan, "Race and Gender in the Early Works of Alice Dunbar-Nelson," 121–38. See also Gloria T. Hull, "Shaping Contradictions: Alice Dunbar-Nelson and the Black Creole Experience," *New Orleans Review*, 15 (1988), 34–37, republished Allain, 250–55. In addition, see Dunbar-Nelson's historical essay "People of Color in Louisiana," republished in Kein, 3–41.

17. Auguste Viatte, *Anthologie littéraire de l'Amérique francophone* (Sherbrooke: University of Sherbrooke, 1971), 305–6, seems to have confused Rodolphe Desdunes with his brother, P.A. Desdunes, a poet. The Choate statement was made at a fundraiser for the Tuskegee Institute. See www.twainquotes.com/1906123.html.

CHAPTER SEVEN

1. *Creole Echoes: The Francophone Poetry of Nineteenth-Century Louisiana*, trans. Norman R. Shapiro, introduction and notes by M. Lynn Weiss (Urbana: University of Illinois Press, 2004), cover 4. Shapiro is a very skilled translator of verse. Unfortunately, American rules for capitalization are applied to French titles, which are thereby marred.

2. Armand Lanusse, ed., *Les Cenelles: Choix de poésies indigènes* (New Orleans: H. Lauve, 1845); rpt., Edward Maceo Coleman, ed., foreword by H. Carrington Lancaster (Washington, D.C.: Associated Publishers, 1945); rpt. with English translations and preface by Régine Latortue and Gleason R. W. Adams (Boston: G.K. Hall, 1979); rpt., ed. Mia B. Reamer (Shreveport: Editions Tintamarre, 2003). The Coleman edition has a substantial introduction. The Latortue-Adams edition has an inadequate table of contents and no index. Its biographical notes are sketchy. In the Reamer edition, the text has been slightly corrected, but there is no new critical material. The comment by Clint Bruce on cover 4 labels the work as the first Afro-American poetry collec-

tion. See Alfred J. Guillaume, "Love, Death, and Faith in the New Orleans Poets of Color," *Southern Quarterly*, 20, 2 (Winter 1982), 126–44; republished in W. Kenneth Holditch, ed., *In Old New Orleans* (Jackson: University Press of Mississippi, 1983). The quotation is on 139. On the original edition, see Patricia Brady Schmit, "Cultural Treasure Acquired," *Historic New Orleans Collection Newsletter*, v, 4 (Fall 1987), 1–4. In 1945 Coleman brought out also, with the same publisher, *Creole Voices: Poems in French by Free Men of Color*, a reworking of his edition of *Les Cenelles* with the addition of two new poets, V. A. (for V. E., i.e., Victor Ernest) Rillieux, the blind brother of the brilliant inventor Norbert Rillieux, and P. A. Desdunes, the brother of Rodolphe-Lucien Desdunes. Under the title *Les Feuilles mortes* (New Orleans: Ateliers du "Daily Crusader," 1895), he rendered into French verse (from, apparently, a prose translation) a collection in Spanish by Gus A. Becquer, *Las Hojas muertas*. See R.-L. Desdunes, *Nos hommes et notre histoire: notices biographiques accompagnées de réflexions . . .* (Montreal: Arbour & Dupont, 1911), trans. and ed., with notes, Dorothea Olga McCants (Baton Rouge: LSU Press, 1973), 59–60, and *Creole Echoes*, 148–53. The Rillieux brothers, sons of Vincent Rillieux and Constance Vivant, a Free Woman of Color, were related to Edgar Degas, whose grandmother was Marie-Céleste Rillieux. An unsigned poem in *La Tribune*, "Le Docteur Noir," concerning a slave physician who refuses to treat his master, may be by Rillieux; see John W. Blassingame, *Black New Orleans 1860–1880* (Chicago: University of Chicago Press, 1973), 136.

3. See Caryn Cossé Bell, *Revolution, Romanticism, and the Afro-Creole Protest Tradition in Louisiana, 1718–1868* (Baton Rouge: LSU Press, 1997), 114–23; *Creole Echoes*, 193–96. There is scanty information on Dauphin in Desdunes, 51–52. See also Gary B. Mills, *The Forgotten People: Cane River's Creoles of Color* (Baton Rouge; LSU Press, 1977), 184. "B. Valcour" is included under that name in *Creole Echoes*. Lanusse is one of three authors of color included in Charles Testut's *Portraits littéraires* (1850). Testut called their poetry monotonous but also refreshing. See Desdunes, 24, n. and Guillaume, 71. On the connections between some of these authors and spiritualism, see Bell, chapter 6; Chris Michaelides, ed., *Paroles d'honneur: Ecrits de Créoles de couleur néo-orléanais* (Shreveport: Tintamarre, 2004), 42–48; and, in the same volume, "Communications spiritualistes," passim. It was alleged that these spiritualists entered into communication with such figures as Voltaire, Napoleon, Abraham Lincoln, and Madame Couvent.

4. Guillaume, 139; Calvin André Claudel, trans., *Louisiana Creole Poems*, ed. Sue Walker (Mobile: Negative Capability Press, 1981), foreword. This is a selection of black patois songs and "Creole slave poems," with an unsatisfactory preface. Claudel's graduate thesis (1947) at the University of North Carolina concerned Louisiana folklore.

5. Bell, 114–15. See also Caroline Senter, "Creole Poets on the Verge of a Nation,"

in Sybil Kein, ed., *Creole: The History and Legacy of Louisiana's Free People of Color* (Baton Rouge: LSU Press, 2000), 280.

6. Michel Séligny also wrote about "l'ancien canal Carondelet." See Auguste Viatte, *Anthologie littéraire de l'Amérique francophone* (Sherbrooke: Université de Sherbrooke, 1971), 288–90. The canal was dug in 1792 to connect New Orleans via the lakes to coastal shipping.

7. Thierry, *Les Vagabondes, poésies américaines* (Bordeaux: Delaporte/Paris: E. Lemerre, 1874); rpt. ed. Frans C. Amelinckx and May Rush Gwin Waggoner (Shreveport: Tintamarre, 2004), 19, 53, 147, 176–77 n. 3; Blassingame, 57. See the introduction to the 2004 edition for other biographical facts and Blassingame, 75, for information on the firm in question. Mercier's poem was published in *Les Comptes Rendus de l'Athénée Louisianais*, 1878. The "Bordeaux" imprint was a formality; the book was printed in Paris. Michel Fabre asserts that the father's occupation was liquor dealer. See his "New Orleans Creole Expatriates in France," in Kein, 183. See also *Les Cenelles*, ed. Latortue and Adams, 134–57. It is generally said that Thierry settled definitively in Bordeaux, his father's city, but Desdunes (32) identifies his residence as Paris.

8. Tinker, quoted by Fabre, 194. See *Les Vagabondes*, 17, 73, 155.

9. See Thierry, 193 n. 7 and 195 n. 16. The friend who killed himself is identified as Eugène Bloom.

10. See Desdunes, 4–8, 61–65, 68. Castra's poem is quoted there (in English) from Roland C. McConnell, *Negro Troops of Antebellum Louisiana* (Baton Rouge: LSU Press, 1968). Bell (90) believes that Castra read the poem before the Société des Artisans. Castra may have been a pseudonym. See Michaelides, 211 n. 1. The lawsuit inspired a novel by Tinker, *Toucoutou* (New York: Dodd Mead, 1928). See Sybil Kein, "One-Drop Rules: Self-Identity and the Women in the Trial of Toucoutou," in John Lowe, ed., *Louisiana Culture from the Colonial Era to Katrina* (Baton Rouge: LSU Press, 2008), 136–46. A famous song on the case is collected in Lyle Saxon, Edward Dreyer, and Robert Tallant, *Gumbo Ya-Ya* (Boston: Houghton Mifflin, 1945), 428. See also Kein's poem in *An American South* (East Lansing: Michigan State University Press, 1996), 25–26.

11. James L. Cowan, ed., *La Marseillaise noire et autres poèmes français des Créoles de couleur de la Nouvelle-Orléans (1862–1869)* (Lyons: Eds. du Cosmogone, 2001). See 89,103 n. 95 on Lamartine. The poems were gathered from archives at the University of Louisiana at Lafayette and Louisiana State University. See also Senter, "Creole Poets . . ."; *Creole Echoes*, 67.

12. The flower metaphor was used by French Renaissance poets most frequently in connection with the carpe diem theme. In the famous "Consolation à Monsieur du Périer," by François de Malherbe, it stands for a dead girl: "Et rose elle a vécu ce que vivent les roses . . ."

13. See Charles L. Dufour, *Ten Flags in the Wind* (New York: Harper, 1967), 182–85. Dufour considers A. P. Dostie a fanatic and demagogue and blames him for inciting the whites and blacks to riot, since he threatened that the streets would run with blood.

14. *Creole Echoes*, 90. Bell (233–40), however, attributes the poem to Henry Rey, a Creole of Color and a spiritualist, as does Ruth Salvaggio in *Hearing Sappho in New Orleans: The Call of Poetry from Congo Square to the Ninth Ward* (Baton Rouge: LSU Press, 2012); Weiss concedes it may be his.

15. *Creole Voices*, 90–93.

CHAPTER EIGHT

1. Alice Hall Petry, "Native Outsider: George Washington Cable," in *Literary New Orleans: Essays and Meditations*, ed. Richard S. Kennedy (Baton Rouge: LSU Press, 1992); J. John Perret, "Strange True Stories of Louisiana: History or Hoax?" *Southern Studies*, 16, 1 (Spring 1977). Kennedy's volume should not be confused with Judy Long's anthology, *Literary New Orleans*, foreword by Patricia Brady (Athens, GA: Hill Street Press, 1999), nor with Kennedy's *Literary New Orleans in the Modern World* (Baton Rouge: LSU Press, 1998).

2. Mark Twain, letter to William Dean Howells, 27 Feb. 1885, in Bernard de Voto, ed., *The Portable Mark Twain* (New York: Viking Press, 1946), 761. Lafcadio Hearn was likewise vexed by Cable's "awful faith." See Christopher Benfey, ed., *Lafcadio Hearn: American Writings* (New York: Library of America, 2009), 820 (hereafter cited as Benfey).

3. See Cable, *Creoles and Cajuns*, ed. Arlin Turner (Garden City, NY: Doubleday, 1959), 2; Cable, "The Freedman's Case in Equity," in Turner, ed., *The Negro Question: A Selection of Writings on Civil Rights in the South* (Garden City, NY: Doubleday, 1958); Anna Shannon Elfenbein, *Women on the Color Line: Evolving Stereotypes in the Writings of George Washington Cable, Grace King, Kate Chopin* (Charlottesville: University Press of Virginia, 1989); William Bedford Clark, "Cable and Miscegenation," *Mississippi Quarterly*, 30 (Fall 1977), 597–609; Demarest, "Creole Days and Ways" (unpublished paper).

4. Anthony G. Barthelemy, "Light, Bright, Damn *Near* White," in Sybil Kein, ed., *Creole: The History and Legacy of Louisiana's Free People of Color* (Baton Rouge: LSU Press, 2000), 261–62; Edmund Wilson, *Patriotic Gore: Studies in the Literature of the American Civil War* (New York: Oxford University Press, 1962), 548–87, 593–604.

5. Robert Tallant, *The Romantic New Orleanians* (New York: Dutton, 1950), 163; Elfenbein, 29; Cable, "The Dance in Place Congo" and "Creole Slave Songs," *Century Magazine*, 31 (February and April, 1886); collected in Cable, *Creoles and Cajuns*, 366–

432, viz. 369 on the bamboula. See S. Frederick Starr, "Young Louis Moreau Gottschalk and the Multicultural Musical Milieu of New Orleans," *Explorations*, 7 (1993), 13–15, for information about Cable's essay and his sources. See also Ruth Salvaggio, *Hearing Sappho in New Orleans: The Call of Poetry from Congo Square to the Ninth Ward* (Baton Rouge: LSU Press, 2012), 64–65, 157, 158 and passim.

6. See above chapter 7 n. 10. "'Tite Poulette" was collected in Cable, *Old Creole Days* (New York: Scribner's, 1879); *Madame Delphine* was added to later editions. See the Signet Classics edition (New York: New American Library, 1961), foreword by Shirley Ann Grau. Both are reprinted in *Creoles and Cajuns*; see 87, 232. "The Solitary," in the same volume, reprinted from Cable's 1899 *Strong Hearts*, includes an account of a hurricane (358–60). For a twentieth-century treatment of the Madame Delphine theme, see "L'Enfant perdue," in Kein, *American South*, 8–9.

7. King, *New Orleans: The Place and the People* (New York: Macmillan, 1895), 350. The Haunted House story comes from *Strange True Stories of Louisiana* (1880).

8. Cable, *The Grandissimes* (New York: Scribner's, 1880; rpt., Kessinger, n.p., n.d.), 43, 237. Page numbers refer to the reprint. On Creole sterotypes, see Merrill Maguire Skaggs, *The Folk of Southern Fiction* (Athens: University of Georgia Press, 1972), 154–88.

9. 90, 287, 334; Kjell Ekström, *George Washington Cable: A Study of His Early Life and Work* (Cambridge: Harvard University Press, 1950), 56 (quoting Cable).

10. *The Grandissimes*, 18, 54, 90, 141, 283; Hjalmar H. Boyesen, "Cable's *Grandissimes*," *Scribner's Monthly Magazine*, 1880, reprinted in Arlin Turner, ed., *Critical Essays on George W. Cable* (Boston: G.K. Hall, 1980), 10–11. Cable has one Creole refer to himself in 1803 as a "good subject of His Catholic Majesty" (36). Napoleon, who then occupied the imperial throne, was known as "Sa Majesté l'Empereur" but not as "Sa Majesté catholique," a term for the previous monarchs. Might this be Cable's slip, or might the Creole, deliberately or without thinking, hark back to pre-Revolutionary times?

11. *The Grandissimes*, 3, 170, 228, 254. There was a historical Agricole Fusilier de la Claire, from the Spanish and French Creole family that built Fuselier in Iberia Parish. The Bras-Coupé episode was originally a short story, which under the title "Bibi" Cable submitted to *Scribner's* in 1873 and elsewhere, without success, although an assistant editor called it a "powerful Victor Hugo–like episode." Readers will recall Louis-Armand Garreau's story about Bras-Coupé. "The Dirge of Saint-Malo," from Cable's "Creole Slave Songs," deals with the same figure. See *Creoles and Cajuns*, 11, 20, 419. A contemporary, Henry C. Castellanos, asserted that Cable's account was "pure fiction." Instead, he claimed, Squier (the name of the slave who served as a model) was treated well by his master, General William de Buys, but was insubordinate and rebellious. His arm was amputated after he was shot. He continued to commit

various crimes, fled to the swamps, and was finally killed by a fisherman. See Castellanos, *New Orleans As It Was: Episodes of Louisiana Life* (1895); rpt., introduction by Judith Kelleher Schafer (Baton Rouge: LSU Press, 2006), 210–11; Lyle Saxon, Edward Dreyer, and Robert Tallant, *Gumbo Ya-Ya* (Boston: Houghton Mifflin, 1945), 253–54.

12. Robert Bush, ed., *Grace King of New Orleans: A Selection of Her Writings* (Baton Rouge: LSU Press, 1973), 26.

13. Dustin Griffin, *Satire: A Critical Reintroduction* (Lexington: University Press of Kentucky, 1994), 1.

14. [Rouquette], *Critical Dialogue Between Aboo and Caboo on a New Book; or, a Grandissime Ascension* (Mingo City [New Orleans]: Great Publishing House of Sam Slick Alspice on Veracity Street, 1880; facsimile rpt., Kessinger Publishing, n.d). Page numbers refer to this edition. The name Mingo is associated with blacks; that was, presumably, Rouquette's reason for using it. It was that of a free black, Jean Mingo, who in 1727 married a slave named Thérèse, with her owner's permission. It is used likewise by Joel Chandler Harris, in *Mingo and Other Sketches in Black and White* (Boston: Osgood, 1884). In the title tale, Mingo is a kindly old black man. Ruth McEnery Stuart later published a story called "Uncle Mingo's 'Speculatioms'" [sic] in *A Golden Wedding and Other Tales* (New York: Harper, 1893; rpt., New York: Garrett, 1969). The name, part of Chef Menteur's appellation, was used among the Acolapissa Indians of Louisiana.

15. On Laveau, see Barbara Rosendale Duggal, "Marie Laveau: The Voodoo Queen Repossessed," in Kein, *Creole*, 157–78.

16. Cable, *Old Creole Days*, foreword by Grau, vii, xiii; Cable, *The Grandissimes*, introduction by Arvin (New York: Hill and Wang, 1957).

17. Biographical details come from Benfey and from Edward Larocque Tinker, *Lafcadio Hearn's American Days* (New York: Dodd, Mead, 1925). Hearn was transcultural before it became popular to be so. See the Hearn archives in the Louisiana Research Collection at Tulane University and the 2012 exhibit, "The Open Mind of Lafcadio Hearn."

18. See Tinker, 88.

19. Ibid, 70; Wilson, 559, 576; *Creole Sketches* (Boston: Houghton Mifflin, 1924); Benfey, 680–90, 757–69, 795; *Ghombo Zhèbes* (New York: Coleman, 1885). See also S. Frederick Starr, ed., *Inventing New Orleans: Writings of Lafcadio Hearn* (Jackson: University Press of Mississippi, 2001). Hearn wrote that he was "a little disappointed," though elsewhere "delighted," by *The Grandissimes* (Benfey, 794). The phrase "Ghombo Zhèbes" or gumbo zhèbes refers to a concoction of greens cooked on Holy Thursday. See Saxon, Dreyer, and Tallant, 167.

20. *Chita: A Memory of Last Island* (New York: Harper, 1889). *Chita* was translated at least twice into French and reprinted repeatedly; a recent edition is by Delia La-

barre, introduction by Jefferson Humphries (Jackson: University Press of Mississippi, 2003). On comparisons with Hugo and Loti, and Hearn's interest in Spencer, see Robert L. Gale, *A Lafcadio Hearn Companion* (Westport, CT: Greenwood, 2002), 31. On the storm, see Harnett T. Kane, *The Bayous of Louisiana* (New York: Morrow, 1943), 53–65.

21. *Chita*, 25–26, 149; Benfey, 85, 128. It will be noted that Hearn mentions oil slicks, "oleaginous patches," that appear on the water from the submarine oil (*Chita*, 32; Benfey, 87).

CHAPTER NINE

1. De la Houssaye, *Contes d'une grand-mère louisianaise*, ed. Jonathan Vidrine (Shreveport: Tintamarre, 2007), 33 and Cover 4 comment (cited as Vidrine, with page number); Wilson, "Neither Devil nor Mystery," *Chronicles: A Magazine of American Culture*, 36, 6 (June 2012), 30. Auguste Viatte called her quadroon series a vigorous protest "contre le préjugé de couleur en Louisiane." It is more properly a defense of *certain* Free Women of Color. See his *Histoire littéraire de l'Amérique française*, 2 vols. (Quebec: Presses Universitaires Laval/Paris: PUF, 1954), II, 295.

2. See J. John Perret, "S. de la Houssaye's Quadroon Tetrology: *Les Quarteronnes de la Nouvelle-Orléans*," *Louisiana Literature*, 11 (1994), 12–44; republished in Mathé Allain, *Louisiana Literature and Literary Figures* (Center for Louisiana Studies, University of Louisiana at Lafayette, 2004), 104–131. See also introductions to Vidrine and to de la Houssaye, *Octavia la quarteronne, suivi de Violetta la quarteronne* (partial reprint of *Les Quarteronnes de la Nouvelle-Orléans* [Bonnet Carré: L.B. Tarlton, 1894]), ed. Christian Hommel (Shreveport: Tintamarre, 2006), 7–10 (future references are in the text). The Louisiana State University Library Archives collection no. 105 contains twenty-one volumes of more than five thousand pages of manuscripts. See the important doctoral thesis (1966), rectifying earlier errors, by Perret: "A Critical Study of the Life and Writings of Sidonie de la Houssaye with Special Emphasis on the Unpublished Works."

3. See Zola, *Correspondance*, ed. Henri Mitterand, vol. 7 (Montreal: Presses de l'Université de Montréal, 1989), 268. She must have written to him, but no letter has been discovered. The phrase on indecencies is quoted by Vidrine, 20.

4. Perret, "Strange True Stories of Louisiana: History or Hoax?" *Southern Studies*, 16, 1 (Spring 1977), 41–53.

5. Perret, "S. de la Houssaye's Quadroon Tetrology," 20.

6. See Vidrine; *Pouponne et Balthazar: nouvelle acadienne* (New Orleans: Librairie de l'Opinion, 1888), rpt. ed. May Gwin Rush Waggoner (Lafayette: Center for Louisiana Studies, University of Southwestern Louisiana, 1983); trans. and introduction by

Perret (Lafayette: Center for Louisiana Studies, University of Southwestern Louisiana, 1983). See also Waggoner, "Sidonie de la Houssaye's *Pouponne et Balthazar*: The Other Side of the *Escalin*," *Louisiana Literature*, 5 (Spring 1988), 61–70, republished in Allain, 97–103.

7. Viatte, *Histoire littéraire*, II, 295. Earlier treatments of quadroons by non-Louisiana authors include L. Maria Child, "The Quadroons" (1842), republished in her *Fact and Fiction: A Collection of Stories* (New York: C. S. Francis/Boston: J. H. Francis, 1845), and William Wells Brown, *Clotel; or, The President's Daughter* (1853). "Beautiful Quadroon stuff," a variation on the "Tragic Quadroon," remained a type of southern potboiler. See Basil Thompson's editorial in *The Double-Dealer*, quoted in William Faulkner, *New Orleans Sketches*, ed. Carvel Collins (New Brunswick: Rutgers University Press, 1958), 16. Donald Demarest similarly encountered family indignation at his use of family information (see chapter 12).

8. Parker, "Evangeline's Darker Daughters," in Dorothy H. Brown and Barbara C. Ewell, *Louisiana Women Writers* (Baton Rouge: LSU Press, 1992), 75–97. De la Houssaye is the only French-language author treated in this volume.

9. See Hazard Adams and Leroy Searle, *Critical Theory Since 1965* (Tallahassee: Florida State University Press, 1986), 163. In 1884 Arthur comte de Gobineau published *Essai sur l'inégalité des races humaines* (1884), widely cited in the following decades, with broad or narrow application, as in the distinction made by Zola in *La Débâcle* between the German and French "races," and the similar distinction in *Colette Baudoche* by Maurice Barrès (1909). It will be recalled that Taine wrote of cultural products as being functions of "la race, le milieu, le moment." As late as 1932, Clifford Sharp, writing about Cecil Rhodes, distinguished the Boers, or Dutch, from the English as two different races. See H. J. Massingham and Hugh Massingham, *The Great Victorians* (London: Ivor Nicholson & Watson, 1932), 428 ff.

10. Harper's phrase is quoted by John Ernest, *Resistance and Reformation in Nineteenth-Century African-American Literature* (Jackson: University Press of Mississippi, 1995), 3. The anonymous traveler is quoted in Edward Larocque Tinker, *Lafcadio Hearn's American Days* (New York: Dodd, Mead, 1925), 92. Names similar to those here—Azuréah, Zibeline—were used by Paris call girls in the twentieth century. See Brooke L. Blower, *Becoming Americans in Paris* (New York: Oxford University Press, 2011), 168. Charles Gayarré and Cable were among those who talked about the elimination of black pigment by careful breeding. See Cable, *Creoles and Cajuns*, ed. Arlin Turner (Garden City, NY: Doubleday, 1959), 12, 193. On women of mixed blood in New Orleans, see Anna Shannon Elfenbein, *Women on the Color Line: Evolving Stereotypes in the Writings of George Washington Cable, Grace King, Kate Chopin* (Charlottesville: University Press of Virginia, 1989), viz. chapter 1.

11. King, *New Orleans: The Place and the People* (New York: Macmillan, 1895), 350.

On *plaçage*, see Joan M. Martin, "*Plaçage* and the Louisiana *Gens de Couleur Libre*" [*sic*] in Sybil Kein, ed., *Creole: The History and Legacy of Louisiana's Free People of Color* (Baton Rouge: LSU Press, 2000), 57–70.

12. Some years after de la Houssaye, Mollie Moore Davis (1844–1909), who had been reared in Texas but settled in New Orleans with her husband, wrote similarly, in her posthumous *The Ships of Desire*, about a New Orleans mulatta, Yvonne du Quesnay, who loves and is loved by a white; when he leaves her to marry, her love turns to hatred.

13. Incest appears also in de la Houssaye's unpublished "Frère et soeur."

14. See Perret, "S. de la Houssaye's Quadroon Tetrology," 28–38, for a summary; the quotations, translated by him, are on 31,38. See also Hommel, *Les Quarteronnes*, 342–45.

15. *Essais littéraires et dramatiques* (Paris: Imprimeries Réunies, 1892). Page numbers are in parentheses. "Un Eté à la Grand'Isle" was reprinted in *Contes et récits de la Louisiane Créole* (Shreveport: Editions Tintamarre, 2000). On the du Quesnay or duQuesnay family, see W. Adolphe Roberts, *The French in the West Indies* (New York: Bobbs-Merrill, 1942).

16. "Men, you will always conceive crime and give birth to sorrow. O Death, perverted instinct of this word, fatal instigator that awakens in us everything that is blamable and vile! Love, your true name is Homicide" (86).

17. Du Quesnay, *A Summer at Grand'Isle*, trans. C. S. Brosman and Paul de Laup, preface by Brosman (Lafayette: University of Southwestern Louisiana, 1997), xiv. It anticipates by a few years André Gide's *L'Immoraliste* and Joseph Conrad's *The Heart of Darkness* (both 1902). Another pertinent parallel is Pierre Louÿs, *La Femme et le pantin* (1898), which joins frame narration to a tale of destructive Romantic passion. A Creole work by Rose Falls Bres (1869–1927) (pen name: Rosetta C. Falls), *Chenière Caminada, or The Wind of Death* (New Orleans: Hopkins Printing Office, 1893), concerning the great Chênière Caminada storm of 1893, bears coincidental resemblances to du Quesnay's novella.

18. See below on the Fortier family. See also Ruby Allen Caulfeild, *The French Literature of Louisiana* (New York: Institute of French Studies, Columbia University, 1929), 229; Gerard Labarre St. Martin and Jacqueline K. Voorhies, *Ecrits louisianais du dix-neuvième siècle* (Baton Rouge: LSU Press, 1979), 49–81.

19. *Vendanges* (Shreveport: Tintamarre, 2007); Viatte, *Histoire littéraire*, II, 292. See chapter 7 above on Thierry. See also Caulfeild, 91, for biographical details furnished by Dessommes.

20. The Geoffroy sequence is based on the story of Jaufré Rudel, a twelfth-century Provençal poet, who celebrated "distant love" and, according to legend (recounted also by Petrarch and Robert Browning), fell in love with the Countess of Tripoli. The

actor named Barrett mentioned in "Afternoon" as having played Hamlet in New Orleans is, presumably, Lawrence Barrett (1838–91).

21. See *Contes et récits de la Nouvelle-Orléans* (Shreveport: Tintamarre, 2006), 107–17.

22. Dessommes, *Tante Cydette: Nouvelle louisianaise* (New Orleans: Imprimerie du Franco-Louisianais, 1888); rpt. ed. Ida Eve Heckenbach (Gretna, LA: Pelican, 2001). The novel was a commercial failure. See George Reinecke, "Introduction to *Tante Cydette* by Georges Dessommes," *Louisiana Litterature* 2 (1985), 19–21; republished in Allain, 46–50. (The remarks on James, below, are on 46–47.) Page references in the text are to the reprint, which includes also more than forty pages of Dessommes's poems, including some mentioned above. See Heckenbach's useful introduction for the symbolic reading of the poem "L'Orage" (20). The publisher of the reprint, the Codofil Consortium, rendered a service by putting out this school edition, but the editing is unsatisfactory.

23. Viatte, *Anthologie littéraire de l'Amérique francophone* (Sherbrooke: University de Sherbrooke, 1971), 301. The *laisser-aller* of Creole mores is compared implicitly to French usages; under the Second Empire the best circles were known for prudery. Andrée Kail spoke of Dessommes's "light and mocking pen" in his descriptions of society (Heckenbach, 17). Reinecke criticizes the impressionistic passage as too long and ornamental and notes inconsistency in point of view (Allain, 48).

24. See Reinecke, "Alfred Mercier, French Novelist of New Orleans," *Southern Quarterly*, 20 (1982); republished in Holditch, 145–76; Estelle Fortier (1866–1968), "Memoirs of a Louisianan," typescript, Howard-Tilton Memorial Library, Tulane University; Estelle Cochran (b. 1898), *The Fortier Families and Allied Families* (San Antonio? 1963). The scholar Edward J. Fortier (1883–1918) was Alcée's son.

25. *Louisiana Folktales in French Dialect and English* (Boston: Houghton Mifflin,1895), ix–x; Tinker, 265. On Compair Lapin and Leuk, see Raphaël Confiant, *Les Maîtres de la parole créole* (Paris: Gallimard, 1995), 8–9. See Barry Jean Ancelet, Jay D. Edwards, and Glen Pitre, *Cajun Country* (Jackson: University Press of Mississippi, 1991), xix. Sarah Morgan Dawson produced a translation of certain tales under the title *Les Aventures de Jeannot Lapin* (1903). Harris lived briefly in New Orleans (1866–67) but presumably did not know Louisiana plantation folklore.

26. See Tinker, 262–67; *Creole Echoes: The Francophone Poetry of Nineteenth-Century Louisiana*, trans. Norman R. Shapiro, introduction and notes by M. Lynn Weiss (Urbana: University of Illinois Press, 2004), 143–47; Donna M. Meletio, "Leona Queyrouze (1861–1938) Louisiana French Creole Poet, Essayist, and Composer," dissertation LSU, 2008. Queyrouze's mss. are in the Hill collection at Louisiana State University. See www.ancientfaces.com/research/story/400425.

CHAPTER TEN

1. Helen Taylor, *Gender, Race, and Region in the Writings of Grace King, Ruth McEnerny Stuart, and Kate Chopin* (Baton Rouge: LSU Press, 1989), 138; Peggy Whitman Prenshaw, "Louisiana and the American Literary Tradition," in John Lowe, ed., *Louisiana Culture from the Colonial Era to Katrina* (Baton Rouge: LSU Press, 2008), 153; Thomas Fleming, "Our Sacred Anticanon," *Chronicles: A Magazine of American Culture*, 35, 6 (June 2011), 11. Page references in the text are to Kate Chopin, *Complete Novels and Stories*, ed. Gilbert (New York: Library of America, 2002). *The Awakening* was originally published by Herbert S. Stone of Chicago. Toth's publications on Chopin include *Kate Chopin* (New York: Morrow, 1990) and *Unveiling Kate Chopin* (Jackson: University Press of Mississippi, 1999). The assertion that *The Awakening* was removed from libraries is refuted by Toth, "What we do and don't know about Chopin's life," in Janet Beer, ed., *The Cambridge Companion to Kate Chopin* (Cambridge: Cambridge University Press, 2008), 24. Toth points out that Chopin was in fact invited to speak at the Wednesday Club's authors' luncheon.

2. See Gary B. Mills, *The Forgotten People: Cane River's Creoles of Color* (Baton Rouge: LSU Press, 1977). The Cane River was created when the Red River changed its course around 1835. In the 1930s the channel was dammed; it is now a thirty-three-mile oxbow lake. The three- to four-mile strip of land between the Cane and Old River, to the west (another Red River channel), is commonly called L'Isle Brevelle. The upper part is often called Côte Joyeuse or Grande Côte. Bayou Brevelle crosses the territory. See chapter 12 concerning Lyle Saxon.

3. Anne Rowe, "New Orleans as Metaphor: Kate Chopin," in Richard S. Kennedy, ed., *Literary New Orleans: Essays and Meditations* (Baton Rouge: LSU Press, 1992). Sand's novel *Lélia* (1833) concerns women's unhappiness with men and inability to satisfy their desires.

4. See *The Complete Works of Kate Chopin*, ed. Seyersted, 2 vols. (Baton Rouge: LSU Press, 1969), I, 26. Seyersted (1921–2005), who came to America to research southern literature, deserves credit for first reviving Chopin's name. He became professor of American literature at the University of Oslo.

5. Seyersted, I, 26.

6. Fuller, *The Letters of Margaret Fuller*, vol. IV, ed. Robert Hudspeth (Ithaca: Cornell University Press, 1987), 256.

7. Alice Hall Petry, introduction to Petry, ed., *Critical Essays on Kate Chopin* (New York: G. K. Hall, 1996), 19.

8. James E. Rocks, "Kate Chopin's Ironic Vision," *Revue de la Louisiane/Louisiana Review*, #1, 2 (Winter 1972), 110–20.

9. Donna Campbell, "At Fault: A reappraisal of Chopin's other novel," in Beer,

38–39; Susan Castillo, "'Race' and ethnicity in Kate Chopin's fiction," in Beer, 59–72; Edmund Wilson, *Patriotic Gore: Studies in the Literature of the American Civil War* (New York: Oxford University Press, 1962), 587–88. See also Taylor, xii–xiii and chapter 3.

10. For another reading, see Cynthia Griffin Wolff, "The Fiction of Limits: 'Désirée's Baby,'" in Harold Bloom, ed., *Kate Chopin* (New York: Chelsea House, 1987), 35–42. See also Ellen Peel, "Semiotic Subversion in 'Désirée's Baby,'" in Dorothy H. Brown and Barbara C. Ewell, *Louisiana Women Writers* (Baton Rouge: LSU Press, 1992), 57–73.

11. Joyce C. Dyer, "Gouvernail, Kate Chopin's Sensitive Bachelor," in Bloom, 66. According to Susan Koppelman, quoted by Toth, 22, "In Sabine" is the only story of its era in which the battered wife escapes, and thus is unique in providing a happy ending.

12. Bloom, "Introduction," 1–2. Drawing comparisons with Stephen Crane's *Maggie: A Girl of the Streets* (1893), Darrin Dykes suggests that Edna displays signs of "severe depression" or an even more deep-seated and self-destructive narcissism. See his "Into the Watery Grave: The Aquatic Escapes of Maggie and Edna," *Louisiana Fictions: Proceedings of the Third Annual Louisiana Studies Conference* (Natchitoches: Northwestern State University/Cane River National Heritage Area, © 2011 [2012]), 126. The Joan Crawford film *Humoresque* (1946) affords an example in twentieth-century popular culture of a wife who deliberately walks into the sea to drown.

13. Seyersted, I, 29; Wolff, "Thanatos and Eros: Kate Chopin's *The Awakening*," *American Quarterly* 25 (October 1973), 449–72; Wolff, "Un-Utterable Longing: The Discourse of Feminine Sexuality in *The Awakening*," *Studies in American Fiction*, 24 (Spring 1996), 3–23; Toth, in Beer, 19, 24. On awakening of sexual drives, see in Wilson, 591–93, an analysis by a British woman. The woman in "The Storm," a previously unpublished graphic story by Chopin (926–31), is similarly sexually frustrated.

14. Demarest, unpublished paper; Wilson, 590; Priscilla Leder, "Kate Chopin's *The Awakening*: Personal Failure as Feminist Statement," *Louisiana Literature*, 6, 2 (Fall 1989), 70–81; Ronald C. Miazga, "The Persistent Romanticism of Edna Pontellier," *Louisiana Literature*, 3, 2 (Fall 1986), 68–76; Helen Taylor, "Kate Chopin and postcolonial New Orleans," in Beer, 158. Chopin's uncollected story "Her Letters" depicts a husband who drowns himself in the Mississippi after his wife's death, because he suspects her (not without reason) of infidelity.

15. Gilbert, "The Second Coming of Aphrodite," in Bloom, 89–113.

CHAPTER ELEVEN

1. Sources differ on her birth date (1851, 1852, 1853). See Anne Goodwyn Jones,

Tomorrow Is Another Day: The Woman Writer in the South, 1859–1936 (Baton Rouge: LSU Press, 1981), 93. On King's house, see Samuel Wilson, Jr., et al., *New Orleans Architecture, Vol. I: The Lower Garden District* (Gretna, LA: Friends of the Cabildo/Pelican Publishing Co., 1979).

2. See Robert Bush, ed., *Grace King of New Orleans: A Selection of Her Writings* (Baton Rouge: LSU Press, 1973), 5, 8, 398; Richard S. Kennedy, ed., *Literary New Orleans: Essays and Meditations* (Baton Rouge: LSU Press, 1992), 2, 11. References to the Bush anthology are in the text. The Louisiana Research Collection at Tulane University holds the archives of the Quarante Club, the Causeries du Lundi, the Ruth McEnery Stuart Clan, and other women's clubs.

3. Helen Taylor calls this account "self-dramatizing" and asserts that her ambitions were obfuscated. See Taylor, *Gender, Race, and Region in the Writings of Grace King, Ruth McEnery Stuart, and Kate Chopin* (Baton Rouge: LSU Press, 1989), 34. See also Edward Larocque Tinker, *Lafcadio Hearn's American Days* (New York: Dodd, Mead, 1925), 257. The phrase on "psychological realism" comes from Jack Trotter, "Grace King's Portrait Miniatures: A Currency of the Heart." Trotter considers some of King's short stories to be among the best produced during her era (unpublished paper, quoted with permission, and e-mail correspondence, 23 July 2012).

4. Taylor, xii–xiii. The term *racist* is used by other commentators also, including Linda S. Coleman, "Race and Gender in Grace King's Short Fiction," in Dorothy H. Brown and Barbara C. Ewell, eds., *Louisiana Women Writers* (Baton Rouge: LSU Press, 1992), 33, 37. The phrase "white-apologist" comes from Coleman, 33. For Weaver's views, see George M. Curtis and James J. Thompson, eds., *The Southern Essays of Richard M. Weaver* (Indianapolis: Liberty Fund, 1987).

5. John W. Blassingame, *Black New Orleans 1860–1880* (Chicago: University of Chicago Press, 1973), 87; Bryan, *The Myth of New Orleans in Literature: Dialogues of Race and Gender* (Knoxville: University of Tennessee Press, 1993), 40, 160.

6. Elfenbein, *Women on the Color Line: Evolving Stereotypes in the Writings of George Washington Cable, Grace King, Kate Chopin* (Charlottesville: University Press of Virginia, 1989), 75–77, 79. See "What Killed American Lit.," his review of *The Cambridge History of the American Novel* (*Wall Street Journal*, 27 August 2007) for Joseph Epstein's rejection of criticism according to which "nothing one has read is as it appears but is instead informed by authors hiding their true motives even from themselves."

7. King, *Monsieur Motte* (New York: Armstrong, 1988; rpt., Kessinger, n.d.). Page references are in parentheses.

8. See Jones, 97–117, for a different approach to the story and the later novella.

9. Taylor, 60.

10. Ibid.; Jones, 117.

11. The second quotation comes from King, *New Orleans: The People, the Place* (New York: Macmillan, 1895), 335–36.

12. The use of *chauvin* to mean "fanatically patriotic" dates from the First Empire, but was publicized widely by Alphonse Daudet's story of the Franco-Prussian War, "La Mort de Chauvin," which King may well have known.

13. King, *Balcony Stories* (1893; rpt., Ridgewood, NJ: Gregg Press, 1968), 35, 180; republished and enlarged (New York: Macmillan, 1925). "Grandmama" is from the enlarged edition; the quotation is on 254.

14. Ann Douglas Wood, quoted by Elfenbein, 79. "Little Mammy's" agility and usefulness are to be compared with those displayed by the badly crippled great-aunt of Ernest J. Gaines. See chapter 12 below.

15. See Jones, 121–26, for a reading of the story as an allegory.

16. Taylor, 75–76, 107; Blassingame, xv–xvi. As late as the mid-twentieth century it was acceptable for cultural historians to write of faithful, devoted blacks and good treatment by masters, with substantiation furnished by quoted statements from former slaves. See Lyle Saxon, Edward Dreyer, and Robert Tallant, *Gumbo Ya-Ya* (Boston: Houghton Mifflin, 1945), 143–47, 229–30, 256–57. See Blassingame, 26, on slaves who did not leave their masters after 1862.

17. King, *La Dame de Sainte Hermine* (New York: Macmillan, 1924), 278.

18. King, *New Orleans: The Place and the People* (New York: Macmillan, 1895), 201. A source for this volume is the narrative of André Pénicaut, who arrived in Louisiana with Iberville. King also drew on historical writings by Alexander Walker (1819–93). See Charles L. Dufour, *Ten Flags in the Wind* (New York: Harper, 1967), 44, 278.

19. These and other details come from Nancy Dixon, *Fortune and Misery: Sallie Rhett Roman of New Orleans* (Baton Rouge; LSU Press, 1999), 1–22.

20. Dixon, 28; Bennett H. Wall, ed., *Louisiana: A History* (Arlington Heights, IL: Forum Press, 1984), 213. Another Creole woman journalist of note was Eliza Jane Poitevent, from Mississippi, who married Alva Holbrook, editor of the *Picayune*, and, at his death, became editor and publisher, the first woman to occupy such positions at a large city paper. She published poetry under the name Pearl Rivers. See W. Kenneth Holditch, "Eliza Jane Poitevent, Pearl Rivers, and the Old Lady of Camp Street," *Louisiana Literature*, 4, 1 (Spring 1987).

21. Dixon, 70. Roman spoke also of Paul Bourget, a moralistic novelist, who, with Zola, "wields the most gorgeous descriptive pen of the period."

22. See Stuart, *Simpkinsville and Vicinity: Arkansas Stories of Ruth McEnery Stuart*, ed. and introduction by Ethel C. Simpson (Fayetteville: University of Arkansas Press, 1983, 1999); Chopin, quoted in Jones, 146. "Blink" was collected in Stuart, *A Golden Wedding and Other Tales* (New York: Harper, 1893; rpt., New York: Garrett, 1969). According to Taylor, 114–16, a faithful black servant in this story views her

depiction by the apprentice writer as a "distortion" of her experience, a misrepresentation, and she "connives" in this "literary exploitation." This is erroneous; the servant does not recognize herself in the portrait, because she has no experience of literary techniques and values, especially selection and shading. Stuart's papers are in the Louisiana Research Collection of Tulane University.

23. Stuart, *The Second Wooing of Salina Sue* (New York: Harper, 1898; rpt., New York: Garrett, 1969), 12, 226. White narrators and observers are used less by Harris. He commended Stuart's approximation of black speech; see Simpson in *Simpkinsville and Vicinity*, 15.

24. Taylor, 84–85; Simpson in *Simpkinsville and Vicinity*, 9. DuBose Heyward similarly imitated black speech, Gullah-inspired, in *Porgy* (1925); its language was praised in the *Times* and by some black writers, including Nella Larsen. Similarly, the black novelist Zora Neale Hurston drew heavily and without mockery upon picturesque types, folkloric elements, and black idiom as she knew them from her Florida childhood. Other black writers continue to imitate unlettered black speech in writing, e.g., Arthur Pfister. Taylor's point would be that Stuart *ought* to have been another Harriet Beecher Stowe. Stuart's black discourse is repeatedly called *dialect*. The concept of dialect, strictly defined, depends upon another language, standard or not, to which the speech in question must be compared. If speakers of the two can understand each other, and yet the forms differ in vocabulary, phonology, syntax, and morphology, they are dialects of another speech or one is a dialect of standard speech. If speakers cannot understand each other, they are different languages; if all forms do not differ, there is no dialect. Stuart's black speech varies in vocabulary only slightly and does not vary in syntax.

25. *The Second Wooing of Salina Sue*, 103–47. According to Blassingame (26), in 1863 there were still fifteen plantations in Orleans Parish.

CHAPTER TWELVE

1. Robert Tallant, *The Romantic New Orleanians* (New York: Dutton, 1950), 262; Ishmael Reed, quoted by Hilton Als, "Playing to Type," *New Yorker*, 23 May 2011, 86; Carl A. Brasseaux, *French, Cajun, Creole, Houma* (Baton Rouge: LSU Press, 2005), 100, 143; Réginald Hamel, ed., *L'Aventure de Johnelle (roman d'Alfred Mercier)* (Quebec: Humanitas, 2004), xxiii.

2. See J. Randal Woodland, "New People in the Old Museum of New Orleans: Ellen Gilchrist, Sheila Bosworth, and Nancy Lemann," in Dorothy H. Brown and Barbara C. Ewell, *Louisiana Women Writers* (Baton Rouge: LSU Press, 1992), 195–210; Daniels, "Porch-Sitting and Southern Poetry," in Jefferson Humphries and John Lowe, eds., *The Future of Southern Letters* (New York: Oxford, 1996), 65. In addition to fig-

ures mentioned above and below, others could be adduced to illustrate the critical positions adopted toward white Creole culture by twentieth-century writers. Jewish authors were ipso facto likely to be critical. Lillian Hellman (1905–84), born in New Orleans, retained her affection for the city.

3. Helen Taylor, *Gender, Race, and Religion in the Writings of Grace King, Ruth McEnery Stuart, and Kate Chopin* (Baton Rouge: LSU Press, 1989), 148; Brooks, quoted by W. Kenneth Holditch, "South Toward Freedom: Tennessee Williams," in Richard S. Kennedy, ed., *Literary New Orleans in the Modern World* (Baton Rouge: LSU Press, 1992), 61–75; Lowe, introduction to Humphries and Lowe, 8. See also Violet Harrington Bryan, *The Myth of New Orleans in Literature: Dialogues of Race and Gender* (Knoxville: University of Tennessee Press, 1993).

4. See Gérard Labarre St. Martin and Jacqueline K. Voorhies, eds., *Ecrits louisianais du dix-neuvième siècle: Nouvelles, contes et fables* (Baton Rouge: LSU Press, 1979), 91–108, 109–118; the quotations come from 95, 96. See also *Contes et récits de la Louisiane créole* (Shreveport: Tintamarre, 2006), 203–209. "Ma Tante Louise" was published first in 1911.

5. Keyes, *Dinner at Antoine's* (1948; rpt., London: Reprint Society, 1951).

6. Merrill Skaggs, "The Louisianas [sic] of Katherine Anne Porter's Mind," in Dorothy H. Brown and Barbara C. Ewell, *Louisiana Women Writers* (Baton Rouge: LSU Press, 1992), 155.

7. Norman German's novel *No Other World* (Thibodaux: Blue Heron Pess, 1992) offers a more recent fictional depiction of the Cane River area and the founding of the Métoyer family by Marie Thérèse (or Thérèze) Coincoin and the Frenchman with whom she formed a union, Claude Métoyer.

8. Saxon, *Children of Strangers* (Boston: Houghton Mifflin, 1937; rpt. with foreword by Chance Harvey, Gretna: Pelican, 2011). The novel was praised in the *Saturday Review of Literature*. The Hughes quotation (1933) comes from Harvey, *The Life and Selected Letters of Lyle Saxon* (Gretna, LA: Pelican [Publishing Co.], 2003), 34. See also James W. Thomas, "Lyle Saxon's Struggle with *Children of Strangers*," *Southern Studies*, 16 (1977), 27–40, republished in Mathé Allain, ed., *Louisiana Literature and Literary Figures* (Lafayette: Center for Louisiana Studies, University of Louisiana at Lafayette, 2004), 264–74; Gary B. Mills, *The Forgotten People: Cane River's Creoles of Color* (Baton Rouge: LSU Press, 1977). For a short but good summary of pertinent racial matters, see Clayton Delery, "Teaching *Children of Strangers*," *Louisiana Fictions: Proceedings of the Third Annual Louisiana Studies Conference* (Natchitoches: Northwestern State University/Cane River National Heritage Area, © 2011 [2012]), 117–22.

9. See Faulkner, *Mosquitoes* (1927); rpt. with introduction by Frederick R. Karl (New York: Liveright, 1997), 10; *William Faulkner: New Orleans Sketches*, ed. Carvel

Collins (New Brunswick: Rutgers University Press, 1958), 49; Faulkner, *Absalom, Absalom!* (1936; rpt., New York: Modern Library, 1951), 74. See also Holditch, "The Brooding Air of the Past: William Faulkner," in Kennedy, 38–50; republished in Allain, 407–14. The *Times-Picayune* quotation above appeared also in *The Double-Dealer* in 1925. See Bryan, 84–85. The term *cliché* originally meant "printing plate" and, as of 1869, "photographic negative" or "snapshot." Such "snapshots" become commonplaces when they are trivialized by reproduction and imitation. They can be inhibiting to a writer, who then seeks a fresh approach, or can be reused successfully. See 323–24 of *Mosquitoes* on the origins of Mrs. Maurier.

10. The statement is quoted in Harrington, 116. Critics repeat that the name Belle Reve means "beautiful dream"—the intention, presumably. The French noun is, however, masculine; the adjective thus does not agree.

11. Information on Feibleman's birthplace (on Pleasant Street near St. Charles Avenue) comes from his widow, Shirley Ann Grau.

12. See William Bedford Clark, "Rage and Order: A Meditation on Hurricanes and the Literary Imagination," Rodrigue Lecture, Lafayette, Louisiana, October 2009.

13. See the author's note to the reprint, *Fabulous Ancestor*, preface by Maurice duQuesnay (Lafayette: Levy Humanities Series, 1991). Parenthetical references are to this edition. Information here comes from Demarest's unpublished papers "Creole Days and Ways" and "Creole." He acknowledged the resemblance between the society portrayed by Cable and what he knew of his Creole ancestors and their circles.

14. Francisco Bouligny, from Valencia, arrived as an aide to General Alejandro O'Reilly in 1769, settled in the Bayou Tèche area in 1779, along with sixteen families he had recruited from Málaga, and married Marie Louise le Sénéchal d'Auberville. His son Ursin maintained a faithful liaison with his quadroon mistress and had their natural children baptized and buried in the family tomb. See Fontaine Martin, *A History of the Bouligny Family* (Lafayette: University of Southwestern Louisiana, 1990) and Gilbert C. Din, *Francisco Bouligny* (Baton Rouge: LSU Press, 1993).

15. On the house image in work by Demarest and other Louisiana novelists, see C. S. Brosman, "The House of the Creoles: The Fiction of Four Louisiana Writers," *Explorations*, 10 (2004), (154–74).

16. Myth indicates here a cultural phenomenon, humanly shaped and variable, even if having a historical basis, but treated like a fact of nature. The South as a "myth" is, of course, a cliché. The southerner, said John William Corrington, knows who his fathers were, knows he came from the soil, knows "that the soil and its people once had a name." "He knows that is true, and he knows it is a myth." See www.frontporchrepublic.com/2010/05/john–william–corrington–a–literary–conservative/.

17. Kane, *Gentlemen, Swords, and Pistols* (New York: Morrow, 1951), xiii.

18. Note that Mercier mocked the Yankees' commercialism; Saint-Ybars reflects

on Bostonians who have inherited property in Louisiana and have put the slaves on the market. "And these are the same people who preach abolitionism, in the name of philanthropy. Hypocrites! But as they say, these saints of the day, business is business." (The last three words are in English in the original.) *L'Habitation Saint-Ybars* (New Orleans: Imprimerie Franco-Américaine, 1881), 9.

19. See Maurice W. duQuesnay, introduction to Grau, *Writers and Writing*, Flora Levy Lecture Series, 4 (Lafayette: University of Southwestern Louisiana, 1988), 6, 9; Elzbieta Olesky, "The Keepers of the House," in Brown and Ewell, 170, 171, 177.

20. Other works of Grau's in which New Orleans and its vicinity appear include "Miss Yellow Eyes," "The Way of a Man," and "Joshua," from *The Black Prince and Other Stories* (1955). All concern blacks or those of mixed race; "Miss Yellow Eyes" includes a voodoo practitioner. They do not emphasize the characters' Creole background, however; "Joshua" has a bit of Cajun French. *The Condor Passes* (1971) has various settings, including New Orleans. *The Hard Blue Sky* (1958) is set on a Louisiana coastal island, Isle aux Chiens. Demarest notes that Grau opposes to city decadence the pastoral virtues of farmers, Cajuns, and black servants and sharecroppers ("Creole Days and Ways"). Like Chopin, she posits the Mississippi Gulf as a sort of quasi-Edenic refuge. It is a place of hurricanes also, however; there are flashbacks to former storms, and a great one approaches as the work ends.

21. C. S. Brosman, interview with Shirley Ann Grau, *Louisiana English Journal*, n.s., 5, 2 (1998), 32–33; Allen-Taylor, "The World According to Grau," *Literary Quarterly, Metro Santa Cruz* 25 Feb.–4 March 1998, 11–13.

22. See Percy's "New Orleans Mon Amour," *Harper's Magazine*, Sept. 1968; Corrington, *The Collected Stories of John William Corrington*, ed. Joyce Corrington, introduction by William Mills (Columbia: University of Missouri Press, 1990). On New Orleans as a setting for Corrington's crime novels, see Frank W. Shelton, "The New Orleans Crime Fiction of John W. and Joyce Corrington," *Louisiana Literature*, 9 (1992), 42–56, republished in Allain, ed., 513–24. The novels emphasize the role of history, and some characters are from old Creole families.

23. On speech in Pointe Coupée, see Thomas A. Klingler, *If I Could Turn My Tongue Like That: The Creole Language of Pointe Coupée Parish* (Baton Rouge: LSU Press, 2003).

24. Gaines's use of Madame Bayonne as narrator recalls Faulkner's narrators, and the fictional community of Bayonne owes something to him. Gaines acknowledged his influence. See Valerie Babb, *Ernest Gaines* (Boston: Twayne, 1991), 12, 143 n. 17. He also mentioned Ivan Turgenev in connection with *Catherine Carmier*. See Ruth Laney, "A Conversation with Ernest Gaines," *Southern Review*, 10, 1 (Winter 1974), 1–6, 10–11. Gaines speaks in this interview of his crippled aunt, to whose memory *The Autobiography of Miss Jane Pittman* is dedicated.

25. *Carmier* resembles closely, however, the name *Cormier*, an Acadian name.

26. Gilchrist, *In the Land of Dreamy Dreams* (Fayetteville: University of Arkansas Press, 1981; rpt., Boston: Little, Brown, c. 1981); *Victory Over Japan* (Boston: Little, Brown, 1984). The first title echoes Lafcadio Hearn's "The City of Dreams" (New Orleans *Item*, 9 March 1879). See Edward Larocque Tinker, *Lafcadio Hearn's American Days* (New York: Dodd, Mead, 1925), 64–66. Details are generally accurate. A blueblood fraternity on Henry Clay Avenue, Garden District architecture and streets, Exposition Boulevard, a record shop with "Mushroom" in the name, and the architect Thomas Sully are mentioned. Gilchrist erroneously places Bayou Lafourche, west of New Orleans (Lafourche and Terrebonne Parishes), in Plaquemines Parish, to the east. It is reported that the events in "Rich" really took place; some locals were allegedly enraged by it. An interesting insight, not exploited, is the snobbery of the black bartender at the Lawn Tennis Club: like older club members, he "hated" the new ones, parvenus (rpt. 68). Gilchrist completed *In the Land of Dreamy Dreams* as an NEA Fellow. Her novel *The Annunciation* (Boston: Little, Brown, 1983) provides further evidence of New Orleans decadence.

27. See Bauer, "Ellen Gilchrist's False Eden," in John Lowe, ed., *Louisiana Culture from the Colonial Era to Katrina* (Baton Rouge: LSU Press, 2008), 192. Other stories in the collection, featuring some sex and adolescent unhappiness, may be responsible for the sales.

28. Joel L. Fletcher, *Ken and Thelma: The Story of "A Confederacy of Dunces"* (Gretna: Pelican, 2005), 10, 66, 69 (the Holditch quote is on 14); C.S. Brosman, "Depictions of Popular New Orleans Culture by Mona Lisa Saloy and John Kennedy Toole," *Arkansas Review*, 43, 1 (April 2012), 47–54.

29. Jack Trotter, "Unreal Bodies, Unholy Blood," *Chronicles: A Magazine of American Culture*, 35, 10 (October 2011), 12–14.

30. Rice, *The Feast of All Saints* (New York: Simon and Schuster, 1979). Page references are in parentheses. Rice borrowed some names, such as the inventor Norbert Rillieux, from Rodolphe-Lucien Desdunes, *Nos hommes et notre histoire: notices biographiques accompagnées de réflexions* . . . (Montreal: Arbour & Dupont, 1911), trans. and ed., with notes, by Dorothea Olga McCants as *Our People and Our History* (Baton Rouge: LSU Press, 1973).

31. Kein, "Use of Louisiana Creole in Southern Literature," in Kein, *Creole: The History and Legacy of Louisiana's Free People of Color* (Baton Rouge: LSU Press, 2000), 148. Kein qualifies a poem of hers as "a plea to be recognized and accepted as a group without imposed labeling" (149).

32. The novel by Charles W. Chesnutt (1858–1932) that takes place in New Orleans, *Paul Marchand, F.M.C.*, composed in the 1920s, an interesting contribution to the depiction of men from this caste, was published by the University Press of Mississippi

(1998). In fact, the hero is white, but has been taken for colored during his earlier life. The debate on the issue is thus all the keener. Chesnutt, a distinguished author, was connected to Ohio and North Carolina, but he knew Louisiana well. See Bryan, 32–41.

33. Bosworth, *Almost Innocent* (New York: Simon & Schuster, 1984; rpt., Baton Rouge: LSU Press, 1996), 18, 92, 120, 133. (Page references are to the reprint.) The novel was translated into French and German.

34. Lemann, *Lives of the Saints* (New York: Knopf, 1985; rpt., Baton Rouge: LSU Press, 1997), 18–19 (rpt.); Woodland, 207.

35. Woodland, 209–10.

CHAPTER THIRTEEN

1. Sir Paul Harvey, *The Oxford Companion to English Literature*, 3rd edition (Oxford: Clarendon Press, 1946), v.; M. M. Bakhtin, *The Dialogic Imagination*, ed. Michael Holquist, trans. Holquist and Caryl Emerson (Austin: University of Texas Press, 1981).

2. Interview by Reginald Dwayne Betts, *Able Muse*, 13 (Summer 2012), 76. Smith, who is black, also emphasizes oral presentation of poetry, for herself and others.

3. Karen Sotiropoulos, quoted in Patricia R. Schroeder, "Passing for Black: Coon Songs and the Performance of Race," *Journal of American Culture*, 33, 2 (June 2010), 139. See also *Dictionary of Literary Biography* 41: *Afro-American Poets Since 1955*, ed. Thadious M. Davis and Trudier Harris (1985). According to John Lowe, Brenda Marie Osbey was influenced by Buddy ("King") Bolden; that would be indirectly, through imitators, since there are no recordings of his playing (he ceased performing in 1907). Grace King expressed the conviction that America would "one day do homage for music of a fine and original type to some representative of Louisiana's coloured population." King, *New Orleans: The Place and the People* (New York: Macmillan, 1895), 340. Note a festival sponsored by Faulkner House Books: "Words & Music."

4. Salaam, *From a Bend in the River: 100 New Orleans Poets* (New Orleans: Runagate Press, 1998). See also Joanne V. Gabbin, ed., *Furious Flower: African American Poetry from the Black Arts Movement to the Present* (Charlottesville: University of Virginia Press, 2004), which includes work by Louisiana poets Alvin Aubert (b. Lutcher, 1930), Quo Vadis Gex-Breaux, Yusef Komunyakaa, Pinkie Gordon Lane, Salaam, Mona Lisa Saloy, and Jerry W. Ward, Jr. Salaam, born in 1947, originally Val Ferdinand, is, like Osbey, associated with the Tremé neighborhood and was interviewed in the film on the district. He also organized The WordBand, a poetry performance ensemble that combines poetry with blues and jazz. See Wikipedia on the Maple Leaf

Bar; see also Ruth Salvaggio, *Hearing Sappho in New Orleans: The Call of Poetry from Congo Square to the Ninth Ward* (Baton Rouge: LSU Press, 2012), 123–30.

5. Arceneaux regularly omits *ne*, uses the indicative where the subjunctive is required, and so on. See Ann Brewster Dobie, ed., *Uncommonplace: An Anthology of Contemporary Louisiana Poets* (Baton Rouge: LSU Press, 1998), 7–8. Numerous poets mentioned in this chapter are represented in this anthology. See also Thomas Bonner, Jr., and Robert Skinner, *Immortelles: Poems About Death and Life by New Southern Writers* (New Orleans: Xavier Review Press, 1995).

6. See Dobie, passim; Salaam; Susan Larson, "New Orleans Writer Finds Poetry in the Morning Light," *New Orleans Times-Picayune*, 4 February 2009; Cooley, "How Hurricane Katrina Made Me into a New Orleanian," *Louisiana Literature*, 29, 2 (2012), 17–23; C. S. Brosman, *Places in Mind* (Baton Rouge: LSU Press, 2000); Brosman, *Under the Pergola* (Baton Rouge: LSU Press, 2011). "Chrétien Point" is in the latter collection. Poems by Matherne such as "Les Fils" are in correct French, but the tone, diction, and mores depicted are typical of Cajun poetry (as illustrated by Bourque). Matherne publishes bilingual editions of her writing. In 1989–1992 Lane served as poet laureate of the state, the first black woman to do so. A poet who evoked the Crescent City in the 1920s was Carl Carmer, in *French Town*, illustrations by Frederic Hicks, preface by Grace King (1928; rpt., New Orleans: Pelican, 1968). For an impressionistic but learned discussion of what Katrina signified, culturally and materially, see Salvaggio, passim. In particular, Salvaggio examines the abundant poetry inspired by the storm; she does not provide, however, a balanced and extensive survey.

7. *L'Herne* [Paris], no. 9 (1967), "William Burroughs, Claude Pélieu, Bob Kaufman," with photographs and Kaufman texts translated by Mary Beach and Pélieu, 256–306 (the Hugo allusion is on p. 299); interview of Saloy by Dayne Sherman, "Louisiana Talks," *Louisiana Libraries*, 75, 2 (Fall 2012), 36–41.

8. Maria Damon, introduction to section on Kaufman in *Callaloo*, 25, 1 (Winter 2002), 103–97, viz. 105–106; Kaufman, *Solitudes Crowded with Loneliness* (New York: New Directions, 1965), 56–61); Kaufman, *The Ancient Rain: Poems 1956–1978* (New York: New Directions, 1981), ix–x.

9. See *The Ancient Rain* and *Solitudes Crowded with Loneliness*; the quotation is from "Walking Parker Home," 5.

10. See Violet Harrington Bryan, *The Myth of New Orleans in Literature: Dialogues of Race and Gender* (Knoxville: University of Tennessee Press, 1993), 131–41.

11. Salaam, 52; Stanford, "A Backward Glance at the New *Southern Review*," *Explorations*, 7 (1993), 161. John Freeman observes similarly that "good poetry should elicit some form of somatic response . . . It is the way the sound effects work on the images that most elicits somatic response" (private communication).

12. See John Lowe, "An Interview with Brenda Marie Osbey," in Jefferson

Humphries and Lowe, eds., *The Future of Southern Letters* (New York: Oxford University Press, 1996), 93–118. An abridged version of this interview appeared in the *Southern Review*, 30, 4 (1994), 812–23. See also Osbey, "I Want to Die in New Orleans," in John Lowe, ed., *Louisiana Culture from the Colonial Era to Katrina* (Baton Rouge: LSU Press, 2008), 248. On "Pailet Lane," see Lyle Saxon, Edward Dreyer, and Robert Tallant, *Gumbo Ya-Ya* (Boston: Houghton Mifflin, 1945), chapter 18. The poem for Rowell is collected in *All Saints: New and Selected Poems* (Baton Rouge: LSU Press, 1997).

13. Osbey also published numerous articles, poems in journals, and miscellaneous publications, including *Qu'on arrive enfin*, a bilingual anthology (Renaissance Noire, 2004), and "Canne à sucre: A Slave-Song Suite," in *American Poetry Review*, 34, 3 (May–June 2005). The title of the 1997 collection recalls that of Anne Rice's novel. It is unfortunate that errors in French spelling and etymology mar Osbey's publications. According to Lowe, *Louisiana Culture*, Osbey wrote an opera libretto, *Sultan au Grand Marais*.

14. Bryan, "Evocation of Place and Culture in the Works of Four Contemporary Louisiana Black Writers," *Louisiana Literature*, 4, 2 (Fall 1987), 50. On Creolism and Africanism, see Lowe, "Interview," 1996, 102. See also Osbey, "I Want to Die in New Orleans" and "One More Last Chance: Ritual and the Jazz Funeral," in Lowe, *Louisiana Culture*, 245–52 and 284–93.

15. Osbey, *In These Houses* (Middletown, CT: Wesleyan University Press, 1980). Page references to this and other collections are in parentheses. The elimination of capitalization is not, of course, new; one has only to cite Guillaume Apollinaire's *Alcools* (1913) and E. E. Cummings's *Tulips and Chimneys* (1923) as well as Kaufman and others. Osbey stated: "I pride myself in the fact that I write about people. . . . I look for characters that are clear, and strong, very visible and very visual. . ." (Lowe, "Interview," 96–97).

16. Osbey, *Ceremony for Minneconjoux* (Lexington: Callaloo Poetry Series, University Press of Kentucky, 1983; reissued by the University Press of Virginia).

17. Osbey remarked that it never occurred to her to write about whites and that she sees New Orleans as a "distinctly black space" (Lowe, "Interview," 116–17). This does not prevent poems of hers from appealing to white readers and appearing relevant to their lives.

18. Lowe, "Interview," 108; Bachelard, *La Poétique de l'espace* (Paris: Presses Universitaires de France, 1958). Osbey stated that she saw New Orleans as "a female place" (Lowe, "Interview," 101).

19. See Lowe, "Interview," 109; Bryan, "Evocation," 49–60. In 1992 Osbey stated that she was a deeply religious person, although she had denied so earlier. She was reared as a Lutheran (Lowe, "Interview," 101). The motif of saintliness recurs in a post-

Katrina poem, "Litany of Our Lady"; see *Southern Literary Journal* (Spring 2008), 13–14, and excerpts in Salvaggio, 179.

20. Osbey, *History and Other Poems* (St. Louis: Time Being Books, 2012).

21. Certain information about Saloy comes from a personal interview, 24 October 2010, and from written replies to questions. Other details come from *Red Beans and Ricely Yours* (Kirksville: Truman State University Press, 2005) (page numbers are henceforth in the text); *Wall Street Journal*, "Words Can't Describe What Some New Orleans Writers Lost," 1 Nov. 2005; interview of Saloy by Rachel Breunlin and Ashley Nelson in *Seventh Ward Speaks*, an oral history and poster project sponsored by "The Porch," August 2005, 1; Saloy, "Native Daughter: Growing Up Black in New Orleans," *Designer/Builder: A Journal of the Human Environment*, Nov.–Dec. 2005; and Sherman, "Louisiana Talks." The name Saloy may be derived from Fr. *loi*. On his first job, as a child, her father spoke little, fearing he would be recognized as "colored" if he did so. In the U.S. Army he served in a black unit, since he did not want to deny his heritage. Commentators mistakenly suppose sometimes that she was named for the song.

22. Sherman, "Louisiana Talks." Saloy is currently (2013) at work on a scholarly book concerning Kaufman.

23. Sherman, "Louisiana Talks"; Saloy, "Native Daughter," 9–11.

24. The brochure, in its third printing, was published by Black Bayou Press, New Orleans, © 1994, rev. 1996, 1999. It next came out in *Ishamel Reed's Konch*, 9 (Fall 1996–Spring 1997), then in Gabbin's anthology and at least one other. The Major quotation comes from Randall Kennedy, *Nigger: The Strange Career of a Troublesome Word* (New York: Pantheon, 2002), 37. See also the pertinent but hostile review of this volume by Hilton Als, *New Yorker*, 11 February 2002, 82–88.

25. See C. S. Brosman, "Depictions of Popular New Orleans Culture by Mona Lisa Saloy and John Kennedy Toole," *Arkansas Review*, 43, 1 (April 2012), 47–54.

26. Lamb's ear is a perennial hedge nettle densely covered with white, silky wool. Cawains are large swamp turtles; mudbugs are crawfish; griots are storytellers; gris-gris are voodoo (or hoodoo) fetiches and charms; loup-garou = werewolf. On the bamboula see chapter 8.

27. See Mary L. Morton, "Creole Culture in the Poetry of Sybil Kein," in Kein, ed., *Creole*, 317–25; Bryan, *The Myth of New Orleans*, 146–50, 157; Salvaggio, 5.

28. Kein, *An American South* (East Lansing: Michigan State University Press, 1996), 19. The melting-pot poem comes from Kein, *Gombo People* (New Orleans: Leo J. Hall, 1981); republished in Ann Brewster Dobie, ed., *Uncommonplace: An Anthology of Contemporary Louisiana Poets* (Baton Rouge: LSU Press, 1998), 123–27.

29. See Salaam, 167–72, and Pfister, *My Name Is New Orleans: Forty Years of Poetry and Other Jazz* (Donaldsonville: Margaret Media, 2009) (with a CD), 280, 303–304.

The diaspora quotation comes from a Katrina poem, "Impressions," 31. See Susan Larson, "'Professor Arturo' Pfister Brings His Poetry Home to New Orleans," New Orleans *Times-Picayune*, 1 July 2009.

30. St. Germain, *Swamp Songs: The Making of an Unruly Woman* (Salt Lake City: University of Utah Press, 2003); *Navigating Disaster: Sixteen Essays of Love and a Poem of Despair* (Hammond: Louisiana Literature Press, 2012), "Prelude." The latter volume contains pieces on New Orleans and Katrina-related matters, as well as a six-page poem on Grand Isle and the oil spill of 2010. See Emily Toth's review of *Swamp Songs* in *Women's Review of Books*, 20, 8 (May 2003), 17–18. See also Jean Arceneaux, *Je suis Cadien*, with translations by Sheryl St. Germain (Merrick, NY: Cross-Cultural Communication, 1994). Personal data above comes in part from an interview, 19 November 2012, and an unpublished essay that the author graciously shared with me.

31. See St. Germain, *The Mask of Medusa* (Merrick, NY: Cross-Cultural Communication, 1987), erotic feminist poems that feature snakes (a swamp motif); *Going Home* (Van Nuys: Perivale Press, 1989); *Making Bread at Midnight* (Austin: Slough Press, 1992); *Let It Be a Dark Roux: New and Selected Poems* (Pittsburgh: Autumn House Press, 2007). The quotation comes from "Scars" in *Going Home* (11), republished in *Making Bread at Midnight* (25).

32. See St. Germain's Katrina essay in Katherine Tracy, ed., *In the Eye: A Collection of Writings* (Alamogordo: Thunder Rain, 2007) and Katrina poems in *Let It Be a Dark Roux* and essays in *Navigating Disaster*.

33. Soniat, *Alluvial* (Lewisburg: Bucknell University Press, 2001). See Salvaggio, 128–29, 139–42. Lalaurie is featured in George Washington Cable's story "The 'Haunted House' in Royal Street" (1887); see chapter 8 above.

34. Grue, *Downtown* (New Orleans: Trembling Pillow Press, 2011), 122. See also *French Quarter Poems* (n.p., Long Measure Press, 1979).

35. See Salaam, 94–97.

SELECTED BIBLIOGRAPHY

Principal works treated in the body of this study are listed just below, some in modern editions or collections. (The original publication data are given in the respective chapters; some original dates appear below also.) Certain other works are included here also. Writings that receive only brief mention in the text or in notes are not generally included, unless they have broad interest. The list of secondary works includes the principal sources utilized and certain additional studies particularly relevant or of documentary interest. For other sources, readers should consult the notes.

PRIMARY WORKS

Allain, Mathé, and Barry Ancelet, eds. *Littérature française de la Louisiane: Anthologie*. Belford, NH: National Materials Development Center for French, 1981.
Bibliothèque Tintamarre, La. www.centenary.edu/french/louisiana.html
Bonner, Thomas, Jr., and Robert Skinner, eds. *Immortelles: Poems About Death and Life by New Southern Writers*. New Orleans: Xavier Review Press, 1995.
Bosworth, Sheila. *Almost Innocent*. New York: Simon and Schuster, 1984.
Cable, George Washington. *Creoles and Cajuns*. Ed. Arlin Turner. Garden City, NY: Doubleday, 1959.
――――. *The Grandissimes*. New York: Scribner's, 1880; rpt. Kessinger, n.p., n.d.
――――. *Old Creole Days*. New York: Scribner's, 1879.
Chopin, Kate. *Complete Stories and Novels*. Ed. Sandra M. Gilbert. New York: The Library of America, 2002.
――――. *The Complete Works of Kate Chopin*. 2 vols. Ed. Per Seyersted. Baton Rouge: LSU Press, 1969.
Cowan, James L., ed. *La Marseillaise noire*. Lyons: Cosmogone, 2001.
Creole Echoes: The Francophone Poetry of Nineteenth-Century Louisiana. Trans. Norman R. Shapiro; intro. and notes by M. Lynn Weiss. Urbana: University of Illinois Press, 2004.

de la Houssaye, Sidonie. *Contes d'une grand-mère louisianaise*. Shreveport: Tintamarre, 2007.

———. *Pouponne et Balthazar*. Ed. and trans. John J. Perret. Lafayette: University of Southwestern Louisiana, University of Southwestern Louisiana Center for Louisiana Studies, 1983. Ed. May Rush Gwin Waggoner. Lafayette: Center for Louisiana Studies, 1983.

———. *Les Quarteronnes de la Nouvelle-Orléans*, I. Ed. Christian Hommel. Shreveport: Tintamarre, 2006.

Demarest, Donald. *Fabulous Ancestor*. Rpt. Lafayette: Levy Humanities Series, 1991.

Dessommes, Georges. *Vendanges*. Shreveport: Tintamarre, 2007.

———. *Tante Cydette*. 1888. Ed. Ida Eve Heckenbach. Gretna: Pelican, 2001.

Dobie, Ann Brewster. *Uncommonplace: An Anthology of Contemporary Louisiana Poets*. Baton Rouge: LSU Press, 1998.

du Quesnay, Adolphe. *A Summer at Grand Isle*. Trans. C. S. Brosman and Paul de Laup. Lafayette: University of Southwestern Louisiana, 1997.

Faulkner, William. *Mosquitoes*. Rpt. New York: Liveright, 1997.

———. *William Faulkner: New Orleans Sketches*. Ed. Carvel Collins. New Brunswick: Rutgers University Press, 1958.

Gaines, Ernest J. *Catherine Carmier*. New York: Atheneum, 1964.

Garreau, Louis-Armand. *Bras-coupé et autres récits louisianais*. Shreveport: Tintamarre, 2007.

———. *Louisiana*. Ed. D. A. Kress. Shreveport: Tintamarre, 2003.

Gayarré, Charles. *Aubert Dubayet; or, the Two Sister Republics*. Boston: Osgood, 1882.

———. *Fernando de Lemos. Truth and Fiction. A Novel*. New York: Carleton, 1872.

———. *The School for Politics: A Dramatic Novel*. New York: Appleton, 1854.

Gilchrist, Ellen. *In the Land of Dreamy Dreams*. 1981. Rpt. Boston: Little, Brown, ©1981.

Grau, Shirley Ann. *The House on Coliseum Street*. New York: Knopf, 1961.

Hearn, Lafcadio. *Chita: A Memory of Last Island*. New York: Harper, 1889.

———. *Inventing New Orleans: The Writings of Lafcadio Hearn*. Ed. and intro. by S. Frederick Starr. Jackson: University Press of Mississippi, 2001.

———. *Lafcadio Hearn: American Writings*. Ed. Christopher Benfe. New York: Library of America, 2009.

Kein, Sybil. *An American South*. East Lansing: Michigan State University Press, 1996.

Keyes, Frances Parkinson. *Dinner at Antoine's*. 1948. London: Reprint Society, 1951.

King, Grace. *Balcony Stories*. 1893. Rpt. Ridgewood, N.J.: Gregg Press, 1968.

———. *La Dame de Sainte Hermine*. New York: Macmillan, 1924.

———. *Grace King of New Orleans: A Selection of Her Writings*. Ed. Robert Bush. Baton Rouge: LSU Press, 1973.

———. *Monsieur Motte.* 1888. Rpt. New York: Armstrong, 1988.
———. *New Orleans: The Place and the People.* New York: Macmillan, 1895.
———. *The Pleasant Ways of Saint-Médard.* New York: Holt, 1916.
———. *Tales of a Time and Place.* New York: Harper, 1892.
Kolin, Philip, and Susan Swartwout, eds. *Hurricane Blues: Poems about Katrina and Rita.* Cape Girardeau: Southeastern Missouri University Press, 2006.
Kress, D. A., ed. *Anthologie de poésie louisianaise du XIXe siècle.* Shreveport: Tintamarre, 2010.
Lanusse, Armand, ed. *Les Cenelles: Choix de poésies indigènes.* New Orleans: H. Lauve, 1845. Rpt. Washington, D.C.: Associated Publishers, 1945. Ed. Edward Maceo Coleman, foreword by H. Carrington Lancaster. Rpt. Boston: G.K. Hall, 1979. Ed. Régine Latortue and Gleason R.W. Adams, with English translations and preface. Rpt. Shreveport: Tintamarre, 2003. Ed. Mia B. Reamer.
Lemann, Nancy. *Lives of the Saints.* New York: Knopf, 1985.
Mercier, Alfred. *L'Aventure de Johnelle.* Ed. Réginald Hamel. Quebec: Humanitas, 2004.
———. *La Fille du prêtre: récit social.* 3 vols. New Orleans: Imprimerie Cosmopolite, 1877–78.
———. *Le Fou de Palerme: nouvelle sicilienne.* New Orleans: Imprimerie du "Carillon," 1873. Rpt. Shreveport: Tintamarre, 2006.
———. *L'Habitation Saint-Ybars.* 1881. Ed. Réginald Hamel. Montreal, Guérin, 1989. Ed. D. A. Kress. Shreveport: Tintamarre, 2003.
———. *Hénoch Jédésias ou l'Avare de New-York.* Quebec and Paris: Stanké, 2004.
———. *Lidia.* Rpt. Shreveport: Tintamarre, 2007.
Michaelides, Chris, ed. *Paroles d'honneur: Ecrits de Créoles de couleur néo-orléanais.* Shreveport: Tintamarre, 2004.
Osbey, Brenda Marie. *All Saints: New and Selected Poems.* Baton Rouge: LSU Press, 1997.
———. *Ceremony for Minneconjoux.* Lexington: University Press of Kentucky, 1983.
———. *Desperate Circumstance, Dangerous Woman.* Brownsville, OR: Story Line Press, 1991.
———. *History and Other Poems.* St. Louis: Time Being Boooks, 2012.
———. *In These Houses.* Middletown, CT: Wesleyan University Press, 1980.
Rice, Anne. *The Feast of All Saints.* New York: Simon and Schuster, 1979.
[Rouquette, Adrien]. *Critical Dialogue Between Aboo and Caboo on a New Book; or a Grandissime Ascension.* Ed. E. Junius (Mingo City [i.e., New Orleans]: Great Publishing House of Sam Slick Allspice, 1880). Rpt. Kessinger Publishing, n.d.
Rouquette, Adrien. *L'Antoniade ou la solitude avec Dieu (Trois âges), poème érémitique.* New Orleans: L. Marchand, 1860.

———. *La Nouvelle Atala; ou, la fille de l'esprit. Légende indienne par Chahta-Ima (de la Louisiane)*. New Orleans: Imprimerie du Propagateur, 1879. Rpt. ed. Elizabeth Landry. Shreveport: Tintamarre, 2003.

———. *Les Savanes*. Paris: J. Labitte; New Orleans: A. Moret, 1841.

———. *La Thébaïde en Amérique; ou, Apologie de la vie solitaire et contemplative*. Paris, 1841; rpt. New Orleans; Imprimerie Méridier, 1852.

———. *Trois âges; suite et fin de l'Antoniade. Poème érémitique*. New Orleans: L. Marchand, 1869.

Rouquette, Dominique. *Les Meschacébéennes*. Paris: Librairie du Sauvaignat, 1839.

Salaam, Kalamu ya, ed. *From a Bend in the River: 100 New Orleans Poets*. New Orleans: Runagate Press, 1998.

Saloy, Mona Lisa. *Red Beans and Ricely Yours*. Kirksville, MO: Truman State University Press, 2005.

Saxon, Lyle. *Children of Strangers*. Boston: Houghton Mifflin, 1937.

Séjour, Victor. *The Fortune-Teller*. Trans. Norman R. Shapiro. Urbana: University of Illinois Press, 2002.

———. *The Jew of Seville*. Trans. Norman R. Shapiro. Urbana: University of Illinois Press, 2002.

Séligny, Michel. *Homme libre de couleur de la Nouvelle Orléans: Nouvelles et récits*. Ed. Frans C. Amelinckx. Quebec: Presses Universitaires de Laval, 1998.

Stuart, Ruth McEnery. *A Golden Wedding and Other Tales*. New York: Harper, 1893.

———. *The Second Wooing of Salina Sue*. New York: Harper, 1898; rpt. New York: Garrett, 1969.

———. *The Story of Babette, A Little Creole Girl*. New York: Harper, 1894. Rpt. Memphis: General Books, 2010.

———. *Simpkinsville and Vicinity: Arkansas Stories of Ruth McEnery Stuart*. Ed. Ethel C. Simpson. Fayetteville: University of Arkansas Press, 1983.

Testut, Charles. *Saint-Denis*. Ed. Courtney Herzog. Shreveport: Tintamarre, 2004.

———. *Le Vieux Salomon*. 1871. Rpt. Shreveport: Editions Tintamarre, 2003.

Thierry, Camille. *Les Vagabondes*. 1874. Ed. Frans Amelinckx and May Rush Gwin Waggoner. Shreveport: Tintamarre, 2004.

Tracy, Katherine, ed. *In the Eye*. Foreword by C. S. Brosman. Alamogordo: Thunder-Rain Publishing, 2007.

Tujague, François. *Chroniques louisianaises*. Shreveport: Tintamarre, 2003.

SECONDARY SOURCES

Abel, Sheri Lyn. *Charles Testut's "Le Vieux Salomon": Race, Religion, Socialism, and Freemasonry*. Lanham, MD: Lexington Books, 2009.

Allain, Mathé, and Adele Cornay St. Martin. "French Theatre in Louisiana," in Maxine Schwartz Seller, ed., *Ethnic Theatre in the United States*. Westport, Conn: Greenwood Press, 1983.

Allain, Mathé, ed. *Louisiana Literature and Literary Figures*. Lafayette: Center for Louisiana Studies, University of Louisiana at Lafayette, 2004.

Beer, Janet, ed. *The Cambridge Companion to Kate Chopin*. Cambridge: Cambridge University Press, 2008.

Bell, Caryn Cossé. *Revolution, Romanticism, and the Afro-Creole Protest Tradition in Louisiana, 1718–1868*. Baton Rouge: LSU Press, 1997.

Benfey, Christopher. *Degas in New Orleans: Encounters in the Creole World of Kate Chopin and George Washington Cable*. New York: Knopf, 1997.

Blassingame, John W. *Black New Orleans, 1860–1880*. Chicago: University of Chicago Press, 1973.

Bloom, Harold, ed. *Kate Chopin*. New York: Chelsea House, 1987.

Bond, Bradley G., ed. *French Colonial Louisiana and the Atlantic World*. Baton Rouge: LSU Press, 2005.

Bonner, Thomas, Jr. *The Kate Chopin Companion*. Westport, CT: Greenwood, 1988.

Brown, Dorothy H., and Barbara C. Ewell, eds. *Louisiana Women Writers*. Baton Rouge: LSU Press, 1992.

Brasseaux, Carl A. *French, Cajun, Creole, Houma: A Primer on Francophone Louisiana*. Baton Rouge: LSU Press, 2005.

Bryan, Violet Harrington. *The Myth of New Orleans: Dialogues of Race and Gender*. Knoxville: University of Tennessee Press, 1993.

Castellanos, Henry C. *New Orleans As It Was: Episodes of Louisiana Life*. Introduction by Judith Kelleher Schafer; bibliographic listing and revised index by George F. Reinecke. Baton Rouge: LSU Press, 2006.

Caulfeild, Ruby Allen. *The French Literature of Louisiana*. New York: Institute of French Studies, Columbia University, 1929. Rpt. Gretna: Pelican, 1998.

Chaudenson, Robert. *Creolization of Language and Culture*. Rev. with Salikoko S. Mufwene; trans. Sheri Pargman et al. London and New York: Routledge, 2001.

Conwell, Marilyn J., and Alphonse Juilland. *Louisiana French Grammar*. The Hague: Mouton, 1963.

Cooke, John W., ed. *Perspectives on Ethnicity in New Orleans*. New Orleans: Committee on Ethnicity in New Orleans, 1979. Rev. and enlarged, 1981.

Cruchet, René. *France et Louisiane*. Baton Rouge: LSU Press, 1939.

Davis, Edwin Adams. *Louisiana: A Narrative History*. Baton Rouge: Claitor's Book Store, 1961.

Denuzière, Maurice. *Au pays des bayous*. 1: *Je te nomme Louisiane*. Paris: Fayard, 2003.

Desdunes, Rodolphe Lucien. *Nos hommes et notre histoire: notices biographiques accompagnées de réflexions* . . . Montreal: Arbour & Dupont, 1911; trans. and ed., with notes, Dorothea Olga McCants. Baton Rouge: LSU Press, 1973.

Ditchy, Jay K. *Les Acadiens louisianais et leur parler.* Paris: Droz; Baltimore: Johns Hopkins; London: Oxford, 1901. Translated in part by George Reinecke in *Louisiana Folklore Miscellany*, II (1966).

Dufour, Charles L. *Ten Flags in the Wind: The Story of Louisiana.* New York: Harper & Row, 1967.

Elfenbein, Anna Shannon. *Women on the Color Line: Evolving Stereotypes in the Writings of George Washington Cable, Grace King, Kate Chopin.* Charlottesville: University Press of Virginia, 1989.

Ernest, John. *Resistance and Reformation in Nineteenth-Century African-American Literature.* Jackson: University Press of Mississippi, 1995.

Fortier, Edouard-Joseph. "French Literature of Louisiana." *Cambridge History of English and American Literature.* 1907–21. http://www.bartleby.com/228/0830.html (20 Dec. 2004).

Gabbin, Joanne V., ed. *Furious Flower: African American Poetry from the Black Arts Movement to the Present.* Charlottesville: University of Virginia Press, 2004.

Gale, Robert L. *A Lafcadio Hearn Companion.* Westport, CT: Greenwood, 2002.

Gayarré, Charles. *Louisiana: Its Colonial History and Romance.* 2 vols. New York: Harper, 1851–52.

———. *The Creoles of History and the Creoles of Romance.* New Orleans: C. E. Hopkins, 1885.

———. *A Louisiana Sugar Plantation of the Old Regime.* New York: Harper, 1887.

———. *History of Louisiana.* 4 vols. New York: Redfield/W. J. Widdleton, 1854–56. 4th ed., with a biography by Grace King. New Orleans: F. F. Hansell, 1903.

Giraud, Marcel. *France and Louisiana in the Early Eighteenth Century.* Cedar Rapids: Torch Press, [1950?].

———. *Histoire de la Louisiane française.* 4 vols. Paris: PUF, 1966–1994. Translated as *A History of French Louisiana.* Baton Rouge: LSU Press, 1974–. Vol 1., *The Reign of Louis XIV, 1698–1715*, trans. Joseph C. Lambert; vol. 2, *Years of Transition, 1715–1717*, trans. Brian Pearce; *The Company of the Indies, 1723–1731*, trans. Pearce.

Griolet, Patrick. *Cadjins et créoles en Louisiane.* Paris: Payot, 1986.

Hamel, Réginald. *La Louisiane créole: Littéraire, politique et sociale, 1762–1900.* 2 vols. Ottawa: Leméac, 1984.

Hirsch, Arnold R., and Joseph Logsdon, eds. *Creole New Orleans: Race and Americanization.* Baton Rouge: LSU Press, 1992.

Holditch, W. Kenneth, ed. *In Old New Orleans.* Jackson: University Press of Mississippi, 1983.

Hubert-Robert, Régine. *L'Histoire merveilleuse de la Louisiane française*. New York: Editions de la Maison Française, 1941.
Humphries, Jefferson, and John Lowe, eds. *The Future of Southern Letters*. New York: Oxford University Press, 1996.
Jones, Anne Goodwyn. *Tomorrow Is Another Day: The Woman Writer in the South, 1859–1936*. Baton Rouge: LSU Press, 1981.
Kane, Harnett. *The Bayous of Louisiana*. New York: Morrow, 1943.
———. *Gentlemen, Swords, and Pistols*. New York: Morrow, 1951.
Kein, Sybil, ed. *Creole: The History and Legacy of Louisiana's Free People of Color*. Baton Rouge: LSU Press, 2000.
Kennedy, Richard S., ed. *Literary New Orleans: Essays and Meditations*. Baton Rouge: LSU Press, 1992.
LeBreton, Dagmar Renshaw. *Chahta-Ima: The Life of Adrien-Emmanuel Rouquette*. Baton Rouge: LSU Press, 1947.
Le Page du Pratz, Antoine-Simon. *Histoire de la Louisiane*. 3 vols. Paris: De Bure l'aîné, 1758. Translated by Joseph G. Tregle, Jr., as *The History of Louisiana*. Baton Rouge: LSU Press, 1975.
Louisiana History (journal).
Louisiana Literature (journal).
Lowe, John, ed. *Bridging Southern Cultures: An Interdisciplinary Approach*. Baton Rouge: LSU Press, 2011.
———, ed. *Louisiana Culture from the Colonial Era to Katrina*. Baton Rouge: LSU Press, 2008.
Lugan, Bernard. *Histoire de la Louisiane française 1682–1804*. Paris: Perrin, 1994.
McVoy, Lizzie Carter, and Ruth Bates Campbell. *A Bibliography of Fiction by Louisianians and on Louisiana Subjects*. Baton Rouge: LSU Press, 1935.
Mills, Gary B. *The Forgotten People: Cane River's Creoles of Color*. Baton Rouge: LSU Press, 1977.
Murdoch, H. Adlai. *Creole Identity in the French Caribbean Novel*. Gainesville: University Press of Florida, 2001.
Petry, Alice Hall, ed. *Critical Essays on Kate Chopin*. New York: G. K. Hall, 1996.
Powell, Lawrence N. *The Accidental City: Improvising New Orleans*. Cambridge: Harvard University Press, 2012.
Read, William A. *Louisiana French*. Baton Rouge: LSU Press, [1931].
Reeves, Miriam G. *The Governors of Louisiana*. Gretna: Pelican, 1976.
St. Martin, Gérard Labarre, and Jacqueline Voorhies. *Ecrits louisianais du dix-neuvième siècle: nouvelles, contes, fables*. Baton Rouge: LSU Press, 1979.
Salvaggio, Ruth. *Hearing Sappho in New Orleans: The Call of Poetry from Congo Square to the Ninth Ward*. Baton Rouge: LSU Press, 2012.

Saxon, Lyle. *Children of Strangers*. Boston: Houghton Mifflin, 1937.
——. *Fabulous New Orleans*. New York: Century, 1928; new ed., New York: Appleton-Century, 1947.
——. *Old Louisiana*. New York: Century, 1929.
Saxon, Lyle, Edward Dreyer, and Robert Tallant. *Gumbo Ya-Ya*. Boston: Houghton-Mifflin, 1945.
Sollors, Werner. *Multilingual America: Transnationalism, Ethnicity, and the Languages of American Literature*. New York: New York University Press, 1998.
Spratling, William P. *Picturesque New Orleans*. Introduction by Lyle Saxon. New Orleans: Tulane University Press, 1923.
Starr, S. Frederick. *Southern Comfort: The Garden District of New Orleans, 1800–1900*. Cambridge: MIT Press, 1989.
Sterkx, H. E. *The Free Negro in Ante-Bellum Louisiana*. Rutherford, NJ: Fairleigh-Dickinson University Press, 1972.
Tallant, Robert. *The Romantic New Orleanians*. New York: Dutton, 1950.
Taylor, Helen. *Gender, Race, and Region in the Writings of Grace King, Ruth McEnery Stuart, and Kate Chopin*. Baton Rouge: LSU Press, 1989.
Taylor, Joe Gray. *Louisiana: A Bicentennial History*. New York: Norton, 1976.
Testut, Charles. *Portraits littéraires de la Nouvelle-Orléans*. New Orleans: Imprimeries des Veillées Louisianaises, 1850. Trans. Olivia Blanchard. Survey of Federal Archives in Louisiana, 1939.
Tinker, Edward Larocque. *Les Ecrits en langue française en Louisiane au XIX siècle*. Paris: Honoré Champion, 1932.
——. *Lafcadio Hearn's American Days*. New York: Dodd, Mead, 1925.
Valdman, Albert, et al. *Dictionary of Louisiana Creole*. Bloomington: Indiana University Press, 1998.
Valdman, Albert, senior editor, et al. *Dictionary of Louisiana French*. Jackson: University Press of Mississippi, 2010.
Viatte, Auguste. *Anthologie littéraire de l'Amérique francophone*. Sherbrooke: Université de Sherbrooke, 1971.
——. *Histoire littéraire de l'Amérique française*. 2 vols. Paris: Presses Universitaires de France, 1954.
Villiers du Terrage, Marc de. *Les Dernieres Années de la Louisiane française*. Paris: Librairie Orientale et Américaine, [2004?], translated by Hosea Phillips as *The Last Years of French Louisiana*, edited by Carl A. Brasseaux, annotated by Brasseaux and Glenn R. Conrad. Lafayette: Center for Louisiana Studies, University of Southwestern Louisiana, 1982.
——. *Histoire de la fondation de la Nouvelle-Orléans (1717–1722)*. Preface by Gabriel Hanotaux. Paris: Imprimerie Nationale, 1917.

Wall, Bennett H., ed. *Louisiana: A History.* Arlington Heights, IL: Forum Press, 1984.
Wilson, Edmund. *Patriotic Gore: Studies in the Literature of the American Civil War.* New York: Oxford University Press, 1962.
Wright, William, ed. *The Southern Poetry Anthology, 4: Louisiana.* Huntsville: Texas Review Press, 2011.

INDEX

Abd-el-Kader, 87
Abolitionists, 57, 65, 67, 224n18
Abortion, 54
Acadians. *See* Cajuns
Adams, Gleason R. W., 82
Adultery, 61, 105, 123, 129
Aegisthus, 113
Aesop, 47
Aesthetics of reception. *See* Jauss, Hans-Robert
Affaire d'honneur. See Duels
Africa, 110, 173, 175, 180
African American Museum, 14
Africans. *See* Blacks
Age des Lumières. See Enlightenment
Aimé, Gabriel (Valcour), 119, 144
Alabama, 155, 159, 170. *See also* Mobile, Alabama
Alciator, Bernard, *La Nouvelle Atala*, 200n16
Alcohol and drugs, 61, 124, 184
Alcott, Louisa May, 123
Algeria and Algerians, 70, 77
Alexandrines, 23, 34, 43, 48, 76, 81, 86, 117
Allain, Mathé, x, 30
Allard, Louis, 30; *Les Epaves*, 30
Allen-Taylor, Douglas, 159
All Saints' Day, 138, 151, 157, 164, 184
Alsatians, 25

Amelinckx, Frans, x, 69
American Folklore Society, 119
Americanization of Creoles, 11, 15, 47, 117, 118. *See also* Antiassimilationism
American Revolution, 45, 47, 195n25
Americans, 11, 12, 20, 74, 96, 97, 101, 128, 141, 149, 158, 164
Amistad Research Center, vii, 196n26
Anarcho-communism, 66, 67
Ancelet, Barry Jean. *See* Arceneaux, Jean
Anderson, Debra L., 189n3
Anglicization. *See* Americanization of Creoles
Anglo-Americans. *See* Americans
Annales school of history, 50
Antiassimilationism, 11, 19, 47, 171
Anti-Christian views, 78. *See also* Anticlericalism
Anticlericalism, 47, 50, 53, 58, 81, 89, 143, 203n13
Antilles. *See individual island names*; West Indies
Anti-Semitism, 76, 77, 78, 162
Apollinaire, Guillaume, *Alcools*, 228n15
Arceneaux, Jean (Barry Jean Ancelet), xi, 171, 227n5
Architecture, 51, 101, 149, 159, 180
Armstrong Park, 10
Art pour l'art, L', 57
Arvin, Newton, 100

Assumption Parish, 32
Atlantic literature, 20–21
Aubert, Alvin, 226n4
Audubon Park, 46
Augier, Emile, 70, 76
Avenues and streets (New Orleans): Bayou Road, 14; Bourbon Street, 177; Canal Street, 101, 116, 149, 181; Coliseum Street, 159; Elysian Fields, 162; Governor Nicholls, 14; Henry Clay Avenue, 225n26; Milan Street, 156; Oak Street, 170; Pleasant Street, 223n11; St. Charles Avenue, 186, 223n11; St. Claude Avenue, 176. See also French Quarter
Avoyelles Parish, 145

Babbitt, Irving, 37
Bachelard, Gaston, 177
Bakhtin, M. M., 168
Balls. See Clubs and krewes; Masking and masked balls; Quadroon balls
Balzac, Honoré de, 66; *La Peau de chagrin*, 50; *Splendeurs et misères des courtisanes*, 60
Bamboula, 95, 112, 126, 181
Baraka, Amiri (LeRoi Jones), 183
Barataria Bay, 145
Barbey d'Aurevilly, Jules, 204n5
Barde, Alexandre, 201–2n1; *Mademoiselle de Montblancard*, 45
Barel, Léona. See Queyrouze, Léona
Barrès, Maurice, *Colette Baudoche*, 214n9
Barrett, Lawrence, 216n20
Barrie, James, 12
Barry, David, xi
Barthélemy, Auguste-Marseille, 43
Barthes, Roland, vii

Bartlett, Louise, 93
Basso, Hamilton, 20, 100, 155
Baudelaire, Charles, 39, 116, 117; *Les Fleurs du mal*, 53
Bauer, Margaret, 162
Bayous, 25, 32; Bonfouca, 206n9; Lacombe, 32, 39; Lafourche, 176, 225n26; St. John, 4, 31, 43, 64; Tèche, 105, 223n14
Beat movement, 172, 183
Beaumont, Joseph, 87
Becquer, Gus A., *Las Hojas muertas*, 208n2
Bedell, Jack, 171
Bell, Caryn Cossé, 82
Béranger, Pierre-Jean de, 43, 44, 81
Berquin-Duvallon, Pierre-Louis, 22; *Mélusine*, 45
Berry, Wendell, 19, 20
Bhabha, Homi, 6
Bibliothèque Nationale, 131
Bienville, Jean-Baptiste Le Moyne de, 4, 143, 144
Bienville, Nouan de, 64
Biguenet, John, 171
Bilingual tradition, 4, 186, 191n1. See also Languages
Biracial system, 125. See also Caste system; *Plessy v. Ferguson*
Bissette, Cyrille, 70
Black Arts Movement, 173, 183
Blacks, 5–6, 7, 9–10, 15, 31, 94, 125, 126, 132, 137, 141–43, 146–47, 152, 153, 158, 159–60, 161, 165, 166, 176; under Reconstruction, 141–43. See also Creoles of Color; Free People of Color; Slavery and slaves
Blanc, Louis, 48
Blassingame, John W., 23, 193n11

BLKARTSOUTH, 173
Bloom, Harold, 128
Blue Room. *See* Roosevelt Hotel
Blues, 169–70, 177, 178, 180. *See also* Jazz
Bogalusa, Louisiana, 171
Boise, Jean, 81
Boise, Louis, 81
Bonapartists, 28
Bonnet Carré, Louisiana, 107
Bon sauvage. See Noble savage
Booksellers, modern (New Orleans): Faulkner House Books, 170, 226n3; Garden District Book Shop, 170; Octavia Books, 170
Bordeaux, 71, 85, 116, 165, 186
Bordelais Gothic. *See* Romantic Gothic
Borders, James B., IV, 174, 198n15
Boré, Etienne de, 46
Borgne, Lake, 8, 101, 193n10
Boston, Massachusetts, 48, 49, 102, 134, 158
Bosworth, Sheila, 150, 167; *Almost Innocent*, 165–66
Bosworth Field, Battle of, 77
Boucicault, Dion, *The Octoroon*, 75
Boudreaux, Beau, 171
Boudreaux, Jean, 182
Bouligny, Francisco, 223n14
Bouligny family, 156, 223n14
Bourbon restoration (1815), 8
Bourbon rule in Louisiana government, 144
Bourget, Paul, 220n21
Bourque, Darrell, xi, 171, 190n9, 227n6
Bousquet, Joë, 201n24
Bradford, Mel, 160
Brainard (quoted by Adrien Rouquette), 33
Brannan, William Penn, 20

Bras-Coupé, 21, 65, 98, 100, 211–12n11
Breaux manuscript, 190n8
Brer Rabbit, 119
Bres, Rose Falls (Rosetta C. Falls), 215n17
Brésil, Jules, 77
Bretonne, Charles de la. *See* Rouquigny, Jacques de
Brevelle. *See* Isle Brevelle, L'
Brieux, Eugène, 25
British Psychic Society, 204n7
Brittany, 119
Brontë, Charlotte, 123, 133, 148
"Bronze John." *See* Yellow fever
Brooks, Cleanth, 151
Brosman, Catharine Savage, 171
Brown, Charles Brockden, 33
Brown, John, 89
Brown, William Wells, 206n5
Browning, Robert, 215n20
Bruce, Clint, 207–8n2
Bryan, Violet Harrington, 133
Bryant, William Cullen, 33
Buchuwa, Louisiana, 32
Burke, James Lee, x
Burns, Robert, 89
Butler, Benjamin, 12, 15, 42, 131, 166
Buys, William de, 211n11
Byrne, Bobby, 163
Byron, George Gordon, Lord, 43

Cabeza de Vaca, Álvar Núñez, 4
Cabildo. *See* French Quarter
Cable, George Washington, ix, 5, 20, 27, 31, 47, 56, 64, 70, 81, 93–100, 101, 102, 105, 110, 112, 120, 122, 129, 132, 156, 164, 214n10, 223n13. **Works:** "Le Café des exilés," 10; "The Freedman's Case in Equity," 94, 124; *The Grandissimes*, 21, 39, 53, 65, 94, 96–99, 100, 112,

155, 157, 163, 212n19; "The Haunted House in Royal Street," 15, 96, 230n33; "Jean-ah Poquelin," 201n24; "Madame Délicieuse," 11; *Madame Delphine*, 52, 95, 140; *The Negro Question*, 94; *Old Creole Days*, 93–94, 95–96; *Strange True Stories of Louisiana*, 95, 105; "'Tite Poulette," 95, 140
Caddo Parish, 160
Caen, Herbert, 172
Caillou, André, 89
Cajun French. *See* Languages
Cajun literature, xi, 106
Cajuns, x–xi, 7, 106, 124, 152, 160, 161, 162, 182, 184, 224n20
Cambridge History of American Literature, 58, 60
Camus, Albert, *La Chute*, 155
Canadian literature, 19, 198–99n1
Canadians in Louisiana, 4, 7, 47, 106
Canary Islanders. *See* Isleños
Cane River, 62, 122, 124, 125, 153, 164, 217n2
Canonge, Louis-Placide, 23, 197–98n13; *Le Comte de Carmagnola*, 23; *France et Espagne*, 45
Capuchins, 4, 143
Caribbean Sea, 113
Carmer, Carl, *French Town*, 227n6
Carnival, 59, 147, 152, 155, 162, 166, 176, 181. *See also* Clubs; Masking and masked balls
Carondelet, Baron François de, 194n15
Carondolet Canal, 84, 209n6
Carpe diem, theme of, 209n12
Carpetbaggers, 11, 12, 51, 141–42
Carver, Ada Jack, 153
Cassette girls. See *Filles à la cassette*
Castellanos, Henry C., 211n11

Caste system, 10, 15, 70, 73, 75, 95, 97, 98, 102, 104, 125, 136, 153, 160, 161, 162, 163–64, 165–66
Castra, Hyppolyte, 87
Cather, Willa, 122, 123
Catholics. *See* Roman Catholic Church and Catholics
Catlin, George, 36
Caulfeild, Ruby Van Allen, ix, 189n4
Celibacy, clerical, 50, 53–54, 82
Céline, Louis-Ferdinand, *Voyage au bout de la nuit*, 60
Cenelles, Les, 80–85, 86, 88, 89, 170
Center for Louisiana Studies, x
Chahta-Ima. *See* Rouquette, Adrien
Champlain, Lake, 191n1
Chapels, 32
Charcot, Jean-Martin, 48
Charente, La, 63
Charity Hospital, 176
Charles IX, 89
Chase, William M., ix
Chateaubriand, François-René de, 19, 31, 32, 33, 37, 38, 39, 40, 42, 48, 54, 55, 65, 67, 69, 100, 116, 200n16. **Works:** *Atala*, 29, 31, 49; *René*, 37, 48, 85
Chaudenson, Robert, 4, 5
Chef Menteur. *See* Mingolabee
Chênière Caminada, 25, 127, 155, 215n17
Cheramie, David, xi
Chesnutt, Charles W., *Paul Marchand, F.M.C.*, 225–26n32
Chessman, Caryl, 173
Chevilles, 41
Choate, Joseph, 79
Choctaws. *See* Indians
Cholera, 12
Chopin, Kate, ix, 5, 62, 70, 102, 110, 121–30, 132, 133, 139, 146, 153, 168; life

Index   245

and background, 121–22. **Works:** *At Fault*, 124–25, 126, 128; "Athénaïse," 127, 129, 130; *The Awakening*, 55, 121, 128–30; *Bayou Folk*, 124, 125–27; "La Belle Zoraïde," 126; "Désirée's Baby," 75, 123, 126–27, 141, 217n1; "Her Letters," 218n14; "In and Out of Old Natchitoches," 126; "In Sabine," 218n11; *A Night in Acadie*, 127–28; "The Storm," 218n12
Chopin, Oscar, 122
Choppin, Jules, 21
Christ. *See* Jesus Christ
Christian, Marcus, 205n12
Christianity, 61, 62, 63, 93, 163. *See also* Celibacy; Christian themes; Gospels; Huguenots; Jesus Christ; Protestantism and Protestants; Roman Catholic Church and Catholics
Christian themes: dialectic of *felix culpa*, 63; eschatology, 62, 113
Churches, 149, 183; Notre-Dame de Bon Secours, 150; St. Ann's, 24; St. Augustine, 24; St. Peter Claver, 24; St. Raymond and St. Leo the Great, 179. *See also* St. Louis Cathedral
Cincinnati, Ohio, 101, 140
City Park, 30
Civilization, 178
Civil rights movement, 169
Civil War, 11, 14, 46, 51, 115, 124, 126, 136, 137, 140, 141, 157, 161. *See also* Butler, Benjamin; Confederacy; Confederate army; Farragut, David; Federal troops; Occupation, federal
Claiborne, William Charles, 10, 96
Clark, Emily, 194n14, 194n16
Classicism and classical literature, 18, 43, 77, 81, 113

Classism and class inequality, 108, 138. *See also* Caste system
Claudel, Calvin, 81
Cliché, 151; defined, 223n9; Renaissance cliché, 88
Climate. *See* Hurricanes and storms; Louisiana: climate and weather
Clinton, William J., 160
Cloutierville, Louisiana, 122
Clubs and krewes: Athénée Louisianais, 25, 47, 67, 106, 115, 116, 119; Boston Club, 150, 152; Causeries du lundi, 16; Francs Amis, 24; Freedmen's Aid Association, 86; Historical Club, 98; Krewe of Comus, 145, 147, 166; krewes, 150, 162; Lawn Tennis Club, 150, 225n26; Pickwick Club, 150, 166; Quarante Club, 131, 144, 145; Société d'Economie, 24; Société des Artisans, 24, 70, 209n10; Société du Cordon Bleu, 24; L'Union française, 67
Clytemnestra, 113
Colleges. *See* Schools; Universities
Code Noir, 9–10, 59, 76, 78, 94, 140
Code of Honor. *See* Duels
Codependency, 167
CODOFIL. *See* Council for the Development of French in Louisiana
Coincidence, 49, 50, 53, 106
Coliseum Square, 131
Collens, T. Wharton, *The Martyr Patriots*, 45
Colonialism and colonial attitudes, 10–11, 114, 124–25, 178
Colonial literature, 18
Columbus, Christopher, 178
Commune, Paris (1871), 50
Compagnie des Indes, 4, 204n10
Compagnie d'Occident, 4

Compère Lapin. *See* Brer Rabbit
Condé, Maryse, 69
Confederacy, 46, 47, 115, 131
Confederate army, 14, 63, 93, 94, 144, 151, 196n28
Congo, Luis, 177
Congo Square, 10, 126
Congress, United States, 10, 11
Conrad, Joseph, *The Heart of Darkness*, 215n17
Conspiracy of 1768, 8, 63–64
Constant, Benjamin, 69
Contemporary Arts Center, 174
Cooley, Peter, 171
Cooper, James Fenimore, 33, 36; *The Last of the Mohicans*, 36
Corday, Charlotte, 47
Cordon Bleu. *See* Clubs and krewes
Corneille, Pierre, 119, 207n14
Cornstalk fences, 101
Correction girls, 6, 97
Corrington, John William, x, 160, 171, 223n16
Corrington, Joyce, x
Corso, Gregory, 172
Côte des Allemands. *See* German Coast
Council for the Development of French in Louisiana (CODOFIL), x, 216n22
Courcelle, Achille, 13
Couvent, Justine (Madame Bernard), 23, 79, 208n3
Cowan, James L., xi, 88
Crane, Hart, 155, 173
Crane, Stephen, 23
Crawford, Joan, *Humoresque*, 218n12
Creole: definitions and use, 4–6, 16; etymology, 4
Creoles, black. *See* Creoles of Color; Free People of Color

Creoles, white, 5, 6, 10–11, 12–13, 16, 20, 22, 27, 28, 69, 94, 96–98, 118, 129, 132, 139–40, 147, 149, 150, 151, 154, 156–58, 159, 160, 162, 163, 164, 165–66, 167; mores, 96, 114, 118, 130, 135, 140, 145, 152–53, 155–58, 166, 216n23; as Other, 96; ties to France, 8, 12–13, 28, 157. *See also Creole*; White supremacism
Creoles of Color (modern), x, 6, 15, 16, 149, 153–54, 160, 164, 185, 186; literary style, 69; poets, 169–70, 172–84; prose writers, 78–79; theme of whiteness and blackness, 106, 150, 154, 161, 165, 186. *See also* Blues; Free People of Color; Jazz
Créolité, viii, 149, 175
Crime novels, x
Critical theory, viii
Croats, 8
Croesus, 49
Crozat, Antoine, 4
Cuba, 6, 8, 42, 79, 111
Culture, definition, 191–92n3
Cummings, E. E.: *Tulips and Chimneys*, 228n15

Dagoes. *See* Italians
d'Agoult, Marie, 123
Dalcour, Pierre, 81, 82–83
Dance, 10, 93, 95, 97, 194n18. *See also* Bamboula; Congo Square
Dances with Wolves, 199n3
Daniels, Kate, 150
Daudet, Alphonse, 67, 220n12
Dauphin, Bernard Désormes, 81
David, Jacques-Louis, 53
Davis, Mollie Moore, 215n12
Day of the Dead. *See* All Saints' Day
Degas, Edgar, 208n2

Déjacque, Joseph, 66–67. **Works:** *L'Humanisphère*, 67; *Les Lazaréennes*, 67
de la Houssaye, Louis Alexandre Le Pelletier, 104–5
de la Houssaye, Sidonie, 27, 95, 104–13, 131, 146; life and career, 104–6. **Works:** *Contes d'une grand-mère louisianaise*, 106–7; *Pouponne et Balthazar*, 106; Quadroon novels, 107–13
Delany, Martin R., *Blake, or the Huts of America; A Tale of the Mississippi Valley, the Southern United States, and Cuba*, 59
Delaup, François, 24
Delavigne, Casimir, 43
Deléry, Charles-Chauvin-Boisclair, 42, 201n17; *L'Ecole du peuple*, 42
Demarest, Donald, vii, 11, 94, 129, 200n10, 214n7, 223n13, 224n20; background, 156; *Fabulous Ancestor*, 155–58, 166, 167
Dent, Thomas C., 170, 173–74, 205n12
Depression, economic, 12
Depression, mental, 218n12
de Pues, Freddy, xi
Desbordes-Valmore, Marceline, 106
Desbrosses, Nelson, 81
Desdunes, P. A., 207n17, 208n2
Desdunes, Rodolphe-Lucien, 79; *Nos hommes et notre histoire*, viii, 22, 79
Désert. See Wilderness
de Soto, Hernando de, 4
Dessommes, Edward, 115, 203n14
Dessommes, George Washington, 85, 115–19, 203n14. **Works:** *Tante Cydette*, 117–19; *Vendanges*, 116–17
Diane de Poitiers, 87
Diaspora, black, 21

Diaspora, Creole, 47, 71, 85–86, 174, 182, 183, 185
Dictionary of Literary Biography, vii
Diderot, Denis, *La Religieuse*, 54
Donaldsonville, 203n15
Dostie, A. P., 89, 210n13
Double standard, 66
Doucet, John, 171
Dove, Rita, 175
Dreyfus Affair, 78
Dryden, John, 199n3
Dublin, 101
Dubois, Sylvie, 6
Du Bois, W. E. B., 79
Duclos, Louis, 24
Dueling grounds, 64
Duels, 51, 64, 67, 94, 97, 98, 101, 164, 165
Dufour, Charles L., 210n13
Dugué, Charles-Oscar, 19, 42; *Essais poétiques*, 42, 200n14
Duhart, Adolphe, 73, 87, 206n10. **Works:** *Lélia, ou la victime du préjugé*, 73; "Simple Histoire," 73, 74; "Trois amours," 73–74
Dumas, Alexandre, père, 45, 48, 49, 53, 54, 70, 71, 75, 83, 105. **Works:** *Le Comte de Monte Cristo*, 111; *Dartagnan*, 48
Dumont de Montigny, Jean-François-Benjamin: "Poème en vers, touchant l'éstablissement de la Province de la Louisiane," 25
Dunbar-Nelson, Alice, 78–79; *The Goodness of St. Rocque*, 78–79
Duperron, Jean, 25
du Quesnay, Adolphe, 102, 113–15, 145: "Un Eté à la Grand'Isle," 114–15
duQuesnay, Maurice, vii, xii, 156
Dykes, Darrin, 218n12

Eagleton, Terry, viii
Earthquake, 57, 62
Elfenbein, Anna Shannon, 134
Eliot, George, 123, 133
Eliot, T. S.: "Hamlet and His Problems," 129; "Notes Toward the Definition of Culture," 192n3
Elizabethan drama, 77. *See also* Shakespeare, William
Ellison, Ralph, 169
Emerson, Ralph Waldo, 123
Encyclopedia Britannica, 94
England. *See* Great Britain
Enlightenment, 18, 21, 35, 37, 98
Epstein, Joseph, 219n6
Eroticism. *See* Sexuality and eroticism
Ethnicity, 3, 6, 126, 147, 149, 181, 190n1. *See also individual group names*; Caste system; Intermarriage; Race; Racial prejudice and oppression
Ethnic speech. *See* Languages
Evershed, Emilie Poullant Gelbois, *Eglantine ou le secret*, 45
Executioner, 64, 204–5n10
Exile and expatriation, theme of, 24, 86, 106, 113, 178, 198n15. *See also* Diaspora: Creole

Fabre, Michel, 209n7
Faget, Jean-Charles, 201n22
Fanon, Frantz, 108
Farragut, David, 12
Fatality, as theme, 86, 113
Faubourgs. *See* Neighborhoods
Faubourg Tremé: The Untold Story of Black New Orleans, 14, 226n4
Faulkner, William, 20, 95, 100, 122, 154, 161, 224n24. **Works:** *Absalom, Absalom!*, 110, 112, 154, 161; *Mosquitoes*, 154; *The Wild Palms*, 154

Favorite, Malaika, 171
Federal troops, 14, 42, 51, 140, 141, 151. *See also* Native Guards; Occupation, federal
Federal Writers' Project, 153
Feibleman, James K., 155, 159
Feminine condition. *See* Women's situation
Feminism: in creative works, 55–56, 104, 120, 121, 133; in criticism, viii, 108, 110, 121, 124, 127, 128–30, 167
Feminist criticism. *See* Feminism
Feminization of literature, 160
Ferney, France, 49
Fertel, Rien, 197n12
Filles à la cassette, 6, 97
Fires in New Orleans, 26
First Backyard Poetry Theater, 170
First Empire, 77
Flaubert, Gustave, 102, 123. **Works:** *Madame Bovary*, 75, 123; *Salammbô*, 123
Flora Levy Series, x
Florida Parishes, 7
F. M. S., "Souvenirs de Bonfouca," 72, 73
Foley, Althea, 101
Folklore, xi, 81, 101, 119, 190n4, 216n25
Fontane, Theodore, 123
Food and cooking, 27, 79, 101, 135, 149, 159, 179, 180, 181, 184
Forest. *See* Wilderness
Fortier, Alcée, 5, 29, 79, 119
Fortier, Edward J., viii, 216n24
Fortier, Florent, 119
Fortier, Louise Augustin, 115
Fort Rosalie, 143, 192n8
Foscue (fermier-général in France), 202n8
Foundlings and orphans, 38, 103, 107, 138
France, Anatole, 102; *Thaïs*, 33

Francis, W. T., 32
François I, 87
Franco-Prussian War, 8, 12, 50, 67, 76, 115, 139
Frankfort School. *See* Marxism and Marxist analysis
Franklin, Louisiana, 104
Freeman, John, 227n11
Freemasonry and Freemasons, 58, 59, 61, 89, 204n7
Free People of Color (19th century) (Creoles of Color), viii, x, 5–6, 9–10, 13–16, 20, 23–24, 27, 46, 68–70, 79, 94, 95, 96, 98, 125, 126, 138, 153, 160, 163–65, 168, 169, 176, 182, 185; cultural achievements and literacy, 20, 23–24, 68–69, 80; in the Battle of New Orleans, 71, 87, 195n25; in and after the Civil War, 14–15, 196n28; legal status, 9–10, 15, 86, 88; literary style, 69; music, 196n27; neighborhoods, 14, 176; as Other, 13; poets, 80–92; population numbers, 10, 195n25; professions and trades, 14, 179; prose writers, 70–79; racial attitudes, 13, 15, 137; relationships with non-mixed-race blacks, 72–73, 110; speech, 13; ties to France, 13, 15, 20, 71, 112; valorization of whiteness, 13, 138–39, 154, 161, 165; wealth, 13; women and writing, 68; writings in general, 20, 68–69. *See also* Code Noir; Creoles of Color; Laws in Louisiana; Mulattoes; Neighborhoods; Quadroons; Women's situation
Free Southern Theater, 170, 173, 174
French Opera House. *See* Theaters
French Quarter (Vieux Carré), 10, 12, 26–27, 70, 109, 113, 114, 117, 139, 149, 150, 153, 154, 164, 167, 170, 181, 183, 185;
Beauregard House, 152; Cabildo, 26; Chartres Street, 139; Decatur Street, 185; Esplanade Avenue, 145; French Market, 27, 183; Jackson Square (Place d'Armes), 26, 116–17, 145, 152; Presbytère, 26–27; Rampart Street, 14, 72, 137, 158, 173; Royal Street, 31, 139, 185; Ursulines Convent, 26. *See also* St. Louis Cathedral; Theaters
French settlers in Louisiana, 4, 6–7; influence, 8–9, 28
Frénière, Nicolas-Chauvin de la, 67
Freudianism, 108
Friedmann, Patty, 150
Fruman, Norman, viii
Fuller, Margaret, 123
Fuselier de la Claire, Agricole, 211n11

Gaines, Ernest J., 160–62, 220n14. **Works:** *The Autobiography of Miss Jane Pittman*, 108, 161; *Catherine Carmier*, 161–62
Galileo, 90, 91
Gallier, James, 166
Gálvez, Bernardo de, 29, 186
García Lorca, Federico, 173
Garreau, Louis-Armand, 8–9, 63–66. **Works:** "Bras-coupé," 21, 65; "Une Créole," 66; "L'Idiote," 66; "Un Jour de noces," 66; *Louisiana*, 45, 63; "Naïda," 65–66; "Un Nègre marron," 64–65
Gascons, 141, 146
Gautier, Théophile, 75, 102, 117
Gayarré, Charles, viii, 5, 22, 31, 45–46, 58, 64, 94, 101, 131, 132, 143, 197n12, 202n2, 214n10. **Works:** *Aubert Dubayet*, 46–47; *Fernando de Lemos*, 46
Gehman, Mary, 14

Gens de couleur libres. See Free People of Color
Gereighty, Andrea, 170
German, Norman, 222n7
German Coast, 8, 55, 171; uprising, 10, 13
Germans, 8, 149
Gers (France), 31
Gex-Breaux, Quo Vadis, 173, 194n18, 226n4
Gide, André: *Les Faux-Monnayeurs*, 109; *L'Immoraliste*, 215n17
Gilbert, Sandra, 121, 129
Gilchrist, Ellen, 150, 151, 162
Gildea, Robert, 24
Gilder, Richard Watson, 132
Ginsburg, Allen, 172
Glasgow, Ellen, 100
Gobineau, Arthur, comte de, 214n9
Georgia (state), 131, 165
Golden Age drama, 77
Gombo (speech). *See* Languages
Goncourt, Edmond and Jules, 75
Good, Charles Hamlin, 80
Gospel music, 180
Gospels, 89, 118. *See also* Christianity
Gottschalk, Louis-Moreau, 9, 22, 200n12
Gracerie, Charles de, *Les Mystères des bords du Mississippi*, 45
Grand Isle, 25, 40, 114, 127, 129, 230n30
Grand Tour, 28
Grau, Shirley Ann, vii, 17, 100, 158–60, 223n11. **Works:** *The Black Prince and Other Stories*, 224n20; *The Hard Blue Sky*, 224n20; *The House on Coliseum Street*, 159; *The Keepers of the House*, 112, 159
Great Britain, 7, 101, 146, 198–99n1
Greece, 48–49

Grenoble, 104
Grima, Edgar, 21
Grue, Lee Meitzen, 170, 185–86
Guadeloupe, West Indies, 57, 59, 60, 61, 62, 71
Guinea, 64
Gulf Coast, 4, 147, 159, 196n28, 224n20
Gulf of Mexico, 4, 25, 102, 113, 114, 115, 129, 130
Guthrie, James Birney, 105

Hachard de Saint-Stanislas, Sister Madeleine, 20
Haiti and Haitians, 6, 10, 71, 73, 80, 82, 85, 165. *See also* St.-Domingue
Halévy, Fromental, *La Juive*, 76
Hamel, Réginald, x, 47, 54, 203n14
Hangman. *See* Executioner
Harper, Frances E. W., *Minnie's Sacrifice*, 109
Harris, Joel Chandler, 25, 119, 146, 147, 212n14, 221n23
Harte, Bret, 25
Hartford, Connecticut, 132
Hayden, Robert, 182
Hearn, Lafcadio, 5, 28, 30, 37, 94, 101–3, 114, 119, 120, 130, 132, 145, 182, 210n2. **Works:** *Chita*, 102–3; *Creole Sketches*, 101; *Ghombo Zhèbes*, 101, 119, 212n19
Hellman, Lillian, 222n2
Hennessey, David, 120
Henri (poet), 90–92
Henry, Cammie Garrett, 153
Henry, O., 139, 150
Heredity, 55, 102, 105, 130
Hero, Danella P., 186
Heyward, DuBose, 221n24
Hippocrates, 44
Historical novel, 19, 50, 60, 63–64, 96

Hobson, Geary, 192n8
Holbrook, Alva, 220n20
Holditch, Kenneth, 162
Home Guards, 14
Homer, 71
Hommel, Christian, x
Hoodoo, 97, 110, 161, 176, 177, 181
Horvath, Barbara M., 6
House, as metaphor, 157, 158, 159, 176, 177
Houssaye, Sidonie de la. *See* de la Houssaye, Sidonie
Houzeau, Jean-Charles, 24–25
Howells, William Dean, 132; "A Modern Instance," 124
Hudson, Julien, 14
Hughes, Langston, 153, 169, 173
Hugo, Victor, 19, 24, 34, 39, 43, 45, 49, 53, 63, 71, 75, 77, 81, 82, 102, 113, 116, 172, 204n7. **Works:** *Bug-Jargal*, 59; *Les Burgraves*, 75; "Ce que dit la Bouche d'ombre," 172; *Le Dernier Jour d'un condamné*, 69; *Les Misérables*, 62, 69, 204n5
Huguenots, 4, 97, 144. *See also* Protestants and Protestantism
Hurricanes and storms, 25–26, 40–42, 51, 58, 72, 86, 98, 102, 113, 114, 116, 117, 143, 155, 185, 211n6, 224n20. *See also* Katrina
Hurston, Zora Neale, 221n24

Iberia Parish, 105, 211n11
Iberville, Pierre Le Moyne d', 4, 144, 220n18
Identity. *See* Mistaken or hidden identity
Identity literature (group-oriented), 17, 159
Illegitimacy, 72, 73, 85

Illusion: fictional, 109; theme of, 53, 117, 123
Imaginaire, 25–26
Immigrants and immigration, 8, 10, 35, 57, 144
Incest, theme of, 38, 47, 49, 74, 110, 201n17, 215n12
Indians, 7, 29, 30, 32, 37, 42, 52, 97, 106, 125, 143, 160, 192n8, 199n3; Acolapissa, 212n14; Attakapas, 30; Choctaws, 29, 31, 32, 38, 39, 42, 55, 63, 176; Houmas, 30; Hurons, 199n3; of mixed race, 97, 125, 146, 193n8; Natchez, 143, 182, 192n8; Seminoles, 66; Tchoupitoulas, 98. *See also* Mardi Gras Indians
Ingraham, Joseph Holt, 201n17, 214n10
Injustice, theme of, 59, 68, 94, 96, 98. *See also* Racial prejudice and oppression; Slavery and slaves
Insanity, 50, 52–54, 78, 87, 111, 126, 155, 177. *See also* Pathological behavior
Institut catholique des orphelins indigents. *See* Schools
Intermarriage, 7, 72, 94, 95, 161, 164–65, 194n16. *See also* Miscegenation; Mixed-race liaisons
International, The, 58
Intertextuality, 22
Intolerance. *See* Racial prejudice and oppression
Irish, 8, 14, 101, 121, 122, 149, 152, 162, 163, 166, 193n12
Irving, Washington, 33
Isle Brevelle, L', 15, 23, 81, 153, 217n2. *See also* Cane River
Isle dernière, L', 25, 40–42, 102, 155
Isle of Orleans, 193n10
Isleños, 8

Italians, 8, 102, 138, 141, 146, 147, 149, 152, 158, 163, 193n12
Italy, 77; Bologna, 77, 78; Palermo, 53; Sicily, 52, 54; Tuscany, 53

Jackson, Andrew, 25, 46, 71
Jackson, Helen Hunt, *Ramona*, 36
Jackson asylum (Louisiana Insane Asylum), 176, 177
Jackson Square. *See* French Quarter
Jamaica, 57, 113
Jambon, Kirby, xi, 190n9
James, Henry, *Daisy Miller*, 118
James, William, 204n7
Janin, Jules, 75
Japan, 101, 120
Jauss, Hans Robert, 108, 168
Jazz, 14, 150, 169–70, 172, 173, 180, 183, 185, 226nn3–4
Jazz and Heritage Foundation, New Orleans, 173
Jazz musicians: Armstrong, Louis ("Satchmo"), 179, 181, 183; Bolden, Charles Joseph ("Buddy"/"King"), 226n3; Byrd, Charlie, 173; Davis, Miles, 173, 183; Doe, Ernie K, 186; Domino, Antoine Dominique ("Fats"), 186; Ellington, Edward Kennedy ("Duke"), 183; Floyd, "King," 180; Gillespie, John Birks ("Dizzy"), 173; Marsalis, Ellis, and family, 183; Neville, Aaron, 183; Parker, Charlie, 173, 183; Ruffin, Kermit, 186; Thomas, Irma, 180; Toussaint, Allen, 180; Washington, Walter ("Wolfman"), 186
Jefferson, Thomas, 10
Jefferson Parish, 42, 47
Jesuits, 54
Jesus Christ, 59, 61, 82, 88, 89, 90, 114, 129

Jews, 9, 46, 76, 77–78, 111, 172
Jim Crow laws, 181, 182, 184
Joan of Arc, 90
John, Elton, 163
John, Madame, 95, 182
Jones, Anne Goodwyn, 136
Joseph, Givonna, 196n27
Juana, Sor (of Lima), 177
Jullien, Adolphe, viii
July Revolution. *See* Revolution of 1830

Kadish, Doris Y., 10
Kail, Andrée, 216n23
Kane, Harnett, 155, 157, 166
Kane, Julie, ix, 170, 171
Katrina (hurricane), 171, 178, 179, 182, 183, 185, 211n6, 227n6, 230nn30–31
Kaufman, Bob, 172–73, 175, 176, 179, 228n15; *Solitudes Crowded with Loneliness*, 172
Kein, Sybil (Consuela Marie Provost née Moore), 164, 165, 171, 181–83. **Works:** *An American South*, 182–83; "Siblings: The Mulatto Slave," 165
Kerchief. *See* Tignon
Kerlérec, Louis Billouart, Chevalier de, 205n10
Kerouac, Jack, 172
Keyes, Frances Parkinson, 151–52, 155, 156; *Dinner at Antoine's*, 152, 166
King, Grace, 5, 11, 23, 28, 31, 95, 98, 110, 122, 123, 125, 131–44, 145, 146, 157, 204n10, 226n3; attitudes towards and portrayal of blacks, 132, 133, 134, 138; attitudes toward and portrayal of women, 133, 136; attitudes toward the South, 137; use of language, 132. **Works:** *Balcony Stories*, 139–41; "Bayou l'Ombre," 136–37, 141; "Bonne Maman," 137–38; "A Crippled Hope,"

140; *La Dame de Sainte Hermine*, 143; "La Grande Demoiselle," 140; "Grandmama," 140; "Heroines of Novels," 133; "In the French Quarter. 1870," 139; "The Little Convent Girl," 140–41; "Madrilène," 138–39, 157; "Monsieur Motte" (story and novella), 77, 132, 133, 134, 135–36, 142; *The Pleasant Ways of St. Médard*, 131, 141–43; *Tales of a Time and Place*, 136–39
King, Martin Luther, Jr., 184
Knopf (publishers), 166
"Know-Nothing" Party, 35
Komunyakaa, Yusef, 171, 226n4
Krewes (Carnival clubs). *See* Clubs and krewes

La Bretonne, Charles de. *See* Rouquigny, Jacques de
Lacroix, Victor, 89
Lafayette, Louisiana, 184
Lafitte, Jean, 67, 144
La Frénière, Nicolas-Chauvin de. *See* Frénière, Nicolas-Chauvin de la
Lakanal, Joseph, 22, 46
Lakes. *See individual names*
Lalaurie, Marie Delphine (Madame), 96, 185, 230n33
Lamartine, Alphonse de, 19, 30, 33, 43, 80, 81, 82, 84, 116. **Works:** "L'Isolement," 83; "Le Lac," 86; *Toussaint-Louverture*, 87
Lambert, P.-A., 44
Lammenais, Félicité-Robert de, 31
Lamotte, Louisa R., 205n1
Landes, Les, 66
Landscapes, 25, 151, 155. *See also* Mississippi River; Swamps; Wilderness
Lane, Pinkie Gordon, 171, 226n4, 227n6
Languages, 21, 126; African languages and terms, 175, 176, 178; Cajun (Acadian) French, xi, 7, 106, 119, 126, 171, 184, 224n20, 227n5; colonial French, 5; dialect, defined, 221n24; elevated style, 69; English, crude, 96, 97, 100, 125, 221nn23–24; French, crude, 125; French as dominant spoken or literary language, 12, 14, 93, 150, 153; *Gombo* or "Creole" (black creole patois), 5, 21, 31, 37, 47, 50, 54, 87, 96, 97, 100, 101, 102, 103, 110, 120, 126, 160, 161, 164, 171, 172, 178, 179, 182, 190n8, 208n4; Haitian Creole, 182; laws on, 12, 25, 195n22; levels of speech, 69; literary French used to record popular speech, 38, 60, 64; quasi-phonetic spellings, 60, 96, 125, 132, 146, 152, 183, 221n24; Sicilian patois, 138, 146; Spanish, 8, 102, 184; West Indian, 178
Lanusse, Armand, 15, 23, 80, 82, 83, 87, 194n14, 208n3; "Un Mariage de conscience," 72, 82
Lanusse, Numa, 80
Larsen, Nella, 221n24
La Salle, Robert Cavelier de, 4, 119
Lasseigne, Charles, 107
Last Island. *See* Isle dernière, L'
Latil, Alexandre, 43, 58, 87; *Les Éphémères*, 43–44
Latin America, 11
"Latin" character and culture, 15, 20, 36, 46, 47, 55, 96, 99, 118, 153, 181
Latortue, Régine, 82
Laveau, Marie, 100, 161, 181, 183, 186
Law, John, 4, 9
Lawrence, D. H., *Lady Chatterley's Lover*, 129
Laws in Louisiana, 4, 46, 72, 88, 105; law of 1830, on seditious speech, 69, 82; statute of 1970, 15. *See also* Code

Noir; Free People of Color: legal status; Intermarriage; Jim Crow laws; Languages
Leblanc, Eugène, 200n12
Le Blanc de Villeneufve, Paul-Louis, 29; *La Fête du petit blé*, 29–30
LeBreton, Dagmar Renshaw, 199n6
Le Clézio, J. M. G., 199n3
Leconte de Lisle, Charles-René, 39
Legion of Honor, 70
"Lélia D." *See* Duhart, Adolphe
Lemann, Nancy, 150; *Lives of the Saints*, 166–67
Le Page du Pratz, Antoine-Simon, 5, 19, 29, 200n16
Lépouzé, Constant, 83
Leprosy, 43, 201n24
Leroy, Fabrice, 65
Liberty Place, Battle of, 12
Lincoln, Abraham, 89, 90, 208n3
Liotau, Mirtil-Ferdinand, 81, 82, 83–84
Literacy: in Louisiana, 23, 24; theme of, 63. *See also* Free People of Color: literacy
Literature in Louisiana: identification, origin, and distinctiveness, 17–22, 198–99n1; milieu, 22–25
Littérature engagée, 69
Local color, 19, 39, 88, 114, 116, 122, 159, 180, 185
London, 75
Longfellow, Henry Wadsworth, 100
Lorrain, Claude, 151
Loti, Pierre, 102
Louisiana: climate and weather, 19, 101, 114, 117, 118, 159, 184; constitution, 9, 92; after 1865, 11; flora and fauna of bayous, 114; history, 3–15; name, 4; population figures, 10; population makeup, 3, 6–9; statehood, 10–11. *See also* Bourbon rule; Hurricanes and storms; Landscapes; Laws in Louisiana; Literacy: in Louisiana; Literature in Louisiana; New Orleans
Louisiana Lottery, 144
Louisiana Purchase, 4, 10–11, 96, 122
Louisiana Research Collection, vii, 193n12, 200n7, 201n21, 219n2, 221n22
Louis-Napoleon. *See* Napoleon III
Louis-Philippe, 35, 38, 46
Louis XV, 7
Louis XVI, 22
Louvre, 179
Louÿs, Pierre, *La Femme et le pantin*, 215n17
Love, as theme, 32, 38, 42, 44, 51, 53, 54, 56, 61, 62, 64, 70, 76, 81–82, 86, 184
Lowe, John, 151
Loyal retainer figures, 54, 125, 137, 143, 147–48, 220n16, 220–21n22
Lucifer and demons, 35, 36
Lussan, Auguste, 202n1; *Les Martyrs de la Louisiane*, 45
Lutherans. *See* Protestants and Protestantism
Lycées. *See* Schools

McAlpin, Robert, 125
McCullars, Carson, 160
McDonogh, John, 182
McKenna, Beverly Stanton, 198n15
McKenna, Dwight, 198n15
Macpherson, James (Ossian), 33
Madame John's Legacy, 95, 182–83
Maddox, Everette, 170
Magazines. *See* Newspapers and magazines
Maistre, Joseph de, 31
Major, Clarence, 180
Malays, 8

Mal du siècle, 30
Malherbe, François de, 48; "Consolation à Monsieur du Périer," 209n12
Mallarmé, Stéphane, 39; "Don du poème," 25
Manchac River, 193n10
Mandeville, Louisiana, 32, 44, 116, 140
Mansion, Lucien (Lolo), 25, 198n18
Mantua, Pennsylvania, 31
Maple Leaf Bar, 170
Marat, Jean-Paul, 47
Marciacq, J. L., 72, 203n15
Mardi Gras. *See* Carnival
Mardi Gras Indians, 7, 176
Margot, Queen (Marguerite de Valois), 87
"Marie" (anonymous), 72, 75, 113
Marigny, Faubourg. *See* Neighborhoods
Marinoni, Ulisse, 151, 157
Marksville, Louisiana, 145
Marriage, theme of, 69, 70, 72, 73, 74, 75, 76. *See also* Intermarriage; Mixed-race liaisons
"Marseillaise, La," 13, 89
Marseillaise noire, La, 87–92
Marshall, Bill, 21
Martial, 30
Martin, François-Xavier, 202n2
Martineau, Harriet, 215n13
Martinique, West Indies, 63, 70, 101, 113, 172
Marx, Karl, 66
Marxism and Marxist criticism, 59, 60, 63, 65, 66, 119, 134
Masking and masked ball, 55–56, 158, 166
Masons. *See* Freemasons and freemasonry
Matas, Rodolpho, 102
Matherne, Beverly, 171, 227n6

Maugham, Somerset, *Of Human Bondage*, 76
Maupassant, Guy de, 102, 123, 125, 130, 132, 139
Maurepas, Lake, 145, 193n10
Mauriac, François, 66
Mechanics Institute uprising, 89, 92
Merchant Marine, 172
Mercier, Adèle, 52
Mercier, Alfred, 22, 47–55, 56, 74, 81, 82, 101, 116, 150, 171; background and life, 47–48. **Works:** "L'Artiste amoureux," 53; *L'Aventure de Johnelle*, 54–55; *Du panlatinisme*, 202n4; "1878," 47; *La Fille du prêtre*, 47, 50, 82; *Fortunia*, 47; *Le Fou de Palerme*, 52–53; *L'Habitation Saint-Ybars*, 15, 21, 26, 27, 50–52, 107, 203n10; *Hénoch Jédésias*, 49–50; *Lidia*, 53–54, 116; *La Rose de Smyrne et l'Ermite du Niagara*, 48–49
Mercier, Armand, 47, 86
Mercier, Armantine, 52
Mercier, Jean-Baptiste, 47
Mérimée, Prosper, "Tamango," 62
Métoyer, Claude, 222n7
Métoyer family, 23, 222n7
Mexico, 73, 113
Michaelides, Chris, x, 68, 69, 74
Michigan, University of, at Flint, 182
Middleton, David, 171
Milton, John, *Paradise Lost*, 35
Mingo (name), 212n14
Mingolabee (Chef Menteur), 99, 212n14
Miscegenation, 52, 94, 95, 101, 110, 122–23, 126–27, 154, 166. *See also* Intermarriage; Mixed-race liaisons
Mississippi (state), 154, 155
Mississippi coast. *See* Gulf Coast

Mississippi River, 4, 7, 25, 27, 33, 39–40, 50, 54, 151, 152, 185, 193n10
Mississippi Valley, 26
Mistaken or hidden identity, 47, 55, 61–62, 71, 73, 75, 78, 103, 111, 147
Mixed-race liaisons, 9, 51–52, 62, 73, 74, 94, 110, 161. *See also* Free People of Color; Intermarriage; Miscegenation; Quadroons
Mixed-race people. *See* Creoles of Color; Free People of Color; Indians; Mulattoes; Quadroons
Mobile, Alabama, 57, 62
Mockingbird, 30, 32
Mocquard, Jean-François, 77
Modern Language Association, 119
Molière, 42, 99, 119
Monarchists, 28
Montaigne, Michel de, 29, 199n3
Montherlant, Henry de, *La Reine morte*, 207n14
Montpellier, France, 174
Moore, Charles, 182
Moore, Thomas, 33
Morel, Amadeo, 40, 201n21; *Récit sur l'Ouragan de la Dernière Ile*, 40–42
Mormons, 35
Morphy, Paul, 152
Morrison, Toni, 175; *The Bluest Eye*, 138
Mortara case, 77–78
Mulattoes, 9, 87, 97, 125, 126, 153, 160. *See also* Creoles of Color; Free People of Color
Multiculturalism, 3
Murdoch, H. Adlai, 6
Muslims, 76, 77
Musset, Alfred de, 82, 85, 116, 117.
  Works: *Les Nuits* (*Nights*), 43; "Tristesse," 49
Myth, 178, 223n16

Nantes, France, 29, 31, 39
Napoleon I (Napoleon Bonaparte), 44, 82, 139, 194n18, 202n1, 208n3, 211n10. *See also* Bonapartists
Napoleonic Code, 45
Napoleon III (Louis-Napoleon), 8, 63, 70, 75, 77
Narcissism, 218n12
Narrative structure and technique, 49, 52, 60, 64, 107–9, 117, 124, 136, 139, 140; analepsis, 50, 60, 77, 97, 141; autotextuality, 60; diegesis, 52, 60, 99, 107, 108; frame narrative and embedded tales, 52–53, 54, 64, 71, 72, 99, 114, 126, 215n17; indirect style, 117; metafiction, 109; paratextual elements, 99–100, 107, 108; prolepsis, 50, 60
Natchez, Mississippi, 33
Natchez Wars, 9
Natchitoches, Louisiana, 15, 23, 58, 153, 182
Natchitoches Parish, 122
Native Americans. *See* Indians
Native Guards, 15, 72, 73, 196n28
Nativist movement, 35, 166
Naturalism (in literature), 50, 74, 109, 123, 130, 145
Natural religion, 30, 37, 42, 65–66
Naudin, Camille, 87, 89
Negroes. *See* Blacks; Slavery and slaves
Neighborhoods, 176, 186–87; "Back of Town," 137; Bywater, 185; as changing, 166; Downtown, 185–86; Faubourg Marigny, 12, 14, 23, 162, 178; Faubourg Sainte-Marie (American sector), 12, 23; Faubourg Tremé, 14, 27, 137, 174, 183, 186, 226n4; Garden District, 154, 155, 162, 166, 167; Kenner, 184; Lower Garden District, 131; Ninth Ward, 185; Pailet-Land, 174, 183; Seventh Ward,

14, 172, 174, 178–79, 182, 202n2; Sixth Ward, 14, 183; Uptown, 150, 153, 154, 162, 185, 186. *See also* Avenues and streets; French Quarter
Nerval, Gérard Labrunie de, "El Desdichado," 87
Nesanovich, Stella, 171
New England, 61, 94, 123, 156, 157, 190n1
New Iberia, Louisiana, 136, 156
New Mexico, 58
New Orleans: as a "black space," 228n17; City Council, 10; as a "female place," 228n18; founding, 4; history, 4, 7, 11–12; name, 4; 19th century cultural milieu, 22–25; population figures, 6, 10, 11–12, 24; reputation and image, 20, 36, 110, 154, 197n7; vestiges, 175. *See also* Avenues and streets; French Quarter; Louisiana; Neighborhoods
New Orleans, Battle of, 38, 57, 71, 87, 144, 162, 182, 195n25
New Orleans Poetry Forum, 170
Newspapers and magazines, English-language, America: *Atlanta Constitution*, 119; *Boston Literary World*, 93; *Callaloo*, 174; *Century Magazine*, 132; *Cincinnati Commercial*, 101; *Daily City Item*, 101; *De Bow's Review*, 25; *Democrat*, 101; *The Dial*, 123, 153; *The Double-Dealer*, 72, 170, 223n9; *Harper's (New Monthly) Magazine*, 102, 132; *Harper's Bazaar*, 131; *Harper's Weekly*, 101; *Louisiana Gazette*, 24; *Louisiana Literature*, 170; *Louisville Courier*, 156; *New Laurel Review*, 170; *The Bee (L'Abeille)*, 24, 25; *New Orleans Review*, 170; *New Princeton Review*, 132; *New York Herald Tribune*, 155; *New York Times*, 155; *Picayune/ Daily Picayune/Times-Picayune*, 5, 25, 48, 93, 154; *St. Louis Post-Dispatch*, 122; *Scribner's*, 93; *South*, 25; *Southern Review*, 170; *Times-Democrat*, 94, 101, 120, 144; *Tribune*, 198n15; *Vogue*, 122; *Xavier Review*, 170

Newspapers and magazines, foreign-language, Louisiana and France, 11, 24–25; *L'Abeille (The Bee)*, 24, 25, 57, 71, 94, 105, 113, 120, 144, 205n1; *Album Littéraire: Journal des Jeunes Gens*, 30, 72; *L'Ami des Lois*, 25; *Le Carillon*, 53, 115, 117; *La Chronique*, 57; *Les Cinq Centimes Illustrées*, 64; *Les Comptes Rendus de l'Athénée Louisianais*, 25, 49, 50, 106, 115, 120, 201n22; *Le Courrier de la Louisiane*, 24, 53, 85, 144; *Le Démocrite*, 63; *L'Epoque*, 49; *L'Equité*, 58; *Le Franco-Louisianais*, 105, 117; *La Gazette* (German), 24; *La Gazette de la Louisiane*, 57; *Le Libertaire*, 67; *Le Meschacébé*, 25, 105, 107; *Le Moniteur de la Louisiane*, 24; *Le Propagateur Catholique*, 32, 37; *La Renaissance Louisianaise*, 24, 55, 64; *La Revue des Colonies*, 70; *La Tribune*, 15, 24, 58, 72, 73, 74, 87, 90, 91, 208n2; *L'Union*, 24, 82, 87, 90; *Le Vigilant*, 55, 203n15; *La Violette*, 55
New York, New York, 46, 59, 62, 75, 101, 102, 134, 146, 170, 172
Niagara Falls, 33, 48
Noble savage, 29, 37, 40, 55
Noomo, 170
Normandy, 50, 126
North Carolina, University of, at Asheville, 185
Northerners. *See* Americans; Yankees
Nova Scotia, 7
Novel, defined, 37

Occupation, Federal, 12, 15, 32, 50, 131, 136, 156, 158. *See also* Butler, Benjamin; Farragut, David; Federal troops

Occupation, Spanish. *See* Spanish in Louisiana

Octoroons, 9, 75. *See also* Free People of Color; Quadroons

Ogé, Vincent, 73, 164

Ohio River, 33

Oil, 213n21, 230n30

Opera house. *See* Theaters

Operas, 23

O'Reilly, Alejandro, 8, 63, 64, 223n14

Orestes, 113

Orphans. *See* Foundlings and orphans

Osbey, Brenda Marie, 7, 14, 151, 171, 174–78, 180, 182, 205n10, 226n3, 226n4, 228n13, 228n15; background and career, 174; religious views, 175, 228–29n19. **Works:** *All Saints: New and Selected Poems*, 175, 177–78; *Ceremony for Minneconjoux*, 7, 175–77; *Desperate Circumstance, Dangerous Woman*, 175; *History and Other Poems*, 174, 178; *In These Houses*, 175, 177

Ossian. *See* Macpherson, James

Oushola, 32

Overall, John W., 25

Ovid, 71

Paranormal phenomena. *See* Insanity; Pathological behavior; Spiritualism

Parker, Alice, 108

Pascal, Blaise, 31, 36

"Passing" (as white), 52, 87, 95, 165, 179, 182, 229n21

Pathetic fallacy, 37, 53, 114, 145

Pathological behavior, 50, 52–55, 204n7. *See also* Insanity; Somnambulism

Patois. *See* Languages

Patriarchal criticism, 129, 133

Pauger, Adrien de, 26

Péladan, Joséphin, called Sâr, 204n7

Pénicaut, André, 220n18

People of Color. *See* Creoles of Color; Free People of Color

Percy, Walker, 155, 166. **Works:** *Lancelot*, 155; *The Moviegoer*, 155

Père Antoine. *See* Sedella, Antonio de

Père-Lachaise Cemetery, 71

Périer, Etienne de, 9, 143

Perret, Hélène. *See* de la Houssaye, Sidonie

Perret, Jean-Baptiste, 104

Perret, J. John, 70, 105, 106, 107, 198n17

Perse, St.-John (Alexis Leger), *Eloges*, 113

"Petite Rose" (anonymous), 55–56

Petrarch, 215n20

Pfister, Arthur, 183–84, 185, 221n24

Philadelphia, 31, 39, 46, 171

Philippe II, duc d'Orléans, 4

Philippines, 8, 156

Pinchback, P. B. S., 42

Plaçage, 9, 72, 82, 110, 194n14

Place d'Armes. *See* French Quarter: Jackson Square

Place des Nègres. *See* Congo Square

Plantations, 12, 119, 126, 131, 135, 144, 151, 152, 221n25; Destrehan, 14; economy, 65, 114; Laura, 119; life, 51, 64–65, 146–47; Melrose, 153; Le Petit Versailles, 119; River Lake, 160

Plaquemine, Louisiana, 185

Plessy v. Ferguson, 6, 15, 79

Plutarch, 71

Poetic forms. *See* Versification

Poetry, 18–19, 25, 32–36, 39–44, 48–49, 58, 80–92, 113, 116–17, 168–87

Pointe Coupée Parish, 29, 160, 182; uprising, 10, 29
Poison, 63, 64, 66, 71, 75, 76, 77, 177
Poitevent, Eliza Jane (Pearl Rivers), 220n20
Pontchartrain, Lake, 4, 31, 32, 44, 55, 83, 155, 185, 193n10
Populus, Auguste, 81
Pornography, 163, 164
Porter, Katherine Anne, 152–53
Postcolonial criticism, viii, 121
Postmodernist criticism, viii
Potter, Paul, 151
Potvin, Charles, 89
Poydras de Lalande, Julien, 29; "La Prise du morne du Baton Rouge par Monseigneur de Galvez," 29
Pre-Romanticism and pre-Romantics, 18, 32, 35, 37
Presbytère. *See* French Quarter
Presentism, viii, 104, 108, 132
Prévost, Antoine-François, *Manon Lescaut*, 29
Prizes and awards, 174, 184; American Book Award, 175; Louisiana Literature Prize for Poetry, 171; National Book Award, 162; National Book Critics Circle Award, 161; NEA Fellowship, 225n26; PEN/Oakland Josephine Miles Award, 179; Pulitzer, 159, 162, 171, 196n28; T. S. Eliot Prize, 179
Progress, philosophy of, 51, 52, 59
Proletariat, 50, 59
Protestants and Protestantism, 8, 35, 47, 61, 89, 97, 98, 130, 132, 140, 152, 156, 157, 159. *See also* Huguenots
Protest writing, 68–71, 72–75, 76, 77–79, 87–92, 96, 169
Proudhon, Pierre-Joseph, 66–67

Provincial literature. *See* Regional literature
Puritanism, 20, 61, 100. *See also* Protestants and Protestantism
Putnam, Walter, 18
Pygmalion, 53

Quadroon balls, 24, 70, 95, 97, 164, 198n15
Quadroons, 9, 46, 70, 95, 97, 104, 105, 108, 109–13, 126, 132, 133, 134, 135, 137, 138, 146, 164–65, 201n17, 214n7. *See also* Free People of Color
Quarante Club. *See* Clubs and krewes
Questy, Joanni, 73, 74, 80, 81, 87; "Monsieur Paul," 74–75
Queyrouze, Léona, 119–20
Quincey, Thomas de, 166

Race, 3, 95, 108, 125, 133, 214n9. *See also* Caste system; Ethnicity; Intermarriage; Racial prejudice and oppression
Rachilde (Marguerite Eymery Vallette), 106, 123
Racial prejudice and oppression, 73, 75, 76, 77, 78, 86, 87, 94, 98, 108, 125, 128, 133, 134, 140, 143, 146–47, 178, 184, 198n14, 207n14
Racial system. *See* Caste system
Racine, Jean, 113, 120
Racism. *See* Racial prejudice and oppression
Rama, Ángel, 21
Raphaël, Jean-Baptiste, 182
Raymond, Louise. *See* de la Houssaye, Sidonie
Reader reception theory. *See* Jauss, Hans-Robert
Realism, 49, 50, 111. *See also* Naturalism

Reasons of state, 76–77, 207n14
Récit, defined, 117
Recognition, theme of. *See* Mistaken or hidden identity
Reconstruction, 9, 12, 15, 42, 96, 125, 131, 132, 141–42, 144, 156
Reed, Ishmael, 180
Regional literature, 17, 122, 146, 150
Régnier, Henri de, 25
Reinecke, George, 18, 117–18, 119, 216n23
Rennes, France, 31
Republicanism and republicans, 28, 45, 57, 203n13
Republic of West Florida, 7
Revolution, 50
Revolutionary virtues, 59, 61
Revolution of 1789, 6, 35, 45, 46, 47, 50, 57, 88, 89, 91, 98, 105
Revolution of 1830 (July Revolution), 8, 45
Revolution of 1848, 8, 45, 49, 51, 57, 64, 67
Rey, Henri, 210n14
Rice, Anne, 15, 22, 157, 163–65; background, 163; *The Feast of All Saints*, 72, 109, 157, 163–65, 228n13; religious views, 163; sales, 164
Richard, Zachary, xi
Richard III of England, 77
Rights of Man (human rights), 51, 57, 88, 98
Rillieux, Norbert, 208n2, 225n30
Rillieux, Victor-Ernest, 201n24, 208n2
Rimbaud, Arthur, 172
Riquet, Nicol, 81
Robespierre, Maximilien, 47
Roman, Alfred, 144
Roman, André, 144
Roman, Sallie Rhett, 144–45
Roman Catholic Church and Catholics, 17, 35–36, 61, 62, 67, 97, 129, 143, 144, 151, 152, 156, 158, 162, 166, 167, 177. *See also* Churches; St. Louis Cathedral
Romance (genre), 60; defined, 36–37
Romantic Gothic, 25, 66. *See also* Southern Gothic
Romanticism and Romantic elements, 18, 19, 26, 30, 32, 34, 37, 39, 43–44, 48, 49, 53, 55, 57, 60, 65–66, 68, 69, 71, 74, 81, 82, 86, 88, 109, 111, 114, 116, 120. *See also* Pre-Romanticism and pre-Romantics; Romantic Gothic
Roosevelt Hotel, 152, 153
Roquigny, Jacques de. *See* Rouquigny, Jacques de
Roquigny, Jean-Baptiste de, 203n15
Rosicrucians, 204n7
Roudanez, Louis Charles, 24
Rouget de Lisle, Claude Joseph, 89
Rouquette, Adrien-Emmanuel, 22, 30–39, 42, 43, 55, 61, 65, 113, 116, 200n12; attitude toward America, 34–36; attitude toward blacks, 31, 100; attitude toward New Orleans, 36; conservatism, 28, 30, 38; life and career, 31–32; political views, 38; religious views, 32, 35–36; support of Union, 31. **Works:** *L'Antoniade*, 34, 35–36; *Critical Dialogue Between Aboo and Caboo*, 38–39, 99–100; "Mokeur Shanteur," 32; *La Nouvelle Atala*, 36–38, 55; *La Question américaine*, 38; *Les Savanes*, 33–34; *La Thébaïde en Amérique*, 34
Rouquette, François-Dominique, 30, 32, 39, 42, 43, 48, 65, 113; *Les Meschacébénnes*, 39–40
Rouquette, Térence, 30, 72
Rouquigny, Jacques de, 203n15; "Le Soulier rouge," 55, 203n15
Rousseau, Jean-Baptiste, 89

Rousseau, Jean-Jacques, 19, 29, 30, 48, 55
Rousseau, Joseph, 85
Rowell, Charles, 174, 175
Rudel (Jaufré), 215
Rylance, Keli E., 202n2

St.-Bartholomew massacre, 89
St. Bernard Parish, 8, 141
St.-Céran, Tullius (de), 57, 87
St. Charles Parish, 42, 135
St.-Domingue, 6, 8, 10, 22, 46, 59, 70, 85, 113, 115, 164. *See also* Haiti
Sainte-Beuve, Charles-Augustin, 33, 197n12
St. Germain, Sheryl, vii, 184–85
St. James Parish, 104, 119, 144
St. John the Baptist Parish, 104
St. John the Divine, 113
St. Louis, Missouri, 121, 122
St. Louis Cathedral (St. Louis King of France) (formerly Church), 24, 26, 32, 46, 84–85, 118, 145, 186
St. Malo (village), 101
St. Martin Parish, 140
St. Martinville, 105
St. Mary Parish, 102, 104
St.-Pierre, Bernardin de, 19
St.-Pierre, Michel, 81
St. Tammany Parish, 31, 32, 116, 152
Salaam, Kalamu ya (Val Ferdinand), 170, 226n4; *From a Bend in the River*, 170
Sallis, James, x
Saloy, Mona Lisa, vii, 6, 172, 178–81, 182, 226n4; background and career, 179; name, 229n21. **Works:** "The 'N' Word," 180; *Red Beans and Ricely Yours*, 179–81
Sand, George, 55, 105, 106, 122, 123, 133; *Lélia*, 217n3
San Francisco, California, 170, 172, 179

San Malo, Juan, 177
San Martín de Porres, 177
Santa Maura, Greece, 101
Sarzant, Anastasie de. *See* Toucoutou
Satan. *See* Lucifer and demons
Satire, 150; genre defined, 99
Savane (savannah), 33–34, 200n12
Saxon, Lyle, 20, 153–54, 161. **Works:** "Cane River," 153; *Children of Strangers*, 72, 153–54, 161; *WPA Guide to New Orleans*, 153
Sazerac Bar. *See* Roosevelt Hotel
"Schneitz," 89
Schools: Académie (Collège) Sainte-Barbe (New Orleans), 23, 70, 71, 85; Collège de Rennes, 31; Collège d'Orléans, 22, 25, 31, 39, 46; Collège Royal de Nantes, 31, 39; Collège Sainte-Barbe (Paris), 71; Ecole Polytechnique, 72; Jefferson College, 42; Institut catholique des orphelins indigents (Couvent Institute), 23, 72, 73, 74; Institut St.-Louis, 131; Lycée (Collège) St.-Louis, 42; Lycée Louis-le-Grand, 22, 42, 47, 71, 115; St. Augustine High School, 183; St. Peter Claver School, 183; Ursuline Academy, 159. *See also* Universities
Scott, Sir Walter, 105
Scribe, Eugène, 76
Scribner's (publishers), 94, 100, 105
Seattle, 179, 180
Second Empire, 216n23
Second Republic (1848–52), 194n18
Sedella, père Antonio de, 46
Segregation, 23, 79, 172. *See also* Caste system; Jim Crow laws; *Plessy v. Ferguson*
Séjour, Victor, 70–71, 75, 76, 80. **Works:** *Diégarias*, 76–77; *Le Fils de la nuit*,

75–76; *Henri de Lorraine*, 76; *Le Martyre du coeur*, 77; "Le Mulâtre," 71; *Les Noces vénitiennes*, 77; *Richard III*, 77; *La Tireuse de cartes*, 77–78
Séligny, Michel, 22, 23, 70, 73, 85, 209n6. **Works:** "Le Pêcheur de la Guadeloupe," 71; "Souvenir de 1815," 71
Senancour, Etienne de, 19, 69
Senate, U.S., 46. *See also* Congress
Sentimentality, 58, 59, 69, 106, 121, 123, 126, 140, 145, 146, 147, 151
Seven Years' War, 7, 198–99n1
Sexuality and eroticism, 61, 65, 108, 110, 118, 127, 128–29, 133, 136, 154, 159, 176, 178, 184, 185, 218n13
Seyersted, Per, 122, 129, 217n4
Shakespeare, William, 18, 75, 77, 199n3; *Hamlet*, 78
Shange, Ntozake (Paulette Williams), 175
Shapiro, Norman R., 76, 207n1
Siberia, 50
Sicilians. *See* Italians
Sicily. *See* Italy
Simpson, Lewis P., 170
Skinner, Robert, x
Slave march and rebellions, 13, 115
Slave markets and trade, 9, 51, 140, 178, 182
Slave narratives, 20
Slavery and slaves, 9, 10, 14, 31, 45, 47, 51, 54, 55–56, 59, 61, 62, 63, 64–65, 94, 96, 98, 100, 104, 106, 122, 123, 125, 133, 136, 137, 140, 158, 161, 176, 178, 182; abolition by the French, 10, 65, 194n18; emancipation in Louisiana, 15, 141–42; population figure, 195n25
Slavs. *See* Croats
Smith, Dave, 180
Smith, Julie, x
Smith, Patricia, 169
Snobbery, 150, 152, 165. *See also* Creoles, white: mores
Socialism, 47, 57, 59–60
Socrates, 49, 90
Somnambulism, 50
Songs and singing, 95, 97, 101, 120, 164, 177
Soniat, Katherine, 185
Soulé, Armantine, 52
Soulé, Nelvil, 52
Soulé, Pierre, 47, 49, 52
Soulier-rouge, 203n15. *See also* Rouquigny, Jacques de
South Carolina, 144
Southern Gothic, 51, 93–94, 145. *See also* Romantic Gothic
Southern literature, 17, 150. *See also* Regional literature
"Souvenirs de Bonfouca." *See* F. M. S.
Spain, 7, 46
Spanish in Louisiana, 4, 7–8, 9, 43, 63–64, 67
Spencer, Herbert, 102
Spiritualism and spiritualists, 58, 61, 81, 176, 204n7, 208n3, 210n14
Spitzer, Nick, 14
Spratling, William, 154
Staël, Germaine de, 55, 106, 123
Stanford, Donald E., 174
Starr, S. Frederick, 23
"Star-Spangled Banner," 13
Stendhal (Henri Beyle), ix, 49, 109, 123; *Chroniques italiennes*, 111
Stereotypes, 71, 78, 96
Storms. *See* Hurricanes and storms
Stowe, Harriet Beecher, 62, 63, 64, 158; *Uncle Tom's Cabin*, 59, 60, 61, 62, 100, 125, 165

Stuart, Ruth McEnery, 60, 125, 145–46, 152, 212n14. **Works:** "Egypt," 147; *The Story of Babette*, 147–48; "Uncle Mingo's 'Speculatioms,'" 146, 212n14
Sue, Eugène, *Les Mystères de Paris*, 49, 58
Suicide, practice and theme of, 38, 51, 52, 53, 54, 55, 66, 69, 71, 72, 75, 76, 81, 86, 87, 98, 112, 128, 129, 141, 161, 165, 176, 177, 218n12, 218n14
Sully, Thomas, and family of architects, 167
Supervielle, Jules, 39
Supreme Court of Louisiana, 144
Surrealism, 173
Swamps, 25, 32, 98, 184, 212n11
Swiss, 8
Switzerland, 52
Sylva, Manuel, 81

Taine, Hippolyte, 3, 19, 105, 117, 214n9
Tallant, Robert, 155
Talleyrand-Périgord, Charles-Maurice de, 47
Tangipahoa Parish, 38
Taylor, Helen, 136, 143, 146, 151, 219n3
Tekahkwitha, Catherine, 34
Templeton, Lucy, 156
Terror, The. *See* Revolution of 1789
Testu, Amable, 58
Testut, Charles, viii, 9, 43, 57–63, 64, 87, 119, 197n12, 204n7, 208n3. **Works:** *Calisto*, 58; *Les Echos*, 58, 60; *Les Fleurs d'été*, 58; *Or et fange*, 58; *Portraits littéraires de la Nouvelle-Orléans*, 22, 58; *Saint-Denis*, 58; *Le Vieux Salomon*, 58–63, 71, 89, 107
Theaters, 22–23; French Opera House, 23, 198n13; Porte Saint-Martin, 70; St. Charles Theater, 23; Théâtre Français (Comédie-Française), 70, 76; Théâtre d'Orléans, 23, 73; Théâtre Saint-Philippe, 23. *See also* First Backyard Poetry Theater; Free Southern Theater
Theodicy, theme of, 63, 114
Thibodaux, Louisiana, 171, 183
Thierry, Camille, 22, 26, 70, 81, 83, 85–87, 116. **Works:** "L'Amante du corsaire," 26; *Les Vagabondes*, 86–87
Thomson, James, *The Seasons*, 32
Thoreau, Henry David, 32, 200n10
Tignon, 194n18
Tinker, Edward Larocque, ix, 18, 86
Tintamarre, Bibliothèque and Editions, x
Tiresias, 61
Tolstoy, Lev, 123
Toole, John Kennedy, 151, 162–63, 184, 197n7
Toth, Emily, 121, 128–29
Toucoutou (Sarzant, Anastasie de), 87, 95, 209n10
Toussaint L'Ouverture, François Dominique, 82
Train, Henri, 90
Travel writers, 29. *See also* Le Page du Pratz, Antoine-Simon
Treaties: of Fontainebleau, 7; of Paris, 7; of San Ildefonso, 7
Trembling Prairies, 67, 116
Tremé, Claude, 14
"Tremé" (HBO series), 195n26
Trethewey, Natasha, 196n28
Tristan, Flora, 123
Trotter, Jack, 219n3
Tudor, Henry, Duke of Richmond (Henry VII), 77
Tujague, François, 67, 139; "A travers

l'océan," 26; "La Frénière," 45; *Le Premier Pas: Essais littéraires*, 67
Turgenev, Ivan, 224n24
Tuscany. *See* Italy
Twain, Mark, 25, 93, 132, 150

Ulloa, Antonio de, 8, 46
Umbra Workshop, 173
Union army. *See* Federal troops
Universities (Louisiana): Dillard University, 24, 173, 174, 179; Louisiana State University (LSU), 153, 170, 174, 179, 209n11, 213n2, 216n26; Loyola University, 174; Southeastern Louisiana State University, 184; Straight College/University, 23–24, 78; Tulane University, vii, 119, 133, 146, 151, 159, 174, 185, 196n27, 212n17, 216n24; University of Louisiana at Lafayette (University of Southwestern Louisiana), x, 209n11; University of New Orleans, 182; Xavier University, 182, 196n27
Uptown. *See* Neighborhoods
Ursuline nuns, 4, 141, 152, 191n2
Ursulines Convent, 26, 44

Vacherie, Louisiana, 144
"Valcour B." (B. Valcour), 80
Vaudreuil de Cavagnal, Pierre de Rigaud, Marquis de, 204n10
Verlaine, Paul, 33
Versaillais, 50
Versailles, 113
Versification and technique, 35, 56, 86, 87, 117, 120, 169, 173, 175–76, 177, 178, 183, 184, 228n15. *See also* Alexandrines
Viatte, Auguste, 39, 107, 116, 118, 213n1

Vice and deviancy, 82, 85, 110, 154, 155
Vicksburg, Mississippi, 63, 162
Vieux Carré. *See* French Quarter
Vigny, Alfred de, 30, 34, 45, 68, 82
Violence, 52, 54, 64, 65, 71, 98, 176, 177, 178, 182
Virgin forest. *See* Wilderness
Virginia, 93, 151, 159, 180; University of, 119, 131, 180; Virginia State, 185
Vitry, Louise, 13
Voix du sang, La, 38, 99, 111
Volstead Act, 156
Voltaire, 7, 49, 199n3, 208n3
Voodoo, 97, 100, 138, 164, 172, 181, 224n20. *See also* Hoodoo

Waggoner, May Rush Gwin, xi, 106
Walden Pond, 32
Walker, Alexander, 220n18
War, theme of, 63. *See also individual names*
Ward, Jerry W., Jr., 226n4
Warner, Charles Dudley, 132
War of 1812, 11, 71. *See also* New Orleans, Battle of
War of Secession. *See* Civil War
Washington, George, 47, 58, 90
Washington, University of, 179. *See also* Seattle
Weather. *See* Hurricanes and storms; Louisiana: climate
Weaver, Richard M., viii, 132
Weiss, M. Lynn, x, 90
Welty, Eudora, 160
West Florida, Republic of, 7
West Indian figures, 178. *See also* Ogé, Vincent; Toussaint L'Ouverture, François Dominique

West Indies, 9, 19, 21, 59, 101. *See also* Cuba; Guadeloupe; Haiti; Jamaica; Martinique; Saint-Domingue
White League, 12, 96, 122
White Supremacism, 46, 98, 107, 132, 144, 202n2
Whitman, Walt, 33, 150; "Song of Myself," 128
Wilderness, theme of, 19, 30, 31, 32, 34, 37, 38, 39–40, 42, 48, 49, 55, 65–66, 67, 143
Williams, John R., 31
Williams, Tennessee, 154–55; *A Streetcar Named Desire*, 154; *Suddenly Last Summer*, 155
Wilson, Clyde, 104
Wilson, Edmund, 95, 129; *Patriotic Gore*, 94
Wolfe, Thomas, 100
Wollstonecraft, Mary, 123
Women's situation, 9, 55–56, 62, 66, 68, 70, 110, 124, 127–28, 145, 146, 159, 176, 177, 218n11
Woolson, Constance Fenimore, 137, 204n8
WordBand, 226n4
Words & Music (festival), 226n3
World War I, 201n24
World War II, 152
Wright, Richard, 169

"Yacoub" (J. Mansion), 87, 88
Yankees, 11, 47, 115, 152, 156, 157, 158, 224n18
Yellow fever, 12, 25, 42, 47, 48, 97, 102, 103, 164, 193n12, 198n19
Yucca House. *See* Plantations: Melrose

Zola, Emile, 50, 55, 67, 102, 105, 109, 117, 120, 123, 145; *L'Assommoir*, 123; *La Débâcle*, 59, 214n9; *Lourdes*, 123; *Nana*, 116

www.ingramcontent.com/pod-product-compliance
Lightning Source LLC
Chambersburg PA
CBHW022003220426
43663CB00007B/941